SNOWBALL'S CHANCE

SNOWBALL'S CHANCE

My Kidneys Failed, My Wife Left Me and My Dog Died (i still miss that dog!)

Don Gordon

SHOTWELL

COLUMBIA · So. Car.

EST. 2015

PUBLISHING

Produced in the Republic of South Carolina by

SHOTWELL PUBLISHING LLC
Post Office Box 2592
Columbia, So. Carolina 29202

www.ShotwellPublishing.com

Cover Design by Boo Jackson

ISBN 978-1-947660-51-9

FIRST EDITION

10 9 8 7 6 5 4 3 2

CONTENTS

DEBI... WHO WAS IN IT FOR LOVE...

MY BRAVE BROTHER JIM WITH HIS FAITHFUL DOG JACK.

ALTHOUGH I WILL ATTEST to the training and skill of the medical professionals who played a role in saving my life, this book is not dedicated to them because none of them would have been present if they weren't getting paid. My book is dedicated to Debi who was in it for love and to my brave brother Jimmy, who volunteered for this mission because of his sense of duty...

FOREWORD

THE STORY THAT YOU ARE ABOUT TO READ is true, told with as little exaggeration and dramatization as possible, however some of the names have been changed to protect the guilty.

While I am the central character this book is not about me, but rather it is about the medical "professionals" that I came into contact with in my successful attempt to save my life. One day you will need "professionals" from this same industry to save your life. I thought that you should know that if you don't understand the rules, then you don't stand a snowball's chance in Hell.

MEDICAL RULES

RULE NUMBER ONE: Play to win because when you are talking about living or dying there is no glory for second place.

RULE NUMBER TWO: One half of all doctors finished in the bottom half of their graduating class in medical school (do the math).

RULE NUMBER THREE: In every graduating class at all medical schools one person graduates last in his class and they bestow a special title to this person. They call him Doctor (Med school joke that is true).

RULE NUMBER FOUR: There is nothing in the Hypocritic Oath about not lying to patients.

RULE NUMBER FIVE: Medical science can save you if medical practice doesn't kill you first.

RULE NUMBER SIX: Medical Science determines what is theoretically possible but your Health Insurance Policy determines what will be done in your particular case.

RULE NUMBER SEVEN: Believe any doctor who says that he can't save you then go out and find one who thinks that he can.

RULE NUMBER EIGHT: When a doctor says that he has never lost a patient in your category that could mean that they know where the patients are buried.

RULE NUMBER NINE: A hospital is a business run by somebody with an MBA not a Ph.D.

RULE NUMBER TEN: He who dares, wins (sometimes).

Chapter 1

IN THE MIDDLE OF A NORMAL LIFE
(TWO DOGS AND A WIFE)

THERE WAS A TIME when my world included no financial, health, or woman problems: then I turned five years old.

The first indication of a medical abnormality was searing pain in my back that would awaken me even from my deepest childhood slumber. Going to the doctor was fun because after failing to find anything wrong, since there was no pain during the examination, the doctor would take out a jar of purple disinfectant and then use it to paint a big heart on my chest, making me the proud owner of a purple heart just like the one that my Daddy had hanging in a frame next to the bullet that a Japanese sniper had shot into his leg.

By the time that I first felt that terrible pain in my side irreparable damage to my kidneys had already been done. It would be six months before the doctors could determine that the pain was a result of a constricted bladder neck. My bladder would overfill, since it couldn't drain properly, with the resulting pressure destroying the valves that prevent urine from backing up into the kidneys. As you might imagine urine back flow into the kidneys is not a good thing.

Basically, I was a poorly drained but otherwise robust active little five- year- old Southern boy. I was taught by my Granddad to hate Yankees and to be polite. I didn't understand exactly what Yankees were but surely they were bad. Even though I heard my doctors talking about me I didn't really understand what poorly drained kidneys would do to you. Apparently, in addition to waking you up in the middle of the night, bad drainage will kill you (whatever that meant).

My prognosis was that I had about twelve months to live before a slow and painful death (unless something changed). If my father had not been in the military a young death would have been my destiny and you would be reading a different book.

I can still remember how I strained to hear my parent's conversation through the partially open bedroom door. My little five-year-old mind was frightened by a sound that I had never heard before: the sound of my Mother crying as she talked with my Father about something that she did not want to hear. Apparently my only chance (whatever that meant) was to go to Walter Reed Army Medical Center in Washington, D.C. . I was more terrified to think about moving away from home than I was of going to a hospital because all the doctor ever did to me was to paint a big purple heart on my chest.

I couldn't stand to hear my Mother cry so I ran into the bedroom to give her a big hug and told her that if she would stop crying, I would go to the hospital. But first I wanted to go visit Mama and Papa (my maternal Grandparents). There was nothing that I liked better than to visit my Grandparents and have all of my cousins come over to play.

Yet, little did I know that Walter Reed Hospital was in Yankee Land. My father was transferred to Fort McNair, right across the Potomac River from the National Airport in Washington D.C., where my brother Jim and my parents would live while I was admitted to the children's ward at Walter Reed. Leaving my Grandparents back home in South Carolina was the hardest part.

My first experience with Yankee food was hospital food, small wonder that I refused to eat. In an effort to stimulate my appetite the head nurse would tell me that I could have anything that I wanted for breakfast. Since I was feeling homesick, I asked for yellow grits saying "that's what my Granddaddy eats." It turned out that I was so deep in Yankee Land that the hospital didn't even have any yellow grits (how backwards can you get).

The hospital staff delivered white grits on my breakfast tray but I wouldn't eat them. I had never seen white grits before and didn't really believe they were grits at all (don't these people know what grits look like). I refused to eat even one bite because the Nurse had said that I could have anything that I wanted for breakfast, and I wanted yellow grits.

When I continued to refuse to eat my breakfast the nurse tricked me into thinking that they had found some yellow grits by mixing some egg yolks in with the grits, and ceremoniously delivering my breakfast tray a second time. I fell for the trick, hook line and sinker, devouring those grits while I sang their high praises. That Yankee nurse should have left well enough alone but she had to prove to me that I must like white grits since that's what those were (mixed with egg yolks).

I learned a valuable lesson that day: a Yankee will trick you if they can.

That was the beginning of a very rough year in which I would undergo nine serious medical operations and in the process discovered that doctors do a lot more than paint purple hearts on your chest.

There were about twenty patients on the children's ward but only one made a lasting impression on me and that was Stanley (the kid with no arms). I never saw Stanley's face because his head was always bandaged up like a mummy except for two bright eyes and a mouth that smiled. Stanley had lost both of his arms when a hot water boiler that was used to heat the building that he lived in exploded while he was standing next to it.

Stanley was amazing because he had learned to do everything with his feet. Opening his bed side drawer was no problem for Stanley. He would reach in and get whatever he wanted just like anybody else except, he picked it up with his bare foot. Stanley's massive wounds created a bad smell so powerful that the other children couldn't stand being near him and they would leave the area when Stanley came over to play. I just learned to breathe through my mouth and Stanley became my best friend.

Stanley never mentioned his missing arms but he must have told me a least one hundred times that he lost his twenty-one-jewel watch when that boiler exploded. Being around Stanley showed me you may as well not complain because other people have situations so bad that you are glad to have your misery instead of theirs. This is when I first learned just how compassionate and loving my Mother really is. Seeing that Stanley's parents were not around my Mother started giving him love and attention.

Stanley was five years old just like me but his parents could never come to visit him since they lived in Alaska. Pretty soon my Mother had just about adopted every child on the ward. I still remember how excited Stanley got the day my Mother brought him a surprise. It was a small red toy car and Stanley grabbed the toy car with his foot and took off pushing it all around the ward making loud motor sounds as he went. Stanley taught me the meaning of perseverance years before I was to hear the word, and also that good friends were more important than a bad smell.

After several operations I could only get around in a wheelchair. There was a tube coming from each kidney and a tube from my bladder draining into two bottles that were with me night and day. Each day I would sit at the main entrance to the children's ward wearing the Rebel hat that my Grandfather had brought me, resting my toy rifle on the arms of the wheelchair as I waited for my mother to come visit me. As each person entered the ward, I would ask them one question: "What state are you from?" determining in my five-year-old brain if they were Yankees or Rebels by their response. If I thought that they were Yankees, I did what my Grandfather would want me to do: I shot them on the spot.

There was one nice lady from North Carolina who would try every single day to convince me that North Carolina was not really "the North." She would claim that North Carolinians were Rebels, but I always shot her anyway just to be safe (knowing how tricky Yankees can be).

Each morning my Mother would push me in my wheelchair around Walter Reed Hospital. My favorite destination was the fire station where the firemen would always put a fireman's helmet on my head, and its weight would make my weak little neck wobble (I loved it).

On nice days we went to the fire station but when it was cold or raining my Mother would take me through the long hallways over to the hospital radio room. It had a large picture window between the broadcast studio and the people who were walking past it out in the hallway.

As my Mother would push me up close to the large picture window so that I could see inside the studio, the radio show host would always say to his audience that: "the Little Rebel has just arrived." Then he would play Dixie over the radio which we could hear on the speaker that was mounted on the wall up above the picture window. The song "Dixie" was a big boost for my homesick spirits because back home whenever there is a parade the people always cheered the loudest when the band played "Dixie." Back then you could play "Dixie" without offending anyone and the song was an expression of Southern pride, which always ended with an ear- splitting Rebel Yell that I loved to help out with.

I had no concept of what death meant back then but sometimes at night the kids on the ward would sit up and talk about death with the central issue being: would death hurt? The other burning issue on our five-year-old minds was wondering if we could stay awake all night (we failed).

To everyone's great relief and surprise my doctors were able to save me. I clearly remember the morning that the Doctors came into my room and removed all of the tubes (I got to go home the next day).

I didn't understand death back then but I had cheated it for the first time. The doctors were able to correct my drainage problem but 90% of my kidney tissue had already been destroyed. My prognosis was that I would probably die before I ever graduated from high school because as my body grew larger my limited kidney function would prove to be insufficient. (bummer). Having enough kidney tissue for today was all that mattered to me and there was more than enough for that. Young boys don't have any quit in them so I tore back into my life without any cares about what the future might bring.

The best advice that I could give anyone facing life's uncertainties is to close your eyes to the probabilities and totally focus on the possibilities in life.

Somehow, I grew from a boy into a man without anything bad ever happening so the Sword of Damocles that had hung over my head since birth seemed remote by the time that I was a thirty four-year old man.

I was in the middle of a normal life (two dogs and a wife). Then one day everything changed and I found myself in the middle of a fight for my life.

Chapter 2

THE SWORD HAS FALLEN

AMONG THE PHONE MESSAGES waiting for me after lunch is an interesting one from Dr. Calm's secretary that says "Dr. Calm wants to see Don Gordon today at 4:00 P.M. to discuss the results of his blood test last week and to review his options." Wow, it's scary when your Doctor calls you to make an appointment, especially, when you didn't call him first. Somehow the fact that Dr. Calm wants to see me today lets me know that something bad is coming down.

I know that I have bad kidneys but to use Pete Maravich's last words "I feel great, I am fine" (at least that's what I was told that he said just before he died during a game of basketball).

Walking into Dr. Calm's waiting room two things are immediately apparent; the first thing is that I am the strongest patient here because all of the other patients look like they have at least one foot in the grave, and secondly every one of the other patients are staring at me for some reason. Before long a nurse comes into the waiting room and calls my name before leading me back to exam room number three. Dr. Calm comes in to see me without the normal fifteen-minute wait that doctors usually subject you to. I have some American Indian in my heritage so I can read the signs of the Universe and I know that when Dr. Calm sees me right away: it's a bad sign.

Talk about a lack of bedside manner, the first words out of Dr. Calm's mouth are, "I want to do a vein reversal in your arm so that we can be ready in case we need to do emergency hemodialysis." I literally shudder and shake to the bone in an involuntary reaction as I visualize the event that Dr. Calm is so casually talking about, of course for him it's just another day at the office, but for me it's a life changing event. Boom! The Sword of Damocles that has hung over my head since my youth has fallen. Me, Don Gordon, on hemodialysis: this is the day that I have lived in mortal fear of since the days of my kidney operations when I was five years old.

Like a vampire sucking your blood through a filter the two giant needles of that dialysis machine have always appeared to be my dismal fate. You get weaker and weaker, like a prisoner in a Nazi concentration camp, waiting on your ultimate fate: which is to die. Now if this mental picture is a bummer to the max you are right on target with me as my brain reels in the first few seconds of shock.

Not yet ready to accept what may be unavoidable I ask Dr. Calm what my creatinine level is at this time (a measurement of impurities in the blood that your kidney should filter out). Dr. Calm tells me that the blood test that I had last week indicated that the creatinine level was 7.2 but it may already be higher because decline in kidney function is rapid at this stage.

This leads me to ask, "just what stage am I in?" Dr. Calm answers "we call it end stage renal function." Oh boy, I wish that I had never asked Dr. Calm that question. "End stage renal function" rings in my ears as I ask Dr. Calm "what are the options that your secretary said you wanted to discuss with me?"

Dr. Calm replies in his normal monotone "If you have a real supportive wife, and we would have to interview her in private before we could consider it, you might be able to use peritoneal dialysis. This is a new kind of dialysis where you are dialyzed through a tube in your abdomen instead of through needles in the arms, and of course we would need to look into the possibility of a transplant."

Immediately I tell Dr. Calm that there is no question that I want to use the kind of dialysis without the needles. Then I go on to ask Dr. Calm what creatinine level would require dialysis to begin. Dr. Calm tells me that it varies from patient to patient based largely on just how fast kidney failure occurs, if it is happening slowly a higher creatinine level may be tolerated but the key word in my case is "soon." Dr. Calm tells me that in my case the creatinine level will probably be around 9 or 10 when dialysis begins and that may be just a couple of months away.

Then Dr. Calm asks me the critical question, "do you have any potential kidney donors in your family?" I know that with both of my parents being in poor health the only possible donor is my only sibling (my older brother Jimmy).

Unfortunately, Jimmy and I have never been all that close as brothers, partially because of the almost six-year difference in our ages, but it goes much deeper than that. Nobody is very close to Jimmy, neither my parents nor his wife seems to be on the same wave length that he is on. Jimmy just marches to his own drummer and he tries to make everyone else get in step.

Don't get me wrong, Jimmy is a good man, being a Vietnam veteran (Marine aviator), good husband and father (two sons), church going, money making, member of the school board type of guy (make that a double church going, almost holy rolling, certainly holier than thou type of guy). Jimmy has always been the ant of our family and I have been the grasshopper. Jimmy has always saved almost every dollar that he ever made being the family pessimist (that he is). The fact that Jimmy is successful in real estate is a testimony that hard work can overcome a negative attitude.

Jimmy is so convinced that one day America's economy will completely fail that he probably has gold in a Swiss bank account. I have always told Jimmy that I have a rifle with plenty of ammunition for that same day (that I feel will not come). I have grown up knowing that my life will be short so every moment is something to savor. Yes, I am the grasshopper in our family living life to the fullest, and living it with gusto. Being optimistic with an outgoing personality is something that I have inherited from both of my parents.

Don't get me wrong, I work hard and I make good money, it's just that I spend it a little more freely than Jimmy would. My red V-12 Jaguar XKE convertible brings me more pleasure than more money in my savings account possibly could. Unfortunately, it has always seemed to me that Jimmy the ant would never be happy with his self-inflicted deprivations unless the grasshopper suffers in the long cold winter of life. This attitude of Jimmy's manifests itself in a lot of different ways: for example, he bought his Life Insurance from somebody else (lest I make a dollar off of him).

Like I said: Jimmy keeps his distance from just about everybody in the world and he is my only hope. I don't want to wait on a cadaver kidney (one taken from some dead guy that you never knew). If I have to go on a waiting list for a kidney from a cadaver it will mean that I have to live on dialysis for a longer period of time (I call that not dying but don't get it mixed up with living). The other bad thing about not having a living related donor would be that I would have to take a lot more medicine after the transplant to keep it from rejecting.

I really don't want to be on dialysis at all (who would). Just picture having your blood sucked through a machine while you waste away. After a moment of stunned silence, I answer Dr. Calm that my brother Jimmy is my only possible kidney donor. Dr. Calm tells me that he wants me to have another blood test and make an appointment to come back to see him in two weeks. Dr. Calm has finished what he came here to say so he stands up and walks out of the door while he is making a note in my file. Dr. Calm has other patients to see and I have to try to pick up the pieces of my life (that was just shattered in exam room number three).

Bam! Just like that and the doctor's visit that I have dreaded my entire life is over. There was just one thing missing (words of encouragement from my doctor). Dr. Calm is a man of science so this is all about logic to him. The words that I need to hear right now would be more like a football coach at halftime, or at least something like: "This is all routine for medical science don't worry we will not let you die."

I sit alone for a minute in exam room number three with Dr. Calm's words ringing in my ears (do I have any possible donors). The only certainty is that life as I have known it is over. There was a virile young man of thirty-four that walked into Dr. Calm's office twenty minutes ago but it is a stumbling zombie that leaves. Making my way down the hall and back through the waiting room I feel everybody's eyes on me but now I understand why they are all staring (they can tell by the look on my face that now I am one of them).

As I stumble out to the elevators, I'm thinking that I will go get in my car and drive around Columbia on the Interstate Highway for a while so that I can try to sort everything out, but never have I seen the subconscious mind so clearly demonstrate its power. Our conscious train of thoughts are just the tip of the iceberg of what really goes on deep inside our brain, and my subconscious mind has already worked out all of my options (I have none except for my brother).

My conscious plan of action is to get out on the Interstate Highway which means that my car should be turning to the right but it goes straight to my brother's office without any thinking by me until my Zombie trance is broken when a parking space comes into view. I park in front of Jimmy's office on Devine Street and I think about the communications class that my best friend, Bill Tulluck, recently talked me into paying five hundred dollars to attend. Right now, it seems like money well spent because this will be the biggest sale of my life.

On the conscious level I think that I will go in and build a little rapport with Jimmy before getting into anything heavy (like they taught me to do in the class). In my mind's eye I see Jimmy immediately offering me his kidney when he hears my plight (but this ain't the movies so forget about that [song lyric playing in my head]).

Like I said Jimmy and I aren't that close so I rarely go to his office (he has never been to mine). This means that I don't know Jimmy's receptionist (maybe that is why she greets me coldly). Perhaps the receptionist sees the dazed look on my face, at any rate, she greets me with just one word: "Yes?"

I ask the receptionist if Jim Gordon is in identifying myself as his brother (as if I need to be worthy to see the great Oz). With rather an incredulous tone the receptionist says "I'll see," as if she doesn't believe me and then she disappears down the hall towards Jimmy's office. I think about what the receptionist just said, "I'll see," (ha) as if she doesn't know if the boss is in or not. It seems like the receptionist has worked here long enough to pick up some of Jimmy's personality traits (or lack thereof). In a minute the receptionist comes back but now she has a big smile on her face (having verified that in fact I am her boss's brother).

The receptionist proceeds to tell me that Jimmy is in his office and although he is on the phone, it is ok for me to go on in. Jimmy is talking on the phone with a client of his so I sit down on the couch and start looking around his office. I am glad for the moment of rest because I am tired (I have been tired a lot lately). Jimmy has done well in business and he has a nicely appointed office with a real leather couch that feels cool to my sweaty skin. There is grasscloth wallpaper that looks expensive on the walls of Jimmy's office and he has two photos framed on his desk. One large picture has his wife (Jill) sitting with their two sons (Scott & Ryan) and, fittingly enough, the other photograph is one of Jimmy sitting in the woods with his famous bird dog, Jack.

While I am lost in thought Jimmy finishes up his conversation, hangs up the phone and spins around in his chair. We are facing each other across his desk when he says "you look tired." Wham! My subconscious mind takes control and all of my carefully laid plans about building rapport go right out of the window, so the net result of my $500 communication class is that I just blurt out "Jimmy, I need your kidney."

Total shock, that's the only way to describe the expression on Jimmy's face as his eyes open as wide as they will go in utter disbelief. Jimmy's eyes search the ceiling and then the floor while he is saying "I thought that the doctors had told you that you couldn't have a transplant because of all of the scars from your old surgery." I respond in a rush telling Jimmy that the only thing that I know is that Dr. Calm just asked me if there was a potential kidney donor in my immediate family. If this was a movie, instead of my life, at this point Jimmy would be making some sort of supportive statement followed by heavy male bonding (but this is reality folks).

I had been thinking that I had already had my shock for the day but upon reflection I must admit that I was wrong. Deep in my heart I always knew that there would be a day like this in my life where a doctor would give me bad news, but nothing in life had prepared me for what I was about to hear.

Suddenly Jimmy stands up behind his desk with his eyes now tightening into little slits while he says, "Well I can't give you a kidney." Now it is me who looks totally shocked, so I just sit there staring at Jimmy in silence (dumbfounded). Jimmy breaks the silence with a string of excuses; he and his business partner just split up leaving Jimmy the burden of running the entire business, etc. I don't respond except with silence so Jimmy stammers on about how he has to look out for Jill and the boys (what about me).

You have heard about tension in rooms that you could cut with a knife, well this room was filling with tension that would cut you back. I continued to sit there without saying a word but the glint in my eye has changed from surprise to hostility. The tension feels like this room could explode when Jimmy says, "You didn't tell me that you were coming by here today and I have a meeting to go to." I can tell by Jimmy's face that there is no love in his heart and I have to suppress my urge to blow up because I can't afford to alienate my only hope (but deep inside I seethe).

There is probably nothing that Jimmy would like better than for us to have a big argument right now so that he can harden his heart and have another excuse for letting me die. Standing up so that we are eyeball to eyeball I look directly at Jimmy and I tell

who

him that I will call him in advance next time, but as I walk out to my car, I'm having bad thoughts about shooting sons-of-bitches that won't give me a kidney.

Outside, as I start up my Jag, I reflect on that moment of brotherly love that failed to materialize and one thought keeps ringing in my ears: Jimmy has a meeting to go to and I have to die. The tears make their first appearance as I drive through the Five Points section of town (other drivers are looking at me but right now I don't give a damn). I make no attempt to suppress the tears until I am almost home to Blythewood, then I spend the last few moments of my journey trying to straighten up my act. As I drive into my garage I am out of touch with reality and it's just as well because reality sucks, but in my fantasy world I'm going to stoically keep this bad news to myself (right). I'm dreaming about not telling Delila, my beautiful wife, but those plans will burst like a soap bubble once I get inside of the house.

As soon as I open the front door to my house the music that is coming from my stepdaughter's room breaks my trance. Sabrina is playing her music loud enough to damage her hearing as young girls will but it is happy music and it makes me feel good to be back home with people that I love. *who*

I can hear Delila vacuuming back in the master bedroom and I can tell that nobody knows that I am home (because of the noise). As I walk through the great room, I feel like some kind of a ghost who is watching my world as an observer (instead of a participant). As I watch my world function without me, I have a creepy feeling and am glad when I catch a whiff of Jungle Gardenia because I love the girl who wears it.

The scent of Delila makes my body relax because I am deeply in love with my wife. I start thinking about all of the things that I like about Delila and it is a very long list. It's not only Delila's beauty that I crave, but she also has a sense of style that satisfies my soul. Delila is very feminine and often wears a flower in her curly auburn hair this time of year, in fact she is everything that I am not (we are like the yin and yang who need only each other to be complete).

14

Even after I open the bedroom door Delila is unaware of my presence because she is vacuuming aggressively with her back to me, and instead of immediately saying anything I freeze for a minute (so that I can admire the view). When Delila catches a glimpse of me standing in the doorway looking at her all Hell breaks loose. Delila shouts over the sound of the vacuum, breaking what for me had been a meaningful moment, saying, "You scared the hell out of me you son-of-a-bitch."

Just when I thought that my surprises were done for the day life gives me another one in the form of a hostile wife. I tell Delila that I didn't mean to scare her but she isn't buying what I'm trying to sell, and she snaps back, "Why do you do things that I hate?" Wow! After the day that I have had to get home only to discover that my wife has pms tells me that I don't need a calendar to know that this is Monday.

My subconscious mind kicks into gear again and any plans that I might have had about how to communicate this complicated tale are instantly forgotten as I holler over the noise of the vacuum, "Dr. Calm told me to line up a kidney donor because I'm going to need a transplant and it won't be long." Delila just stands there for a minute in a state of shock. She cuts off the vacuum and I tell her the rest of the story about how Jimmy doesn't want to give me a kidney because he has to look out for Jill and the boys (sure).

Delila hugs me tightly as she says the first encouraging words that I have heard today: "Don't worry sweetheart I will give you one of my kidneys." On the logical side of my brain the thoughts were that they almost never do transplants from non-related living donors and Delila, being as smart as she is, probably knows this too; but on the emotional side of my brain I can feel the love that I so desperately need. As we embrace it is Delila's love, not her offer of a kidney, that comforts me.

Chapter 3

SEARCH FOR AN EXIT THAT DOES NOT EXIST

MY MIND SEARCHES FOR AN ESCAPE from this trap of dialysis or death. The only option Dr. Calm mentioned was which kind of dialysis machine to use, and apparently, I don't even control that choice. It would have made me feel better if Dr. Calm had said "maybe we can use" instead of "maybe I would consider" when referring to the kind of dialysis without those huge needles. Dr. C. knows that I would do anything to avoid those vampire needles, so what does he expect me to do? Beg? Suddenly I am on a path that I don't want to walk, but walk it I must because it's literally: DO OR DIE!

Years ago, I had gone to Duke University Hospital for medical tests and they determined that I 'would not be a good transplant candidate' because of all the old scar tissue from my childhood surgery. That's how they tell you NO in the medical business. My probable future is simply dialysis until I die (bummer).

Pondering my fate, I wonder if death is the best way out of my misery. My only real option, the only factor that I seem to control, is whether and when to exercise the death option. I can't picture myself being able to make a living selling life insurance if I look weak and frail like the people in Dr. Calm's waiting room and I don't even want to think about how they must feel. Why should

I go through all the heartache and pain just so that I can suffer a miserable slow death when one option is just to blow my brains out. BLAM! The lights go out and it's all over.

Doctors may have some different medical name for what I am going through mentally but I call it justifiable depression. Anyone who would not be depressed in a situation such as the one that I find myself in either doesn't understand the ramifications or they are insane.

Selling on commission means not having the financial security of a regular paycheck (if I stop selling the money stops). In the end the world runs on cash, and while I only have about $11,000 in the bank, the only debt that I have is a small home mortgage. One of my major worries is the financial challenge because I don't know how much longer I will be able to work, and at this time Delila is not working either.

Thankfully, money is only a problem if I live because when I die my $275,000 Life Insurance policy will take care of Delila and Sabrina for a while. I'm intensely emotional about Delila and Sabrina's financial security because as I look at the distant future I'm not in the picture. Plus in the immediate future I'm going to be a major financial and emotional burden for both of them (Oh, just shoot me, I'm so worthless, woe is me; etc.).

Seeking some positive thought to balance against all of the negatives that surround me, I grasp at the hope that perhaps it was a faulty blood test (sure). There are a lot of ways that the lab could be off on my creatine level; maybe I'm not as sick as Dr.C. thinks. creatine is a measure of the impurities in the blood that a healthy kidney filters out (lower is better when it comes to your creatine level).

I still feel O.K. The fact that I play softball and basketball proves that I'm healthy (doesn't it). I try to convince myself that I am not sick by looking in the mirror (the doctors would call this denial but I call it clinging to my only hope).

The day for me to get another blood test had already arrived. I went back to Dr. Calm's office and as was I sitting in the waiting room, a new wave of fear swept over me making my heart race as my entire body began to worry. Suddenly the hair on the back of my neck bristles in the primitive flight response but life isn't that simple. I wish that I could just run out of the waiting room door but I would have to run right out of my skin because the problem is me. This is one of those problems in life that we all have to face at some point in time.

Then I snap back to living in the present instead of the future because at this moment I'm sitting in a nice room looking at magazines that I have no interest in (things could be worse and they will). I look around the waiting room at people who share my fate (They look pitiful, all skinny and weak). Then I realize that everybody is looking at me again (it gives me the creeps). I guess these other patients realize exactly what stage of this process that I am in now because each one of them had a day just like this in their lives too. I'm the before picture and the other patients are the after picture (oh dear). That thought stuns my brain until the nurse comes walking into the waiting room calling my name.

As I follow the nurse back towards the exam room I am hoping that I get a 15-20 minute wait before Dr. Calm comes in to see me maybe that would mean that Dr. Calm has patients who are sicker than I am (small comfort). Knowing that any fantasy about the blood test being wrong was about to be dispelled, I grasped at the concept that perhaps my kidney function had stabilized allowing my life to go on (at least for a while). I had now accepted the high creatine level that made me desperate just two weeks ago. The human mind can adapt to almost anything if it has enough time (I don't). Naturally, I was hoping for some improvement in the creatine level but that is not in the cards.

Without much waiting Dr. Calm comes in from the hall looking at the contents of a manila folder with my name on the front. Dispensing with small talk, Dr. Calm glances down as he tells me that my other body chemistries are looking bad too (oh great). Apparently my potassium level is extremely high which could lead to a heart attack and that is on top of my troubles with my creatine level (which is higher by the way).

Now I have to start taking two huge pills before each meal and a different pill, that would choke a horse, after every meal. Dr. Calm also wants me to make an appointment with his dietician because she has a list of foods that I have to avoid (no problem these pills should fill me up). I'm still thinking about the possible heart attack while Dr. Calm is telling me that he wants my brother to have blood work done to see if he is a possible kidney donor. Dr. Calm wants me to bring my wife in with me next week when I come for my blood test because he wants to talk to both of us.

If you have ever totally lost control of your car on a rain slick highway then you know how I feel but in my life that feeling lasts all day long. My immediate problem isn't dialysis, a transplant, or even money. My number one problem is Jimmy.

Jimmy is going to be hard to handle because he changes slowly and I'm changing fast. Getting Jimmy comfortable with this situation in time to do me any good is going to be tough (I don't blame him). I haven't talked with Jimmy since I asked unsuccessfully for his kidney (wait until he hears that I might need his heart too). I was hoping that Jimmy would feel a little guilt and phone me to volunteer his kidney to save my life, but from Jimmy I have heard not a peep (I shouldn't blame him but I do).

My Mother and Father along with my wife give me the strength that I need to go on (the power of love: old song that was right).

Remembering that in my original conversation with Jimmy, when I asked him if he would give me one of his kidneys, one of the things that he used as a defense was that "I hadn't called him before I came by." (good grief). So I phone Jimmy to make an appointment to see if he would mind if we cut one of his kidneys out of his body (I hope that phoning in advance helps to make it easier). WOW! Make an appointment to see my own brother when my life is at stake, what a concept! The phone call is brief and right to the point. I stammer into the phone, "Jimmy, this is Don, I would like to know when would be a good time for me to stop by and talk." Jimmy surprises me when he agrees without a fight by saying, "What about right now?" So I hang up the phone and drive right over to see Jimmy at his office as fast as my car could go.

I sit down on Jimmy's leather couch and get right to the point as I explain that Dr. Calm wants both of us to have blood tests done just to see if we are a match or not. "I'll have to pray about it," is Jimmy's reply. Fuming at the lack of brotherly love I say to Jimmy in a loud tone of voice, "You have to pray about it. Jimmy, I will die without your kidney!" Jimmy glares at me as he shouts right back, "You won't die. Dr. Calm says that you could live on dialysis for a long time."

The thought that it would be O.K. for me to live on dialysis for a long time makes me blurt out, "Jim, dialysis is worse than dying!" Jimmy finishes our conversation since he is in control when he tells me, "I'll have to pray about it. Call me next week!"

I can see that Jimmy's face is all wrinkled in anger and I realize that my face is too. Knowing that I have to be careful not to alienate my only hope, (any further than he is already). I smile to break the tension, as if a smile could help (it does). The tension in the room is explosive. What I say is, "I'll call you the first of next week," but inside my tortured brain what I want to shout out to the world is something about shooting sons of bitches who don't give me their kidneys as I storm out of his office.

Thoughts of my monetary situation fill my head as I drive down Forrest Drive with the top down on my Jag, while I hurry on over to Dr. Calm's office for another consultation. One thing is clear: the longer that I am going to be out of work the bigger my financial problem will turn out to be. I just wish that I knew how long that it would be before I could reasonably expect to be able to get back to work after my transplant (if I am lucky enough to have one). I don't need any fancy financial planning, I just need to "make hay while the sun shines," as my Father would say.

Limited amount of money meets unlimited need (the vast unknown is disconcerting). Recalling that my Father had recommended that I refinance my house to improve my cash flow. I conclude that once again, "Father knows best." I decide to go see my softball buddy, Wade Watson, down at the savings & loan right away because a bank may not lend me money for thirty years if I look like I may be dead in thirty days.

As soon as my troubled mind has dealt with my financial issues it turns to assess my emotional needs, so my thoughts turn to my parents. I have been blessed when it comes to parents. I can't even imagine what it would be like if they weren't here to help me (I don't even want to think about that). My Mother has always been my closest friend; we still talk on the phone every day and she is the bedrock of my life. My Father has always been a great male role-model and I respect his sage advice (although I don't always follow it).

My life snaps back to its petty pace of day to day as I pull into the parking lot at Dr. Calm's office. I walk into Dr. Calm's depressing waiting room filled with the living dead and after I take my seat with the rest of them I realize that everyone who is seated in this room is really just waiting on their turn to die (I told you that it was depressing). When the nurse finally calls my name, I am eager to follow her (anything to get me out of this room).

The nurse takes me down the hall to exam room three and as soon as Dr. Calm comes in to examine me, I start trying to probe his Life Insurance policies (that's what I do). Dr. Calm doesn't want to hear anything about what he ought to be doing (neither do I). Yet still I press on and so does Dr. Calm which makes for a rather stressful situation. I insist that Dr. Calm understand that when he dies all of the cash values in any of his non-par Whole Life Insurance policies will revert to the company instead of his wife (you can have the face amount or the cash value but not both [catch 22]).

Dr. Calm insists that I understand that without dialysis or a transplant I will be dead in less than one year, not two. Cash value life insurance is a screw job for the consumer if you compare spending the same amount of money each month on Term Life Insurance and putting what you save on premiums in an appropriate investment, but a doctor hates to look dumb (especially to his patients). Dr. Calm hears my words but he doesn't care about the implications, so he tells me that his life insurance policies are staying where they are and I tell him that he is acting like a little knowledge will hurt him.

I don't sell any life insurance but what does occur is Dr. Calm becomes tense and uncomfortable so when he finally gets to talk about what he has brought me in for today he is uncharacteristically aggressive and demonstrative. Dr. Calm starts by berating me as if I were an employee about to get fired because I still haven't made an appointment to see his dietician so that she can show me which foods that I have to avoid. Then he tells me that he wants Jimmy and me to go to the dialysis clinic in the next few days so that we can determine if my blood type matches that of my brother (or not). This leads me to ask Dr. Calm what the chances are of two siblings not being a proper match. His answer of 75% stuns me back into silence.

I don't know why they save the big bombshells until last, but just when I think that we are finished Dr. Calm says, "I want to go ahead and schedule you for outpatient surgery to do a vein reversal in your arm so we have a shunt in place for hemodialysis just in case of an emergency." Dr. Calm's words sear my brain as I reel from the thought of those dialysis needles. I tell Dr. Calm that I definitely want the kind of dialysis without the needles, so I don't want to reverse a vein in my arm (lest it be too easy to start me on the wrong kind of dialysis).

Dr. Calm answers me in his dry monotone as if this is all strictly routine (maybe for him but not for me). He looks totally unconcerned as he says, "I haven't decided what type of dialysis to use on you but we need to be ready in case things happen faster than we anticipate, just to be on the safe side." I think about what Dr. Calm just said to me and I truly wish that there was a safe side that I could be on in this situation, but every scenario that I am aware of scares the heck out of me.

Since I am uncomfortable with every single apparent course of action, I use the line on Dr. Calm that had always been the most frustrating for me to deal with when I ran into it during the course of a sale. I look straight at Dr. Calm and tell him that I have to think it over.

Apparently medical school doesn't spend much time teaching prospective doctors how to deal with frustration because instantly Dr. Calm's face turns red and I can see that he is steaming mad (I guess that he isn't used to patients thinking). How dare a patient question a procedure that the doctor says is necessary?

I can remember seeing patients sitting in Dr. Calm's waiting room with grotesque veins bulging in their arms (most of them wear long sleeve shirts even in the summer just to cover them up). Reversing a vein in your arm can't be good for all of those muscles that are used to receiving that blood supply. I want to avoid hemodialysis and everything connected with it (I'll take the kind of dialysis without the needles thank you). I'm not about to make it convenient for Dr. Calm to plug me up to a hemodialysis machine so we sit there in silence for a few seconds until I tell Dr. Calm for the second time that I will have to think things over before I do something like reverse a vein in my arm.

Dr. Calm is obviously not calm as he holds up his two index fingers, each one pointing down like a big fang, as he pokes them at my neck saying, "Fine, in an emergency I'll just have to stick big needles right in your neck." If he is trying to scare me then it's working but if he is trying to rush me into making a decision without giving it some thought first, then it isn't working at all. It seems like Dr. Calm is treating me as if I were a five-year-old child instead of reasoning with me, so once again I tell him that I'll have to think about it. As I stand up to leave it appears to me that Dr. Calm is somewhat dazed (welcome to the club).

Driving home in my Jag I burst out crying because I don't see any way out of this mess except to suffer my way through it. The worst part of all of this is the feeling that I am totally out of control of my life. I don't have control of anything what-so-ever. I'm just being swept along by events. I can't make my brother give me one of his kidneys any more than I can make his blood match mine. I don't even control what kind of dialysis that Dr. Calm will use on my body. I'm going through mental torture because I know that I am going to go through physical torture and there is no way that I can avoid it. My life is spinning out of control and I wipe away the tears as I pull into my driveway thinking about how much I love Delila.

Chapter 4

SOUL ON FIRE

STARTLED FROM MY SLUMBER by the incessant ringing of the telephone I look to see what time it is and when I see that it is only 6:32 AM I immediately know that it has to be Jimmy (no else would call this early). My brother gruffly tells me to meet him for lunch today at the Lion's Den restaurant in Five Points. Realizing that we need to spend more time together and hoping in my heart that Jimmy is going to tell me that he will give me his kidney, I happily agree.

I offer to pick Jimmy up at his office so we can ride there together but Jimmy keeps me at arm's length by saying "meet me there at 1:00 pm sharp" before hanging up the phone without waiting for my response (same old warm hearted Jimmy).

As I am walking down the sidewalk towards the Lion's Den I see Jimmy coming from the other direction and both of us are dressed like we are here on business (we are). I knew that Jimmy would be wearing a business suit so I wore one too (just to look more worthy in his eyes).

Right after we are seated Jimmy says "Let's pray" and as we bow our heads Jimmy prays loud enough to let the Lord and everyone else in the room know that he is present.

We eat a pleasant meal together and that makes me feel good because this is the first time in quite a while that we have been nice to each other. Then Jimmy tells me that he has prayed about giving me his kidney and he has talked it over with Jill (the turmoil in my body is enormous as I wait for Jimmy to get to the bottom line). Holding my breath while leaning forward in my chair I listen to Jimmy tell me that he will get the blood test to see if he is a possible donor (my pounding heart is filled with joy).

Jimmy goes on to tell me that he is only agreeing to have his blood tested to see if he is a possible donor and he makes it clear that he is not ready to commit to actually giving me one of his kidneys.

The fact that Jimmy has not agreed to give me his kidney yet does not dampen my spirits because it has been so long since I have had any good news at all that I will take it even if it is conditional.

I respond to Jimmy with a double thank you, "Thank you, thank you" I gush giving Jimmy extra praise (since it's free and he deserves it). I can feel my body relax as the tension flows out of me but then Jimmy drops the other shoe by saying, "What worries me is that you are not a Christian so when you die I know where you are going to and I don't want my kidney to burn in Hell"!

My mind is spinning at Jimmy's remark about me not being a Christian as he continues on in a condescending tone of voice telling me that we need to study the Bible together.

My mind goes from joy to anger in a heartbeat. It takes every bit of my self-control not to yell out the thoughts that are swirling around in my brain: you sanctimonious son-of-a-bitch who are you to tell me that I'm going to Hell, but I can't say what I am thinking (if I want to live).

What does Jimmy expect me to do? Beg? My brain tells me that there is no time for Bible study because I need to be earning money.

I want to scream: judge not, but I realize that my life is at stake here and I want desperately to live so I cheerfully agree that Bible study would be a good thing (that's begging but so be it).

We are waiting for the waitress to bring us our check and I am sitting there thinking that I have already had my big shock for the day when Jimmy drops a bombshell saying, "Don, I just want you to know that I don't see that woman that you are married to sticking with you through all this". I am so shocked that I can't believe what I am hearing.

The thought that Delila is being smeared by this hassle rat makes me want to explode. Jimmy has always felt that Delila was a bad influence on me spiritually but to question her loyalty is going too far. We have been together for eight years and I would die for that woman (as she would for me).

I feel like just knocking the hell out of the son-of-a-bitch right now but after getting a partial commitment from Jimmy I don't want to blow it but my subconscious mind is in charge of my audio output and I blurt out "You're crazy as hell! This conservation is over! I have a meeting to go to!"

I storm out of the restaurant with my soul on fire. I drive like a wild man all the way home to Blythewood seething at my brother's remark about Delila.

Driving along on the Interstate Highway at about 90 miles per hour I suddenly burst out laughing in a mood swing of epic proportions. The laughter seems appropriate to me because I have just realized that the traffic police can't scare me anymore.

I can drive as fast as I damn well please because I'm probably not going to be alive much longer so a speeding ticket doesn't mean a thing. When you accept the fact that you are probably going to end up dead it sets you free from a lot of life's little details.

The emotions of my lunch meeting with Jimmy are swirling around in my brain like oil and water. I'm happy that Jimmy is going to have the blood test to see if he is a possible donor at the same time that I am deeply disturbed by my brother's remark about my wife.

My tires crunch the gravel in my driveway as I pull up to my house and I can tell you that it feels good to be coming home to someone who really loves me.

Chapter 5

PUNCTURE WOUNDS

I HAVE ALWAYS CONSIDERED myself to be a deep thinker and I feel that this must be a result of my childhood illness. People who almost die at a young age grow up more afraid of missing life than of losing life (at least I did). Spending time trying to understand what I would not experience if I were to die young leads me to have a natural respect for anything old, man, woman, dog, or tree; in fact, being sick once again makes me philosophical about everything.

I see the beauty in large trees and feel that these trees should be satisfied with life since they survived to be full grown trees; which leads me to the feeling that I too should be satisfied with my life since I am full grown and at least I know what it is to be a man. Seeking satisfaction with life by totaling my accomplishments I decide that life's ultimate competition for a man is to be totally in love with his wife. I declare myself to be the winner while I pretend to be happy with my sorry state of affairs. The doctors call this the end of the denial stage and the beginning of acceptance, but I call it losing hope.

When you have end stage renal disease the resignation stage follows the acceptance stage by about one second. This leads to what I call "the last time syndrome" where each experience is savored as if it's being done for the very last time. Is tonight the last time that I make love with Delila? Will this weekend be the last time that I ever drive to Lake Murray to visit my parents? Then after wondering if I will ever water ski again, I start the familiar "why me routine," which I am able to shake off by shouting, "Why not?" followed by crazy laughter (hey it works for me).

Snapping back to thoughts about the fiscal realities from worries of physical reality I make a mental note to phone my friend Wade Watson to see if he can hurry up with the refinancing of my home. The amount of money in my bank account is diminishing and we all know that banks won't loan you any money if they think that you need it.

No matter what thought that is on my mind when I go to sleep, upon awakening my first instinct is always to look down at my ankles to see if the swelling has gone away (it hasn't). I can see the decline in my health with my own eyes every morning. Recently my blood pressure has become more erratic (if it isn't one problem it's two). Dr. Calm has started me on medication to manage these symptoms but he ignores the fact that with the end of denial comes deep dark depression. The days grow more wearying as my kidney function declines.

Blood work is being done once a week now and it leaves small bruises on my arms. It becomes important to rotate which vein they draw the blood from so that I can make sure that each one has the maximum time possible to heal before they stick it again. With my attention drawn to this subject I begin to notice that when having my blood work done at Dr. Calm's office there is a lot more vein damage than when I use the independent laboratory.

Then I realize that the two labs are using different types of syringes which I believe accounts for how much more bruised my arms are when I have my blood drawn at Dr. Calm's office, where they are still using those old plunger type of syringes instead of the syringes that use vacuum tubes like the independent lab does. The nurse can keep a steadier hand when she uses the type of syringe with vacuum tubes to draw my blood. With the plunger type syringe there is a lot of inevitable shaking that goes on as they pull back on the plunger, and it is this shaking that leads to tearing the vein every time that they are used.

I make a point of explaining this to Dr. Calm's nurse when I ask her to order the syringes with vacuum tubes so that she will have them in time for my next blood test. Although Dr. Calm's nurse tells me that she will order them I would have been wise to attach more significance to the way that she rolled her eyes. You know the deal; next week comes but the new syringes don't. Every week Dr. Calm's nurse bruises another one of my veins and she promises that the new syringes will be here soon. I keep clinging to the hope that my decline in kidney function will reach a plateau and maybe I can live like this for a while before I have to face up to these grim realities (denial is trying to make a comeback).

With the emotional roller coaster that my life has become I can't believe that Dr. Calm hasn't thought of giving me a mild, no make that a strong, anti-depressant. I still have not given up hope of somehow avoiding my fate if only for a short while (still working my way through the denial stage). This is all happening so fast that I can make my body show up where it is supposed to be, the doctor's appointment or whatever, but I still cannot make my mind admit that this is definitely happening to me and happening fast.

Now that I am having a blood test done each week Dr. Calm wants all of the blood work to be done at his office. The reason that Dr. Calm gives me is that he can get the results of the blood work faster if I have my blood drawn at his office. I tell Dr. Calm that I don't mind having my blood drawn at his office so long as they have the syringes with the vacuum tubes because the only reason that I have been going to the independent lab downtown is because they damage my veins less.

Naturally when I go back to Dr. Calm's office the following week, I find out that once again they don't have the syringes that use vacuum tubes, and once again I leave with a badly bruised arm. I don't mind telling you that in regard to this issue my glass is full. As I leave Dr. Calm's office, I tell his nurse that she has bruised my arm for the last time because in the future I will be having my blood work done downtown at the independent lab where the technology is better (oh how the truth hurts). Dr. Calm's nurse is livid as she tells me that she will order the syringes with the vacuum tubes herself and they will be here when I come back next week, and like a fool I believe her.

Wishing that time would slow down changes not one thing, and in a week, just like clockwork, I am back at Dr. Calm's office waiting for his nurse to draw blood from my arm. I'm thinking about what this blood test means to my life when my eyes fall upon a discomforting sight: the old plunger type syringe that Dr. Calm's nurse has in her hand. Feeling betrayed I remind Dr. Calm's nurse that she had promised to have the syringes that use vacuum tubes in stock by today, and when her attitude turns sour, I tell Dr. Calm's nurse that I am going to the independent lab downtown to have my blood drawn today because of their superior technology.

It is clear that my words have struck a raw nerve as Dr. Calm's nurse tenses up as she says, "Look, if it's a needle that you are afraid of, I'll just replace it with a little tiny needle." The little tiny needle on the rather large syringe looks out of place and it is, as I am about to discover. The little needle that is sitting on top of that rather large syringe was designed for injections and blood platelets are too large to fit easily through this tiny tube. As with many of man's blunders on this earth I make this one when I don't follow my own instincts.

I knew in my heart that I needed to get out of there but I didn't want to make Dr. Calm mad because he is the best that there is in his field and it would be his nurse's version that he would hear first, so he would believe her (chapter & verse). Trying to extract myself from this uncomfortable situation, I tell Dr. Calm's nurse that I am not afraid of the size of the needle, I'm afraid of the size of the bruise that you leave (like you do every week).

Without even answering my statement, without further ado, Dr. Calm's nurse sticks her tiny needle right into the vein in my arm. I've been stabbed and there is no use arguing now that Dr. Calm's nurse has a needle in my arm, so I have to endure it. Dr. Calm's nurse didn't intend to hurt me but that is exactly what is going on as she tries gamely to pull back on the plunger, but despite her best efforts in this ill- fated mission the syringe refuses to fill with blood.

When no blood passes through the sharp, tiny needle into the tube, Dr. Calm's nurse makes a reasonable observation that more pressure is needed as she strains to pull back on the plunger that still will not move. It is at this point that a reasonable person would terminate this attempt because it obviously is not working, and that is exactly what I do (or rather I try to). Even though Dr. Calm's nurse is doing her best to hold the syringe steady, all of her straining to pull back on the plunger makes the needle shake in my arm, causing a tear in my vein that swells up like a golf ball under my skin. So I tell Dr. Calm's nurse to remove the needle from my arm.

This is the point at which medical practice diverged from medical science and I started receiving the kind of care that you will not find in any textbooks. Dr. Calm's nurse acts like she never heard me and without saying a word she pulls even harder on the plunger that still refuses to yield. This increased effort to pull back on the plunger brings a little of my blood into the shaking syringe, but nothing compared to the amount of blood that is swelling up in my arm. Yet still Dr. Calm's nurse has not responded to my repeated demands that she remove the needle from my arm.

The swelling under my skin has reached frightening proportions so I order Dr. Calm's nurse in a calm but firm manner to terminate this blood test, but she just ignores me as if I had never said a word. What would you do if this happened to you (old Beatles' song)? I am considering what would happen to my transplant chances if I took my free arm and knocked out Dr. Calm's nurse, which I am confident that I could do, when she abruptly pulls the needle from my arm.

It's hard to win an argument with someone who has a needle stuck in your arm but now that it is out, I intend to see that Dr. Calm hears about this and I am sure that he will have her head when he learns what his Nazi nurse did to my arm. The only reason that I didn't knock this Nazi nurse across the room is because I knew that I would forfeit my life, but now that she has destroyed my left arm she should forfeit her job.

As I walk out with my damaged arm, I turn around and tell Dr. Calm's nurse that she will never see my face here again, and I make sure that she knows that I am going to file a formal complaint. She doesn't even bat an eye. Little did I know that while I was in my car driving home, Dr. Calm's nurse was filing a preemptive complaint of her own by phoning Dr. Calm to make sure that he knew that I was "uncooperative" today.

Dr. Calm would be furious if he knew what really went on here today, but the phone call from his nurse will confuse him about which one of us that he ought to be mad at. Dr. Calm provides the absolute best in medical care and he is in no way responsible for the fact that one petulant employee turned the best of intentions into a medical Gulag for me today.

I learn through my painful experience one of the unwritten laws of medical care: medical science can save you if medical practice doesn't kill you first. I paid in blood to learn that lesson; I hope that reading this difficult chapter causes you less pain.

As soon as I get home, I phone Dr. Calm to protest the fact that his nurse would not terminate the blood test when I ordered her to stop. I make sure that Dr. Calm knows that I want to lodge an official complaint about his nurse. The main thing that I want to make clear to Dr. Calm is that a patient has the right to terminate any medical procedure that is causing injury and the medical "professional" has an obligation to stop when they are harming a patient (first do no harm). Dr. Calm responds by telling me that his nurse is starting a new job next week anyway (I hope that it is far away).

The medical industry has a protocol for handling unhappy patients: it's called burial.

Chapter 6

WHAT ARE THE ODDS?

RETURNING HOME FROM ANOTHER DAY of trying to earn our daily bread I discover that there is a message on my telephone answering machine from Jimmy. He tells me that we have an appointment at 10:30 a.m. this Friday at the dialysis center to have blood drawn from both of us for testing to see if my body would reject one of his kidneys (if he were to offer me one). This is a classic Jimmy maneuver; I have been at my office all day long and Jimmy probably knew that when he decided to call my house to leave a message on my answering machine.

The first thing that I do is to phone Dr. Calm's secretary to ask her to check with the dialysis center to be certain that they have the syringes that use vacuum tubes, and her assurances come so easy that it gives me an uneasy feeling. You wouldn't think that something as minor as what type of syringe is used would really matter. If it didn't make any difference they never would have developed the vacuum tube syringes. The issue has a new sense of urgency now that one of my arms has been messed up. Dr. Calm's secretary tells me that she is sure that the dialysis center will have everything that we need but her voice lacks conviction.

I live in a fog until Friday comes haunted by the thought of what happens if this blood test shows that our blood doesn't match. When I drive into the parking lot at the dialysis center on Friday, I see Jimmy getting out of his car so we walk in together.

Take my advice and don't ever go to a dialysis clinic alone because, trust me, you aren't ready for what you would see. Inside the clinic there are about 25 (un)easy chairs with roughly half of them occupied. Hemodialysis machines stand behind each occupied chair with their clear plastic tubes full of bright red living blood (I stare in stunned silence).

The hemodialysis machines pulsate as they suck the blood through their mechanical filters. The clear plastic tubes full of red living blood quiver and shake as the machines do their jobs but the weirdest thing is the sound that fills the room. The dialysis machines seem to strain as they pull in a fresh supply of blood and they relax as they slowly pump it back in. This motion, coupled with the sound, makes it seem like the machines are breathing. One thing is for sure: the machines look more alive than the patients.

I know that I said that the weirdest thing was the sound but that was before I saw the guy curled up in the fetal position in the corner on the floor (I kid you not). I start looking at the patients who are hooked up to those misery machines and I can tell that some of them look like they came from the state mental institution (like the guy curled up on the floor). Too bad that Dante' couldn't see this, he might have gotten some fresh ideas.

This blood work could have been done anywhere so why did Dr. Calm send me here to this room with the soon-to-be-dead and their combination mechanical-biological beings from Hell. I can't tell if the dialysis machines are sucking the life out of these patients or pumping it back in. Jimmy and I are directed to sit in the two (un) easy chairs, up at the front of the room, that sit side by side facing this chamber of horrors.

My mind makes my body walk to the front of the room and sit down on the edge of that chair, but oh how my soul wants to flee. I have to sit there despite an overpowering feeling of impending doom (that I am sure is well founded). I feel like a condemned criminal who is being strapped into the electric chair, but with a strange twist: most of the witnesses are crazy.

Has no one considered the psychological impact of forcing me to sit in front a room full of suffering hemodialysis patients? Hemodialysis has always been my greatest fear but I find that my imagination was unable to prepare me for the horror that is here.

Several of the normal looking patients are holding one hand up in the air as if they are in a high school class and they know the answer to the teacher's question. It is surprising when all of the nurses just walk right past these people without even asking them what it is that they need. Possibly they need to be unhooked from the hemodialysis machine to go to the bathroom or maybe they are thirsty. It could even be that having done their time in hell they just want to be unhooked so that they can go back home, but no one pays them any attention (except for me and I'm not saying a word).

I continue to find it quite disturbing that the nurses don't inquire as to why the patients are raising their hands but they just walk past them like they aren't even there (very strange). Then it hits me that the nurses are here to tend to the machines. After a while I turn to the closest patient asking him why he is holding his hand up in the air and he tells me that his circulation is bad so he is holding up his arm trying to get it going again. Then he makes a face of desperation, that tells me more than any words ever could, as he says, "When I'm hooked up to this dialysis machine it feels as if my heart is going to beat right out of my chest, and after they unhook me, I'm so tired that I have to rest before I can walk to my car."

Right then and there I make the irrevocable decision that no one will ever reverse a vein in my arm because I will take my chances with the type of dialysis that doesn't use needles (no matter what). Dr. Calm's discussions of dialysis never got to the part about having to go around with one hand held up in the air and I failed to hear anything about my heart feeling like it might beat right out of my chest. Even though this is a terrible experience, it is a good thing that I came here because now I know the truth about hemodialysis, and it is a lot worse than anything that I ever imagined.

I shiver at the thought that this could be a glimpse of my future as I look at this chamber of horrors. Then I realize that I have made an irrevocable decision: I will not use hemodialysis (some things are worse than death). This gives me a little peace because it is one of the few things that are certain in this uncertain world.

About this time my sub-conscious mind kicks into gear and I start trying to quantify the odds of having a successful kidney transplant from my brother (not good). Last week Dr. Calm had told me that there is only a one in four chance that two siblings will have blood that matches well enough for a transplant.

So, to begin with, there is only a 25% chance that my Brother could actually give me a kidney (even if he wanted to). Worse still is the fact that seven years ago I was told that I was not a good transplant candidate due to all of the scars from my childhood surgery. In the medical industry 'not a good candidate' is code for: go home and die. I can't work out the exact odds but let's just say that if I were a horse, I would be a very dark one.

There I am sitting in a state of high anxiety when a very young nurse comes up to me ready to draw my blood with one of those old-style plunger type syringes topped with the biggest needle that I have ever seen (Houston, we have a problem). Using my nicest tone of voice, lest I be labeled a troublemaker, I explain to the young nurse that Dr. Calm's secretary phoned the dialysis center yesterday to be certain that they would use syringes with vacuum tubes on me today. Then I show the young nurse my damaged left arm so that she can see how important of an issue this really is.

This real-life drama is being played out in front of an audience of dialysis patients and the ones who are close enough to hear the conversation have knowing smiles on their faces. They probably remember the day that they had to face the big needle for the very first time.

The needle that is facing me today is smaller than the huge ones that they use for dialysis but still it is a lot larger than what I am used to and I don't feel like having my only good arm messed up by that needle shaking while the nurse is pulling back on the plunger.

I insist that the young nurse go check with her supervisor about the phone call from Dr. Calm's secretary, but she comes right back needle in hand with her supervisor along to make the excuses.

To be honest, my glass was pretty well full before the Supervisor ever said one word. But the words that she did say brought me no comfort because they were all about how "professional" the staff is around here. When the supervisor got to the part about, "They know what they are doing," I blew a gasket, and said in a loud voice "I know what I'm doing too I'm getting out of here."

Leaping from this chair of agony I am ready to exit this man-made Hell, but I can't get Jimmy to come with me even when I show him my damaged left arm as an example of what could happen to him. A man has to do what he has to do, so Jimmy stays and I go. As I walk across the room towards the portal to the outside world my mind has completed a subconscious review of the overpowering smell that pervades this place, and the odor reminds me of embalming fluid (the smell of death is in the air).

Once I get outside in the bright sunshine where I can breathe the fresh air, I marvel that this beautiful world is just a doorway away from Hell. I drive straight to the independent lab downtown where they draw my blood in a professional manner as if they do this all of the time (using vacuum tubes).

On my way home to Blythewood, I reflect on today's events and I feel now that Jimmy and I have had the blood work done to see if we are a match or not, whatever the outcome, the die is cast. I know that Jimmy is on his way home right now, too, and he is probably thinking about these very same events but from a totally different perspective. I'm thinking that there is only a 25% chance that our blood types match and Jimmy is probably thinking that he has a 75% chance of being completely off the hook (I don't blame him). I can tell you that after what I went through today it feels good to get home to where I am loved.

Chapter 7

THE CAROLINA CUP

ON MONDAY MORNING I feel tired in spite of a restful weekend. Drinking massive amounts of coffee seems to be the only way to get my system going these days. The weekend had not been very emotionally satisfying because it had been my intention to spend some quality time with Delila but it was not to be. Things started going downhill when I reminded Delila that she needed to be thinking about getting a job (for obvious reasons). I must have hit a sensitive subject because after that remark Delila gave me the cold shoulder all weekend long.

Things have never quite gotten back to normal between Delila and me since our bad day at the Carolina Cup. It was supposed to be a great day, one of those that would qualify as going out in style. The Jag had been in the shop for over a month getting repainted a bright fire engine red and the guys down at Sussex Motors were working hard to complete the job in time for me to drive the Jag with its new coat of paint to the Carolina Cup, which is one of the best social events of the year.

The Carolina Cup is one of those horse races where the fillies that everyone comes to see have two legs and a beverage. The in place to be is the infield of the race track where the real show is the elaborate tailgating parties that go on. Conspicuous consumption is the order of the day and the fine silver champagne buckets set the tone for some fine dining that goes on at car after car as far as the eye can see. The objective is to wander around from party to party in between races. I have heard about people who come to the Cup year after year without ever seeing a horse.

Infield parking spaces are all reserved and ones that are on the front row provide the best view of the race, so they are a highly coveted item. This year we are in high cotton since Delila's good friend, who works for the South Carolina Department of Parks, Recreation and Tourism, is going with us. She has one of the front row infield parking places for me to show off my freshly painted Jag and two babes. Oh, what a wonderful day it is (so far).

It was planned to be a day to end all days and it just about was. We went by Sussex Motors to pick up the Jag on the way to the Cup. There was the Jag in all of its splendor, a cherry red chariot which was ready for the mission. Then things started to go haywire.

When I drove into the infield at the Carolina Cup, I did it in style. The Jag looked great as did Delila and her friend. There was a pretty major problem, though, since there was a car already parked in our reserved space. The car that was parked in our space had been locked up and left, which was basically what I thought should be done with its owner.

I rounded up two of the plentiful highway patrolmen but one thing that they were not dispensing was justice, since they would not have the car towed from my space (no revenue in that). The highway patrolmen wouldn't do anything at all because they said that no law was being broken, and with a chuckle they just drove away. In some areas of the country perhaps people may put up with behavior like that but not down South. I parked sideways behind the offending car so that I could have a word with its owner after the race.

We partied heartily, but I always had one eye on that car as I waited for my chance to teach the owner some manners, which I must say he badly needed. Long after the end of the last race when most people had already gone home, I waited in vain for the owner of the car to return.

Delila wanted to leave and I wanted justice, so sparks started to fly. I thought that I had a brilliant solution when I let the air out of one tire on the offending machine, but Delila just thought that she had a dumb husband; so all the way home it was just yap yap yap (if you know what I mean).

That was the beginning of a very long night and Delila and I have needed a weekend out of town together ever since that time. I have been missing the warmth of Delila's smile, so I am feeling just a little bit blue as I look out of the window. I am glad to see the crew drive up to survey the lot because that means things are moving along with the refinancing of the house.

My spirits rebound somewhat with the realization that progress is being made towards financial security even if it is borrowed money. My softball teammate Wade Watson is making things happen fast considering that I only told him a couple of days ago that I wanted to refinance my house. Other than my family good friends like Wade are the real treasures of life.

Knowing that money is on the way puts me in a better frame of mind as I drive over to Jimmy's office for our first Monday Bible study together (oh boy). I'm not looking forward to this drudgery but knowing that Jimmy and I need to bond in a deeper manner this is probably the best thing that could happen. I arrive at Jimmy's office on time and we go back into his conference room for our Bible study, and as soon as we sit down Jimmy says, "Lets pray." Jimmy's prayer was so long that I thought we were doing the entire Bible study class with our eyes closed, so when he finally got to the end, I add a hearty "Amen!" which Jimmy does not appreciate.

Then Jimmy presents me with the surprise gift of a new American Standard Bible that has my name in gold letters on the front cover, and this gesture touches me deeply (I think that we have bonded but we haven't). As I look at my new Bible Jimmy tells me to open it up to the beginning of the book of Matthew. It's not like he tells me the page number, and I'm not familiar with the sequence of the books in the Bible, so it takes me a long time to find the right page. Jimmy just sits there without offering any assistance looking at me like I'm failing some sort of religious test (which I am).

Jimmy glares at me as if I'm not worthy while he gives me instructions to read the first couple of paragraphs in the book of Matthew, so I begin to read silently. Jimmy interrupts me with a gruff tone of voice saying, "No, no, no, read aloud." I proceed to read aloud in my very best voice, but after the first two paragraphs Jimmy interrupts me again with a strange quizzical look on his face as he says, "Do you know what it all means?"

I didn't know if Jimmy meant what do these two paragraphs mean or what does the entire Bible mean; it was a vague question and so I ask him, "No, Jim what does it all mean?" Somehow my tone of voice seems somewhat insincere. My response obviously irritated Jimmy as he glares at me over the top of his notebook before launching into a lengthy dissertation about what the first two paragraphs in the book of Matthew mean. As I listen to Jimmy drone on and on about the first two paragraphs in the Book of Matthew the tension keeps building up inside of me, and I have to bite my tongue so that I don't just stand up and scream.

I am so frustrated that I finally interrupt this sermon saying, "Jimmy, if we take this much time on every couple of paragraphs it will take a year just to get through the book of Matthew." I'm sure that Jimmy has to feel this tension as much as I do, but he sticks to his prepared script and just ignores my remark as he repeats his original question saying to me, "Well, what do you think it all means?" I don't know what answer Jimmy wants and I am trying to be conciliatory when I say, "Well I guess everybody has their own interpretation."

Jimmy takes my answer as a great insult to his biblical scholarship and in righteous indignation Jimmy shouts back at me, "The Bible is NOT open to individual interpretation!" Then, not meaning to insult Jimmy, I say, "Then why did you ask me?" Jimmy is livid, his face turns red and he stands up shouting something about our Bible study being over for today (hallelujah). Jimmy tells me to just take the Bible home and read the rest of the book of Matthew before next Monday (can do).

Leaving Jimmy's office, I reflect on the total lack of brotherly bonding that I had expected to take place here today. At least the session was brief, which is good because I need to make money while I can.

The following Monday I trek back to Jimmy's office at the appointed time for Bible study again. Unfortunately Jimmy's first question is "Have you read all of the book of Matthew?" I tell Jimmy quite honestly that I had meant to read it, but because I have had so much on me there wasn't enough time to read all of it but I have read some (the first two paragraphs).

Jimmy gets hostile right away and starts shouting "Don, what do you mean you haven't had time to read the Bible. It's been a week and I'm trying to keep you from going to Hell." Jimmy's last act of Christian charity of the day is to stand up and issue me an ultimatum saying, "Don, you better go read all of the book of Matthew and be ready to talk to me about what it means next week or you will never get one of my kidneys."

As I leave Jimmy's office I start to worry about my relationship with my brother because we are not growing closer like I thought that we would. These Bible study sessions have been a lot more intense than I thought that they would be (and a lot briefer). Driving home to Blythewood my mind is occupied with the happy thoughts about where I will invest the money that we are borrowing on the house. Jimmy's hostility today is worrisome, but I don't dwell on it because I know that I will have read the entire book of Matthew by next Monday.

I can't take big risks with this borrowed money because it's all the money I have in the world but I can't be too cautious either. Pondering my possible investment options keeps me from dwelling on what went on at my brother's office today because it wasn't very comforting. Jimmy and I are supposed to be bonding but I know that it's not happening.

Pulling into my driveway as the garage door starts to go up, I am glad to see that Delila's Mercedes is here because I can't wait to tell her what a jerk Jimmy was today.

Chapter 8

EVIL HAS ITS DAY
(THE BIG WHEEL CAME BACK AROUND)

FINALLY, THERE IS A DAY OF PLENTY in my life. We close the loan on the house and Wade Watson hands me a check for $87,000 (hallelujah). This brings with it some peace of mind (at least the fiscal worries are over). "It's called liquidity and it's lovely," I sing to Delila as we drive home to Blythewood after leaving the Bank. Having sufficient amounts of money in the bank takes the edge off the world. This is the first time that I have been able to relax in a long time. Actively managing this money will give me something to do while I recover from the transplant (that I hope to have).

After receiving this big morale boost the bummer of going to Dr. Calm's dietician tomorrow will be easier for me to handle. I know that the trip to the dietician will be a bummer because I'm sure that she will tell me to avoid all of the foods that I like to eat (that's what dieticians do for a living).

The next day Dr. Calm's Dietitian exceeds my expectations by giving me a list of foods that I have to avoid which contains virtually every food known to man. After I glance over the list of foods that I can't eat anymore, I look up at the dietitian and say, "Why didn't you just give me a list of both foods that are ok for me to eat?" It is depressing when I put the taboo food list on the refrigerator door because I had been expecting just one page, but I was given four (it's like I am wall papering the refrigerator).

Taking comfort from Delila's statement that she will help me watch my diet I still have the feeling that this is a situation that we can handle together. Even though Delila and I now have some sort of financial security there is still some tension between us because of everything that is going on. I guess that a lot of the tension is because I have been pressuring Delila to get some sort of a job until I get well. Having a transplant is different than having regular surgery because you have no idea how long it will take to get well (if at all).

Longing to regain that loving feeling with Delila that has been missing these past few weeks, I suggest that we drive down to Myrtle Beach for the weekend. It would be nice for just the two of us to spend some time together. Delila tells me that Sabrina can spend this weekend with a friend and I have something nice to look forward to as I kiss Delila goodbye for the day.

I'm going on a mission to sell some life insurance in Bishopville with my friend Al Holland today. Al sets up the appointments and I go in and play the role of expert from afar (which I am). It's always a long day when I go to Bishopville, but Al's stories are so entertaining that I have fun and we make some money too.

There is another dimension that makes my journey to Bishopville worthwhile and that is because I feel useful to society when I make a sale. The clients usually already have a life insurance program that is working just fine (for the agent who sold it). After I explain the financial pitfalls of what the client already owns, Al sets up their new life insurance program and we are all done (except for getting paid).

Al and I usually make the sale because the math is on our side and Al is one of the most likeable guys in Lee County, where he owns the local farm supply store. Today is no different and when it is over, I am driving home on the interstate highway with a nice sale in my briefcase. Normally I would just call it a day at this point but these aren't normal times. So, I think that I will make one more sales-call on a successful businessman that I have known for a long time in a small town named Camden because it is on the way home.

This mission is to pick up his life insurance policies for review (that's how Life Insurance salesmen do what they do). I don't know for sure but it has always seemed to me like my prospective client has some sugar in his boots, if you know what I mean. So, when he starts telling me that his life's ambition is to establish a home for runaway boys, the irony hits me as being extremely funny. It is all that I can do to not burst out laughing right in the client's office but thankfully I make it out to my car before I succumb to the urge to laugh.

Delila knows this client too, so I know that she is going to get a laugh out of this story. Let me tell you that there hasn't been much to laugh about in my life recently so I can't wait to get home to Blythewood so that I can tell Delila all about it. Even though I try hard to keep my mind off of my troubles in the back of my mind, I'm still worried because I don't know how much longer I will be able to work. I'm also not sure how long it will be before I can return to work once I stop.

There is also the issue of the pain to contemplate. Since I have never had a transplant before I have no frame of reference for how bad I will hurt. (What if I can't stand the pain?) A few weeks ago, Dr. Calm had told me that I could expect to be out of work for six months or more, and it's that 'or more' part that bothers me. I don't want to even think about the physical hell that I am about to go through because even the best- case scenario means that I am going to hurt like hell (ouch).

When I get home and turn into my driveway, I push the button on my radio control for the electric garage door to open but nothing happens (the power must be out). Then I notice that the bench that sits on the front porch is gone (some thief must have helped himself to our porch furniture)! I stop my car in front of the unresponsive garage door, and I get out and stare at the vacant spot that would normally be occupied by the bench.

Then I see the note that is stuck in the front door. As soon as I open the unsigned note I recognize Delila's handwriting, but I can't stand to read the words because I already know what the story line will be (girl leaves boy). I fumble with my key as I unlock the front door and step inside the darkened house with my heart about to beat right out of my chest. I reach over and flip on the light switch but nothing happens, which adds to my state of confusion.

I say, "Hello, I'm home," even though I know that I am all alone. I stand perfectly still while my eyes adjust to the dim light but it will take a lot longer for my heart to adjust (I know the deal and it stinks). Instinctively I flip the light switch again before looking up to see what the problem might be, but instead of seeing the antique light fixture, there are just two bare wires sticking out of the wall. I take a few steps into the great room and I can see that the antique love seat is missing but the couch that the cat had pissed on is still here.

There I am standing in the dark in the midst of the ruins of my life when I remember that Dr. Calm had warned me that I might start hallucinating as my body chemistries get out of whack. Just last week I had put the milk in the kitchen cabinet, where the glasses go, instead of back in the refrigerator.

Hallucinations, what a relief, my heart jumps for joy as I walk through the great room (dead cat bounce). Then I see that the ceiling fan is gone and I know that any delusion took place before today. I was briefly in denial but now I realize that I couldn't hallucinate in this much detail, so I try to read the note in the fading light (it's an age- old story but it's new to me).

I read the first few words of Delila's note and my heart sinks right to the floor with my body collapsing on top of it. As I go down, I make a sound like a wounded beast that I have never heard before or since. I cry out in the darkness, "Delila, I'm home" (then I just cry).

I would have laid there on the floor crying forever if it would have brought Delila back home to me but I know that I am the only one who can hear me so I get back up on my feet and begin to survey the damage as the setting sun's rays cast their long shadows.

I stagger into the bedroom trying to understand why this has happened but my grief is so profound that I can't even express it to myself (much less to you). I try collapsing again to see if it will do any good, but it doesn't. My bones feel heavy as I lay on the floor, then I cry out, "Et tu Delila." I know how the mighty Caesar felt when he saw his friend Brutus' hand gripping the knife that was in his chest.

I will tell you that lamenting on the floor loses some of its appeal when you are all alone but what else could I do (not much). After a while I struggle to my feet again in the fading light of the setting sun and I walk around in silence surveying the destruction that evil has done.

I think about the money that I have just borrowed from the bank and like a nuclear negative I realize that just last week I had put Delila's name on my money market account. I know in my heart that if Delila is gone then the money is too. A man never likes to admit that he is scared but my hand is shaking like a leaf while I dial the phone trying to reach my friend at the bank to see if there have been any recent rather large withdrawals. My friend explains that banks do all of their check clearing with other institutions at night so he can't tell me for certain what the deal is until first thing in the morning (I know the deal, I'm screwed).

I spend the sadist night of my life sitting all alone in the darkness feeling utterly betrayed (and I am). I wonder how things could possibly be worse than they are right now, then I think of the answer: wait until I start trying to pay back all of the money that I just borrowed from the bank. No longer having the comfort of deluding myself, I start wondering just how big of a check Delila wrote to herself to go (severance pay I suppose).

Then I phone my best friend, Bill Tulluck, who lives in Orangeburg, which is a small town that is about an hour's drive from Blythewood. I tell Bill about my shattered dreams. As I pour my heart out into the phone Bill tells me that he will come over to my house early in the morning (the calvary is on the way).

Bill is cut from the same cloth as the Americans who built this country (He owns a construction company). We are talking about the kind of man who means what he says and has the ability to see that it happens. Everyone probably has just one friend that can be counted on when push comes to shove, and I'm glad to have a friend like Bill on my side because I've been pushed pretty hard.

From what I have observed of this world I'll bet that Heaven is full of best friends and parents along with their dogs. Dogs never lie and if they leave home, we never question that they are lost. Maybe Delila is lost (no that would be me).

Before we say goodnight, Bill tells me that he has a friend in Columbia who owns a cleaning company and Bill will phone him first thing in the morning to get someone to come over to my house to clean the place up. It feels good to have a friend like Bill because about the only other thing that I have right now is the couch that the cat had pissed on.

I know that Bill will be a big help to me in this situation with his engineer's mind and his well- placed connections besides he has just gone through his own divorce so he knows the ropes. I look forward to seeing Bill pull up in his big Lincoln Town Car but that will not happen until tomorrow morning and I still have to make it through the night. I can see why they call this being heart-broken because it feels like I have a weight on my chest and maybe a pain (I guess that is from where Cupid pulled out his arrow).

Then I phone both of Delila's brothers to find out if they know where she is, but they don't and there is no answer over at her parent's house so I do the next logical thing: I call my own parents to tell them what came down here today at my house. I tell my Mother that it feels like the contents of my life are gone and I've been left with the box that it all was in. I talk to my parents as long as I can since I don't dare cut the power back on until I tape up all of the loose wires.

After talking to my mother for hours on end I sit alone in the darkness and much to my surprise a little humor comes creeping back into my brain. I think about one of my favorite sayings, like I have always told Sabrina to do her homework because "the big wheel comes around," and I realize that the big wheel had come around for me today (squish).

They say that sleep never comes to a troubled mind and I can verify that since I stay awake all night long. When the dawn's early light starts filtering into my miserable world it surprises me that the sun even bothers to come up today (but it did). As I start to shave I am startled by the face I see in the mirror looking back at me. I know desperate eyes when I see them and this is even worse because I recognize these (it's me).

I still cannot believe that Delila doesn't love me. A sane man would have taken the hint but I find denial more comforting. I picture Delila upset and crying with her parents there keeping her from phoning me to make up (what other explanation could there be). I'm so full of hurt that there's no room for anger, then I hear the sound of a car's tires rolling on the gravel driveway.

Deep in denial I think that it's Delila coming back home to me, so I run to the front door. My bubble is burst as soon as I look outside but it still feels good when I see Bill Tulluck's car sitting in my driveway (the calvary is here). After we take a tour of the desolation Bill starts putting some logic into this emotional situation by telling me that getting in the first shot in a divorce case is really important, as he gives me the phone number of some hotshot attorney.

It rankles my soul to hear Bill talking about me divorcing Delila (I don't want to divorce Delila, I want her back). Yet still I know a bad sign when I see one and all of your stuff being gone when you come home is one of the worst signs that you can have. Even though I don't want to listen I know that Bill is right. Inside of my heart I know that tomorrow will be better because surely evil has already had its day.

Chapter 9

CLINGING TO DELUSION
(AS MY HEART SINGS THE BLUES)

LATER IN THE MORNING some primal instinct forces me to seek food. I don't need to worry about what might be in the refrigerator (it's gone). No need to waste time thinking about something to heat up in the microwave oven since it's gone too. Even the electricity is gone since the pillagers had the good sense to cut off the electric breakers before they took the antique light fixtures.

At 8:30 a.m. my friend at the bank phones me to let me know that Delila wrote herself a $60,000 check (to go). At this point I'm just glad that Delila left me any money at all and I wonder if this could mean that she still cares about me (oh sure). I have big money problems for sure, but that's somewhere off in the future and I may not be around for that long. At least Delila left me with enough money for now and that's all that I am going to focus on (the glass is 10% full). The $60,000 check cleared my bank account on the 26th and my furniture cleared the house on the 27th (Ha Ha).

Denial may get in the way of one's efforts to deal with reality but that still might be better than being paralyzed by depression. Feeling somewhat better by clinging to my current delusion, that Delila could actually still love me, I drive into Columbia and eat breakfast at Lizard's Thicket. Events often demand that you make important decisions on the spur of the moment when your only real choice in life being whether you make it happen or let it happen. If you go through life just letting things happen you end up with what is left over after everything that was worth fighting for is gone (that can't be good).

If I could give you just one rule to live by it would be: don't let it happen, make it happen.

So instead of just eating my breakfast I'm forced to sit there pondering monetary choices like should I mail a check to the I.R.S. and deplete my assets or should I just file for another tax extension. Then it occurs to me that there is a good side to my medical woes: if I'm dead I don't have to pay the I.R.S. (small comforts are all that I have). I could be dead by the time the tax extension runs out. The eternal optimist in me has found the silver lining (such as it is). I realize that this is a no brainer and I decide to file an extension with the I.R.S. because it's probably smarter to hold on to whatever cash that I still have. Don't forget to enjoy the good that comes with the bad in life (such as it is).

The entire time that I spend thinking about the I.R.S. and my money problems is time that is totally devoid of any thoughts about Delila. Maybe emotions are stored in a different part of the brain than financial problems and the short break from the "Why, Delila, why?" routine leaves me feeling a little better as I arrive at the office of the lawyer that Bill Tulluck had recommended (Jim McLaren).

When I walk into Jim McLaren's office, he is sitting behind his desk with a cigarette hanging down from his mouth at a 45-degree angle giving him sort of a Humphrey Bogart tough- guy look which reassures me (Lord knows that I need a tough guy on my side right now). After I finish explaining the particulars of my current situation to McLaren he shouts, "We'll get the bitch! We'll get the bitch!"

The hair on the back of my neck bristles when he refers to Delila as a bitch. I can't get used to Delila being my enemy but she is. Just yesterday morning Delila was the love of my life. Getting used to the new reality may take some time.

I almost choke when McLaren tells me that he needs a check from me for $5,000 up front for his retainer. Then he starts talking about other people that I should get ready to pay like the photographer and, for some reasons, he recommends that I retain two different private eyes. While he is phoning the photographer, telling him to get out to my house right away, I'm sitting there thinking about having to pay two private eyes and wondering why. Maybe this lawyer is going to try to sock it to me and run up his fee (stranger things have happened).

Feeling the need to probe McLaren's logic, I ask him why two different detective agencies are required. He lights up another cigarette and says, "Some dicks excel in surveillance while others are better at getting action pictures of the perpetrators." The word perpetrator being applied to my wife makes me mad but I know that he is right, so I write out the checks.

McLaren keeps talking in a detached monotone that makes me wonder how many times he has watched the movie Casablanca, because he has the Humphrey Bogart persona down pat.

According to him, our primary objective is to locate Delila's hideaway so we can serve legal papers on her for desertion and abandonment before her lawyer can serve legal papers on me. McLaren phones both of the private eyes putting them on the trail (the hunt for Delila had begun).

I drive back home to Blythewood arriving just in time to unlock the front door for the photographer who pulls into the driveway right behind me. It occurs to me that there really was no need to lock the house when I left this morning since everything of value had already been pilfered. While the photographer is doing his thing, I phone my mother putting her on the case (to find Delila). At my mother's suggestion I call my cousin who works with the power company to see if Delila has opened an account in her name.

While I'm waiting for things to develop, I drive across town to see another one of my cousins, Billy Taylor, who owns a restaurant appropriately named Bill's Restaurant. Billy knows everybody and their daddy too that's why he is the Chairman of the Richland County Council. I just hope that this is one of those deals where it's not what you know but who, because I don't know anything except that Delila it gone and it makes me blue.

Walking into Bill's Restaurant reminds me of a scene from the movie "the Godfather." I see Billy sipping coffee in the far corner booth and he motions for me to come join him, so I do. Then I start pouring out my story about what I found when I got home from work yesterday or more correctly what I failed to find and after I had finished my tale of woe Billy tells me to finish my coffee while he goes to make a phone call.

Billy walks through the door behind the counter that leads to the kitchen area and he is only gone for a couple of minutes before he comes back to the booth to tell me that Sabrina is not in school today. Billy tells me to call him back in a couple of hours so that he has some time to find out if Sabrina has enrolled in any other school in the area, and if she has enrolled, we might be able to get her address (it feels good to have the Godfather on my side).

Driving home to Blythewood I find some dark humor in the old saying,'Life is such that things could always be worse.' Yesterday I had financial security that lasted 24 hours and now I have a 30- year mortgage to remember it by. The good news is that my financial problems are of such magnitude that there is no time left to worry about my health, and since I'm so absorbed with thoughts of Delila there is no time to worry about money.

When I get back home to Blythewood the people that Bill Tulluck got to come clean up my house are waiting on their check. After the cleaning crew leaves my house the silence is deafening (I would cut on the t.v. except that it is gone). Oh, how I long to hear Sabrina playing her music too loud.

The nothingness magnifies my desperation until it is broken by the sound of the telephone ringing. Delusion comes quickly when a man hears what he wants to hear and as I rush across the room, I'm hoping that the phone call is from Delila (but it's not). I am brought back to reality as soon as I say, "Hello," because the phone call is from Bill Tulluck, calling from Orangeburg just to see if I'm ok. I talk with Bill for a long time and we do some much-deserved gender bashing but I still hurt inside.

I go to bed early since I didn't sleep any last night, but early the next morning I am awakened by someone pounding on the front door to my house. I don't have to wonder who that might be aggressively knocking on my front door at 7:15 in the morning. It has to be Delila's process server trying to serve legal papers on me but I realize that with the garage door down the process server can't tell that I am here (so I act like I'm not). Bang all you want, I think, but I'm not answering the pounding at my chamber door (E. A. Poe turns over in his grave). One of the concepts in life that is important to master is knowing when delay is on your side and today it is on mine.

After the process server gives up, I phone my friend Charlie Branham to tell him about the need to locate Delila's new address and Charlie tells me that he dates a girl that works at the Highway Department. She can check their computers to see if Delila has changed the address on her driver's license. It feels good to have the hounds on Delila's trail after all her hounds are on mine.

As soon as I hang up the phone it starts ringing. This time I'm not thinking that it might be Delila calling me to say that she loves me (that's progress, I suppose). Chancing that the ringing phone isn't the process server I pick it up. It's my cousin who works at the power company letting me know that he can't find anything in the power company's computer that looks like it could be Delila (dead end).

Then I remember that I was supposed to call Billy Taylor back to see if Sabrina had enrolled in a different school, so I phone Bill's restaurant only to find out that the Godfather has come up empty handed too (dead end number two).

When the phone rings again the search for Delila is over. My Mother has Delila's address and her unlisted phone number too. My Mother will not tell me how she got what I needed but I know that one of Mom's best friends has worked for the telephone company for years (and one plus one is two).

The search for Delila took less than one day and when I call Jim McLaren to give him the information, he is impressed, and so am I (way to go Mom). Delila's new address is on Garden Path Lane (how fitting since I have definitely been led down the garden path). An ecstatic McLaren gives me clear instructions not to phone Delila until after we have served her with legal papers and that will not happen until early tomorrow morning. He is excited but the concept of serving legal papers on Delila brings me no joy.

The temptation for me to phone Delila is too great to resist (I know that I have to call her). The clock drags around all day long and I finally dial Delila's number at nine p.m. My heart pounds as it rings once, if her parents answer I'll just hang up, my heart pounds faster as it rings a second time (if a man answers I'm going to flip out).

Delila answers her phone on the third ring and the music of her voice brings a smile across my face. I utter, "We need to talk sweetheart." Delila responds coldly, saying, "Tell it to my attorney". Not until this moment do I realize that there is no hope of reconciliation. Delila really doesn't love me anymore (how can this be).

I say to Delila, "Does this mean that your offer to give me one of your kidneys is off?" (Ha! Ha!). Delila slams the phone down in my ear without giving me an answer (her sense of humor has always been somewhat deficient).

My heart aches while my soul cries the blues.

Chapter 10

TORMENTED BY THE PROCESS (SERVER)

MY GUTS ARE TIED UP IN KNOTS, all night long, as I am constantly tormented by the vision of Jim McLaren's process server pounding on Delila's door. At 7:30 a.m. sharp I am awakened by the sound of Delila's process server pounding on my door again (to no avail). Small wonder that my queasy stomach refuses breakfast.

Cup after cup of coffee help me to pass the time while I am waiting for McLaren to get to his office so that I can get a report on our early morning attempt to serve Delila with some legal papers of our own. When Jim McLaren drives into the parking lot at his office I am already there waiting on him so we walk up to his office door together.

Even before McLaren can unlock the office door we can hear the sound of his telephone ringing. The insistent ringing turns out to be his process server phoning in with a report on all of the details about how he successfully served legal papers on a very surprised Delila this morning at 7:32 am.

McLaren had just hung up the phone and had barely begun to gloat when the phone rings again, but this time the caller is Delila's attorney who is loudly demanding to know how we got Delila's address and unlisted telephone number. Hearing Delila's attorney demanding an answer over the speaker phone, my sense of humor overrides my brain and I shout out, "We got them by asking my mother."

Delila's attorney is obviously perturbed. She must have phoned him as soon as she was served with our little surprise. Even though

Delila's attorney "officially" is outraged, "unofficially" he is very impressed (thank you Mom). After the normal unpleasantries Delila's attorney concludes the conversation by telling McLaren, "We will see you in court" (which is how lawyers tell each other hot-dog we are both going to get paid).

McLaren is arching up one of his eyebrows, as he turns slowly in his chair until he is directly facing me, then he says, "What the hell is this business about knowing Delila's unlisted phone number?" Somewhat meekly I explain by saying, "McLaren, I love the woman so I had to call her." His knowing eyes tell me that he understands even before I hear him say, "It doesn't matter because we served Delila with our legal papers first, so you are in the driver's seat."

Having already heard what I came here to find out I stand up to leave while I am responding to McLaren by saying, "Too bad that it is the driver's seat of a gasoline tanker that is stuck on the railroad tracks." (I wish that I could jump out and run but I can't).

The comment that Jim McLaren just made about me being in the driver's seat sticks in my mind as I drive aimlessly around the city trying to prioritize my problems. The one constant is that they are all going to require money.

Depression paralyzes me for days on end but I know that I am going to be even more depressed if I run out of money, so eventually I decide that I had better go make a sale. If I am going to make a sale, then it may as well be a big one, I'm thinking as I drive into Columbia to pay a little visit on Burney Nix, who owns the local Porsche dealership.

I know that someone who has as much money as Burney Nix does must get called on by a lot of salesmen wanting part of it (like me). Somehow, I have to get through his defensive screens and decide that my chances are better if Burney thinks that he might be the one who is making the sale.

Wheeling into the Porsche dealership I'm glad that my car looks sharp, it might blow my cover if I were pulling up driving a wreak. I walk into the dealership and sit down in their most expensive Porsche. I tell the car salesman that wins the sprint over to me that, "I'm here to see Burney" (that sends him scurrying away). While I am sitting there, thinking that a car that sells for this much money should come with a garage, (if not a house). I see a beautiful young lady making her entrance through the showroom door.

Mesmerized, as I am, by the sound of high heels clicking on the hard tile floor it surprises me when the young lady stops right in front of me. I look up at her trying to take it all in but the only things that I see are big gold earrings and ruby red lips. Then I hear her telling me in an angry little voice that her Porsche is overheating (so am I).

Ah-ha! A damsel in distress and she must think that I work here. Seizing the moment, I decide to play the role and I take her back to the service department where they can take care of the problem. When the service manager tells her that it will take a couple of hours to fix her Porsche since they have to wait until it cools down before they can begin, I see the smile on those ruby red lips turn upside down.

I know opportunity when I see it, and it is right here. I break the silence by saying, "My Mercedes works just fine, why don't we go to lunch while they take care of your car?" Her reflexive smile is somehow good for my soul, but it could just mean that she has subconsciously estimated my net worth based on the list price of the Porsche that I was sitting in. She accepts my chivalrous offer with two blinks and a smile (her name is Monica). About that time the Porsche salesman returns with the news that Burney Nix is not in today, but I don't really care because I've already made a sale so to speak. I leave my business card for Burney and drive away with Monica (what a great day).

Momentarily forgetting all of my troubles, I pour all of my charm and several beers into Monica during our lengthy lunch. We eat at Annabel's restaurant in Columbia Mall, but the main things that are served are goo-goo eyes and footsie. Monica thinks that I am rich and I think that she is beautiful (sounds like the basis of a relationship to me).

When we return to the Porsche dealership, I'm really relieved that Monica's car is ready for her to pick up because, even though lunch was fun, I'm not ready for a relationship yet. Even if I were ready to fill the void in my heart I'm not in the mood for another flashy woman. When the day does come for me to bond with a woman again, this time I want a woman of pure values and subdued beauty instead of the other way around (once down the Garden Path is enough for me). Driving home to Blythewood I marvel that medical science can't make you feel younger but going to lunch with a beautiful woman can (thank you, Monica).

I wake up the next morning to a mild case of the blues (go figure). In the shower it is my soul that I'm trying to cleanse as the warm water beats against my pitiful head. My heart heard the phone ringing before my ears did at least that's how it seemed as my spirits soar skyward before the second ring (it could be Delila or I could be in denial [probably the later]). By the time that I can race from my bathroom to the kitchen the ringing has stopped but they have left a message on my answering machine.

When I pushed play my heart was sitting up in my throat wanting to hear soft words spoken from Delila's lips, but my bubble is immediately burst by the sound of Dr. Calm's nurse telling me to phone her sometime today, preferably this morning if I can. That part about calling her back this morning is a piece of advice that I'm going to just have to ignore because I am going to stop by the Porsche dealership to see Burney Nix, and I don't want reality getting in the way of the sale (woe is me if I don't sell).

Walking into the dealership I notice that I have a little more spring in my step than I normally would, and I think that perhaps the little red Porsche isn't overpriced after all, considering how well it worked for me without even starting the engine. I pause for a moment next to the red Porsche on the show room floor and just about the time that I was wondering if they could work out a thirty-year mortgage, Burney Nix appears by my side inviting me back to his private office.

While Burney and I walk through the Porsche dealership on the way to his office I think about the importance of the next few minutes. I spent, or wasted, a lot of time for whatever results this meeting brings, so I want to make my point clearly (I can save you money). and get any objections out on the table. Burney is easy to talk with (especially when you might be buying a Porsche) and he gives me his life insurance policies to review. I feel like it's been just a little too easy (when you catch a big fish you expect a big fight). At least I'm leaving here with what I came in for (Burney Nix's life insurance policies). I wonder how all of this would have turned out if instead of sitting in the $83,000 red Porsche, I had just gone up to the secretary and tried to make a sales appointment with Mr. Nix (right).

Flush with victory my mood soars and I decide to roll with this tide of emotion and see if there isn't someone out there who would love me (if we had only met). I know that the woman who I fell in love with no longer exists, and love is what my soul craves as time dwindles away. When you look back at this world with your own fate close at hand you find that life's true treasure is love, and it's something that you cannot do alone. Compelled by my empty heart I look for worthy women wherever I go (like I would know one if I saw her).

It helps my broken heart to be around people who are having a good time, even if they are not talking to me the sound of their chatter helps me to not dwell on my blues. It is important in life to know when delay is on your side and with my declining health delay is the enemy in my quest to find love once more. Using my business education, I start doing "market research" in the search for Miss Right. While making business calls I cast an eye on the clerical pool, when I am shopping at the mall what I'm really after is companionship, as I continually search for something that I have never found but surely exists (true love).

Needing to cover a lot territory in a short period of time I go in to bars for a one beer experience. My favorite watering hole is a restaurant named the Loft which is located in Five Points. As I sit at their oyster bar it feels good to be in a room full of people chattering and having a good time, but I'm looking for magic not waiting for magic to find me. So I chug my beer and go back into the night wondering if I love Delila so much that falling in love with someone else might not be possible.

Concentrating once again on life's possibilities instead of its probabilities, I stop for another beer at a late-night club named New York, New York. Quickly deciding that this crowd is too young for me I chug my beer in preparation for a speedy exit, and then I see HER dancing on the lighted dance floor. Making this a two beer experience I move closer to the dance floor to better observe this evocative free spirit dance into my psyche. I am mesmerized as she dances to a unique rhythm, happily smiling as she cast her spell over me without knowing of my existence. I'm enthralled by the way she moves, her means of locomotion is smooth and uninhibited, exhibiting a spirit that is in harmony with something deep inside of me.

Soon after the song ends her dance partner, (yielding to the axiom: beer in, beer out) heads to the men's room and acting on instinct, I sit down in his vacated chair not having a clue as to what I am about to say. This brief moment of silence is more effective than anything I might have uttered, as looking at her with genuine appreciation brings a smile across her face just as a new song begins beckoning our unintroduced souls to bond.

She is one with the music and I am one with her. Too soon the song is over and not wanting our budding cosmic relationship to end with the music, I tell her that I'll get us a couple of beers. She responds that her nose needs powdering as she disappears into the crowd.

The first five minutes that I wait are those of blissful ignorance because she never returns to my table. Scanning the crowd in vain I suddenly feel like a fool. Denial gives way to anger for allowing myself to be hurt by someone whose name I don't even know. Chugging both beers, I make a mental note to walk my dates to the lady's room in the future.

Driving home in a stupor once again, I marvel that a pretty girl can make a man feel younger but medical science cannot (it seems profound after seven beers). My drunken mind visualizes life as an interstate highway where the car is going so fast the road signs are impossible to read, then the truth hits me (lost in a trance my car is going 85 m.p.h. and being a bit under the influence I can't read the signs). A rush of fear sweeps through my body which is taken as a good sign as it proves to me that on the subconscious level it is clear that I still want to live.

The next day, knowing that my money may give out before my kidney does, I decide to drive back to Bishopville to work with Al Holland. Even if we don't sell a thing, I know that his funny stories about small town life will take my mind off of my problems at least for a while. The drive on the interstate to Bishopville gives me time to put things in perspective (I am in deep doo doo).

A few weeks ago, there would have been audible boo-hoos and tears as I listened to B.B. King singing "The Thrill Is Gone" all the way to Bishopville. Now the trip can be made without crying as long I don't play B.B. King. There is a sense of emotional healing and to nurture this progress I feel a need to withdraw from negative stimuli (doctors). I go get my blood work done on schedule but not wanting to be brought down, I don't call to find out the results, nor can I bring myself to return Dr. Calm's phone call (depression paralyzes in an attempt to protect). The week is happily plodded through with all images blocked out other than those of my smiling dancer.

When Saturday night finally rolls around, I am drawn to one place only, the club New York, New York. I must find my smiling dancer like a pretty, little needle in a hay stack. To increase the probabilities that we find each other in the teaming crowd, I wear the same cream colored linen suit that I wore the night we danced along with the same light lavender shirt and thin red tie.

Hopefully, this will help her to recognize me if she wants to because if she isn't on the dance floor, I might not spot her even if she is in the club. As I scan the dance floor my heart sinks when she is not there. Having a beer as I curse the power of a woman whose absence can bring me down, suddenly my knees buckle (someone has popped my knees from behind like in elementary school). Turning to smite whoever has jostled me I see the beautiful eyes of my smiling dancer (she found me)!

The smile breaking across my face erupts into a laugh as we spontaneously head into the throbbing mass on the lighted dance floor. Deliriously happy we dance song after song bonding in bliss (at least I was). Over drinks she tells me that her name is Debi and that she is twenty- four years old, having recently moved back home to Columbia after living for a year in New York City in an unsuccessful attempt to be an actress.

When we reach the point in the evening where Debi has to go powder her nose, I ask her if it will take seven days. Debi's eyes stop their carefree sparkling and peer deep into mine. "I'll level with you, "She says, pouring out the intimate details of how she is living with a guy named Sandy who is six-four and jealous to the point that He could be dangerous. Then Debi tells me what happened last week. She ran into one of her friends in the bathroom who said that Sandy was in the club looking for her, so she had to sneak out the side door. Debi goes on to tell me that she is here tonight with friends because Sandy is out of town, as I walk her to the ladies' room.

More dancing leads to more bonding until Debi confides that she is no longer in love with Sandy because he runs around on her, but since she lives with him and works for his company there is no alternative until she finds a new job. Wanting to be sure of Debi's phone number before she disappears again, we leave the noise of the club to sit in my Mercedes talking for a minute, with the music playing softly as the sunroof opens allowing the moon and stars to work their magic.

Debi's relaxed smile invites my kiss but no amount of coaxing or promising can get her to come home with me. Dismay over my lack of power to induce love into my lair turns to devastation as Debi divulges that she would love to go home with me but it is out of the question. In fact, the only reason that she came outside with me is to make it clear that we can never see each other again because Sandy would kill both of us.

Before I can find fault with that logic Debi's girlfriends giggle their way out of the club causing Debi to whisper "They might tell Sandy" so she better go right now before they see us together. When I tell Debi to just duck her head down so that they can't see who is in the car she responds that riding to the club with her friends obligates her to ride home with them, or else Sandy might get the idea that she is seeing someone else. With an intimate squeeze and a quick kiss Debi hops out of my car and skips to join in the giggling throng.

Stunned at having played my best card to no effect, I drive home to Blythewood singing the blues. Yet Debi's eyes had been saying yes the entire time that her words were saying no, and then there was the strategic squeeze which gave new life to the dreams that she had just finished destroying. The enigma of Debi's actions contradicting her words intrigues me.

Sunday upon awakening, to dry mouth and a headache, I look down at my ankles for the morning reassurance only to discover that the swelling has not gone away (small wonder). I have a tiredness that is unfamiliar and frightening as it's all that I can do to get up long enough to grab a bite to eat before collapsing back into the scant relief of my bed. Maybe the swelling will never go away again; what if this means it is time for dialysis (bummer).

Now I see what makes the special diet a requirement instead of an option. I vow that if my ankles get back to normal Dr. Calm's orders will be followed to the letter (I pray but they are prayers of hope not prayers of faith).

Monday begins a new ritual of a quick prayer just prior to looking at my ankles for the latest update on my medical condition (apparently prayer works because the swelling is gone). My exuberance over normal ankles is tempered by the knowledge that today is Bible study day with Jimmy at his office.

Arriving on time for Bible study dressed in a nice suit (to look worthy). I feel good about this mission until Jimmy's first question to me, "Have you finished reading all of the book of Matthew?" Even someone whose faith is weak has to pause at lying about the Bible, but my disclosing to Jimmy the simple truth that I had been too busy to do my homework elicits an unexpected reaction. Jimmy shouts, "How can a dying man not have time to read the Bible?" Startled by his description of me as a dying man, in an attempt to defuse the situation with humor, I retort, "Jimmy, I resemble that remark." But Jimmy is unimpressed by my humor or my honesty. With facial expressions of a high priest whose golden calf has just been blasphemed, Jimmy stands up adjourning our brief meeting with the statement, "You are hopeless: there is no need for us to ever have Bible study together again!"

I leave Jimmy's office with a sense of accomplishment because I can barely stand his inquisitions. I head straight to the independent lab for my blood work knowing that this is one set of lab results that can't get to me fast enough, because my ankles have been telling me that I'm not getting any better (none of this pretending it doesn't matter stuff; I'm scared). When I finally do get the results of my blood work they really scare me because my creatinine is over 10 for the first time, and I remember Dr. Calm had at one time indicated that dialysis would be required when my creatinine level reached 8 or 9 (oh dear).

Feeling my biological clock winding down as never before I don't want to waste my last days trying to earn a buck, but needing money I make business calls in the afternoons only to discover that there is a different feeling as I scan the clerical pool looking for love. I'm looking for one particular pretty face. At that moment the conscious mind realizes that the subconscious mind has already begun the search for Debi. There is now a new mission in my life. I must find Debi!

The search for Debi begins with a call to Charlie Branham because he used to work for the company that Debi said her boyfriend Sandy owns and I want to know how to spell Sandy's unusual last name. Charlie sells insurance for the same company that I represent, so in the course of this conversation Charlie agrees to move his stuff into Sabrina's old bedroom and help me make the house payment; plus he has couches and other furniture that along with his company could help me to maintain (or attain) sanity.

Looking Sandy's name up in the phone book I remember Debi's description that he is six foot four and jealous, but figuring there is a fifty percent chance that she will answer the phone I dial the phone number planning to ask to speak to Leroy if a man answers. My senses are on full alert but I hear only the sound of endless ringing as no one answers the phone. Several times every day I phone only to have the ringing go unanswered.

When Saturday finally comes around, hoping that Debi is a creature of habit, I return to the dance floor at club New York, New York only to find the club packed but no sight of Debi.

Thinking that, since it's now Sunday, perhaps Sandy is playing golf, I drive to the address in the phone book to reconnoiter. Pulling into the Bayou apartments my heart is pounding as my conscious mind reminds me of the stupidity of this mission. The master plan is for me to knock on the door while praying that it is Debi who answers, and if a man opens the door, I'll ask if Leroy lives here loud enough that if Debi is around at least she will know that I'm trying to find her. God must protect fools in love because no one is home.

Helping Charlie Branham move his furniture into Sabrina's old bedroom I mention the quandary of trying to talk to Debi without inciting Sandy's jealousy (please remember that I am not breaking up a happy home but rather saving a maiden trapped by an ogre). Charlie has always been a good source of information (one of his female friends who works for the telephone company had provided Delila's unlisted phone number just two days after my mother got it for me) and he comes through again when he tells me that he still knows everyone who works for Sandy's company, so we will just stop by their office so that Charlie can say hello to everyone while I reconnoiter (look around and see if Debi is working at that location).

As we enter Sandy's company there is a very pretty receptionist that Charlie engages in chit chat while I look around the office in vain. Returning to the front desk I tell the receptionist that I'm a friend of the owner's fiancé, Debi, and I'm wondering if she works at this location. The receptionist's pretty face contorts as if I had just said a very nasty word as she exclaims that she (the receptionist) is engaged to Sandy and the marriage is next month!

The receptionist has her dander up and now she becomes the one asking the questions, and I'm the one who is glad that Sandy isn't in his office because the receptionist is now looking as if she is ready to kill someone. She asks me "Who the hell are you talking about" (the proverbial hornet's nest has been disturbed)!

When I tell the receptionist that all I know is that a girl named Debi told me that she works for and lives with Sandy, the receptionist looks at Charlie and says the only Debi that ever worked here was Debi Hollis, but she never lived with Sandy and she doesn't even work here anymore.

Quite innocently I ask the receptionist if Debi lived at 38-D in the Bayou apartments (the home address of Sandy and perhaps that of the receptionist). The response is another facial expression of anguish as she shouts, "Hell no, Debi doesn't live at the Bayou apartments. She has an apartment on the corner of Pickens Street and Hollywood Drive." Then she aggressively starts dialing the phone to beep Sandy's pager as she asks me to repeat my name (time to exit the craft before it explodes). "My name is Don" is all that I volunteer as Charlie and I get the hell out of Dodge.

In the car headed back home to Blythewood I'm feeling good about having a last name for Debi as well as a home address, but now I'm more confused than enlightened. Have I been on a quest over another lying woman? Opening the phone book, I see the listing D. Hollis Hollywood Drive.

The ringing phone is answered by a familiar melodious Southern voice. "Debi," I exclaim only to hear Debi's sister tell me that Debi is at work. Rolling with the events I tell Debi's sister that I am a friend of Debi's, before casually asking where Debi is working these days. The response that Debi is a waitress at A. J.'s restaurant on Devine Street shocks me since I was operating under the impression that Debi works for Sandy's company and lives with him. For the first time I realize that everything that Debi has told me, except her first name, was a lie! She fed me a line and I took it, hook, line and sinker.

There would have been anger in me except that I know that all is fair in love and war (I just don't know which of those two I'm dealing with yet). I am more intrigued than ever as I drive into Columbia on my way to A.J.'s restaurant. Pulling into A.J.'s parking lot I rev the engine of my car hoping Debi will hear the noise and look outside, recognizing my car.

Seated by fate in Debi's section she sheepishly approaches the table to take my order, her face glowing from embarrassment. Looking up at Debi our eyes lock on to each other wanting to embrace as I intone, "Pickens and Hollywood is a long way from the Bayou Apartments." Debi's face is now fully flushed, she says, "Oh, I am so sorry!"

The prying eyes of everyone in the restaurant prevents me from leaping up and kissing Debi so I settle for a club sandwich. I didn't come for the sandwich I came for the server, if only to let her know that in spite of the lies, she had been found (and I'm glad). Taking just one bite of my sandwich I leave Debi a twelve- dollar tip (as a sign of approval) before I leave the restaurant without any further conversation (I know her phone number).

Out in the parking lot, turning to the sound of rapid footsteps, I see Debi running out of the kitchen door with her arms wide open to hug me. Our embrace reminds me of a shampoo advertisement, except there is no slow motion. Smiling eyes meet smiling eyes as we kiss. Then I break the silence saying, "I am doing nothing tonight if you want to do nothing with me." Nodding vigorously in agreement, Debi tells me to pick her up at 8:00 p.m. as she races back into the kitchen. Overjoyed I float back home to Blythewood.

Hollywood and Pickens, eight o'clock sharp, the sounds of my feet pounding up the steep metal stairway announces my arrival. Debi opens the door to her world revealing brick walls painted white, covered with posters advertising Broadway musicals and Greek tragedy masks on either side of a large white couch, centered in front of an antique coal burning fireplace insert. The visual impact of the white on white suggests a purity that goes well with Debi's youthful 106 pounds of exuberance.

Bells go off in my head with our first kiss but the growl from my stomach sets our agenda as I ask Debi if she would like spaghetti for dinner (since just having one bite of lunch has left me famished). Not wanting to take Debi on our first date to a restaurant that I associate with Delila my mind sorts through all of its crevasses to come up with Tony's Restaurant on Saint Andrews Drive. It is a cozy place with high backed booths offering a little privacy for lovers of discretion such as myself out courting a fair maiden (ideal for those with a nasty soon to be ex-wife still at large).

It can only be karma that leads me to the far side of Columbia for Italian food from a Greek restaurant. Walking behind Debi and the waitress who is seating us, my peripheral vison picks up a familiar aura that sends my subconscious mind on to maximum alert. There in the next booth is Delila! The first time my eyes have fallen upon her since she kissed me good-bye the morning my life disappeared along with my furniture.

Delila is all snuggled up sitting on the same side of the booth as her lover man. My eyes are stretching open in excitement that Debi perceives as I tell her that my wife is in the next booth with a strange man. The instant that I said strange man my mind sorts through all the shapes and postures stored in the subconscious mind to the startling realization that even though I haven't seen his face, I know exactly who the dirty rat is.

Leaping to my feet and leaning into the next booth so that my face is only inches away from the two lovers, I verify that the dirty rat in question is none other than my very good friend who lives across the lake from me in Blythewood, Benedict Arnold. I say "This is not healthy," I grab Debi's hand and storm out of Tony's restaurant to my Mercedes.

Understanding for the first time the expression 'twisted mind,' I can feel my brain trying to twist inside of my skull. I open the glove compartment, starting momentarily at the rubberized grips on my Colt Python .357 magnum revolver wanting to just waste the son-of-a-bitch, but I know that this is my fault not his.

Instead of freaking out and screaming Debi says lovingly, "They aren't worth it." Don't tell me that deterrence won't stop crimes of passion because my thought process went something like, no jury in the world would convict me but Jimmy would never give his Christian kidney to someone awaiting trial for murder. So, listening to Debi's sweet voice saying WE have too much to live for, I close the glove compartment but the fire in my soul burns on. I don't want to die and shooting Benedict Arnold would blow my chances of a transplant, so I drive out of the parking lot instead of putting that guy in the ground.

Benedict Arnold had been over to my house a couple of times since Delila split just to check on me. I'll bet he was pumping me for information to pass on to Delila (my good buddy my ass)! I had noticed a lot of his cigarette butts in the ashtray located in the sun room at my home in Blythewood, which told me that he had been talking to my wife for a long period of time while I was out trying to make a living. But there had never been one of his cigarette butts in the bedroom (good thing for him). I always gave my good buddy the benefit of the doubt, plus he seemed too ugly to interest Delila, but she looked pretty interested sitting next him in the booth. I poured my soul into Debi's heart as the car headed for Blythewood but something deep in my being called for vengeance.

The inside story that had eluded me is that the bastard who had been disguised as my friend coveted my wife. He deserved to be in the cold, cold ground! Rage is more powerful than love or the desire to live. Throwing my shotgun in the trunk just in case he went for his pistol, (superior firepower seems prudent). I tell Debi to wait for me in Blythewood. I drive into the night to have a little discussion with my good buddy, the bastardly Benedict Arnold. The normal man is a different beast than the man with nothing left to lose who, when escape is impossible, is seized by the burning desire to take the oppressor with him to the grave to continue the struggle in Hell.

Driving out on the interstate, armed and on a mission that could have terminal results, it is my probability of surviving the immediate medical challenge that my mind dwells on, going over all the statistics in order to determine exactly what it is that I would be putting at risk. Then a smile breaks across my face telling me that my subconscious mind believes that in spite of the odds, I will live through this mess. Even if there is just a seven percent probability of survival, if I do make it, I'll be one hundred percent alive.

At this point I realize that I'm just armed and mad, instead of armed and dangerous, so breaking a rule I do a u-turn across the median of the interstate and turn my car towards home. I wonder if Debi will be able to handle this incredible display of everything short of violence and insanity that has been our first date (no one could blame her if she gets the hell out of my life). Debi opens the front door as I pull into the driveway, our embrace on the barren front porch reminds me of Rhett and Scarlet as our bond is, at last, forged in furry and passion.

The body can do amazing things on just breakfast and one bite of lunch but the results can be equally amazing. Much to my dismay the swelling of the ankles is still with me upon awakening from what had passed for sleep (go figure). Everything works out for the greater good as Debi spends the weekend in Blythewood nursing me back from the edge. Sunday the beautiful weather entices me to take Debi across the small lake in my canoe to show her the elegant blossoms of a huge wild azalea bush growing out over the lake so the clear water reflects the delicate pastel blossoms. This tranquility seems far from the turmoil of the realities that await me on land.

Elated by awakening to the sight of ankles that aren't swollen I try my best to talk Debi into calling in sick declaring today a spontaneous holiday. Alas, she insists that people are counting on her at work so I drop Debi off at her apartment and drive over to Jefferson Square on Main street to make a sales call on Bobby Hendrix at Hendrix Construction.

With emotion (Bobby is a family friend) and logic on my side, Bobby comes through when the chips are down, buying a one-million-dollar face amount term life insurance policy from me (I don't know if he bought because of his need or mine). Leaving Bobby's office feeling more self-assured in a sea of uncontrollable events, with my usefulness to society being validated by the business world and the female side of the species, I take several steps (enjoying the afterglow of success) before the pain that shoots from my ankles to my groin jolts me back to reality. My ankles that were fine this morning are more swollen before lunch than they would normally be in the evenings.

It seems like a good idea to drive over to the independent lab to get some blood work done during one of these swelling episodes, and since I have found Debi as well as made a big sale, my mind can stand the bad news that will surely come. It doesn't take modern medical science to tell me the results will reveal a further decline in kidney function with the pain in each step telling me to get off my feet.

Waiting until 7:30 P.M. to call the lab for the results, the ringing phone gives me a few seconds to contemplate my anguish. If the creatine is more than 10 it's bad news, less than 10 and it's great news. Dialysis isn't something you do to extend the last of your natural kidney function. Once you give in one time to the machine it's over forever as the kidney gives up and atrophies, leaving you totally dependent on torture to stay alive. My hand has tremors holding the pen to write down the results. My heart races as the lab transfers my call to Alan Oakey who will give me the numerical interpretation of my chemistries, as he would say. When Alan tells me that the numerical interpretation of my creatine level is 12.3, I nearly poop in my pants.

The suspense of having to wait until my appointment with Dr. Calm on Wednesday to get the word that it is time for dialysis makes me feel like a condemned convict on death row waiting for the phone call from the Governor that I know won't be coming (if it's not one problem, it's two).

Responding to the doorbell just as I hang up the phone, Delila's process server shocks me with a change in tactics and serves her evilness' legal papers on me which claim: that she had fled the marital residence out of fear since I was violent and had beat her up.

What a liar Delila is, I tell my attorney on the phone. He snaps me back to the reality of how the divorce game is played by deadpanning, "What did you expect her to say, that she left with all of your household goods and took your money because you are a great guy?" This objective observation defuses the emotional charge of the moment with humor, as I'm laughing instead of crying as we set up a time tomorrow for me to drop these legal papers by his office.

Tuesday my attorney and Wednesday my doctor, life creeps its petty pace from day to day (my apologies to the bard for butchering his words but these are my thoughts). This life of mine has been swept up by events that are out of my control and lyrics from a song play in my head, "like a river that has overflowed, I took a wrong turn and I just kept going."

The appointment with Dr. Calm that I had so dreaded passes without the word dialysis being mentioned (I wasn't going to bring it up if he didn't). Dr. Calm concentrates on the symptoms of my swelling ankles by increasing the dosage of my diuretic and then he drops the bombshell on me that I need to stop by Columbia Boot and Brace shop to pick me up some support hose! Will the humiliation never end? I have a brand-new girlfriend and I'm pretty sure that I'm not supposed to be the one wearing hose.

Oh, the agony of the support hose. It begins with stopping off to buy them on the way home as I feel so out of place in this store filled with old people and their parents, only to be further horrified to discover that support hose are like thick pantyhose and they are available only in white. They make me look like a fat nurse with poor traction as my foot slips and slides in my shoe especially since I'm wearing dress socks over the support hose to disguise them. Debi will never see me in this getup I vow as I take the support hose off before heading over to Debi's apartment to escape from my world into hers.

With both parties in a divorce in no mood to delay the legal system moves swiftly to the day for the court hearing on the temporary property settlement. There is no real reason to refer to this as a temporary property settlement as it's only temporary until this same division of your assets becomes permanent. It's not temporary until something fair can be worked out, like it sounds. This becomes permanent automatically unless you reopen the case with compelling new evidence, and it is this shifting of the burden of proof that causes this to be your final settlement. This is judgement day: the legal system gives your life's work a numerical equivalent and requires that you pay your ex-spouse one half of that amount or the court will liquidate your ass(ets) in any manner the judge sees fit.

The tension at the Richland County Court House suits the occasion as both sides to today's divorce hearings are sitting on pew like benches in the same large hall. This is so stupid to have both sides to this emotional struggle seated in the same area. I wonder how many divorces will end right here in murder before they change things. I try to match up the unhappy couples out of this random seating as the eyes of the other people waiting seem to be playing the same game and then Delila comes down the hall walking right in front of me without a word.

This is only the second time that I have seen Delila since she left me and she looks beautiful, promenading down the hall in Her almost a virgin look with an off-white dress, stockings, shoes and purse. This outfit of Delila's makes me think of this as a reverse bridal procession (I guess this must be a bridal recession.)

At last my lawyer ushers me into a conference room where the deal is cut with the two lawyers picking over the carcass of what had been our marriage, as they haggle out the details of an agreement with the bride and groom in separate conference rooms prior to the final matrimonial ceremony in front of the judge. It is cold to see your possessions divvied up but colder still to hear the judge's gavel fall on your marriage.

When the bailiffs open a pair of doors, the attorneys and the newly un-weds start moving in unison without instruction to exit the courtroom, down a wide sloping ramp that has a waist high railing providing a panoramic view of the empty lobby one floor below. Feeling somewhat like Solomon's justice had just given me one half of my child I wonder how many despondent unrequited lovers will take a dry dive to the hard tile floor, when I hear a familiar voice saying, "I will not be needing this anymore." This causes me to turn around with my back to the railing to find Delila standing right in front of me holding out her closed hand palm down, as if to hand me something (the two aggrieved parties that had to be sequestered in separate conference rooms are now face to face over a lovers' leap).

Holding out my open hand palm up to receive my final gift from her evilness, Delila drops the gold wedding ring that I had given her into my palm with the verbal admonishment, "I didn't think you would be such a liar!" In my best Rhett Butler 'frankly my dear, I don't give a damn' personification, without averting my eyes (remembering her cold retort of "tell it to my attorney"). I toss Delila's wedding ring over my right shoulder (for good luck) saying, "Tell it to the judge." With the ping of Delila's ring bouncing off the tile floor below providing the final bell for our marriage. Delila's jaw drops open in amazement, providing me with a smile where before there was none. I walk outside into the Southern sunshine a free man.

Feeling a little blue as I leave the courthouse it seems like there is an emotional need to stop by my brother's office to tell him that the evil princess and I had our day in court. When a smile breaks across Jimmy's face upon my entering his office it is obvious that something is up, because Jimmy has been wearing a tense frown ever since I asked him to have one of his living organs cut out of his body (go figure).

I'm worried that his relaxed look means that for some reason he is off the hook then Jimmy stands up giving me a vigorous handshake as he says, "Dr. Calm just phoned with the results of our blood studies to see if we match well enough for a transplant to take place and we are what is known as a half-match which is not perfect but it means that a transplant could work."

Then Jimmy continues by saying, "More importantly while praying with my prayer group about this quandary one of them told me that we are supposed to follow the teachings of the Bible and Jesus would give the gift of life so I have decided, reserving the right to change my mind if it doesn't look like it will work, that I will give you one of my kidneys."

In an involuntary spasm of joy, I shout, "Hallelujah! Thank you, thank you!" Realizing that what Jimmy is doing (giving me his spare kidney) coupled with blood studies indicating that we are a match will mean life instead of death. My heart leaps with joy and looking into Jimmy's eyes, I feel a brotherly love that has been missing for some time as we both have had defensive emotional blocks that are now removed, allowing a full expression of unconditional brotherly love.

Feeling like a double lottery winner I phone my parents and Debi before driving home to Blythewood on cloud nine to discover that the traitor Benedict Arnold is out mowing his back yard down by the lake. It's amazing how fast the hostility changes my mood as the last time that I saw the low life he was with my wife.

Since Benedict Arnold has been trying to sell his house, he hasn't been around much lately and I don't blame him. He ought to be afraid of what could happen if I go crazy since I caught him snuggled up to my wife in the booth at Tony's restaurant. Back when Benedict and I were good buddies we purchased identical Colt Python .357 magnum revolvers which we would shoot from my wood deck every chance we got. So it seemed natural as I sent a special message to Benedict by firing a thirty round clip from my brand new AR-15 rifle into the lake between us to let the son-of-a-bitch know that I had superior firepower (no need for him to share my joy).

I never knew that someone in my medical condition could be this happy. Surfing a huge positive emotional wave that could only swell up from someone who had been in the depths of deep depression I try not to slow my surging spirit with negative thoughts like; statistical probabilities of survival, financial Armageddon, projected pain or lost love. It feels so good to break out of depression that I understand why I spent so much time in denial before slipping into it.

I won't bother my troubles if they won't bother me. I understand the manic mind fleeing the fire in their brains (depression) in any way they can. It feels so good not to feel bad that the week goes by without my guts being knotted; in fact, I'm looking forward to my appointment with Dr. Calm because finally he is going to be telling me something I want to hear (that my blood is a half-match with Jimmy's).

Dr. Calm is smiling as he enters the examining room dispensing his medicine without the normal tension that usually pervades these meetings between us. I wonder if it has anything to do with Dr. Calm thinking that maybe he will end up with a satisfied customer instead of a dead one. Dr. Calm, to his credit, explains the process called end stage renal disease so that I understand not just what action we are going to take but also why it has to be done.

The new issue is that I now have to start taking four pills before each meal, which in view of my diminished appetite, should just about fill me up. The pills are potassium blockers that will keep me from absorbing too much potassium because my kidneys are no longer cleansing the excess potassium from my blood stream which could lead to a sudden heart attack (pretty good reason to follow doctor's orders). I will also be taking calcium blockers to keep my blood pressure from getting out of control.

Just as I feel like the news from the medical front isn't that bad, Dr. Calm delivers the coup-de-grace to my struggling spirits, by telling me that I need to go up to Duke University Hospital to see the urologist to make sure there is no other clinical reason that a transplant couldn't be successful. How quickly small problems that have been in the background take center stage with full control of my destiny. My spirits crash through the floors below like the meteor that cast its shadow briefly but changed the dinosaur world for all time.

The old Catch-22 is that this same laboratory answered this same question in the negative manner (saying that I was not a good transplant candidate because of all of the scars from my childhood surgeries) and I still carry the same scars now as I did back then. Leaving Dr. Calm's office, the emotional roller coaster is at the bottom when just thirty minutes ago it had been at the top.

When I phone Debi to tell her that Dr. Calm's office is making an appointment for me at Duke University Hospital, she insists that she go with me but I have to tell her no (some journeys a man must make alone). I'm shaking in my boots and I need to spend the time on the interstate driving to Duke University Hospital thinking about everything. I might need to do some crying on the way back home because if they give the thumbs down to the transplant, we are back to dialysis until death do you part.

As I pull into the parking garage at Duke University Hospital it feels good to know my way around; as a matter of fact, the primary reason that I would like to have the transplant here is that the surroundings are familiar. The native stone structure with its gothic arches has a cathedral like feel. As I go inside the building a chill runs up my spine as the exterior doors seal off the outside world behind me, leaving me in the main lobby of a hospital teaming with college students as well as patients and staff.

Going with the flow of people through the doors leading to the hallway with the various outpatient clinics, one of the students reaches out tweaking the nose on the brass bust of the hospital benefactor (traditionally done for good luck on the way to exams). Since I am going in for an exam that I had flunked once before, I tweak that shiny bronze nose thinking that all of my chips are on the line.

The hallway leading to the various clinics has color coded lines painted on the floor that you follow if you don't want to get lost. The red line leads to the heart clinic, the blue line to the pulmonary area and the Purple line takes me to the urology clinic (they should have used a Yellow line). The time has come for one of my most dreaded crossroads: my appointment with the head urologist, Dr. Wienrith, who now holds the life-or-death decision in his hands alone.

The clinic waiting room is full as it turns out that everyone has the same appointment time and the doctors see patients on a first come first served basis. After expecting to see the doctor right at the time of my appointment, the thirty-five minute wait is filled with tension causing me to break out in a sweat. This makes me wonder if I'm worrying myself into high blood pressure. So I go out into the hallway and walk down to the lobby and back trying to break the tension, because high blood pressure will look bad on my physical exam.

Finally, the nurse calls my name before she leads me to an exam room where she weighs me and takes my blood pressure, (155 [diastolic] over 101 [systolic]) which is a little high but not alarmingly high (I hope). Dr. Wienrith, the chief urologist, comes in and his relaxed manner and cheerful personality make me feel comfortable. I put on my most outgoing personality trying to make sure that the man holding my life in his hands likes me.

After an extensive physical exam Dr. Wienrith tells me that all he wants before sending me on to the laboratory for blood work is to insert a catheter, in order to run some dye into my bladder for empty and full x-rays. When the x-ray with my bladder full of dye is taken, Dr. Wienrith pulls the catheter out telling me to go to into the bathroom and fully drain the bladder before the last x-ray.

The realization that this must be the part of the exam that I failed when I came to this clinic for evaluation a few years ago fills me with fear as I go into the bathroom. All of my hopes and dreams rest on one flush of a strange toilet. Stretching and leaning in every direction to make sure that I am fully drained before going back for the critical x-ray, I think about how my life will change if it turns out bad like it did the last time that I was here.

After the x-ray, the nurse tells me to get dressed and go to the lab for my blood work before returning for my final interview with Dr. Wienrith. Walking to the lab I'm hoping that I didn't just piss my life away, as I try to get a laugh out of myself to break the tension.

After giving enough blood to put out a small fire I trudge back to the urology clinic for my final interview. When I think about the significance of what Dr. Wienrith is about to tell me my knees wobble and I feel like a prisoner that has just been tried in a capital punishment case, waiting to hear the jury's verdict.

Soon the nurse takes me back to Dr. Wienrith's business office where he greets me warmly and tells me right away that, "He sees nothing that would preclude a successful graft." I feel like grabbing and hugging Dr. Wienrith. Thumbs up, I live! Hallelujah! Thank you, Lord!

Walking out to the lobby feeling that the world isn't so bad after all, I phone Debi from a payphone and when she answers, I say, "Rejoice, we conquer," finding it hard to beat the original Marathon man's brief commentary. I give her the details, asking Debi to phone my parents and my brother with the glorious news.

Driving home on the interstate highway even listening to B.B. King sing the blues can't get me down. I don't feel bad for a guy with one foot in the grave.

Chapter 11

WE ALL HAVE TO PLAY THE ODDS
(SOMETIMES)

JUST AS I'M DRIFTING OFF to sleep for the night my eyes jolt open as it hits me that my brother was having his check up with Dr. Calm this afternoon, just to make sure that there is no medical reason why Jimmy couldn't give me his kidney. Wouldn't you think that my brother should phone me to let me know the outcome of his physical exam? I decide to wait until tomorrow to phone Jimmy to see what happened because he goes to bed with the chickens (as soon as it gets dark).

The insistent ringing of my telephone startles me awake and as soon as I see that it is only 7:00 a.m., I figure that it has to be Jimmy calling to tell me the results of his medical tests. I am glad because even though it would be unusual, sometimes the doctors discover a medical problem that the potential donor never knew existed, and if that happened it would be fatal (to me).

When Jimmy talks to someone on the phone, he usually skips the normal pleasantries like: good morning, how are you; so instead of answering my phone by saying hell-o, I pick up the receiver and say "thumbs up or thumbs down?" Jimmy responds "thumbs up," but before I can relax and savor the moment, he goes on to tell me that Dr. Calm told him that I have missed several appointments, and that my blood work hasn't been done on schedule. So Dr. Calm has made an appointment for me to sit down and talk with the social worker at the dialysis center today at 11:00 a.m.

Before I can express my displeasure over having appointments made for me without my knowledge, Jimmy goes on to say that they have to give me three transfusions of his blood to see if there is any allergic reaction in my body. We are supposed to do the first transfusion today at noon, so Jimmy tells me to look for him in the waiting room of the dialysis clinic when I get finished talking to the psychologist.

Forgetting about the minor details like who made the appointment for whom, here is another low probability but potentially disastrous hurdle to get over that until now has been unknown to me. Now in addition to everything else I have to deal with a psychologist when I need to be out making a living.

Walking from my car into the dialysis center for the appointment with the psychologist, I spot Jimmy in the parking lot so we go inside together. Instantaneously, the brotherly love that I have felt deprived of flows into me as Jimmy's presence is a surprise. It's still an hour before the time of my appointment for the blood transfusion from him and there is some relief in knowing that at least I won't be walking into the dialysis clinic alone, because this place gives me the creeps.

The tension in my gut tells me that there must be a hundred different places in Columbia where this transfusion could be done and psychologically none of them could be worse for me than the dialysis clinic. If this psychologist was any good, we wouldn't be having the transfusion here at the hemodialysis clinic. I see this appointment with the psychologist as an opportunity for some mid-level administrator to justify their job by saying no to my transplant request. I mean, if they don't ever reject anybody on psychological grounds why have this interview in the first place.

Why haven't they thought about the psychological impact of having a transfusion in a dialysis clinic (it seems like they are trying to get me acclimated to this environment.) Dr. Calm knows that I do not want to use hemodialysis since it is the one thing on this planet that terrifies me (stalking me, as it has, from my youth).

Dr. Calm seems to be forcing me to have this transfusion at the dialysis clinic perhaps to prove his power over the course of my treatment, and over me, since he knows that this is the same place that I stormed out of four weeks ago when they didn't have the proper needles for my blood matching test.

As I am pondering this the nurse comes into the reception area to take Jimmy back where three units of his blood will be drawn while the psychologist interviews me. I go into the psychologist's office for the interview, the forced rapport, and sit down across the desk from the plump little woman with short hair that will be judging me today.

I am thinking that here is another opportunity for someone else to throw my transplant plans in the trash. If I don't form some kind of rapport with the psychologist and play the game, I could lose my life. When the psychologist begins our interview by calling me Donald instead of Don, it is obvious to me that she is not qualified to judge me since she doesn't even know my name.

Then the psychologist asks me how my wife is coping with the situation. Good grief, why do I have to share my most painful personal experience with this stranger. I don't feel like playing this game so I answer with what I take for humor by telling the psychologist that my wife is coping quite well (which is true, I just don't mention the fact that my wife has left me because it isn't one of the psychologist's questions).

Then the psychologist asks me if my family is supportive to which I respond, "Yes, unless my brother backs out as my donor, in which case the answer would be no." Of course, my parents have been consistently supportive, I am just trying to be funny (I'll bet that they don't get many laughs around here).

The psychologist then looks at me over her reading glasses and says, "Mr. Gordon, we are not used to our transplant patients being uncooperative." Yeah, you're used to them laying down and dying quietly is what I want to say, but knowing that this lady is in a position to ruin my life I tell her that, "I'm not trying to be uncooperative, I'm just trying to stay alive."

So goes our forced rapport until a nurse knocks on the door and says, "We're ready for Mr. Gordon," then the nurse leads me back into the dialysis clinic as I look around the room for my brother (but I don't see him anywhere). My skin crawls the instant that I'm seated in one of those big reclining chairs at the front of the room which is full of patients hooked up to dialysis machines.

The nurse tells me that Jimmy has completed having his blood drawn so he has already gone home. Suddenly I feel very alone in this strange environment (and I am). The nurse explains the procedure to me: they have taken three units of blood from my brother and they are going to give me one unit of his blood per week starting today to see if there is any allergic reaction.

Part of the protocol for this part of the process of having a kidney transplant is that I am supposed to take an anti-rejection medicine called Imuran to reduce the chances that my body's defenses will attack my brother's blood. The news that I am going to be taking an anti-rejection medication is a complete surprise and seems like a big step that I didn't think would come until transplant time.

As I'm internalizing what all of this will mean the nurse tells me to sign a release form, which makes me worry about whatever is worrying them so much that they want a release from liability. So I start reading the release form when a second nurse comes up with a container of my brother's blood that has a tube coming from it terminating with a needle that seems too big to use on humans.

I know that they use even bigger needles around a dialysis clinic but this one is meant for me and it looks pretty imposing. I feel a light sweat break out on my forehead as I contemplate the size of the hole in my arm that needle will leave. The nurse starts acting impatient just as soon as I begin reading the release form until before long, she is trying to hurry me up by saying, "It's standard procedure, just sign the form." A little wave of resentment swells up inside of me as I answer back, "It's standard procedure for me to read anything that I sign." The nurse doesn't say anything else while she waits impatiently for me to review the form, but the look of exasperation on her face lets me know that she isn't used to patients thinking for themselves.

In the end it turns out that the nurse is right, there was no reason for me to read the form because I don't have any choice if I want to live. But if I hadn't read the last paragraph of the form then I would have missed being aware of something that I should worry about (if I didn't have all of these other worries taking up all of my time). By signing this form, I am acknowledging that I understand the procedure of transfusing the donor's blood into the recipient carries with it a five percent probability that it will make the recipient have an allergic reaction to the donor's blood. As if I didn't have enough to worry about already, now I have to take a one in twenty chance of becoming allergic to my brother's blood.

I can picture a twenty round revolver that I put one bullet into before spinning the cylinder for a game of Russian Roulette. I don't like this even though there is a 95% probability that it will not create a problem (it's not the odds that bother me, it's the stakes). I would still like to understand what my options are but after the psychologist has just referred to me as "uncooperative," I realize that there is no real option other than taking this risk. So I sign the form and say, "Stick it to me."

The nurse gets ready to start poking that big needle into my arm and all of the dialysis patients in the room have their eyes fixed on me, waiting to see how I am going to hold up under the pain of the big needle. Then I recognize the knowing smiles of the dialysis patients and terror floods through my brain. My God, they've got me trapped this time. I can't walk out on them no matter what happens to me, not after just being referred to as "uncooperative" by the psychologist. Shouldn't this transfusion at least be done with some privacy instead of right in front of a room full of dialysis patients. The nurse wraps the rubber strap around my arm to get the vein bulging and then sticks that huge needle into my arm.

The instant that my brothers blood begins to flow into my body a feeling of warmth sweeps through my arm then quickly up to my face, and immediately the odd warmth goes down through the trunk of my body out into my legs. Sweat starts to bead-up on my forehead and I begin to feel like I'm going to throw up, making me worry that I must be having an allergic reaction to my brother's blood! (oh no, I'm a dead man).

Simultaneous heartbreak and nausea allow a slight moan to escape from my lips bringing a different nurse from across the room, who turns a valve which slows the flow of blood into my arm, immediately relieving the burning sensation around the needle that I had been almost unaware of due to the overwhelming nature of the nausea, which also subsides. As the nurse tilts the reclining chair back so that my feet are up, she wipes my face with a damp paper towel until my nausea dissipates just enough for me to whisper that I must be having an allergic reaction to my brother's blood. She answers, "No you aren't, they just let the blood flow into you too fast."

Then my original nurse comes back to check on me, and once she sees the situation she says, "You will get used to it," in an uncaring, almost flippant tone of voice (no, I will not!). This is the last time that you will ever see Don Gordon in this place are what my thoughts are as I close my eyes so that I don't have to look at the room full of dialysis patients who are all looking at me. The thought of having that big needle in my arm and having a tube of blood running into me while I watch dialysis patients in their easy chairs makes me feel like I am halfway to hemodialysis already. The only thing that I need now is to have a needle in my other arm sucking blood out (reality is so terrifying that it makes me long for denial).

Seizing control of what is left of my life I vow to myself that I will never come back to this clinic again no matter what happens to me. I keep my eyes closed and wait for this psychological terror to pass. Walking my wobbly self out to my car in the parking lot after the transfusion is complete it strikes me as odd that the sun can shine down on such a beautiful world just a doorway away from Hell.

The next day a strange eagerness controls my spirit and instead of the usual anxiety I am at peace while I wait for Dr. Calm to come into the examining room for my regular visit. In this vast sea of uncertainty, the one thing that is certain is that Don Gordon is not going back to the dialysis clinic from Hell for my last two transfusions of my brother's blood and I can't wait to tell Dr. Calm.

When Dr. Calm comes into the examination room and I make him aware of my intentions, the subtle change in my status is evident from his lack of outrage at me exerting a little control. They must

90

teach desensitization in medical school so that doctors and nurses can deal with the death of people on a regular basis, at least that's the way it seems to me because the medical staff that I have been in contact with has not interacted with me in the normal manner that I would expect. It seems as if they don't want to form interpersonal relationships with patients who might be denied some life-saving procedure (I don't blame them).

Now that I have passed many of the medical industry's tests of exclusion Dr. Calm's staff is treating me more like a good customer should be treated (I'm not talking about major things, just the subtle way that they look at you).

The pendulum of control continues to swing back my way when Dr. Calm tells me that I need to make a final decision on which hospital that I want to use for the transplant. This signals a shift away from doctors and hospitals checking my qualifications to one of me judging their qualifications (I like this much better).

Once I get back home to Blythewood, I decide to call around to the various hospitals that I could potentially use to see which one I am more comfortable with. I phone long distance information to get the main phone number for Duke University Hospital and it isn't hard to reach the Kidney Transplant Coordinator who is very enthusiastic once she finds out that I already have a donor in mind.

I expect to be most comfortable with Duke University Hospital since I had some surgery there some years ago and at least I know my way around the hospital. I feel like there may be less overall stress if the transplant can take place in familiar surroundings.

Dr. Calm has indicated that he feels Duke University Hospital would be the best choice since he has a good working relationship with the doctors up there. I liked the urologist that I met when I went up there for x-rays recently, so unless I feel uncomfortable after getting to know the rest of the transplant staff that is where I want to have my transplant. The decision to have my transplant done at D.U.H. has already been made on the subconscious level and with just a little more research my conscious mind should be comfortable with the choice.

Just to have something for comparison in case I don't like the vibes that I get from D.U.H. at some future point in time, my next phone call is to Vanderbilt University in Nashville, Tennessee. After the Kidney Transplant Coordinator there cheerfully tells me that she will put some literature in the mail to me, I cheerfully inquire as to what sort of historical mortality experience their facility has (trying to use an uninterested sounding tone of voice so that the Kidney Transplant Coordinator will not feel defensive as I search for answers about my own probability of survival).

She responds in a casual, almost proud sort of manner, informing me that almost half of all living related kidneys that are transplanted are still working after ten years (this sounds pretty good to me). After my phone conversation with the Kidney Transplant Coordinator at Vanderbilt University is over, I try to internalize these abstract numbers and I sink right past denial into depression as I worry about what happens to the other half of the patients whose kidney transplants don't last ten years. It's not really death that bothers me the most right now because that is something that may or may not be in my immediate future, but any way that you look at it, pain is inescapable and I have no idea how bad it will be.

My sudden plunge into depression is interrupted by a phone call from my mother with fantastic news about a new wonder drug for transplants that she had just heard about on the Larry King radio show. The drug is named Cyclosporine and it is supposed to revolutionize the transplant field, according to talk radio, and from what I just heard about the mortality experience from the Transplant Coordinator at Vanderbilt University I would have better odds of living through a revolution. My spirits swing up from the pits of depression to near manic excitement as I pin my renewed hopes on this wonder drug. Such is the emotional roller coaster that one rides through the transplant world.

It is with excitement instead of the usual dread that I approach my regular appointment with Dr. Calm. A new eagerness drives my steps as I walk into Dr. Calm's waiting room refusing to be brought down by the images of the walking skeletons around me. I now have a new mental picture of what my future may look like and I no longer see these forms as models of what my life will be like, but rather as living reminders to use the new wonder drug.

When Dr. Calm comes into the exam room, before he can tell me about the results from my most recent blood work, I tell him that I have decided to have the transplant done at D.U.H. and that my mother has heard about a new drug named Cyclosporine on talk radio that we should explore using. Dr. Calm's right eyebrow arches up as he tells me that, "He feels it would be wise to let the professionals make that decision." Dr. Calm is very aware of Cyclosporine and all of its great potential, but he tells me that he will have to consult with D.U.H. in regards to the use of Cyclosporine in my particular case.

Dr. Calm tells me that he feels more comfortable using the medications that they use every day. Remembering the sobering statistic that more than half of the kidney transplants fail before the tenth year, I ask Dr. Calm what makes him feel more comfortable with the existing medications. He answers that with the existing medications they will be dealing with known problems that have known solutions and with Cyclosporine being brand new they would be dealing with the unknown.

I have lived much of my life hoping for advances in medical science and in my gut it seems the known statistics about the mortality experience using the old medications is far more frightening than the threat of the unknown associated with the new wonder drug. Somewhat unnerved by Dr. Calm not sharing in my excitement over the prospects of using Cyclosporine, I stick with my gut feeling and say to Dr. Calm, "I think I'll take some of the unknown." After a long pause and a cold stare, Dr. Calm informs me that he will consult with D.U.H. to see what they think about the possibility of using Cyclosporine in my case.

Leaving Dr. Calm's office emptied of my newly acquired enthusiasm and filled with doubts about everything my spirits drag me down all the way home to Blythewood. Here I am at the crossroads of my life facing the same two choices that have been with mankind since the beginning of time: let it happen or make it happen. I don't know anything about kidney transplants but I do know that if you just sit back and let things happen in life you end up with what is left-over after everything that is worth fighting for is gone. So I decide to try to make things happen instead.

Without even knowing what questions I want to ask, I pick up the phone to call the Transplant Coordinators at Duke and Vanderbilt to pump them for information about Cyclosporine. I decide to call Vanderbilt first so that when I talk to the doctors at Duke, who will probably be doing the surgery, at least I might know enough to understand what my choices are (if any). The feedback that I got about Cyclosporine was that it is a tremendous breakthrough for medical science that dramatically improves the chances of success (hot dog). In the course of conversation with the Kidney Transplant Coordinator at Vanderbilt she tells me that the research on Cyclosporine was done at Stanford, Minnesota and Pittsburgh.

Pittsburgh did the studies on transplants with cadavers as donors and Minnesota did the studies on living related donors (like Jimmy). Since Minnesota had done the research on transplants like ours, I got their transplant coordinator on the phone hoping to hear wonderful things about Cyclosporine, and I was not disappointed because she had that missionary zeal in her praise for the drug.

At last I have found somebody who is saying the things that I want to hear, so I ask to speak with the main doctor involved with the Cyclosporine studies, and much to my surprise the Chief of Staff for the transplant program picks up the phone. I feel like the Tin Man in the "Wizard of Oz" before he saw what was going on behind the curtain, and I know that I can get a truthful opinion to any question, but I have to know which one to ask. I put my one question to this medical guru in the only terms that matter when I ask him directly, "Are my odds of survival improved if I use Cyclosporine?"

"Like night and day," came his response (the night would be a long one). The medical guru goes on for several minutes but I have already heard everything that I need to know. All the stuff that he tells me about Cyclosporine revolutionizing the transplant field with patients recovering faster and going home faster was just icing on the cake, because I want some of that "day" stuff. Don't underestimate the value of having a Doctor who is enthusiastic about his ability to save your life (it feels good).

When I get off the phone with the doctor in Minnesota I feel like a kid at Christmas, if not better. I go ahead and phone the transplant Coordinator at the University of Pittsburgh, who tells me that Cyclosporine is so good that she wouldn't be surprised if in a few years hospitals almost stop doing transplants from living related donors.

Well, after hearing all of those glowing reports on Cyclosporine I was just sitting there in my kitchen floating on Cloud Nine for a minute, smiling at the improvement in my prospects for the future when my telephone rings ending my current state of delusion.

When I answer the phone I am surprised to be talking to Dr. Calm, but before I can tell him the great news, he lets me know that he has some of his own: Dr. Calm has talked with the doctors up at Duke and it turns out that they are not planning on using Cyclosporine in my case. I'm too stunned to react: I just stand there in a state of emotional shock as I hang up the phone a broken man.

Like a zombie I sit down at my kitchen table, motionless, pondering my fate. I can't really concentrate, it's like looking at a puzzle where none of the pieces fit. Totally devastated, absolutely exasperated, I sit in my kitchen looking for the bright side that doesn't exist. I feel like one of those early explorers who spent their lives looking for the Northwest Passage around Canada that they knew had to exist, and it did, too bad that they were in sailing ships when it required a nuclear submarine (Catch 22).

This new twist haunts my every thought. I had made up my mind to have my transplant at Duke using the new wonder drug Cyclosporine, but now I find out that Duke would not advise using Cyclosporine in my particular case. I have to decide if I want to have my transplant at a different hospital that would use Cyclosporine or go ahead and have the operation at Duke using the old anti-rejection medications (medical quandary).

A wrong choice here and everything that I have struggled so hard for would mean nothing. The wrong choice on my part would negate all of the medical advancements that have been made during my lifetime and the efforts of the most gifted surgeon. I could spend years researching this 'life or death' choice, but in fact there only exists a few days until I must follow the advice of Dr. Calm and the transplant team at Duke, or listen to my mother who got her information from talk radio which was backed up by two brief phone calls to people that I don't even know (the transplant coordinators at Minnesota, Pittsburg and Vanderbilt Universities).

The thought of my downfall coming from me overruling my doctors in some arbitrary emotional decision keeps me awake thrashing in my bed for most of the night. The next morning Bill Tulluck and I have to attend a business meeting where I tell him about the new wonder drug with all of its potential and of the conflicting recommendations that I have gotten. When Bill hears all of the details of the quandary that I face he sticks a pin in my balloon by questioning whether the doctor that I choose to believe is the one telling the truth or the one telling a lie.

Bill reminds me that I might expect a bias from some doctors in favor of using Cyclosporine because it might be part of their job to promote it, since they rely on funding to do research, and the money could be coming from the drug company that makes Cyclosporine.

Bill and I sit in the back of the room during the business meeting and Bill takes out a piece of paper drawing a line down the middle of the page labeling one side advantages the other side disadvantages. On the advantage side we list: faster recovery from surgery, shorter hospital stay and lower probability of rejection; on the disadvantage side the only thing we have is unknown long term problems to which Bill says, "If you don't make the short term you don't have to worry about the long term, and future advances can take care of future problems." (sage advice).

I phone my mother after the business meeting to tell her about Duke's reluctance to use the new drug in my case, to which she recommends that I call Dr. Reed who had helped with the surgery in my youth and was now the head urologist at the big hospital in Champagne, Illinois.

I get the phone number from long distance information and call the Urology Department in Champagne Illinois, reaching Dr. Reed on my first phone call. Dr. Reed is glad to hear from me after all of these years and I am amazed that he even remembers exactly who I am. I know that I will get some good, clear, unbiased advice from Dr. Reed because he doesn't have a dog in this fight (he doesn't have a financial interest to cloud his judgment and he probably does really care whether I live or die).

I get right to the bottom line as I ask Dr. Reed if I should try Cyclosporine or stick with the old drug, and he tells me that there is no question that I should use Cyclosporine if I want to live. That remark sends a shiver up my spine because I know that since I am tired, there has been a weakening of my resolve about overruling the "professionals" at Duke and self-doubts had worried my soul to the point where I might have chosen the door with the tiger behind it.

Then I start questioning Dr. Reed as to whether I should have the transplant attempt at Duke since they have been in favor of using the old medication which appears to be faulty logic. I inquire from Dr. Reed as to the best hospital in the United States for kidney transplants to which he answers firmly, "any place that will give you Cyclosporine."

I thank Dr. Reed for saving my life a second time and hang up the phone to call Dr. Calm, while musing that I would gladly trade life expectancies with Dr. Reed. It is just as well that we don't get everything that we wish for because a couple of months later my mother hears a rumor that Dr. Reed lost control of his Porsche trying to miss a deer and hit a tree: thereby preceding me to the grave.

When Dr. Calm comes to the phone, I inform him that I have made the decision to go ahead and take my chances with Cyclosporine, then after a long pause he asks coldly, "Then what hospital are you going to use since Duke has said they would not use Cyclosporine in your case?" I respond, "any hospital in the United States that will give me Cyclosporine." Dr. Calm indicates that he will inform Duke of my decision and we leave it at that. Then Dr. Calm reminds me that I am scheduled to have the second transfusion of my brother's blood tomorrow and they have it set up for Richland Memorial Hospital instead of the dialysis clinic (hooray). Be thankful even for small favors (I am).

Debi goes with me to have the transfusion just in case I feel too weak to drive home after it is over. Going into the hospital feels much less threatening than going into the dialysis clinic and a nurse leads us into a carpeted room on the first floor. The room looks more like office space than a hospital room, which is fine with me, but the easy chair that the nurse seats me in gives me a weird feeling since it is the same style and color as the chairs in the dialysis clinic.

The nurse hangs up a bag of my brother's blood behind the easy chair and gently inserts a large needle into the vein in my arm, allowing my brother's blood to start flowing slowly through my body. When I realize that I'm not getting nauseated my spirits are boosted and I tell Debi that this is the proper way to handle blood transfusions.

Just as I am reflecting on the lack of mental torture associated with this transfusion compared with the one done over at the dialysis clinic, my blissful state implodes since it requires total ignorance which I am about to lose. Sitting in the easy chair with my feet up, waiting for my brother's blood to drain into my arm, I flip through a medical periodical that the nurse had left for me to read because one of the articles is about Cyclosporine. I am horrified to read that the research referred to in the article concludes that it is unwise to give preoperative transfusions of the donor's blood to kidney recipients who are going to use Cyclosporine since there is no improvement in rejection experience in conjunction with Cyclosporine immuno-suppressive therapy. Therefore, the five percent risk of developing an allergic sensitivity to the donor's cells is not worth taking.

The happy mood in my brain shatters in an instant as my mind fills with rage. Wanting to yank the damn needle from my arm and cast it, along with all of the other tormenting devils from my life, I sit instead. I'm seething as each drop marks time until I can get back outside of this hospital and stop resisting the powerful urges running through me to shout profanities, calling my doctors bad names. I have to sit still and endure it even though it's a medical error (lest I get labeled as "uncooperative" again).

The one positive thing that I get from this miserable experience brings a little smile to my face as I realize that at least there will be no third transfusion of my brother's blood like the doctors are planning to do. It feels good to have this transfusion stuff complete instead of hanging over me for another week. I am through with transfusions, but this time I'm going to handle my doctors in a better manner by getting them to agree with me that having the third transfusion is unnecessary (without pointing out how stupid it would be).

Driving home to Blythewood on the interstate highway the cursing that the occasion calls for takes place so that I'm calm and quiet by the time we get home, where I phone Dr Calm's secretary to seek concurrence on canceling the final transfusion. Trying to be diplomatic I ask Dr. Calm's secretary to find out what Duke says we should do regarding the last transfusion in light of this new research. Wanting to accomplish my mission without further alienation of my doctors seems like an internal sign that I am gaining wisdom, but it has come at the cost of frazzled nerves from the emotional ups and downs.

Just after collapsing in my bed I receive a phone call from the transplant coordinator at Duke, and though her tone of voice is friendly, her choice of words sends little prickles up the back of my neck. "We understand that you have spontaneously decided not to have the final transfusion of donor blood, so you can stop taking the medication that we have been using to suppress your immune system," she says. After taking the time to carefully word my concerns to Dr. Calm's secretary, it is interesting that the way it's phrased to me is that I made the decision "spontaneously" so if my body ends up rejecting my brother's kidney it will be all my fault. As I gently try to make my position clear to the transplant coordinator, she alters her verbiage, saying she was just calling to let me know to stop taking the immuno-suppressive drug since they aren't going to do any more transfusions. This little bit of doublespeak troubles me, but I let it drop so that the transplant coordinator will not label me as "uncooperative." When the conversation is over a rush of joy comes over me now that I can stop taking the medication, and with great flourish the remaining pills are thrown in the trash.

Once again, my happy mood exists only through total ignorance. Debi awakens me with the news that a doctor from Duke is on the phone wanting to talk with me. It turns out to be the chief of staff for transplant services at Duke, Dr. Big, who is calling to let me know that Duke will use Cyclosporine in my case since that is what I have requested (hallelujah). Dr. Big tells me that he wants to welcome me to The Duke Transplant Program and he offers to answer any questions that I might have.

Dr. Big's personable manner makes me like him right away even before he tells me that he has heard that I am very well informed, and that's how they like their patients to be. Then Dr. Big gives me his office phone number with instructions for me to phone him if any problems arise or if I have any questions. Dr. Big inspires confidence in the institution and he makes me feel more comfortable with the human side of the equation at the same time.

Before we hang up I tell Dr. Big that, "I do have one question: what made Duke make the decision to go ahead and use Cyclosporine in my particular case?" Dr. Big's answer blows my mind as he explains that until now Cyclosporine has only been approved for use at the hospitals that were doing the research projects, but that the results have been exciting. Now that Cyclosporine has been released to regional centers such as Duke, they are happy to provide it for me; in fact, the staff is looking forward to it as I am scheduled to be the very first kidney transplant recipient that will get Cyclosporine at Duke.

My mind is racing, filled with mixed emotions, while I am overjoyed that Duke will give me Cyclosporine, I am uncomfortable in the role of being their first patient to use it. What bothers me the most is that the whole time that Duke was saying that they would use the old medicine instead of Cyclosporine in my particular case, they never mentioned the fact that Duke wasn't approved to use Cyclosporine. Make no mistake about it, doctors consider it bad form to lie to your face, but they have no qualms about not disclosing something that you don't ask about. There isn't one word about telling the truth in the Hippocratic Oath.

Then in closing, Dr. Big tells me to be sure to taper off slowly over a period of several days before I stop taking the medicine to suppress my immune system that they gave me because of the blood transfusion from my brother. If I were to stop cold turkey the chances are increased for developing an allergic sensitivity to my donor which could preclude a transplant.

Cold chills shoot up my spine as I picture my pills in the trash, so I tell Dr. Big that his transplant coordinator never mentioned one word about tapering down on the dosage over a period of several days. She had just said that I could stop taking the medication. Dr. Big fumes as he tells me that the transplant coordinator shouldn't be instructing patients on medical procedures anyway. Naturally I let it drop right there lest the chief of staff for transplant services label me as "uncooperative."

Hanging up the phone I shout out to Debi, "Hallelujah, Duke will give me Cyclosporine," but inside my mind there is an uneasiness about the way that the decision was made that will keep me awake for many nights to come.

Chapter 12

DEATH'S DOOR

THE DAY OF RECKONING is approaching rapidly and I am powerless to stop the hands of time. My mood swings up when Dr. Calm tells me that he will use peritoneal dialysis on me for a few weeks before my transplant to stabilize my condition, and it's a big relief to know that I will not be subjected to the agony of hemodialysis, but when the man comes to my house to deliver the peritoneal dialysis machine there is no joy in my heart. We put the machine in the third bedroom until I need it but I can feel its presence through the walls. I have a lot to be thankful for but I have a lot to worry about also. Once I start dialysis there is no turning back because as soon as my body is hooked up to the machine, my own kidneys will atrophy leaving me totally dependent on the machine to keep me alive until my transplant.

I wish that I could just keep on living the way that I have been for a while longer but that is not in the cards. I concentrate on living in the present so that worrying about tomorrow doesn't ruin today. Debi and I take a short walk everyday as I try to get in shape for what I know will be the fight of my life and our dog Spats loves to go along as he explores the world as young dogs do. Spats has made this trip around the neighborhood enough to be comfortable with his surroundings until one day there is a pallet of bricks on the side of the road that has been delivered to a new house that is under construction. Spats is walking along having a great time until he spots that pallet of bricks and then he comes running back to me afraid that whatever it is it might eat him. I put the leash on Spats and try to get him to walk on past the bricks, but he doesn't want to go anywhere near it because he has never seen anything like this before. I can only hope that my own fears about what I have to face are just as unfounded.

Like an outlaw that can't run anymore, the day finally comes when I have to go have the peritoneal dialysis tube surgically inserted into my side. Depression makes my legs feel like they weigh a ton as Debi and I drive down to the hospital to have the tube inserted into my side.

Walking through the automatic doors of the main entrance to Richland Memorial Hospital my mind drifts away from the hum-drum of daily life to more profound concerns, like wondering if this means that I am at death's door. My subconscious answers my own question with a resounding "YES!" that shocks the conscious part of my brain. Without kidney dialysis, death would take me in less than a month; so yes, I guess that I really am at death's door.

Searching for a comforting thought when there are none I muse that death probably doesn't use this door very often, preferring instead to enter the hospital through the emergency room doors and exiting through the doors down on the loading dock. It would be bad for business to roll dissatisfied customers through the main lobby dead, so hospitals use the back door for final exits.

The first thing that hits me upon entering the main lobby is the heavy antiseptic smell, as if they are killing germs with the same air they expect me to breathe, or perhaps they are trying to cover up some serious stink. The less time spent thinking about what that stink might come from the better. It has been said that hospitals kill more people accidentally each year than cars and handguns combined and part of the problem is probably that patients have to breathe hospital air.

Only under a threat of death would I have a two-foot long catheter [drain tube] installed in my gut, but that's the deal, so here I am. It was this or hemodialysis, so the choice is a no brainer. I'm lucky to be here (the tough choice would be between hemodialysis and death). Happily, I go through all of the questions involved with hospital admission which essentially gets down to who will pay the hospital bill in case of an emergency (patient dies).

Upon arrival to my designated hospital ward the head nurse takes charge of my life, and her first instructions to me are to change out of my street clothes into pajamas. The reality of not being in control of even what clothes I wear brings into sharp focus the fact that I am in deep trouble, and the only way out is to go through whatever I have to so that I can be normal again.

When Dr. Calm's nurse had been instructing Debi and me in the science of peritoneal dialysis and the art of staying alive while doing this at home, she had showed me a Tenckhoff catheter (named after the doctor that had the first patient to survive the procedure). I examined it closely at that time and I intend to look at the one that they are going to put into me tomorrow morning, especially since this type of dialysis has only recently become available.

We all know that doctors make bigger mistakes than just putting the wrong tube in somebody. It's good to remember that if anything goes wrong, the doctors get paid and you get hurt; in fact, if something does go wrong the doctors will probably make even more money while they work to correct the problem.

The pain begins with the man from the laboratory wanting to draw blood from my arm. After making the man from the lab assure me that he would only draw blood one time from me today, he takes a sample of my blood and goes on his way only to return again in less than ten minutes, apologizing as he sticks my other arm for a blood test that he claims wasn't on his first work order (not his fault). Only after having both of my arms incapacitated do I realize that my bladder is totally full. Until this moment I had always taken my arms for granted but I now have a new appreciation of just how vital they are.

The nursing staff does a wonderful job of seeing that I go to surgery rundown and tired by waking me up every four hours to take my blood pressure and temperature, with an extra waking thrown in to weigh me at about 5:00 a.m. After getting my weight the nurse tries to get my autograph on the bottom of something she calls a standard release form, but when I start to read the one page document, the nurse becomes impatient. Telling me that, "It's just standard procedure," to which I reply that, "It's standard procedure for me to read anything that I'm going to sign" (life repeats itself).

I can see why the nurse is not anxious for me to understand that basically the form tells the patient that if anything goes wrong during surgery (you die) it's not their fault. Two guys in funny pastel blue outfits complete with matching hats and shoe covers interrupt my enlightenment, so I sign the release form and get on the rolling gurney for the trip to the surgical holding area where a pretty nurse gives me a preoperative shot to relax me.

Just as I'm feeling cozy, reality comes in the form of a freezing cold operating table pressing against an area of my body that a hospital gown will not cover. Restored to my senses I ask one of the surgical nurses to show me the Tenckhoff catheter that they are getting ready to put in me.

Startled by seeing a different tube than the one that Dr. Calm's nurse had shown me during dialysis training, I alert the surgical nurse to the problem but it doesn't seem to alarm her like it does me. I'll bet that the surgical nurse would be more concerned if the wrong tube was about to be put in her gut. One of the other nurses chimes in, "He has already had his shot," as if I am confused and the surgical nurse that I had been talking to just gives me a pep talk about how "professional" the staff is here at Richland Memorial Hospital. "Professional" must mean that they profess to know what they are doing. The nurse continues by telling me how good my surgeon is, which I agree with or I wouldn't be laying on this cold, black table to begin with, but the issue is the catheter, not the surgeon and the catheter is wrong.

The Tenckhoff catheter that the surgical nurse is showing me is a clear tube with a disc in the center and one on the end of the tube, but the catheter that Dr. Calm's nurse had shown me only had one disc in the center. This surgical nurse and I really didn't have a personal problem until she picked up the little black rubber mask that is placed over a patient's mouth and nose to administer anesthesia (gas the patient that will shut him up). When I insist on speaking with the surgeon before they put me to sleep the surgical nurse tells me that they are supposed to have the patient under anesthesia before the doctor comes into the operating room or he will not stay on schedule.

Now the entire surgical team, except for the surgeon, has gathered around the operating table to see what the controversy is as I persist in my request to speak with the surgeon. A different nurse tells me that he is "unavailable," to which I reply, "He is supposed to meet me here in a few minutes, so I'll just wait on him." It's hard to read the facial expressions of someone who is wearing a mask, but I swear that it looked like the surgical nurse was sticking her tongue out at me just before she spun around and huffed out of sight. Almost instantaneously the "unavailable" surgeon storms into the operating room gruffly demanding, "What is this about you being uncooperative?"

One of the last things that I would want to do would be to argue with a surgeon who is about to cut me with a knife, but the very last thing that I want is to have surgery in order to implant the wrong catheter.

Seconds before I had been merely a mass of apprehension trying to stay awake, but being labeled as "uncooperative" by my surgeon has made me defensive. I get a little indignant as I try to shake off the effects of the slow-me-down shot to do some demanding of my own with a, "What's this about you getting ready to implant the wrong Tenckhoff catheter in me!?!"

People don't take you seriously when you slur your words but that doesn't change the fact that they are about to put the wrong tube in me, which is a possibility that the surgeon refuses to even consider as he growls, "There is only one Tenckhoff catheter" (wrong).

Realizing that no patient has ever won any argument with a doctor in front of his staff I try to bypass this whole mess by asking for a telephone so that I can talk to Dr. Calm (seems reasonable to me). Apparently, asking to speak with another doctor to confirm that there is an error being made is a very big deal. It is like throwing gasoline on a fire as the surgeon's eyes bulge above his mask while he gets very uncooperative, telling me in his hell-fire-damnation bedside manner that Dr. Calm's office isn't even open yet (unavailable?).

Then the surgeon gives me an ultimatum as he tells me again that there is only one Tenckhoff catheter, which he says that he will insert into me right now or he will walk out of the operating room and cancel this surgery. Good grief, I'm being threatened as I lay on the operating room table. Anger is the first emotion to sweep through me as I want to shout out, "You are fired!" but I know that those three words could mean my death. Jimmy has mentioned several times that the only time of the year that he could be out of work this long is in December, and if I reschedule this surgery so that I can change surgeons Jimmy might get cold feet and use this incident as a reason to call off the entire transplant.

Looking up at the angry eyes of my surgeon and those of the hostile surgical nurses, a feeling of being trapped pervades me as I utter, "Go ahead and gas me."

As conciseness begins to seep back into my being bit by bit after surgery the first thing that I'm aware of is that the sickening smell from the plastic oxygen mask that is strapped to my face is about to make me throw up. Struggling against the anesthesia, my eyes flutter open to a blurry world, then close again as I slip back towards the blackness. The anesthesia says sleep but the nausea forces me to fight it or I might choke, since I am about to throw up into the foul-smelling plastic oxygen mask unless I can lift it up and breathe some fresh air, but my hands will not move (they are tied down to the bed railings).

I felt trapped when they put me to sleep and I feel trapped as I begin to wake up with my arms tied to the bed: trapped by the white bandages that bind my arms, trapped by this foul-smelling oxygen mask and trapped by the events which lead me here in the first place.

There is no feeling of pain although there is a very definite fullness that is getting worse by the moment, and I can't seem to breathe deeply. Trying to speak I finally manage a moan, bringing a nurse who lifts my mask and wipes my face with a cool damp paper towel, as I gasp in all of the air that I can. Even the smelly air of the hospital seems mountain fresh compared to that delivered by the green translucent plastic oxygen mask.

Trying to make the nausea subside I attempt to breathe slowly and deeply however something as simple as a good deep breathe eludes me. Before my eyes can focus there is a beep from some devise to my left that sounds remotely familiar, as I'm overcome with a warmth from my abdominal area that triggers a new wave of nausea. When the machine to my left makes that sound again it reminds me of a microwave oven: then it hits me that a peritoneal dialysis machine makes the very same noise and my eyes spring open.

I can clearly see the little red lights on the dialysis machine (like beady little eyes) indicating that it has starting the drain cycle and as the warm fullness drains from my tender abdominal area a feeling of betrayal permeates my very soul. The dialysis machine is hooked up to me and they have started me on dialysis while I was knocked out cold.

It was never made clear to me that this surgery was supposed to do anything more than implant the Tenckhoff Catheter in me so that I would be ready when the time came to begin dialysis. I thought that there would be a period of about two weeks for me to heal up from the surgery before beginning the dialysis; in fact, Al Holland and I have a big life insurance sale scheduled in Bishopville four days from now that I really need to close.

Now I know that by any regular medical measurement dialysis is long overdue, but trust me, beginning dialysis is a pretty significant day in someone's life, so I would have made a mental note of it if the doctors had ever let me know that it was about to begin. I'd like to take another look at that standard release form that I signed just before surgery. I'm not going to make a big deal of it now since it would be like trying to change yesterday's weather, but still, I should have at least known that they were going to start me on dialysis.

Finally, there is some solace for my soul as Debi and my parents appear next to my bed. I know that it is just a damp paper towel that I feel on my face but it changes the way that I feel because the hand that holds it is driven by love. The first relaxation of tension eases through my body while Debi wipes my face, while telling me that she loves me.

Love is a healing thing for body and soul so I'm lucky to be surrounded by people who love me, in fact I pity those patients who have to go through something like this without support from someone that loves them. I would be willing to bet that it hurts their chances of survival.

I don't have the energy to go through the process of explaining my concerns to Debi that the surgeon might have put the wrong catheter in me but I can tell you, the reader of this story, that this surgeon and I would share a painful lesson on Tenckhoff catheters in the future (the surgeon got the lesson while I got the pain). It turns out that there are two types of Tenckhoff catheters in use, the single cuff type for short term use and the double cuff type for permanent use (Murphy's Law: they put the wrong one in me).

I don't want Debi to worry any more than necessary, her big beautiful eyes are already full of concern as it is and nothing is going to change the fact that they put the wrong catheter in me. I just want my nausea to subside, so I tell Debi that I feel tired (little did I know that when you are on dialysis the best that you ever feel is tired.)

After a restless night I'm settling in to deal with a justifiable bout of depression, but my negative mood is being disturbed by the upbeat, even happy, male nurse that takes over my care from the night shift.

How does anyone hum a happy tune as they measure urine output at 7:00 a.m.? This irrepressible spirit of the male nurse brings a smile to my lips so I tell him, "Hey, turn down the volume on those happy sounds, I'm busy trying to be depressed over here." A positive attitude is contagious and the enthusiasm of the male nurse is refreshing, so as he begins to change the bandage over the surgical incision, I say to him, "If you don't hurt me, I will tell you something that no life insurance agent would disclose unless he were on his deathbed."

The male nurse, I learn his name is Bill, wears a short, well-trimmed beard. His eyes are full of expression telling me that I had piqued his interest, so as soon as Bill completes his part of the deal, I ask him who he thinks will receive the savings part of his life insurance policy whenever he dies. Bill answers my question the way that I thought he would, by telling me that he thinks the cash values that had built up in his life insurance policy would go to his wife (seems fair). I shatter Bill's misconception that an insurance company would do what he thinks is fair by telling him that, "The big print giveth and the small print taketh away."

Bill is justifiably outraged when I tell him that in a whole life policy the company pays the face amount of the policy at death, but they keep the cash values that have built up over time for themselves (catch 22). After Bill agrees to bring his life insurance policy to the hospital for me to review my spirits soar, and I vow to myself to never give up as long as I can be useful to society by helping people to avoid financial pitfalls. A sense of purpose and a feeling of worth to society returns to my body, invigorating my soul.

It feels good to get back to my old self, if not in body at least in spirit. Thankfully my bio-chemistries have been altered from justifiable depression to modest optimism in just a matter of a few minutes thanks to Bill.

Just at that moment I notice a six-foot five-inch man wearing a dark business suit who is standing in the doorway to my room, blocking the bright light from the hall as he hesitates to see if I am asleep. Then I recognize the man who is standing at my door as my brother's minister, Terry Crimm (holiest of holies).

Lifting my head up off of my pillow, displaying a purposeful weakness I call his name, "Terry," and then softly I tell him, "Come closer." When Terry comes over and stands next to my bed I repeat, "closer," so he bends at the waist turning his ear to me and I whisper, "Terry, bring me your life insurance policy, you will not believe how much money you can save." No military recruit has ever snapped to attention faster or straighter than Terry did. The shock frozen on his face tells it all as he stammers something about praying for me while he backs out the door to get away (he should have known better than to get near a wounded life insurance agent).

Just as I'm discovering that it hurts to laugh in walks Debi and my parents. Needless to say, they are surprised to find me laughing all alone in my room. When I ask Debi to bring me some of my literature on life insurance back to the hospital this afternoon, it takes considerable effort to convince Debi that I'm really serious. I tell her that, "If I had known dialysis was going to be this good for business, I would have done it a long time ago."

Now my tired brain has to watch closely as the nursing staff goes through the process of setting up the peritoneal dialysis machine because when I go home from the hospital the day after tomorrow, my life will depend on Debi and I doing this procedure correctly. We have to maintain sterile conditions at all times because if I were to become infected, it would send me to the hemodialysis machine. That's when we would get to the penalty phase of my stubborn refusal to allow Dr. Calm to reverse a vein in my arm for emergency dialysis.

Bill is the only member of the staff that can see the humor in the irony that the cutting edge of medical science (peritoneal dialysis) is decidedly low-tech. The nurse hangs up five bags of saline solution (salt water) above the peritoneal dialysis machine allowing the fluid to flow into the machine where it is warmed up to body temperature by what looks like a waffle iron (so the patient doesn't go into shock). Then the warm salt water flows into me and after a few minutes it all drains out, taking the toxins with it. This whole procedure is basically just a gut-gargle (but it works). The machine that is supposed to save my life looks like it is designed around an off-the-shelf waffle iron with a timer and a pump. This is a good time to believe in God if this is all that medical science has to offer.

After several fill and drain cycles they finally shut off the machine and unhook the umbilical cord so that I can stand up for the first time after surgery, where I discover that instead of having a couple of inches of tubing sticking out of my side there is about three feet of tubing that I have to wrap around my waist. It feels like I have an electric extension cord under my pajamas as I take small tentative steps out into the hallway for a little exercise. As I start plodding toward the nurses' station a giggle escapes from my lips causing a little pain, so I have to suppress my urge to laugh even though each time that I take a step my body gurgles as if I had water in my boots.

It's a good thing that humor is the dominant feeling in my brain because if I were to be honest, I would have to tell you that just below the humor lies disappointment. I had been thinking that with just a short tube coming out of me, it could be taped back so that I could pass for a normal, healthy person; but with three feet of tubing wrapped around my waist that illusion is lost. Being normal has to be one of the universal desires of longing souls no matter what affliction torments them. With my left hand holding a bag collecting urine from my bladder and my right hand clutching the tubes around my waist, any dreams that I held for normalcy faded with each sloshing step.

I wonder how this sloshing sound will affect sales. The funny half of my brain muses at the absurdity of my having a big life insurance sale scheduled with Al Holland in Bishopville three days from now; better postpone it for a week is the message from the logical lobe while the humorous side lets out a giggle at the bleak prospects for any such journey even ten days from now.

Debi wants to know what's so funny, but I can't waste my energy explaining everything if I'm going to make it all the way to the nurses' station and back to my room without collapsing on the floor. My energy is dwindling rapidly. When I reach the nurses' station all of the nurses react as if I were a puppy who had just done his business outside for the first time. I must say that it makes me feel like 'a good boy' to have my humble accomplishments so enthusiastically reinforced.

One look back down the hall tells me that I may not have the energy to make it back to my bed. Sloshing my petty pace (apologies to the bard) leaves me covered in sweat as I enter my room, only to discover the man from the lab is waiting to draw some blood from my arm.

The happy muttering of Bill, the morning nurse, announces the beginning of my last full day at Richland Memorial Hospital, with the glorious news that Bill has brought his life insurance policy for me to review. The morning walk to the nurses' station is a walk in the park with Debi compared to the marathon race that it felt like just yesterday. Tomorrow morning, as soon as dialysis is over, I get to go home. Even if I do have to live with a three-foot umbilical cord wrapped around my waist, this is still one step better than being dead and two steps better than hemodialysis.

The improvement in my stamina would be more noticeable if I could stand up straight, but fear of pain makes me walk bent over like an old man until I see my good friend from work, Tony Crumpton, coming up the hall. Greeting me with the big smile that he always has, and as I relax talking with Tony, I straighten out as if some faith healer had slapped me in the forehead.

It impresses Tony that I have actually picked up someone's life insurance policy while I have been in the hospital and it impresses me that Tony has come to visit with me.

After my morning fill and drain gut-gargle routine, Nurse Bill gives me a very serious lesson on how to properly care for my incision at home. First my hands must always be washed in Betadine solution to kill any bacteria before it kills me, and we have to use surgical masks and latex gloves because this is different from a regular surgical incision. The Tenckhoff catheter provides an opening for any opportunistic bacteria to enter directly into my peritoneal cavity and any infection could be fatal.

When Debi arrives to take me home, I want to walk out of the hospital the same way that I walked in, but Nurse Bill insists that protocol requires that I must ride in a wheel chair out to the car. Once again I pass through the automatic doors in the main lobby (death's door) out into the glorious October sunshine where I can hear a mockingbird's happy song. I think how nice it would be if the patients inside the hospital could open up their windows so that they could breathe this fresh air and hear the happy sounds of life.

Chapter 13

I WOULD HAVE TO GET BETTER TO DIE

HOME FROM THE HOSPITAL at last, I quake in fear when my mind tries to fathom how bad I will feel after the transplant if the wimpy surgery that I just went through, to insert the Tenckhoff catheter, makes me feel as bad as I feel right now. Nothing satisfies sleep deprivation like the comfort of your own bed after spending a few sleepless nights on one of those hard hospital beds. I almost miss the old Foley catheter with its ability to handle certain functions without interrupting my sleep.

When I start to shave in the morning, I am shocked by what I see looking back at me from the mirror. I look smaller than I normally would, and I look much older. I had been wanting to get older but not this fast. What I need right now is a long hot shower but even this simple pleasure is denied to anyone right after surgery. It takes a lot of effort to get to get cleaned up, but I feel so much better when I pull on a sweater and a pair of blue jeans that it is worth all of the effort, even though I can't button the jeans. When I walk by my bed my body wants to fall back into it but my brain says you just got up fool.

I go into the kitchen where Debi has my breakfast ready, but all that I can think about is that I have a thirst worthy of a French Foreign Legionnaire after a march through a waterless desert. I am surrounded by water, but I cannot slake my thirst because people on dialysis have a maximum fluid intake set only slightly higher than the minimum amount of moisture required to just stay alive.

In a few days I will discover the painful consequences of drinking too much water. I only wish that the doctors had told me what I am about to tell you: Do not drink anything that has a diuretic effect like hot coffee and ice tea if you are on kidney dialysis because you are going to need every drop that the doctors allow you to have (and not one drop more).

Debi's eyes look huge behind her surgical mask as we prepare to set up the peritoneal dialysis machine for the first time without a nurse being in charge. There is a special thrill when you know that any screw up could mean that you end up dead. Each bag of saline solution is hung on the dialysis machine with great care before it is plugged up to the clear plastic tube that threads it through to the warming reservoir. It is the uncontaminated connection of these sterile areas that separates the sick from the dead. The big finale comes right after the removal of the bulky blue cover on the end of the Tenckhoff catheter. Feeling very much like a moment that might be painted on a chapel ceiling the sacred connection is finally made between man and the life-giving machine.

Debi is sweating from the tension as we peel off our surgical gloves and masks now that the Tenckhoff catheter is plugged into the dialysis machine. Before pushing the start-button we share a quick hug, knowing that if either one of us made a mistake, I will end up just as dead as Julius Caesar. There is a certain bond formed out of danger that makes love stronger than love that has gone untested.

With a click of the switch (roll of the dice) the machine comes to life pumping some of the fluid from the hanging bags into the machine to warm up. Climbing into bed my body is so tired that it feels like this dialysis session had better work or I may never wake up again. Only when the warm fluid begins flowing into my abdominal cavity do I discover something important that they fail to mention in the little handbook that comes along with every dialysis machine. Hear me well future kidney patients: use the bathroom before pushing the red start button on your dialysis machine.

Falling back into bed I kiss Debi good night, laughing that I look pregnant and marveling that the stitches are holding the incision together under all of this pressure. Just as I'm drifting off to sleep, I am awakened by the gentle rocking of my body as the machine changes cycles and the tide starts to go out (catch 22 is that the hours that you spend on dialysis are the same hours that they expect you to sleep).

After unhooking from the machine in the morning Debi and I fill a large black plastic garbage bag with the medical debris of just one day of my extended existence. There is a powerful need that fills my soul to just be normal like everyone else but this need will go unfulfilled because I have three feet of plastic tubing wrapped around my waist. I decide to do something that normal people might do: like drive into the office to pick up my paycheck and to show my friends down at work that there is life after dialysis.

Just getting into my car separates me from the regular healthy folks because each leg has to be lifted by grabbing my trousers just above the knee in order to swing them into the car. Driving down the Interstate Highway I motor along in utter amazement at the progress that can be achieved by the human body in just one day. When I reach the bottom of the steep flight of stairs that leads up to my office on the second floor, I pause to survey the challenge at hand. In the past I had never given these stairs a second thought but today they stand before me like a mountain that is in my way.

Stepping up on the first step with my right foot then dragging my left foot into place before repeating the process, I make my petty pace on up the stairs. Halfway up the flight of stairs my heart is pounding so fast that I have to stop for a brief rest, but I must press on after just a few seconds lest someone come up the stairs behind me and have to wait as I make my way to the top with my elderly gait.

The water fountain at the top of the stairway gives me a clear goal because I'm sweating and thirsty when the summit is finally attained. The clear stream of water revitalizes me and I decide to step into the men's room in order to straighten up my tie. The face that I see in the mirror looks like a heart attack getting ready to happen. The flushed red shade makes me realize that perhaps my body needs more time for recovery, and that I had better take better care of myself, but I have bills to pay so I must press on.

Entering the office, doing my best imitation of how someone would walk if they didn't have a stiff tube stuck in their gut, I greet Sue, the receptionist, loudly (volume may be confused with health). Upon hearing my familiar voice Ted Rentz and Jim Doolin come out of the back office to greet me and I have to tell you that friends like these are a part of what makes life worth living.

The big surprise is that they aren't surprised to see me since everyone had been under the impression that it was just very minor surgery instead of the actual beginning of dialysis. Having just been scared by the image in the bathroom mirror I know that they are all liars when they tell me how healthy I'm looking, but their good intentions are well appreciated. Feeling my energy dwindling without further delay the accumulated mail is scooped up and back down the stairs I waddle away.

Emerging into the sunlight I realize that my energy has dissipated to the point where the short drive on the interstate highway back home to Blythewood will be difficult, and in fact, it turns out to be quite a challenge to not fall asleep at the wheel (an ominous omen for the trip to Bishopville for the big sale two days from now). Arriving home to the welcome sight of my parents carrying in a car full of my mother's home cooking, I know that her vegetable soup will do my body good and they have brought enough food to feed a small crowd.

At last, my appetite is restored, and the next morning so is my energy, so Debi and I take this opportunity to walk down to the edge of the small lake that we live on. I relax in the late October sunshine watching the beautiful dragonflies hovering just inches above the lilly pads, defending their territories against other dragonflies for the privilege of eating any mosquito that happens to come this way. The entire lilly pad area is organized into a patchwork of well-defined territories in the dragonfly world, showing me that there is order in nature even though it may be unrecognized by man, and this concept brings some peace to my worried mind. Debi brings me lunch down by the lake, so we put down a blanket for a picnic and discover that there is romance after dialysis.

Each day I feel a little stronger than I felt the day before and this progress is balm to my soul. On Sunday I feel well enough to walk up the hill to the mailbox for the newspaper before spending the rest of the day down by the lake with Debi watching the dragonflies and falling deeper in love. Monday morning we hurry into our surgical gloves and masks for the disconnect ceremony from the dialysis machine. It seems unnatural to rush through the procedure but we have to if I'm going to be on time for the big sale in Bishopville today.

By the time that I'm finished putting on a business suit a light sweat covers my body. It surprises me that the yellow tint to my eyes and skin that I have had for the last few months is completely gone in less than one week after starting dialysis.

The image in the mirror doesn't look sick but all the rushing around has left me feeling like a one hour nap would be more beneficial than a one hour drive on the interstate highway, but a man has to do whatever it takes to make a living, and I have to go to Bishopville today. Out on the interstate highway, as I drive towards Bishopville, I put on a B.B. King tape with the volume turned up loud. It relieves me to find out that the song, "The Thrill is Gone," no longer makes me cry.

I'm looking forward to seeing Al and Janice Holland again because on every trip that I make to Bishopville they fill me in on everything that has been going on since my last visit. Don't think that life in a small town is boring because these people have the funniest stories that I have ever heard and if nothing is going on, they create their own fun. Al and I make a call on a big farmer named Mendel who sees the logic of our proposal when he finds out that his existing cash values will be absorbed by the life insurance company rather than being paid to his wife when he dies.

Only when we start to fill out the application do I realize the full extent of the hand tremors that come from high doses of Cyclosporine (my hands are shaking so much that I'm afraid that the client might think that I am a crook). Al finishes up the application and we leave with victory in my briefcase.

I leave the music turned off during the drive home listening instead to the steady drone of my diesel engine which soon has me feeling like a World War II fighter pilot struggling to stay awake on the long flight home to his base after a successful mission deep in enemy territory (too bad this machine can't do a victory roll).

Once I make it back home to Blythewood, I discover that when you are tired and worn out, putting on the surgical masks and gloves to set up the dialysis machine loses some of its glamour. The monotony associated with any routine, combined with the hand tremors which are reinforced by weariness, causes me to touch the sterile part of the tube from the dialysis machine to a nonsterile surface which could be a fatal error if the event were to go unnoticed (so, we are forced to trash the entire dialysis setup and start all over again). I am so tired from the long day that when it is finally time for me to fall asleep, I find myself trying to fight off slumber instead of falling happily into it, fearing that instead of sleep this may be death tugging at my soul.

After a restful day of dragonfly watching along with Debi's tender loving care, I feel renewed enough to phone Bill, the male nurse, to set up an appointment to return his life insurance policy along with the computer printout illustrating my proposal. If logic and emotion were both aligned on the same side of the issue more often, then everyone would want to be in sales. Bill and his wife greet me like an old family friend and they see the logic of my proposal right from the start. After getting Bill's autograph in the appropriate place, I say my goodbyes and drive over to my office to turn in this sale, along with the big one from yesterday's trip to Bishopville.

Delivering two sales at the same time just days after starting dialysis does wonders for my morale. As I scale the flight of stairs up to my office dragging my left foot, I discover that having to rest halfway up the flight of stairs no longer embarrasses me, because in this arena your worth is measured by what you can produce and I'm still bringing home the bacon, even with one foot in the grave. I bask in the glow of a job well done on the drive home to Blythewood but my joy is brief because the tingling sensation in my left arm has me concerned. I make a mental note to start spending more time addressing the physical challenges at hand instead of just the fiscal ones.

With the transplant just five weeks away, if all goes well, it is apparent to me that I had better get in better shape while I can to the maximum degree that I can (I don't want to die from a heart attack while they are saving me from kidney failure).

Debi and I decide to start taking walks together again in the mornings right after we unhook me from the dialysis machine. The next morning when we go out for a stroll, I become worn out by the time that we walk up the driveway to the road. Alarmed by my rapid decline I press on instinctively trying to make my way down to the end of the block, but that is obviously a physical impossibility, so I set my sights on the telephone pole that is about halfway to my goal. Pressing on with a stagger in my step, I tell Debi that I feel like a fleeing prisoner who is being pursued by very slow hounds. I make it all the way to my telephone pole goal and I feel the sense of accomplishment that comes from any goal that we attain, but I'm not all that certain that I can make it back home (good thing that it is all downhill).

As these walks become a part of our everyday routine my goal is to walk to the point where I go past one more telephone pole than I did on the previous day (pretty soon we are covering a lot of ground). Debi and I take a short cut home through a thicket of trees where we come to a gurgling brook. It seems odd but I'm quite sure that I would call this a stream if it weren't for the fact that it makes a gurgling sound (somehow that magically changes a stream into a brook).

With this thought as the connection to a contemplative state, I widen my scope and contemplate life in general, as I marvel that I can hear a pretty sound that requires something alive to appreciate it but not to create it. Then I start thinking about other things that

I have appreciated during my life and it seems that relationships have brought me more happiness than material possessions in this world. It seems strange that something intangible would have more value than silver or gold, but after all, the only thing that you really get from riches is the feeling of being rich.

Then I think about one special friend that I had shared some moments in time with, my old Boxer dog Sebastian (God rest his bones). Sebastian had always been such a happy spirit that it was impossible to feel depressed with him around because he would always be ready to play, that's why we had recently gotten our new boxer puppy: Spats (he has some big paw prints to fill).

No man's life is complete without the love of a good dog (they never lie, cheat or steal).

My parents had located Spats when I told them that I wanted to get a Boxer puppy. They found Spats at a kennel in Tennessee and he was just what we were looking for: a male Boxer from good bloodlines with all of his shots and with his ears already trimmed.

I remember the day when Debi and I drove up to the Charlotte airport to pick up our new Boxer puppy. Just thinking about Spats (love-dog that he is) brings an instant smile to my face something that has been scarce in the Gordon household. On the trip home from the airport, we name our puppy Spats in honor of his four white paws.

Our morning walks now become an hour of training Spats as he explores his world instead of another hour of introspection about mine (no wonder pet owners live longer; pets keep their owners minds off of negatives things, focusing instead on a world of love and problems that we can solve). Spats' enthusiasm for life is contagious and when I do turn introspective, I dwell on the fact that Spats lives in a world of total happiness not bothered in the least by the limited life span of a dog.

Each day is better than the day before and much to my surprise there is happiness after dialysis. Now for the first time I understand what makes some people elect to remain on dialysis instead of attempting a transplant. I find that the twilight of my life isn't so bad, in fact, remaining in this pause between life and death could be enjoyable if only the world would stop changing around me. For me, living on dialysis is a temporary state that I have to go through to get my slim shot at being healthy and normal.

The first hint of trouble in dialysis land is a sudden fullness disturbing my slumber (it seems like maybe the dialysis machine skipped a drain cycle). Listening to the steady hum in the dark it sounds normal but I feel completely full. Convincing myself that I am just acting paranoid is easy (it's going back to sleep that's difficult since I'm worried and uncomfortable). Finally the crack of dawn says it's time to get up. Standing by my bed, wondering what made me slosh and gurgle more than normal, I know that something isn't right as soon as my eyes fall upon my protruding belly which looks like I'm nine months pregnant.

First, the assumption is that somehow the dialysis machine must have malfunctioned, but before that can be determined my brain is wracked by terror when I notice that the Tenckhoff catheter is full of little strands of cream-colored matter that shouldn't be there if things weren't terribly wrong. As my eyes quickly scan the catheter up to my body it startles me when I see that one of the thread-like things is half outside of my body and half of it is inside of me (oh oh). The damn things are coming from inside me! The recognition of immense danger leads to the instantaneous response to flee. Yet even if I weren't tethered to the dialysis machine how do you run away from something that's coming from inside of you.

A closer look leads me to believe that these fiber-like strands are clogging up the Tenckhoff catheter, preventing proper drainage. A quick phone call to alert Dr. Calm's office to the new situation thrusts Debi and I into a car race as we drive into to see Dr. Calm. Riding down the interstate, I think about my choice to not have a vein reversed into an artery to create a place to stick me with huge needles for emergency hemodialysis just in case "something" goes wrong with peritoneal dialysis (which it is). Now I wonder if that choice to not have a vein prepared for hemodialysis could end up costing me my life. How ironic if I die from some cream-colored fibers that I never even knew existed until today. Think of all of the good quality time in life that we waste worrying about things that will never happen (expect the unexpected).

Dr. Calm examines me as soon as I arrive (now it becomes clear to me why doctors can't stay on schedule). Dr. Calm tells me the little strands that are stopping up my catheter are called 'fibroids' and they are part of the body's response to a wound. Dr. Calm tells me that the solution for this fibroid problem is an injection of Heparin which is normally used as a blood thinner. I'm just happy that these little fibers don't scare Dr. Calm as bad as they scare me, and it thrills me that these injections that Dr. Calm is talking about go into the Tenckhoff instead of my arm. After giving me the initial mega-dose of Heparin, Dr. Calm gives me a prescription for needles with syringes and Heparin, sending me home sloshing happily as Dr. Calm hurries on to his next crises.

As soon as the physical worries are put to rest the mind turns back to fiscal worries, but that's only a problem if I live. Then what can only be described as divine intervention occurs when I get a phone call from Don Coker of Coker Builders in Turbeville, South Carolina, wanting to know if I can come to their office in Turbeville tomorrow in order to give them a quote on some life insurance that they are going to buy for the owners (millions and millions worth of life insurance). So, with visions of earning big money right when I need it most, the appointment is made. It is hard to look at this without coming to the conclusion that this has to be the answer to a prayer, because in the life insurance business they don't call you.

Debi and I are so excited that it is very difficult to concentrate on the mundane procedure of setting up the dialysis machine, but we have to be careful least the smallest mistake contaminate me (make me dead). The alarm clock seems to go off as soon as sleep comes, but in fact it is 5:30 a.m., which is when I need to begin all the steps required in order for me to launch from Blythewood with plenty of time for the ninety-minute drive to Turbeville. As we hurry through the unhooking process there is a lot of stress, but we do it in record time so that I launch for Turbeville on schedule, but I discover that I am absolutely exhausted as I drive out of my driveway into the cool morning rain.

The drive is therapeutic as I reflect on each problem area of my life: health, wealth and love life. Deciding that love problems hurt the deepest, I'm lucky to have found Debi to heal my heart. Now if the doctors can just heal (replace) my kidneys, then I can earn money (what has been earned once can be earned again).

The excitement of the big sale carries me to Turbeville with no problem but during the wait in Coker Builders lobby my stomach starts making sounds like distant thunder just when Don Coker walks in and asks me to go with him to his house for lunch.

Laughing at the thunder, Don says, "I take that as a yes," so we head to lunch which provides me with an opportunity to bring Don Coker up to date on my health situation. He asks me if I have time to visit a fifteen-year-old girl who is experiencing kidney failure and is frightened because she is just before needing dialysis herself. After a nice lunch which Don's wife has waiting for us, we stop by the young girl's home and I try to alleviate her fears without showing how I tremble at the prospects for her future.

Back at Coker Builders I calculate the rates on five large life insurance policies and make my presentation to Ray Coker, (Don Coker's brother) along with Don and their brother-in-law who is the corporate treasurer. The joy of hearing that I had their business increases my feeling of worth to society, and gives me a measure of financial security because the commissions will arrive after the transplant when I will need it most.

Taking five life insurance applications isn't quite as easy as it sounds since each one is a mini sale, with each partner having to settle any misgivings without the comfort of time. At the end of the day shall we say that I am feeling the absence of my power nap, making the drive home a tortuous ordeal as I fight to stay awake. The little fantasy about the fighter pilot doesn't help but loud music, alternating with no music and the windows down, keeps me alert as the sun sets quickly in the mid November sky with the darkness calling my body to sleep.

When I finally pull into my garage back home and cut my car motor off, sleep takes me where I am until Debi comes out to see why I haven't come inside. Stumbling inside we try to go through the dialysis procedure but there is no way that I can stay awake. I remember that one of the dialysis patients had told me that you could skip one night of dialysis if you had to (the doctors can't tell you this because there is some risk, but there is also a risk of contamination if you screw up because you are too tired). I make a command decision to skip dialysis tonight and go straight to lovely sleep.

Morning finds me unrenewed and bone weary (go figure) nurtured slowly one meal at a time by Debi's loving hand. In the evening, I'm up to feeling terrible. This leads me to make one of those decisions that have a logical origin but lacking practical experience result in disaster due to the law of unintended consequences.

Since dialysis went undone last night, the reasoning goes that my system has more toxins than normal, so I sweeten the mix by adding one extra bag of the more concentrated saline solution (just gut gargling with a little saltier water). Then, after restful sleep had me in lullaby land, my right leg locks up in a cramp that thankfully is beyond the experience range of the normal person.

Leaping to my feet in the dark, I stand on my cramping leg with all of my weight while massaging it vigorously with both of my hands. The cramp from hell will not let go; instead, my other leg begins to cramp, so I yell to Debi for her to cut on the overhead light and to push the stop button on the dialysis machine. Even though I'm standing right next to the dialysis machine, both of my hands are totally occupied going from leg to leg in frantic massaging efforts trying to keep from having both legs cramp up at the same time.

Standing up with my legs straight, I bend over at the waist while I massage my legs, telling Debi to phone Dr. Calm as sweat beads up on my forehead. Fortunately, Dr. Calm has given me his home phone number so I don't have to go through the answering service and wait for a return phone call. A frantic Debi talks to a sleepy Dr. Calm because both of my hands are too busy to hold a telephone. Dr. Calm tells Debi that he will call in a prescription for quinine, which should stop the cramping, but he warns me not to take more than two or it could lead to a heart attack.

After four years of living in Blythewood I discover a negative to the nouveau-country living (that being the nearest pharmacy that is open 24-hours is a forty-minute round trip drive). Debi rushes to pick-up the quinine, leaving me to fight off the cramps until she can come back with the medicine that Dr. Calm has called in for me. After Debi races out of the driveway, I think about being alone at a time like this and I'll tell you that I don't like it one bit.

Maybe the heart attacks associated with higher quinine dosages occur when the heart muscle cramps for the same reason the leg muscles cramp (dehydration). Quickly hobbling to my bathroom sink I start drinking as much water as possible while bent over massaging my legs. After a few minutes that seem like forever, the cramps begin to subside leaving me covered with sweat and still drinking water. My legs and back are sore as I lay back down to rest my weary body, but as soon as the weight is off of my right leg, it starts to cramp again sending me back up on my feet.

Feeling like a contestant in a dance marathon I struggle to stay on my feet to prevent the cramp from starting all over again. Even sitting on the bed for a moment makes the muscle in my right leg tighten up, keeping me on my feet until Debi comes roaring down the driveway like a NASCAR driver at the finish line, as she skids to a stop at the front door. Within seconds of swallowing two of the magic capsules the leg muscles relax, allowing me to collapse in bed, saved by Debi and her midnight medical express.

Night cramps return each time sleep tries to take me for many evenings to come. The fear of the cramps that often wake me makes total relaxation a difficult state to get into, because it's only after drifting off to sleep that the cramp will seize my leg. Quinine by my side I lay me down to sleep. I now see the delicate balance that must be maintained for life on dialysis (life offers no safe havens)

I find myself living in a dangerous world which exposes me to risks without any possibility that these risks could improve my situation. At least the risks associated with having a transplant bring with them a chance for victory: (a normal life).

After being on dialysis for a while the one thing that is certain is that I'm sick and tired of being sick and tired. Life gets down to making the best choice among imperfect options, like my father always says, "Do the best you can with what you have."

PHOTOS

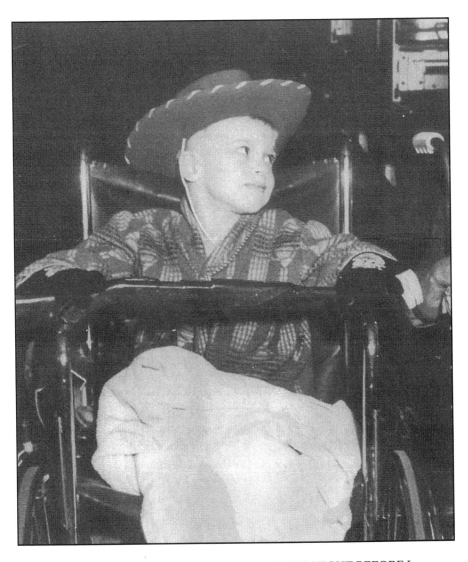

MY FATHER WOULD VISIT MY BEDSIDE THE NIGHT BEFORE I
WAS TO HAVE SURGERY TO LET ME KNOW AND I WOULD START
TO CRY SO HE WOULD TELL ME TO "BE A GOOD SOLDIER"
WHICH MADE ME MAN UP (FOR A 5 YEAR OLD).

SEE THE VIDEO AT
HTTPS://VIMEO.COM/555783500

1974 V-12 JAGUAR

DON & DEBI SUPER HEROES

DON WITH SPATS:
PHOTO BY DEBI

Chapter 14

THIS WAS ORIGINALLY PAGE ONE OF MY BOOK

I AM UP EARLY READING THE PAPER and having a cup of Columbian coffee. Knowing that this could be the last really good coffee that I ever taste, the moment is being savored as my brother's car rolls into the driveway at 6:15 a.m. for the trip to Duke University Hospital for our kidney transplant attempt. At this point Jimmy is still reserving the right to say NO up to the very last minute if he feels uncomfortable after we meet our Doctors at D.U.H., so I don't know if this trip is to see my savior or my executioner, but after six weeks on dialysis I am ready for either one.

As Jimmy pulls his car up to the house, I take my luggage outside and ask Jimmy to come inside for one cup of coffee. It's surprising how little one needs to pack for a trip to the hospital that could be for the rest of your life. I have packed two bags, one of which is full of dialysis supplies that I brought along because Dr. Calm had warned me to be prepared (just in case). Everything else fits into one small black leather bag because I am only carrying the bare essentials: medicine, shaving gear, pajamas, all of my good underwear and my .357 Colt Python revolver (just in case).

The .357 Colt Python revolver was included in my list of bare essentials, not because of a sense of malice towards anyone, as it has never even occurred to me that a doctor might need shooting (ha! ha!). The revolver is just a personal termination device for the unlikely possibility that I could end up lying in a hospital bed all hooked up to machines, too sick to recover and too strong to die.

There are situations that are worse than death, an eventuality for which some people might choose sleeping pills, but I don't want to feel the horrible torment that must come after the pills have been swallowed but before they take effect. Think of the unbelievable agony of trying to decide whether or not you push the button to call a nurse before you pass out. Of course, if you did call the nurse they would save your life by pumping out your stomach, but then you would be back in the same situation without any way to end it.

At least my way if I can't stand the pain the lights just go out (bam!). I am determined that I am not going to live just so that the doctors can see how long they can keep me alive. There is a sense of control that comes with knowing that if the doctors can't stop the pain, I can. Once I realize that the worst case scenario is not going to happen, my mood improves tremendously and who knows, I might just make it back home alive.

The cup of coffee sounds good to Jimmy, so he comes into the kitchen and I pour us each a cup before I pour the rest of the coffee into a thermos for the trip to D.U.H. After a couple of sips of the coffee I go back to the den so that I can give Debi one last kiss (just in case). As we are getting ready to walk out to the car Jimmy says, "Lets pray," and launches into a loud request for divine protection (maybe the volume helps God know exactly where Jimmy is praying from).

Even though I am part Catawba Indian, many times the signs of the universe are seen but not understood; for example, after we have traveled about two miles from my house there is an entire flock of wild turkeys moving on the edge of the field to our right. When I tell Jimmy to slow the car down so that we can look at the wild turkeys, he doesn't even glance their way, much less pause to let me watch them. Maybe Jimmy thinks these are just farm turkeys, or perhaps he is so lost in his own thoughts that he doesn't even hear me.

Suddenly three turkey hens come gliding across the road from the right immediately in front of the car. "Jimmy slow down, the turkeys are on both sides of the road!" I shout to no avail. This is by far the largest flock of wild turkeys that I have ever seen, but Jimmy just continues looking straight ahead as if he is in a trance. While pondering Jimmy's lack of wonderment I miss the sign the universe is trying to give me, which is that I am about to be surrounded by a bunch of turkeys!

The three hour drive up the interstate highway to D.U.H. is good for my relationship with Jimmy as it brings us closer together, reducing the chance that Jimmy might back out at the last minute and not give me his kidney.

Being tired from the trip leaves me short on patience when the lady at the hospital admissions office is long on forms. When I ask the lady who is admitting me why referring hospitals don't provide all of this information, so that tired transplant patients don't have to go through all of this after a long trip, she gets a little huffy with me.

Then the admissions lady tells me, somewhat smugly, that my name is not showing up in the computer and her attitude goes from bad to worse. In a condescending tone of voice the admissions lady asks me if we are sure that we have come to the right hospital, so I let my words drip with sarcasm as I respond, "We are beginning to wonder." I think that I'm being pretty funny but I can see Jimmy starting to shake his head back and forth, giving me a nonverbal signal to stop being uncooperative.

I respond gently to the request from the admissions lady for my social security number for the third time only to be told that I am still not showing up anywhere in her computer, not even on the Medicare active list. With great authority in her voice the admissions lady tells me that there is no way to admit anyone for a transplant if they are not eligible for Medicare. Then the admissions lady gives me a snooty look and tells me to go back home and consult with my local physician.

The reason that Medicare benefits are an issue is that this is how the hospital gets paid (show them the money). Medicare takes over from regular health insurance when someone goes on dialysis and it continues for two years after transplantation, or until death, whichever comes first.

The admissions lady's attitude makes the hair bristle on the back of my neck and without saying a word I put my Medicare card on her desk, as if it was a winning ace in a high-stakes poker game (which it is). Then I tell the admissions lady that perhaps she should consult with the local physician here by calling Dr. Big's office (head of the transplant center) to tell him that we tried to be admitted but we were instructed to return home. The admissions lady reluctantly phones Dr. Big's office, but her eyes are sending me the message that she is just calling my bluff.

The brief phone conversation that follows consists of just a few words, then looking only slightly chagrined and without any explanation, the admissions lady tells us to go wait in the lobby until transportation sends someone over to escort us to our rooms. The joy of being right on time diminishes when no one is expecting you. When I get to the kidney transplant ward the head nurse has an expression on her face like she just discovered that her car has a flat tire. To the head nurse I represent extra work, especially since my file with the doctor's orders has not been delivered to the ward.

Just as I'm thinking that I don't want to get off on the wrong foot with the staff, a young nurse comes into my room and her shoes squeak every time that she takes a step. It's not a loud squeak, but it's definitely there and it causes a little smile to break across my face. In this brief moment of levity, I give this young nurse the nickname "Nurse Squeaky" and the best thing about it is that it would be perfect even if her shoes didn't make a sound. Nurse Squeaky doesn't wear any make up and she has her hair pulled back in a bun, in fact she looks so well-scrubbed that her forehead shines (we are talking squeaky clean).

Nurse Squeaky starts to ask me the exact same set of lengthy questions that the admissions lady just finished going over with me (starting with my name). The whole process grinds on my tired nerves, so I ask Nurse Squeaky if she couldn't just get all of that information from the admissions office, but Nurse Squeaky doesn't even acknowledge my question. She just gives me the evil eye and starts asking her questions again. I guess that glare is meant to let me know who is in charge around here, so I put on a happy face and this time I cheerfully respond to Nurse Squeaky's questions lest they label me as "uncooperative."

We are progressing nicely until Nurse Squeaky gets to the part about what medications I'm currently taking, because after writing them down she asks to see any medicine that I may have brought with me to the hospital. Upon handing over all of my prescription bottles to Nurse Squeaky, she announces with the voice of high authority that, "All future medications will come from the hospital pharmacy." Without any further explanation, Nurse Squeaky starts to walk out of my hospital room still clutching the medicines that she had only asked to "see."

Calling out to Nurse Squeaky, "Wait just a minute," causes her to pause in the doorway to my room, and as she turns to look back at me I tell Nurse Squeaky that I feel like I'm being robbed. This doesn't seem to bother Nurse Squeaky as much as it bothers me because she just says, "You can get these back when you leave the hospital." She then leaves without even waiting for my response. I'm sure that Nurse Squeaky is aware of the fact that when I leave the hospital, all of my medications will be different, but I have to acquiesce because they have me by the medications (balls). Giving up control of my medicine makes me feel lousy and I'm glad that none of Nurse Squeaky's questions were regarding what weapons I may have brought with me to the hospital.

The last medical hurdle that I have to get over before the transplant is a final blood test to make certain that my brother's blood still matches mine. I have to wonder if this last-minute blood matching isn't just a means by which the doctors provide a graceful out for reluctant donors (how could blood that matched a month ago not match now?).

Alone in the hospital room pondering my current state of affairs, I quickly come to the conclusion that I had better start being nice to the hospital staff since in a few days I'll be depending on them to save my life. With that in mind I put a smile on my face just in time to meet a large, older nurse who comes into my room holding a little white paper cup in her hand.

When God made this nurse, He made the perfect army drill sergeant (with an extra Y chromosome). One good thing is that this nurse doesn't need any special nickname because her real name is Nurse Crabb. When she introduces herself to me, she doesn't say that she will be my nurse, she says, "You will be my patient."

Then Nurse Crabb hands me the little white paper cup that she has in her hand telling me that it contains the medications that the hospital pharmacy has sent for me to take. Trying to act cheerful I start to take the pills in the white paper cup, but they don't look like any of my normal medications. The only pill that I take, except at meal-time, is my blood pressure pill and neither one of the two pills in the white paper cup looks anything like it.

In my most deferential tone of voice, as politely as possible, I point out to Nurse Crabb the apparent mistake. Instead of sharing my concerns Nurse Crabb insists that she has to see me take both pills (as if I had never said a word). Since Nurse Crabb makes no effort to answer my question I know that I need to be more direct. I tell Nurse Crabb that I'm no expert but I'm pretty sure that I can still count, and there are two pills in the cup when there should only be one, so I'm not taking anything until the pharmacy can explain that.

I don't care how you sugar coat it, people get mad when you tell them no and it is pretty clear that Nurse Crabb wasn't expecting anything like this when she came into my room (neither was I). Nurse Crabb just glares at me for a couple of seconds as if she would like to make me do some push-ups with a little help from her boot and then Nurse Crabb storms out of my room slamming the large wooden door as if she just had an argument with her spouse (how professional).

One of the best ways to judge something like a hospital is to see how the staff responds to the unexpected, but instead of sharing my concerns, Nurse Crabb had just reacted as if I were a troublemaker (uncooperative).

My interaction with the hospital staff today makes me feel like a square peg that is being pounded into a round hole. I'd like to run down the hall and just keep right on going but there is no escaping the issues that I have to deal with, but that doesn't change the fact that this place gives me the creeps.

In about five minutes Nurse Crabb comes storming back into my room huffing and puffing as if she was right all along, but her words tell a different story. There should be an apologetic tone in Nurse Crabb's voice, because what I am hearing is that when she checked with the hospital pharmacy they said that my blood pressure pill was the correct medication, it was just two milligrams when it should have been one. Then in a condescending tone of voice Nurse Crabb tells me that all that I have to do is to break the pill in half.

I am not particularly impressed with this explanation so I ask Nurse Crabb what about the other pill that was in the cup. She acts like it should make me feel better when she tells me that the pharmacy doesn't have any idea how a second pill got in with my medication. That leaves Nurse Crabb standing in front of me with one half of a strange pill in the white paper cup and a half-baked story about it got there (I'm still not convinced).

Nurse Crabb is waiting for me to swallow the medication along with her explanation but the whole thing just seems "unprofessional." In my nicest tone of voice I decline to take the pill while pointing out to Nurse Crabb the obvious fact that an error has been made, and the only safe thing to do is to give me one of the blood pressure pills that I brought with me while we straighten things out.

Nurse Crabb isn't trying to understand my logic, she just wants to see me take the pill. I know that I need to be more direct, so I remind that just five minutes ago she had been in here insisting on watching me swallow a 100% overdose of my blood pressure medicine along with a mystery pill that she can't even identify.

Nurse Crabb looks me in the eye as if she were a Southern Sheriff about to say, "You in a heap of trouble boy," as she tells me that she is certain that this pill is the correct medication because she talked to the pharmacist herself. Just to be easier to get along with I take the strange pill so that they don't get the idea that I'm "uncooperative."

I'm tired from the trip and tired of dealing with these turkeys here at D.U.H. I get Jimmy on the phone and we decide to go down to the hospital cafeteria to get something to eat. I wish that I could tell Jimmy how slack these people seem but I don't want to make him "uncomfortable." Jimmy tells me that he will come by my room so that we can go downstairs together and just as I hang up the phone a female intern comes into my room. I don't know it yet but I'm about to meet the biggest turkey of them all. The female intern introduces herself as Dr. Frau and tells me that she is here to give me my physical exam.

Dr. Frau isn't a bad looking woman and when she tells me to drop my pants, I ask her if we can't just be friends. I knew that something wasn't right when Dr. Frau didn't even crack a smile, I just didn't know what. Then in a tone of voice that you don't expect a woman to use to a man who has his pants off, Dr. Frau tells me to lay on my side with my back to her (let's just skip the small talk).

Striped of more than my dignity, I lay on my side in the bed as tense as a field goal kicker in the Super-Bowl. Dr. Frau snaps on a pair of latex gloves and says, "This is called a prostate exam." Dr. Frau goes much too fast for my muscles to relax and she handles me roughly. This exam feels much closer to a rectal assault, so I tell Dr. Frau that it hurts. She is lost in her work and shoves her finger harder still, making it appear to me that Dr. Frau doesn't know what she is searching for. Yet again I tell Dr. Frau that it hurts but she continues with her rude behavior, making me wonder if this exam could be retribution for the way that I talked to Nurse Crabb earlier (professional courtesy).

I can assure you that I have never had a male doctor examine my prostate with such vigor. I'm not sure what Dr. Frau may have learned from this physical exam but I learned to never have a doctor check any body part on me that they don't have themselves (it takes one to know one).

Dr. Frau must have missed the day the class went over that 'first do no harm' part of the oath. After Dr. Frau is gone I get dressed to go down to the hospital cafeteria just in time because Jimmy walks into my room announcing that we need to pray together. Jimmy prays loud enough for God to know exactly where we are currently located (third planet from the sun).

We then go downstairs to the hospital cafeteria where Jimmy feels the need for another loud prayer of thanks to let God know that we are now in the basement (if he needs us). Two prayers in ten minutes, for me that could be a personal best (Jimmy has got that old time religion). Jimmy and I go over our schedule of events to see what happens first. Tomorrow morning we are going to have blood work done to make certain that our blood type matches, then we will meet with our doctors.

This is Monday evening and the transplant is supposed to take place Thursday morning at 7:00 a.m. if everything goes as planned. I like being the first surgery of the day because the doctors will be fresh. I point out to Jimmy that the doctors are much less likely to be drunk early in the morning than they would be after lunch. I get a laugh out of this but Jimmy is all business and fails to see the humor. He just sits there glaring at me as if I'm not taking all of this seriously enough (trust me I am).

It will be good to see Debi when she gets here Wednesday along with my parents and Jill (Jimmy's wife). I am already getting tired of being surrounded by strangers. One thing that medical science can't do for you is to make you feel loved.

I am surprised but not disappointed when Nurse Squeaky tells me that I do not have to deal with dialysis tonight. If everything goes as we plan, then I only have to worry about dialysis two more times in my entire life (yes!). Going to bed early does not guarantee getting a good night's sleep and I could sure use some rest. It's hard to go to sleep with a troubled mind and when I do finally drift off to dreamland, the night nurse makes it her job to disturb me every four hours to check my blood pressure and temperature.

Since the night nurse knows that she will be waking me up every four hours to check my vital signs, then that would be the logical time to give me my blood pressure pill or to see how much I weigh (if she had any common sense). I'm sure that common sense is something that we would see a lot more of around hospitals if they could only figure out how to charge for it. The morning finds me tired and ornery, it seems like they haven't figured out that sick people need rest (duh).

Standing at the door to my room I gaze down to the other end of the hall. My attention is drawn to a gaggle of white coated interns who are following their leader as he makes his rounds, while dictating instructions to his female administrative assistant. I watch this scene unfold as this small group of doctors makes their way up the hall one room at a time. There is no question which doctor is in charge because everyone's eyes are on him as he strides majestically up the hall giving his lecture on the go.

The white coated Interns stay closely packed together as they walk briskly up the hall making notes of important things that are being said. I can't hear a word that is being said but I know that this is the modern equivalent of Pharaoh inspecting the construction of the Pyramids followed by his engineers and scribes.

The first time that I called this Doctor "Pharaoh" I didn't know that I was going to write a book. I just did it because it fit the occasion. Dr. Pharaoh does have an imperial bearing and, apparently, he has a pretty high opinion of himself (which he should). Years later I would meet a doctor that studied under Dr. Pharaoh and he told me that all of the medical students called him Dr. God behind his back (because of the way that he treated them in surgery).

All eyes are on Dr. Pharaoh as he enters my room (especially those of his attractive administrative assistant). Dr. Pharaoh explains my situation to the wannabe doctors as if I were just an inanimate classroom exhibit (which it turns out that I am). Maybe it's expected that transplant recipients should just be quiet and look grateful in the presence of the surgeon who will save their life (but I have some questions).

Dr. Pharaoh is thumping my chest like a ripe melon while he listens to my heart. I tell the group of wannabe doctors who are standing around my room that the night nurses should coordinate activities so that the patients can get more rest. I go on to tell them that giving medications and weighing the patients in the mornings should be done at the same time that they take the patients vital signs in order to minimize the disruption of the patients sleep (duh). Much to my surprise all of the interns except for one look shocked. The administrative assistant looks offended, but Dr. Pharaoh just continues his lecture as he leads the group out of my room as if I had never said a word.

I don't want to spend another sleepless night so I walk out in the hall after them and yell to Dr. Pharaoh, "Hey, how about consolidating all of the wake-up calls." Dr. Pharaoh doesn't even turn around; he is already talking about the next case. The last intern in line turns back towards me with a smile as he whispers, "Good luck."

Looking out of the window I see people corning to work in a cold rain and I wonder if they know how lucky they are. What I long for is a normal life with regular problems (that is the theory but I am brought back to reality by a light knocking on my door).

I hear a shrill good morning and it's coming from a skinny little woman in a white coat. She introducers herself as the transplant coordinator and I recognize her distinctive voice. We have had a couple of phone conversations but what stands out in my mind is that this transplant coordinator is the person that screwed up a few weeks ago when she was giving me instructions about my medicine over the phone. It was an honest mistake but it could have cost me my life. This could account for the transplant coordinator's rather defensive tone of voice as we go through the pleasantries, but I am really trying to get along (lest I be labeled as "uncooperative").

I listen with genuine interest to her spontaneous explanation that this hospital's mortality experience would be better, except that they take patients that other hospitals would reject. I guess that would be a relief to me if I had been worried about this hospital's mortality experience to begin with, but I wasn't (until now). In fact, if that bit of information had ever come to my attention before, I might be having this conversation with a transplant coordinator at a different institution.

Someone needs to tell her that making excuses for this hospital's mortality experience does not instill confidence. I think that she may have noticed a look of concern on my face because, in an

143

attempt to reassure me, she says, "Of course the hospital's average numbers aren't your numbers and those are the ones that it's all about " (how true).

Before her visit I had all of the worries of a man in my position. Now that she is gone, I'm paralyzed by fear wondering just how bad this hospital's average numbers are, and whether in the end I will bring the average up or down (up above the earth or down in it, that's what it's all about).

It's hard to get any satisfaction out of being grumpy when someone else around you is happy. So, it is a total mood reversal just to meet John Carter who has come from the lab to draw blood from my arm. It's difficult to see how going around sticking sick people with sharp needles is a job that someone could enjoy, but the nature of the work doesn't dampen his spirits (of course, he isn't the one that feels the pain).

John is on top of his game and his upbeat style is guaranteed to dispel any gloom in the immediate vicinity. Even though Mr. Carter has a professional manner, I feel compelled to ask him to call back down to the lab to confirm that no other blood studies have been ordered for me. I tell him about how Richland Memorial Hospital drew blood from my arms three different times when I was admitted there, showing him my wounded arms to illustrate the point. I have to like his sense of humor even if I don't like his answer, when he asks me the rhetorical question, "Does the sign in front of this building say Richland Memorial or does it say DUH?"

Then Mr. Carter goes on to say, "You aren't dealing with the second string around here; just relax and let us do our thing." He settles the issue by telling me that he will draw an extra tube of blood (just in case). He leaves me smiling as he backs out of my room telling me that he was born at night but it wasn't last night.

I'm beginning to feel like a chassis on a Ford assembly line, except that the factory comes around to me (the longer that you are in a hospital the more it resembles a factory).

I keep meeting new people, one after another, and as soon as John gets all of the blood that he needs, Dr. Wienrith the urologist comes by with a couple of young wannabe urologists in tow.

I met Dr. Wienrith when I drove up to the transplant clinic a few months ago to see if D.U.H. would accept me into their transplant program. A person couldn't ask for a doctor with a better bedside manner than Dr. Wienrith, with his empathetic eyes peering through wire rimmed glasses, doing what no one else around here has tried (asking me if there is anything that he can do to help me).

I jump on that invitation like a mockingbird on a June bug and tell Dr. Wienrith that I need someone to coordinate all of my wake-up calls tonight so that I can get some sleep.

Dr. Wienrith explains my physiology to his throng of interns while listening to my chest with his stethoscope. With all of these doctors floating around it's hard to tell who is in charge of what. They ought to give patients a program that would explain who is playing what role, but I will lay it out for you the best that I can:

Dr. Pharaoh is the star of the transplant program here at D.U.H. and is in total charge until all of the surgical issues are resolved.

Dr. Wienrith, as chief urologist, has basically the same duties as a plumber Unless there is a problem with drainage, he is just assigned to the case until the new kidney starts working.

Then after Dr. Wienrith leaves I meet the guy with the hardest task of all, Dr. Bravo. It's his job to keep my new kidney in me after Dr. Pharaoh puts it there. Dr. Bravo is in charge of regulating my medication levels to see that my new kidney does not reject, and this job requires both science and art.

Dr. Bravo is a nice enough guy, but he will not look me in the eye. Back when I used to play softball we had a saying that hitting is all about confidence but you can't fool yourself. I hope that Dr. Bravo is more confident than he looks because his uneasiness gives me the creeps. When you are flat on your back in a hospital bed the doctor needs to be tall and confident, but I get short and shifty. Before I can get comfortable with Dr. Bravo's strange personality, we are interrupted by John Carter, back from the lab wanting to stick me again.

Mr. Carter should never have taken this job of drawing blood from people because he should have been a doctor, a spin-doctor, because the way that he delivers negative news makes it seem like he is doing you a favor. As Dr. Bravo says his goodbyes, Mr. Carter tells me that my blood was so fine that they want some more of it down at the lab just to show off. I realize that he is not the one who is at fault in this situation but rather just someone else trying to deal with the medical bureaucracy, so I spare him the 'I told you so routine.' (yet still I am the one who is on the sharp end of the needle around here).

There I was alone in my room cursing my luck, when the public address system called out Code Blue. About that time a couple of nurses went running by my door, so I thought that I would get up and look at some problems that weren't my own. I stood in my door so that I could look down the hall, thinking that I was about to witness something like they have on tv, but the only action that I see is one nurse who is rushing down the hall closing all the doors to the patient's rooms. When she gets down to me I can tell that her strange facial expression is meant to convey some sort of admonishment as she mutters Code Blue before slamming the door in my face.

The patient with the problem must be a goner or the nurse wouldn't be so sensitive. I guess now it's just a matter of extracting the last insurance dollars before they pull the sheet up over the face of another dissatisfied customer. Internalizing the probable death of a fellow patient just a few rooms away I wonder if that's how I will end up. My reflections are interrupted by a nurse that is wearing street clothes under a white coat like the doctors wear.

I know that this nurse has to be special because wearing street clothes under your white coat is a status symbol around here (Pharaoh does that). The nurse introduces herself as the transplant nurse, which as I understand it, means that she doesn't do any real nursing at all. A transplant nurse's job is to tell the other nurses what the doctor wants done when he is not around.

The transplant nurse does her job well but without any apparent feelings so I call her Nurse Spock. The comforting thing about Nurse Spock's visit is that she gives me the phone number of the hospital switchboard with instructions to have her paged anytime that I have a question or concern. It's really good to have someone's phone number to call if I have a question because it is a little unclear who is in charge of my overall care. As Nurse Spock is leaving, she tells me that someone will be around pretty soon to start me on dialysis, and if I have any questions don't hesitate to have her paged.

When Nurse Crabb comes by my room later on to start me on dialysis she begins by hanging one bag of dialysis fluid from the IV pole next to my bed. I look up at Nurse Crabb and ask her where the peritoneal dialysis machine is? When I get a puzzled look to such a simple question it hits me that the initials of this place spell my stepdaughter's favorite word (duh).

Nurse Crabb explains that D.U.H. doesn't use machines, they just hang up one bag of dialysis fluid at a time. They then let gravity do its thing until all of the fluid is out of the bag. After that, they clamp off the empty bag and I can go about my business for about thirty minutes; then they put the bag down on the floor and let everything drain back out of me.

Nurse Crabb tells me that this is called ambulatory dialysis but I call it primitive. Now the puzzled look is on my face and what has drained out of me is any confidence that I had in this place. Very diplomatically I tell Nurse Crabb that I would like to have Nurse Spock paged before we begin dialysis because I have a question and a concern.

Dr. Calm had told me to bring my own dialysis supplies but I never dreamed that I needed to bring the machine. You wouldn't think that Columbia, South Carolina would be more advanced than an internationally known medical center when it comes to something like peritoneal dialysis, but good grief, even my house is more advanced than this place is because I have a peritoneal dialysis machine in my bedroom.

Nothing scares you like a good dose of the unknown when your life is on the line. Peritoneal dialysis is something that I thought that I understood, and one thing I am sure of is that the primary purpose of the machine is to preheat the dialysis fluid so that the patient doesn't go into shock (we are talking about me here people).

Nurse Crabb glares at me like I could just go to Hell, then she leaves my room without uttering a word (I know that this will not look good on my administrative review).

Immediately I call the hospital switchboard to have Nurse Spock paged but the hospital operator says, "It's after four o'clock and they all go home at four o'clock, Honey" (that must be why Nurse Spock told me not to hesitate to have her paged). We have a scared camper in room number 212 who wishes that he could just go home (alive). Abandoned, concerned and confused I push the button to call Nurse Crabb to find out who can answer my questions in regards to dialysis. Nurse Crabb tells me that she has just written a note in my chart saying that I had refused dialysis. Seething inside at this untrue statement, I contain my anger as I tell the Crab that I am ready for dialysis now.

Nurse Crabb comes back to my room with one bag of dialysis fluid and a red sign that says, "sterile procedure in progress," which goes on the door. As Nurse Crabb closes out the clatter of the outside world we both put on surgical masks while we go through the routine of soaking the sterile end of my Tenckhoff catheter in Betadine solution to kill all of the germs that would otherwise kill me.

It feels very strange to be doing this in front of hostile eyes and it makes me realize just how much I miss Debi. It is clear to me that living with your mind and body in a relaxed state is probably a lot healthier than going around full of tension (like I am now). It sure will be good to see Debi and my parents when they get up here tomorrow afternoon. I can't wait to hold Debi in my arms and smell her sweet perfume instead of the stale disinfectant that fills the air around here. It is hard to believe that I have only been away from home for two days when I miss it so much. A lyric from an old Beatles song plays in my head, "get back to where you once belonged," and I know that my only chance to do that is through this transplant process that is part miracle and part abattoir.

At the end of the Betadine bath Nurse Crabb plugs the tube from the bag of dialysis fluid into my Tenckhoff catheter, snapping a blue plastic cover over the immaculate connection before she takes off her mask and says, "That's all there is to it," as she throws her gloves in the trash.

Wow, that didn't take long when I compare it to all of the effort that Debi and I used to go through to set up the dialysis machine. But it seems to me that, at the very least, the patient would lose energy as the body expends calories to compensate for the fact that the dialysis fluid is at room temperature. We all know that room temperature is something that you want to avoid if you are a patient.

Operating under the old saying 'you can get forgiveness easier than you can get permission,' I wait until Nurse Crabb is gone before I pull out the electric heating pad that was originally intended to relieve pain. It becomes a warm cocoon for the dialysis fluid with the help of a role of surgical tape (if warm fluid is what we need then warm fluid we shall have).

My moment of admiring this advance in technology that Rube Goldberg would be proud of is interrupted by the gasp that came from Nurse Squeaky when she comes through the door. I can tell that Nurse Squeaky is horrified by what she doesn't understand because she is frozen in place with her mouth hanging open.

If this had been Nurse Crabb that had interrupted me things might have gotten ugly, but since Nurse Squeaky didn't start me on dialysis I know that this is not her responsibility. I say two words to keep Nurse Squeaky from interfering with my plans, "It's approved." (magic words and true ones too, since I approve of it). I see the tension flow from Nurse Squeaky's body as she goes about her business without disturbing my medical marvel.

There I am lying in bed feeling like McGyver, while the warm dialysis fluid flows inside of me, when Dr. Pharaoh comes walking into my room without the normal entourage (it's just Dr. Pharaoh and his pretty female administrative assistant).

I realize that it might be wise to build some rapport with Dr. Pharaoh because two days from now he will quite literally hold my life in his hands, so I compliment Dr. Pharaoh on his colorful shirt. His administrative assistant beams with pride as she says, "I gave that shirt to him for Christmas." Her eyes are full of admiration and they almost never leave Dr. Pharaoh.

Getting down to the business at hand I ask Dr. Pharaoh what the protocol is for the Cyclosporine dosage? (protocol is what medical professionals call standard procedure and they have standard procedures for everything that goes on in a hospital). The expression of shock on the administrative assistant's face immediately lets me know that somehow, without intending, to I have committed blasphemy.

Dr. Pharaoh's face turns red and his voice gets loud as he says, "I know patients like you, patients like you end up messing with their medicines and they end up killing themselves." Now the shocked look is on my face and Dr. Pharaoh continues, "I'll have you know that we don't have a protocol for Cyclosporine, every patient is different." I can't believe it, but I have elicited anger from Dr. Pharaoh just by asking to look at the Cyclosporine protocol. My father has always told me that discretion is the better part of valor (whatever that means) and this comes to my mind as I decide not to press the point.

As soon as Dr. Pharaoh goes on down the hall to his next patient I clamp off the bag of dialysis fluid and nonchalantly slosh my way out to the nurses' station, where I ask to see the protocol for Cyclosporine. The nurse who is sitting behind the counter hands me a blue notebook labeled: Cyclosporine Dosage Protocol.

I take the blue notebook back to my room and quickly begin copying the information as if I were a spy with the enemy's code book, because I know that since Dr. Pharaoh just lied to me when he denied its existence, heads would roll if he knew that I am now aware of its contents. Haunted by his words that patients like me end up killing themselves by messing with their medicine, I complete my mission and return the sacred blue notebook to the nurses' station with Dr. P. none the wiser.

Reflecting on the experience that I just had, I am disturbed by Dr. Pharaoh's reaction to my question. I am mad that my doctor would lie to me when it is my life, not his, that is on the line. He may be in charge around here, but I am in charge of my life. Dr P. is just someone that I have employed in my attempt to save it (a concept that doctors fail to grasp).

Chapter 15

NIGHT OF THE TENCHOFF

DR. WIENRITH SUCCEEDED in getting the night nurse to let me sleep instead of checking my blood pressure in the middle of the night yet, she still managed to disturb my rest several times. What really woke me up this morning was the lady that came around from the lab to draw blood because she lacked John Carter's finesse (ouch).

Life isn't too complicated, I'm just sitting there in my room hoping that they aren't going to hurt me today. After breakfast Nurse Crabb comes by with the welcome news that they don't have any x-rays on schedule for me this morning.

As Nurse Crabb hangs up a dialysis bag she tells me that when we finish with the dialysis, I can go downstairs to the hospital cafeteria for lunch or she can have food service bring me up a tray. I just stare blankly out the window like it's no big deal as I say to Nurse Crabb, "I guess that I'll just go downstairs then," but even in that blink of an eye my subconscious mind already knew that I was going on a mission. As soon as the dialysis fluid had drained back into the bag from whence it came, Nurse Crabb leaves me alone. Wrapping my Tenckhoff catheter around my waist, I shed my pajamas for some blue jeans and a sweater.

I open the door to my room just enough to look down the hall to see if the coast is clear (like any fugitive would). My heart races with the fear of discovery because hospitals don't like their patients walking around in street clothes looking like well people. Once I make it to the stairwell unchallenged a smile breaks across my face and my body relaxes, because this means that now, for an hour at least, I get to pretend to be normal. Exiting the stairwell into the hallway on the first floor it feels good to blend into the throng. It's interesting that the people that I walk past can't sense the anxiety that fills every cell in my body.

Then I notice one disadvantage of not using a machine for your dialysis, because without the machine's pump you end up with a lot of fluid inside of you which makes a sloshing noise every time that I take a step (I'll never laugh at Nurse Squeaky's shoes again). I almost start laughing out loud as I hustle down the hall trying to keep up with traffic, because I am gurgling like a mountain brook and the other people have to be able to hear it.

Then I see the sign on the door of the hospital cafeteria and for the first time my conscious mind realizes that I never wanted to eat there so I walk on by going with the flow. I have a song playing in my head that expresses my feelings as I slosh along: like a 'river that has overflowed, I took a wrong turn and just kept going.'

The crowd in the hall spills out of the building through two large wooden doors and suddenly I'm walking in the sunshine on the college campus along with the students who are going to class. I immediately feel the foreboding atmosphere of the hospital give way to the happiness of a college campus.

I see some students playing frisbee next to a young couple holding hands as I walk down the brick pathway. The feeling that I am getting out here with these carefree students is so profoundly different than the way I felt when I was inside the hospital that it is surprising that humans cannot sense the distress of other humans on the opposite side of stone and mortar. In fact, the other side of those gothic walls have been exposed to so many tormented souls over the years that I am surprised that the stones don't weep.

Walking down the brick pathway just before the campus cathedral there is a large statue of the school's benefactor which students have wrapped from head to toe in tinfoil, complete with two antenna sprouting from the statue's head, making him look like the proverbial man from Mars. The spontaneous laughter that rolls through my body is medicine for my soul (you have to love the irrepressible irreverence of youth).

The campus dining hall sits next to the cathedral and I follow the flow of students inside, going through the buffet line before sitting off to myself where I can watch the chattering students that make me reminisce about my own college days. Oh, how quickly we become old fogeys of thirty-five, but it is not the distance from the beginning of life that is the issue here (it is the closeness to the end of life that makes me different from the other diners).

Returning to the Temple of Doom is difficult but I feel renewed by my brush with youth. When I get back to my room I find that my parents and Debi are waiting on me along with Nurse Crabb, who looks a little chagrined that she couldn't produce her patient on demand. Debi and I must have set some kind of record for the longest hug while we were waiting for Jimmy to get here from his room. In due time, Jimmy arrived at my room with his wife Jill and everybody held hands while they prayed for Jimmy to finish up his long prayer (I guess).

Then we all took the elevator down to the first floor and reassembled in the hospital cafeteria, where everybody held hands again before we ate our supper, while Jimmy said a prayer that made up for in volume anything that it may have lacked in eloquence. After what could be our last supper together as a family we all sit around visiting in my room until we hear the announcement that visiting hours have ended. I am left alone again to ponder my future.

Sitting on the john, using the peace and quiet to do some really heavy thinking, my mind wanders. Tomorrow will be my last day on dialysis (hooray!). That is if Jimmy doesn't change his mind and back out on me here at the last minute. I am lost in a world that is far removed from my immediate circumstance as my mind tries to fathom the vastness of what is unknown.

Often times in life one choice precludes another one so there can be a lot of anxiety over whether you are doing the right thing but this is not an issue in my current situation because there is only one course of action that can lead me back to anything resembling a normal life.

If my luck is good, then two days from right now I will hurt in ways that have gone undreamed of in places that don't even exist in my body today. If my luck is bad then I'll never wake up from surgery unless my luck is terrible (wake up from surgery go through mental and physical hell then die).

Pondering the probabilities of me dying in surgery abruptly ends when I glance upon something, deep in the recesses of refuse that appears to be manufactured instead of digested. Fear beyond terror seizes my brain and I feel an involuntary spasm deep in my gut, as if I had realized that I had just swallowed a fatal dose of poison. Instantly I realize that I am looking at the sky blue plastic cover on the end of my Tenckhoff catheter outlined against a background of brown. How could this be possible? The Tenckhoff catheter with its sacred sterile end is down in the toilet (the most contaminated unsterile environment possible).

Some organisms could move right up that catheter with it's warm, salty fluid providing a perfect conduit into my peritoneal cavity. If I got peritonitis that would doom this transplant attempt (and possibly me). Then it occurs to me that this contaminated catheter could lead to a situation that would be a lot worse than anything that I have been worrying about. If something bad does get into me through this contaminated catheter it will be crunch time, because if I get peritonitis the only choice would be between the hemodialysis machine that has stalked me my entire life and the gun.

Oh boy, this is the scenario that Dr. Calm was telling me about where they would have to stick big needles in my neck for dialysis because I wouldn't let him put a shunt in my arm. I feel an icy chill go down my back, buckling my knees once I understand Death's plan for me. My body trembles as I quickly wash the end of the catheter in the sink using plenty of Betadine soap. I am trying hard to suppress my urge to cry because I know that if I panic I'm a dead man. I glance up in the mirror above the sink and I am startled by the desperate eyes that are staring back at me.

Somewhere past desperation on the scale of human emotion lies a state of sheer terror, and that is where I am now (it is written all over my face). Running out of the bathroom into my hospital room

I try to go over in my mind what action I need to take right now to save my life. I open the suitcase that has my dialysis supplies and pull out three plastic clamps that I quickly attach to my Tenckhoff catheter to create a barrier between death and me.

Forget that stuff about pushing a button to call the nurse. It's time to go get one! Approaching the nurses' station I blurt out, "My Tenckhoff catheter is contaminated. It was in the toilet, so it needs to be changed right away." Much to my disbelief the nurses tell me that none of them has ever changed a Tenckhoff catheter (this has never happened before [right]). Wow, I am dumbfounded and what is worse, so are the nurses. You come to a large, internationally known medical facility putting your trust and your very life in "professional" hands. You have a right to believe that if poop hits the fan they can handle whatever comes up in a "professional" manner (usually).

There I am standing in front of the counter at the nurses' station waiting on years of experience and training to spring into action, but all that I get are blank stares. Before I made the decision to have my transplant done here at D.U.H. I had gotten a phone call from their chief of staff, Dr. Bigg, and he told me to call him if I ever needed his help. Well this is that moment because, if I don't need him now, I never will (HELP!).

I look straight at the nurse who seems to be in charge and say, "Call Dr. Bigg. I need his help right away, this is an emergency" (we have a problem Houston). We actually have two problems, I just don't know it yet. The nurse that I was addressing stands up and tells me to go back to my room and they will "handle the situation."

I race back to my room as fast as I can go, and the first thing that I do is to phone Debi because she is the only one who will know what this means. The Tenckhoff catheter that Debi and I had worn masks and gloves to keep sterile had its immaculate connection down in a foul toilet for an unknown length of time (atomic tragedy). Debi is just as frightened as I am and she wants to stay on the phone with me until help arrives, but I tell her that we have to get off the phone because Dr. Bigg will be calling at any moment (that's the theory). After assuring Debi that I will call her back as soon as they finish changing the exterior part of my catheter, I hang up the phone and start waiting for it to ring (but there comes not even so much as a ding).

Anyone who has ever had to call an ambulance knows the anxiety associated with waiting for medical help to arrive, but, good grief I am already in the hospital (how far away can help be). Apparently the only thing making rounds around here tonight is the clock on the wall. Even if none of the nurses who are on duty tonight knows how to change the exterior part of a Tenckhoff catheter, they ought to know how to wash one off. What the heck about protocols, there has to be one that would cover this. I keep waiting for Dr. Bigg to save the day but nothing happens, so after twenty agonizing minutes I decide to walk back down to the nurses' station to see what is being done.

I don't want to walk I want to run down the hall, and I would, too, except that I don't want to scare the nurses (but they are beginning to scare me). I casually walk down to the nurses' station as if my life weren't on fire. When I get there I politely ask the nurse, who had told me that they would "handle the situation," if she had been able to reach Dr.Bigg? When the nurse answers back, "We can't call the doctors unless there is an emergency," I nearly flip my lid. It's the nurses who are being "uncooperative."

I remember the old saying 'that whom the Gods would destroy first they anger,' and I know that it applies here, so I try hard not to look hostile as I calmly ask the nurse, "What do you call a contaminated Tenckhoff catheter?

Instead of answering my question the nurse launches into a lecture about how the doctors need their rest because they have to be here at the hospital so early in the morning. I ask the nurse a direct question when I tell her to give me Dr. Bigg's phone number, but she flatly refuses saying, "We don't call the doctors unless it's something that we can't handle" (like a corpse).

It is disheartening to think that the microbes could be working harder than the staff but I want to find out for myself what is being done, so I ask the nurse to tell me what she is doing to "handle it?" I'm afraid that I could die and my nurse is afraid to disturb my doctor.

The nurse tells me that they have everything under control. They have someone coming down from the third floor who knows how to change a Tenckhoff catheter. Then the nurse tells me to go on back down to my room and relax so that they can find me when help comes.

I huff back to my room wondering if it is even possible to relax while you are terrified. In my room I start thinking that at least the nurses should act like they care. It has now been over an hour since I reported this emergency and none of the nurses have even bothered to come to my room. I phone Debi and tell her that this hospital's motto must be 'patient heal thyself.'

Absolutely distraught at the total lack of action in the face of a potentially life-threatening emergency, I casually walk back down towards the nurses' station. Trying, as best that I can, to look calm and reasonable on the outside, I struggle to control this explosive mixture of fear and rage that fills my brain. Before I even get close enough to the nurses' station to say anything to them, I can tell that something isn't right. These nurses should be looking at me with sympathetic eyes but instead their eyes are avoiding mine.

I use a calm steady voice as I say to the nurse, "It has been over an hour since I reported to you that my Tenckhoff catheter was contaminated, how long will it be until somebody gets here to change it?" The nurse has a defensive tone of voice as she tells me the nurse from upstairs had just called to say that as soon as she got caught up with her patients she would be right down.

I can't believe that there is only one nurse at Duke University Hospital (D.U.H.). that can change a Tenckhoff Catheter in the middle of the night and she happens to be too busy to deal with me. I insist that the nurse give me the name and phone number of the nurse from upstairs that I have been waiting on to come save my life.

I want to scream things about checking to see if D.U.H. has a protocol for a contaminated Tenckhoff catheter. I'm pretty sure that the nurse is supposed to try to do something about it (like wash it off). It takes everything that I have to remain silent in the face of this total incompetence but I don't want them to label me as 'uncooperative' (I want them to save my life).

I am beginning to understand the reality that the three night nurses appear to only be concerned with getting their shift over, and quite frankly, it scares the hell out of me. I hustle back down the hall to my room and phone the nurse who is supposed to be coming to save my life (change my contaminated catheter).

It is a stroke of good luck when the nurse that I am seeking answers the phone (too busy to see me [sure]). Since she is the one who answered the phone, that probably means that she is just sitting there at the nurses' station doing paperwork while she chats with the other nurses on her shift.

Since it is now almost 10:00 p.m. I want to scream things like: why aren't you here and where the hell have you been? But I know that making the nurse feel defensive would impede my rescue, so in my most calm imploring voice I say, "Are you about to come downstairs to change my contaminated Tenckhoff catheter?"

Before any words are uttered I know that something has gone awry by the odd silence from the other end of the phone. I have reached one of those moments in life when it is time to be quiet and listen. So I don't say another word until the nurse that I am counting on to save me breaks the silence, along with my heart, when she responds with the cold logic that, "Your nurses have Tenckhoff catheter replacement kits right there on your floor".

The realization that no one is on the way to save me blows me away. I feel like a gladiator who is flat on his back in the arena pleading with my unseen emperor to spare my life. I want to scream things about liars because this means that the night nurse on my ward has betrayed me. How could my nurse lie to me about what could be a life-or-death situation?

I plead my case with the nurse from upstairs that none of the nurses on my ward have ever changed the exterior part of a Tenckhoff catheter before (but it falls on deaf ears). Then I hear the words that are the mortal equivalent of Saint Peter consigning you to hell as the nurse from upstairs says in a condescending tone of voice, "I can't do anything without a doctor's order" (catch-22: I'm a dead man waiting to happen).

I feel a sense of betrayal of Biblical proportions as I tell the nurse from upstairs that she is supposed to be on the way to help me but she blows me off by saying, "I can't even talk on the phone to patients who are not assigned to me" and then she hangs up the phone (click).

A tidal wave of indignation swells up inside of me as I think about how stupid the night nurse must have thought that I was (like I wouldn't notice when no one came to help me). Here I am in a life-or-death situation and the only action so far has been the lie that the night nurse told me.

Forget about walking casually down the hall to the nurses' station, this little camper is making the trip just as fast as my feet will carry me without breaking into a full run (wouldn't want to spook the nurses). I make my way to the nurses' station in order to confront the night nurse who has been lying through her teeth (but of course, she is gone).

The two nurses who are sitting at the nurses' station now claim that they don't have any idea where my night nurse has gone, but one of the nurses tells me that perhaps she went down to the x-ray room (sure). It is obvious that my night nurse is dodging me (along with her responsibilities). My brain is fuming mad because my night nurse's lies have given the microbes a two hour head start. I want to scream things about liars and night nurses that are so slack that they don't even bother to wash off a contaminated catheter, but I don't want to be labeled as 'uncooperative.'

Even though I haven't had time to think of any kind of plan, my subconscious mind already has things worked out as I try to establish myself as a sympathetic figure to the two nurses who are sitting behind the counter at the nurses' station.

In a teaching hospital there always seems to be a rookie nurse on duty who is just getting her hours in. As I begin to tell them my tale about how I had discovered my catheter in the toilet over two hours ago, the older nurse tunes me out but the young rookie nurse looks deep into my desperate eyes. I tell her that my night nurse told me over an hour ago that someone was on the way to my room to change my catheter. I tell her I would like to look at the Tenckhoff catheter replacement kits that they keep on this ward, "just to make certain that it's the same model as the one that was put in me."

The older nurse shows no emotion, like she has seen it all before, but I see real concern in the younger nurse's face and she hands me a white plastic container with a sealed paper lid. Once I have possession of the catheter replacement kit I tell the nurses that since they don't know how to change a Tenckhoff catheter and the nurse from upstairs won't replace it without a doctor's order: I'll do it myself.

The look of total shock on the older nurse's face lets me know that she has never seen this maneuver before and I know that I have to do something fast to keep her from interfering with my plans, so I tell her not to worry because this is all being done under a doctor's supervision over the telephone, with my regular doctor back in Columbia, South Carolina. Like two addled ducks the nurses sit there behind the counter, looking totally confused as I start to make my getaway back to my room. Then the young rookie nurse who had handed me the catheter replacement kit calls out, "I'll assist you."

The thought of this young rookie nurse putting her whole career on the line by volunteering to help me almost makes me break down and cry. This is like 'The Bells of San Pedro' where the poor woman's pittance had made the bells ring after the gifts of princes and kings had failed. I had started looking for someone to help me at the top of the chain of responsibility, but I found it on the bottom.

When we get to my room the rookie nurse puts a sign on the door that says "Sterile Procedure in Progress" and she puts on a surgical mask while I pick up the phone to call Dr. Calm at his home back in Columbia. My life hangs in the balance as the phone starts to ring... Thank God Dr. Calm is home and he answers his phone. Immediately I say, "This is Don Gordon and I have a real emergency." I explain to Dr. Calm about the contamination of my catheter in the toilet and the fact that the staff here at D.U.H. has done nothing about it, not even so much as washing it off. I tell Dr. Clam that since D.U.H. can't find anybody to replace the exterior part of my catheter, I am going to do it myself.

Then I tell Dr. Calm that I would appreciate it if he would talk me through this procedure as I change the contaminated tube. I am glad that Dr. Calm doesn't waste any time (or my dwindling energy) trying to talk me out of this course of action because my mind is made up that it has to be done.

I want to take a minute to say how proud I am of Dr. Calm as a man for not dumping the responsibility of my care back to D.U.H (along with the liability). By talking me through this procedure Dr. Calm knows that he is breaking every protocol in the book, and he is taking a huge financial risk if this mission goes bad. If I were to die without the help of this rookie nurse and Dr. Calm there would be one victim, but if I die with their help there will be three, because the negligent night nurse would blame them for any adverse outcome.

What follows is some of the best doctoring that I have ever seen and the doctor isn't even getting paid. Step number one is to wash my hands and put on some latex gloves, but when I pick up the phone to see what step number two is, I mess up step number one because the phone isn't sterile, so I contaminate my left glove as soon as I touch the phone. Now is a good time for me to tell you how important my assistant is to the success of this mission, as she changes my latex glove and then holds the phone to my ear as I listen to Dr. Calm's instructions.

Next, I peel back the paper lid off of the white plastic tray that holds the catheter replacement kit. A lot of people wouldn't have noticed that I contaminated both of my latex gloves just by touching the outside of the white plastic tray (they would all be dead). As soon as the rookie nurse has changed both of my gloves, I follow Dr. Calm's instructions to pour the Betadine solution into the small cup that is provided with the supplies in the white plastic tray. I can now soak the new titanium fitting in the liquid for five minutes to kill all of the germs (so that they don't kill me).

I know that all of this sounds easy, and it would be except for the pressure of knowing that if I make one wrong move, I'm a dead man. The hard part was figuring out how to soak the old titanium fitting in the Betadine solution since it is on the end of the interior part of my catheter, just five inches from my skin. Every time that I would lean forward over the top of the cup of Betadine solution to put the old titanium fitting in for a soak, my hospital gown would start to fall into the cup which would have contaminated the whole thing.

I know that there are a lot of ways to solve this problem but I can only think of one, so I drop my hospital gown to the floor and lean forward against the wall while I wait on the germs to die. Five minutes is a long time when you are in the awkward position that I was in and for a while I wasn't sure who would break first, me or the germs. Finally, the titanium fitting had been in the Betadine solution for more than five minutes so we could go on to the next step, but I discovered that I had to keep leaning against the wall to be sure that the sterile fitting did not touch anything (like my skin).

It was the longest period of time in my life that I was ever naked, except for gloves and a mask, but with Dr. Calm and the Rookie Nurse's help I muddle through until I complete what I set out to do (in fact I set some sort of a new record for the number of gloves used). By the time that we had finished our mission I was covered in sweat and probably would have had some dry heaves, but I knew that would hurt with a Tenckhoff catheter stuck in my gut. I congratulate Dr. Calm and the rookie nurse on the completion of a successful procedure before I fall exhausted into my bed. As I lay there drifting off to sleep, I smile when I think that now the young rookie nurse will have a story to tell in some future year that will top them all.

Very early the next morning, when what I need most is the rest that I'm getting, I am awakened by the shrill voice of the transplant coordinator as she comes into my room waving her arms while she shouts, "We've got to change the outside part of your Tenckhoff catheter." Now this is the sort of action that I had expected last night when I first reported my emergency so I tell the transplant coordinator that she ought to go get my night nurse to listen to this lecture because she obviously missed it in school.

I tell the transplant coordinator that the night nurse was so slack that she never even washed my contaminated catheter and that in the end, I had to change it myself. The transplant coordinator looks at me as if I am a fool and says, "You must be delirious, that has to be done by a professional." When I insisted to the transplant coordinator that I had indeed changed the titanium fitting and the exterior tubing, she stops long enough to say, "Are you a crazy man?" She then storms out of my room (without waiting on my answer).

I thought that I had made it pretty clear to her that my catheter had already been changed, so I was surprised when a nurse showed up to change it. I told the nurse with the Tenckhoff catheter replacement kit in her hand that she wouldn't be needing that because I have already replaced it last night. She isn't taking no for an answer because she says that her job is to follow doctor's orders. She has come to change my catheter and it has to be done before the doctors make their rounds.

I try to use logic on the nurse. If I had contaminated myself already, then putting a new catheter on was not going to help. If I had replaced it without contaminating myself, then to replace it again right away would just needlessly expose me to risk. I knew that the night nurse had to make me look bad in her report and I didn't want this nurse that I had never seen before to say that I was 'uncooperative,' so I let her change my catheter ten hours late.

I will admit that this nurse was able to change my catheter faster than I was able to change it last night, but then again, she didn't have to do it leaning against a wall while she was naked.

Chapter 16

BANZAI

I HEAR SOMEONE HUMMING a happy song out in the hall and I know that the food service lady is about to bring me my breakfast tray (the other members of the staff around here have trouble breaking into a smile much less a song). I reflect on the fact that if things go as scheduled, I will be in surgery by this time tomorrow morning and that means that if things don't work out this could be the last breakfast that I will ever have.

I start feeling like a convict on death row waiting for his last meal, but when I see my breakfast tray I take it as a sign that I am going to be spared (surely a condemned man would eat better). I savor my warm white blob that they claim are grits as well as the yellow stuff that is sort of like eggs, but what I really appreciate is the toast (you can't mess up toast).

I develop another case of the Last Time Syndrome but it docsn't bother me because I know that this time it could really be true. I use it to my advantage when John Carter from the lab comes by to get four test tubes full of my blood to see if it still matches my brother's. You have to wonder if one of the reasons that they do these final blood matching studies is to give any donor that is getting cold feet a graceful out here at the last minute. If my blood matched my brother's three months ago how could it not match now. Then I remember the form that I had signed back when I was about to get the first transfusion of my brother's blood that said: there is a five percent chance that having a blood transfusion would make you have an allergic reaction that would make a transplant impossible.

Back then when we were talking about sometime way off in the future five percent seemed very small, but now that we are talking about calling off the transplant here at the last moment five percent seems like a lot. I can just see someone rolling an oversized pair of dice with twenty numbers on them and if mine comes up: I'm a dead man. The irony would be that the transfusion that created this risk isn't considered necessary if you are going to use Cyclosporine.

When Debi arrives at my room it takes all of my energy to tell her about the *Night of The Tenckhoff,* so when I get to the part about the final blood matching studies I don't even have enough energy to sit up and worry, so I drift off to sleep. Dozing lifelessly, with Debi curled up next to my bed in the big, overstuffed chair, I can barely hear a distant call using my name to pull me from my slumber, "Donald, Donald, time to wake up." Every muscle in my body is tense before I even open my eyes because none of my friends calls me Donald. I'm just laying here with my eyes closed hoping that whatever it is it will not involve pain.

The cheerful nature of the nurse's voice is a good sign, so I open my eyes and am surprised to see that it is Nurse Crabb. I would normally recognize Nurse Crabb's voice but the cheerful part threw me off. One thing that I know is that if something looks like a trick, it is probably a trick, so I glance at Nurse Crabb's hands to see if she is holding a needle (she is not). Had I understood the deal, the chocolate milk that Nurse Crabb is holding would worry me more than any needle, but her words are the ones that I have been waiting to hear. Nurse Crabb tells me that my blood still matches my brother's, so the transplant is on for first thing tomorrow morning.

I know when it's time to celebrate and this is definitely one of those times, but before I can really enjoy it Nurse Crabb says, "Oh yeah, there's one more thing."

It's time for me to taste the medicine that I will be taking every day for the rest of my life (Cyclosporine). I know that it has to taste bad, but I'm so happy that I can drink it instead of having a needle to look forward to everyday of the year that I don't care what it tastes like. If this is what it takes for me to get off of dialysis, then bring it on. That is when I take another look at Nurse Crabb's medication tray with the carton of chocolate milk and the small white box that holds the wonder drug (Cyclosporine).

Nurse Crabb takes a clean glass off of my bedside table into which she pours the chocolate milk before telling me to take the bottle of Cyclosporine out of the carton. At first I'm surprised to learn that I am the one who is supposed to mix the right amount of the wonder drug into the chocolate milk, but if I'm going to be doing this every day for the rest of my life, then I guess that I may as well start learning how. I take a small brown bottle out of the carton and draw up the prescribed amount of the wonder drug into a tiny syringe. When I squirt it into the chocolate milk, I can tell that this isn't the kind of stuff that a person would normally drink because the Cyclosporine beads up on top of the milk like cooking oil would on water. I'm watching this mixture swirl around in the glass as I stir it when I catch my first whiff of this brew, and let me tell you that the smell alone would knock the hair off of your dog.

Swallow this stuff? You have to be kidding! I'm just hoping that it doesn't ignite, because with fumes this strong, it would probably blow me right into Heaven (I hope). I know that I have to act quickly so I hold my nose and hoist the glass up high in the air saying "Here's to my health" as I chug the foul-smelling cocktail (while figuratively holding on to my seat). Nurse Crabb is saying something about a small percentage of patients having an allergic reaction to the Cyclosporine, just as it hits my stomach like a punch in the guts.

My body tries to puke back up this foul mixture so fast that it seems like it bounced off of the bottom of my stomach, but my brain is in a desperate struggle to prevent the body's instinctive response to being poisoned, because I know that it will look bad on my administrative review if I puke on Nurse Crabb (wouldn't want to look like the small percentage of patients who have allergic reactions to the wonder drug). Instantaneously my head is covered in sweat as I begin this unnatural struggle between mind and body that would never take place in a normal life. I start trying to exhale completely in an attempt to purge the noxious vapors from within me as I fight back the nausea.

Usually if the body needs to heave the brain is only too happy to comply, but now my very life may depend on my conscious mind's ability to override this involuntary response. Waves of heat originate from deep within my brain pulsating through the rest of my body like exploding fireworks on a dark sky (you would think they would come from my stomach). Reaching up to unbutton the collar on my shirt so that I can breathe easier I'm startled to discover that I'm not wearing a shirt. Heavy sweat now covers my body from head to foot as Nurse Crabb tells me that there may be some initial discomfort, but I will get used to the medicine.

Then without any trace of human compassion, Nurse Crabb tells me to call her if I have any problems as she exits the room, leaving the real nursing to Debi who is armed for this struggle with a wet paper towel (this is state of the art medical technology). My throat is parched and my mouth is so dry that it feels dusty, but I can only have a few sips of water (this is the special hell of being a kidney dialysis patient).

Debi puts a fresh wet paper towel on my forehead and she slips a small piece of ice into my mouth. I am thankful for this relief yet still the suffering is almost unbearable, so I lower the electric bed to its lowest height trying to escape the oppressive heat, since I know that hot air rises (but there is no escape from something that's coming from inside of you). Just as I'm thinking that a fire in my stomach could be considered a problem and perhaps I should call Nurse Crabb, the sweats are replaced by arctic chills.

Stumbling out of bed I try to dry the sweat from my body with one of those thin white hospital towels while Debi changes the sheets on the bed. I can't help but wonder what happens to the patients who experience an allergic reaction to the wonder drug.

Dry pajamas, a sip of water and it's back to bed only to realize that the thin white summer blanket on my bed is totally inadequate to warm my body in this deep freeze. Debi frantically rushes out of my room to find more blankets as I clutch the electric heating pad to my chest longing for the electric blanket that is on my bed at home in Blythewood. Before Debi can return with more blankets, the sweats have returned and my room feels more like an oven (and I feel like a cooked goose).

When Debi finally comes rushing back into my room with two blankets, the cycle of feeling hot is beginning to fade, but round number two of the nausea takes its place (thankfully, the second cycle of negative side effects aren't as severe as they were the first time around). I get my thermometer and put it into my mouth to see just how hot I really am and much to my surprise the thermometer indicates that my body temperature is normal even though I feel like I am near the gates of hell.

I reflect on Nurse Crabb's statement about how there may be some initial discomfort but I would get used to the medication. Nobody wants to get used to feeling this way. I knew that there had to be a catch to this transplant business (they come up with a drug that keeps you alive but it makes you feel so sick that you wish you were dead). After a while my chills and fever stop just as though someone had thrown a switch (they don't slowly fade away they stop completely all at once).

Just before lunch Nurse Crabb comes into my room to begin my final dialysis session, but I have a great fear that some contaminant may still be in the part of the Tenckhoff catheter that we couldn't change, and beginning dialysis would just wash it right into my gut. I know that you can occasionally skip a day of dialysis, and tomorrow morning I should have my brother's kidney cleaning my blood, so I urge Nurse Crabb not to require this final gut gargle. She gives me a stern rebuke saying "I'm just following orders" (that defense didn't work at Nuremburg).

Logic doesn't stand a chance of changing hospital procedure and I don't want to be labeled as 'uncooperative,' so I wrap my electric heating pad around the bag of dialysis fluid (going with the flow). Come hell or high water this is my last peritoneal dialysis session because if the kidney that I get from my brother tomorrow doesn't work then my only hope would be hemodialysis. Just the thought of hemodialysis sends a shiver down my spine, but the big shiver comes when I think about the fact that I wouldn't let my doctors reverse a vein in my arm for that very possibility. If it comes down to worst case scenarios then my goose is cooked, but I don't really care because I'm playing to win.

I guess if I do reject my brother's kidney, then that would bring about the day that Dr. Calm warned me about, where the doctors would be forced to stick big needles right into my neck (for dialysis). Yet still, with everything considered, as I look at the veins in my left arm I know that I made the right choice. I'm the only one who has any chance at all of ever being normal again. Every other kidney transplant recipient is going to spend the rest of their life wearing long sleeved shirts and wishing that they could have normal circulation again.

One word comes to mind expressing the all or nothing nature of my current circumstance: "BANZAI" (shout as you say this word). You don't do a Banzai charge if you have a better option but if it gets down to it you don't hold back.

After the last of the dialysis fluid has drained out of my body, Debi and I give each other high fives and a hug because we know that we have successfully completed a difficult chapter of my life (no more dialysis).

The plan for this evening is to get the entire family together in the hospital cafeteria so that we can all have supper together. To eat or not to eat, that is the question (Shakespeare needs no footnote from Don Gordon). The young intern who is making the afternoon rounds does a last-minute check of all of my vital signs and I take this opportunity to ask him if it would be ok for me to eat a light evening meal (the night before transplant). The intern tells me what I want to hear, so I don't question his wisdom when he says that a small preoperative meal might be beneficial because you don't know when you might be able to eat again.

Realizing that the best-case scenario calls for my next meal to be several days from now, my stomach easily convinces my brain to eat supper with the rest of my family. Putting on my blue jeans and a sweater in an attempt to look normal, I get ready to go down stairs with Debi. I can feel my mood elevate when I think about how Nurse Crabb wouldn't like it if she were to catch me in street clothes. Glancing down the hallway, to make sure that none of the Gestapo Nurses are watching, Debi and I make a break for the elevators. I giggle out loud when the elevator doors close behind us with Nurse Crabb none the wiser.

I'm still in this strange happy mood when I sit down with my family in the hospital cafeteria and we all hold hands as Jimmy begins praying loudly. I can smell the food on the table which I take as a good sign because surely a condemned man would eat better than this. Then in a surprise move, Jimmy starts saying the Lord's prayer, and I find myself praying louder than anyone else (including Jimmy).

My father takes one look at the food that I have on my plate and he tells me that I shouldn't eat anything solid tonight. Dad goes on to say that I ought to just stick with Jell-O and ice cream (but my stomach and the intern disagreed). I think about how hungry I am and how long it will be before I will be able to eat again as I dig into what could be my very last meal. Fortunately, this is a decision that I will live to regret. I should have listened to my father but I don't know that yet. I savor every bite of my Salisbury Steak and I love my macaroni and cheese, but it never occurs to me how much rearranging they are going to have to do to make room for my brother's kidney.

No one is doing much talking right now, we are all lost in our thoughts. My parents could be thinking that they stand a chance of losing both of their sons and I'll bet my brother is thinking about how much he is going to hurt. As for myself, I'm thinking about an ashtray that I have back home in Blythewood that has these words around the outside rim, "Health, Love & Wealth and the time to enjoy them."

Some people seek out wise men to learn the secrets of life. I found it on sale for ten bucks in Charleston, South Carolina. The ashtray has everything spelled out in the proper order because if you have your health then you have just about everything. Love is more valuable than wealth because even the rich can't order someone to love them. I think about how lucky I am to be surrounded by people who love me. The doctors are in this fight for the money and I am not the hero of this story either, because I am just a man who is trying to stay alive.

Jimmy is a hero because he didn't have to take this risk; he is here at this table tonight because of his sense of duty, something that Robert E. Lee said was the most sublime part of man. Debi is a hero, too, because she didn't have to dance into my life. She is here at this table tonight for love, something that is more valued than wealth (and probably the most sublime part of woman). My parents have always given me unconditional love and I have always tried to be a good son, but we didn't choose this lot in life, it chose us. I'm thankful for everyone who is at this table tonight including Jill, because she is risking the life of her husband.

I feel blessed by life even though I only have love among all of life's treasures, but I have a shot at health and with that I can pursue wealth. One gets a little philosophical the night before transplant, but that's alright because, if things go poorly in surgery these will be some of the last thoughts that I ever have.

Upstairs in my room with all of the hugging going on it makes me think of a family who is saying goodbye to a son as he is about to board a ship that will take him off to war perhaps to never return (someone going off to war probably has a better chance of survival than someone who is going into a transplant). Looking deep into Debi's beautiful eyes as I kiss her goodnight I see genuine love that I want desperately to have time to enjoy. Hugging Debi as I think about the journey that I will be taking in the morning: it's not very far but it could keep us apart for a very long time (like maybe forever).

Alone in my room, I'm standing by my window looking out on a night sky as my thoughts turn again to love and I think about how strange it is that something that is intangible, like love, would be more highly prized than gold (but then again, think about which one is more rare). Love is the world's most precious commodity and it only exists in our hearts and minds.

Then I start thinking about the other things in my life that I would have hated to have missed and it would have to be my friends, because they have meant so much to me.

At that very minute I hear someone calling my name like they know me and I recognize the voice as that of my best friend Bill Tulluck, but it is so confusing that I wonder if I'm having hallucinations. I spin around to look at the two figures standing in the dimly illuminated hall at the door to my room. I'm shocked to see Bill Tulluck in person, along with his pretty girl friend Donna Philips.

This is the last thing that I would have expected not to mention that visiting hours were over a long time ago. That little detail would have stopped a lot of people, but not Bill. He has an engineer's mind by training and birth. But what I like the most about Bill is that he has a noble heart, and Donna Jean, as she is called, is a lovely Southern girl who happens to be a nurse.

I still remember the first day that I met Bill back when I made a business call on Tulluck Construction in Orangeburg, South Carolina. Bill got a kick out the fact that I had on a lavender shirt when I thought that it was funny that someone would think that a lavender shirt was any big deal.

At that time I owned the Overhead Door Company of Columbia and Bill's construction company built warehouses that needed a lot of large doors. Like everything else in life the overhead door business was very competitive (we used to call them "Door Wars"). My big competitor in the Overhead Door business was Chuck Nealey, who naturally said that his company sold the best brand of doors in a similar fashion that I claimed the same honor for my company.

In my eleven years of owning Overhead Door only one person ever ran a scientific test to see who was speaking with a forked tongue when it came to warehouse doors. Bill's construction company erected a metal building that was going to be used as a warehouse for a local tire company and the plans called for two large warehouse doors (one on the front of the building and one in the back). What Bill did that was totally unique is that he had my

Company install one of the large warehouse doors and he had my competitor's company provide the other one, so that he could see with his own eyes which door held up the best.

Tulluck Construction became one of my best customers and Bill became my best friend. It touches my heart deeply that two wonderful people like Bill and Donna would care enough about me to drive this far so that we could have what might be our last conversation.

I'm excited to be able to talk to someone from the outside world so that I can tell them what it has been like around here. Then Bill makes one of those comments that puts everything back in perspective when he tells me that the staff has just been acting like employees (which they are). Then Bill says that he bets that the staff would act differently if it was their life that was on the line.

Several years ago, Bill had described me as "a collector of experiences," which I think is a pretty good thing to be. I remind Bill of that conversation and I tell him that out of all of my experiences that I have had in my life this visit is one of the best. We talk for a long time using hushed tones so that we wouldn't be discovered and it gets my mind off of my troubles (at least for a while).

I remind Bill about the old saying, 'too soon old, too late smart.' I tell him that I am a lot smarter than I was when I first came here and I hope to be a lot older after I leave. Too soon comes the time for Bill and Donna to leave but we all know that I have to get my rest, so I hug Donna Jean goodbye before Bill shakes my hand. The last thing that he tells me is to, "Hang in there" (good advice from a great friend).

I stand over by the window looking at the night sky again as I ponder the infinite universe of things that could go wrong in surgery tomorrow morning. I think about what the worst-case scenario could possibly be when it hits me that because I don't have a shunt in my arm for emergency hemodialysis: they might get confused thinking that I am the donor.

I would hate to wake up to discover that they had put one of my kidneys into my brother (stranger things have happened in hospitals before). I pull a long piece of surgical tape from the roll and I write the word "recipient" on it with a black magic marker before placing the tape across the skin of my chest. I'm trying to be humorous about a serious matter. I just hope that the surgical nurses think that it's funny, too, when they take off my pajama top in the operating room tomorrow morning. I go to sleep thinking about my visit with Donna and Bill, replaying in my mind all of the things that were said, and I think that it is a very good thing that I can dwell on how lucky I am at a time like this.

I sleep like a rock until the early morning hours, when the squeaking shoes of a certain nurse announces the beginning of a new day on the transplant ward. The big day has finally arrived and I can feel its dramatic presence I just don't know if it represents an end or a beginning. Nurse Squeaky is here to give me a shot that she says will relax me, but I tell her that being asleep is just about as relaxed as it gets. Nurse Squeaky lets me know that this shot is not optional (not that I was wondering).

As the shot begins taking effect I'm wondering why they don't give it to the patients on the night before transplant so that they can get a good night's sleep, then all of a sudden I start giggling about Nurse Squeaky waking me up to give me a shot for the purpose of relaxing me (it's working).

Then I see a sight that would normally drain all of the humor out of your body because it's the two guys from transportation who have come here to take me to surgery, but with their matching pastel green outfits, including shoe covers and hats, it hits me as funny because they remind me of the Tams. I tell the two guys from transportation that it would suit me better to walk but they tell me that since I've already had the shot to relax me it wouldn't be safe. I hop-up on the gurney for the ride to the operating room, and the two guys from transportation put wide brown leather straps across me just to be sure that I don't fall off on the way to surgery. I'll tell you that it gives me the creeps to be strapped down.

As we are rolling along down the hall, I have a better understanding for the need to relax the patient. I must say that this shot works so well that I wonder if this is how they get a condemned prisoner to voluntarily take those last few steps from his cell to the gallows (a shot of this stuff and the prisoner would probably whistle on the way).

Suddenly my cart stops moving in the hallway just outside of the operating room and a Surgical Nurse appears wearing the same pastel outfit as the two guys who brought me here from my room (I wonder how Surgical Nurse feels about the guys from transportation having on the same color outfits as hers). About this time it occurs to me that Surgical Nurse has a very serious look in her eyes above her mask and then I see the needle in her hand. Turning my head towards the sound of the guys from transportation who are wishing me good luck as they leave, I feel the sting of the needle in my arm and I realize that I have just been given my go to sleep shot without any comforting words (I really feel like I should know this nurse better before sleeping with her [must be the shot]).

When Surgical Nurse disappears through the pair of large swinging doors that lead to the operating room, I find myself completely alone and I feel very lonely as the shot starts to take effect. As I start getting woozy strapped down on this cot out in the hall all by myself, I think about the stark contrast to the way that this same situation was handled back in Columbia at Richland Memorial Hospital. There they had a pretty nurse stay with me, holding my hand, telling me that everything was going to be fine as I drifted off to sleep (nice touch).

Thinking what I realize could be my very last thoughts, (might not wake up) my overwhelming emotion is that no one should ever be left alone at a time like this. As I start to nod off to sleep under the power of that shot, strapped down as I am on a cart that is parked in a lonely hallway, my sense of humor flickers to life as my mind flashes back to the piece of tape that I have on my chest that says "recipient." I hope that the staff gets a chuckle out of it because I am. A smile cracks across my face just before everything goes dark and I only have time to say one word: "BANZAI!"

Chapter 17

AWAKENING

BOOM! BOOM! BOOM! My first awareness is that of a sound so loud that it is hurting my ears. The nurses must have a machine right next to my bed since with each boom comes pain. My eyes will not open so all that I can do for now is to lay here and hope the nurses move the loud machine away from my bed whenever they finish doing whatever it is that they do with a maddening mechanism that just goes boom, boom, boom.

It sure seems inconsiderate to have something that loud right next to my bed. Boom, boom, boom, as my mind regains more of its normal functions, I realize that the pain that comes with each boom is not centered on my eardrum but rather on my temples. Frightened and bewildered, I try hard to open my eyes to no avail. I am wondering what would make a noise like this when suddenly it hits me that a pump would make a sound like that, and a hemodialysis machine has a pump (maybe the surgery was unsuccessful [bummer]).

Clang (sound effects, no charge). My eyes pop-open without any conscious attempt to do so, yet still, I cannot see clearly as my eyes are dilated to the point where the focus isn't even close. Driven to see if the noise is coming from a hemodialysis machine next to my bed, with great effort, I turn my head to the side only to see nothing except a bare wall.

Since there is no hemodialysis machine on this side of my bed, I turn my head slowly to the other side searching for the source of this sound that won't let me rest. When I see no sign of any hemodialysis machine on this side of my bed either. I feel relieved but it is all very confusing. While my brain tries to come back online, I search for the source of that maddening sound, yet still my vision is blurred.

At that instant I realize that this tormenting sound pounding in my head is the sound of my heart as it beats (*boom!*) and the pain that I'm feeling is coming from my temples as they throb with every beat (how do you get away from a sound that is coming from inside of your head?).

Fear has me in its grip but panic does not, at least I'm waking up and that is something to be thankful for. What is worrying me right now is the fact that my headache alone is just about as much pain as I can stand: what is going to happen when the anesthesia wears off and I start to feel the big hurt (oh boy)!

Trying to understand the world that I'm waking up to is not easy through eyes that still can't focus clearly. As the fog begins to lift things slowly come back into focus, allowing me to see the room that I am in, which looks sterile and barren with the clock on the wall being the only sign of life (other than the pain).

I can tell that the red second hand on the clock is making its rounds as it is the only thing that is moving in the room, but try as I might no amount of effort helps me to be able to tell what time it is (knowing how long that I was unconscious will at least give me some idea of how long that the surgery took). Right now, I just hope that I don't slip back into unconsciousness before I can talk to my nurse to find out how things went in surgery.

Since the knowledge gained about my current state of affairs through my visual senses is inconclusive, I try to access just exactly how my body feels on the inside (damage control report). After careful concentration, I find that there is no report what-so-ever from anywhere below my chest, so the only clue that I have about how I am doing is coming from what I can hear, and the Jungle Drums say that Bwana's head hurts (Boom! Boom! Boom!).

My sense of humor starts working even before I can see clearly. I just hope that when the pain does hit me that I don't cry like a sissy (what if the pain is more than I can handle?). I become aware of a nurse who is walking around in my room like she thinks that I am still asleep, so I try to speak to her but no words come out of my lips (it takes a lot of effort just to produce my first moan).

"Mumlahaaa" finally escapes from deep inside my body (victory comes in many forms). Notified of my existence, the nurse comes to my aid wiping the sweat off of my forehead with a damp paper towel (state of the art technology for a variety of symptoms, all of which are bad). It is nice to have a pleasant sensation to direct my energies towards, even if it is only a cool, damp paper towel on my forehead (be thankful for small favors).

I fight back against the fog in my brain as I try to wake up long enough to find out how my brother is doing (I could easily fall back asleep if I just had some reassuring words). My most immediate concern regarding myself is: will I be able to stand the pain? But since my mind can think before it can feel right now, all that I want to know is how is my brother.

I'm getting more information right now from my toes (can't wiggle them). than I am from my nurse, who isn't saying a word even after I moaned hello. Which even in my subdued state, the humorous side of these events (such as they are) remind me of the old Spanish proverb that I learned deep in the heart of Dentsville High School. Very loosely translated, (that's the only way that we learned Spanish at Dentsville High) the proverb goes something like this, "He who knows nothing, yet understands that he knows nothing, knows something," and that is about all that I currently understand (that I know nothing).

Wishing to ask the nurse my first question leads instead to my second moan, eliciting the first words that I am to hear after my transplant: "Do you hurt too much Mr. Gordon?" asks the nurse who has been moving around the room. Then the nurse walks over next to my bed and as she leans over top of me I can see her bright eyes for the very first time, sparkling like two big green diamonds up above her mask.

I still haven't been able to say my first word, but my sense of humor is already at work as I nickname my nurse "Bright Eyes" (thank you, "Planet of The Apes").

Bright Eyes is leaning over me so that we are face to face as she says, "Would you like some more of the medication for your pain, Mr. Gordon?" The staff psychologist must tell these nurses what to say at a time like this because Bright Eyes' question pulls from my body the easiest word to say in the English language as I murmur, "No."

The terse response from Bright Eyes lets me know right up front just who is wearing the pants around here (not me). Quite firmly Bright Eyes tells me that she is about to give me a shot of Morphine to help bring down my blood pressure, (boom! boom! boom!) but I'm feeling just a little grumpy so I snap back with a weak, "Why did you ask me if I wanted the shot if you were going to give it to me anyway?"

Ouch! (my arm stings). Bright Eyes turns away from me as if I had never said a word and I can hear her say to some unseen accomplice, "He's got an attitude." (boom! boom! boom!). Then the deep sleep that I had fought so hard to break free of starts pulling me back into its dark embrace, leaving me with just enough time for one parting thought (that was probably just enough morphine to get Bright Eyes through her shift).

With each deep slow exhale I try to expel the noxious fumes left over from the anesthesia as I begin to wake up again. I lay there trying to relax away the pain for a long time and it seems to be working since the pain does not increase as I start coming around. I'm pretty excited that I can stand the pain but I am still wondering what time it is and my primary endeavor is to stare at the clock on the wall until I can bring it into focus well enough for me to be able to tell time.

I have a powerful need to wake up so that I can find out exactly what is going on around here, so every time that Bright Eyes comes over to my side of the room, I have to close my eyes in order to keep her in the dark. I think that it is better if Bright Eyes stays none the wiser, because if she sees that I am awake, she might decide that it is time for me to get another shot of Morphine (a sleeping patient means less work).

Long before my mind is up to full speed fear stakes its claim on my limited cognizance as I wonder if I'm rejecting my brother's kidney (oops, it's my kidney now if it is inside of me). Thank you Jimmy. I would suffer in silence if it weren't for this booming in my ears. I guess that it isn't quite as loud as it was which could mean that I am getting better (or weaker). Waking up as I am with my auditory senses leading the way, I'm just happy that the pounding in my head is fading somewhat (small comfort is still some comfort). I guess that I'm making some progress, I just need to make sure that Bright Eyes isn't aware of it because they work some very long shifts around here (the poor dear).

When I wake up to the point that I can see back behind the headboard of my bed I can tell that this is the repository of all knowledge as to whether I'm living or dead (with all of the fuzzy little red lights of the digital displays telling me that I hurt in ten different ways). When at last I can make out what the little red lights have been saying I am more frightened than ever (the blood pressure is going to blow my head off).

Oh God, help me! is my primary thought (now that I can read all of the numbers, they are not very comforting). I can now see what time the clock says that it is but this only adds to my confusion because, since there are no windows in my room I still can't even tell if this is day or night, so I have no idea how long that I have been asleep.

Then I decide to moan to get Bright Eyes' attention, and when she comes over next to my bed I grunt out, "What day is this?" Leaning over the top of me so that we are face to face, Bright Eyes says sweetly, "December 8th, the morning of day two."(the first day is behind me).

When I see that Bright Eyes is in the mood to communicate with me, I try to orient myself to the realities of today by going ahead and popping the big questions, "How is my brother doing and do I have his kidney?" (let's just get to the bottom line). Then I hear one of the sweetest lines to ever play across any stage, "Your brother is doing fine and, yes, you have his kidney." (oh what a happy man I am!).

As I process this happy news my eyes flutter and lock on the little red lights that signal my condition (not good). I can see that my blood pressure is 235 over 159 and a little moan comes out of my body as that knowledge goes in (no wonder my head has been hurting).

I'll bet that they lose some of their transplant patients right here at this point due to heart attacks. These are the thoughts that are filling my head as a familiar face appears next to my bed. Dr. Pharaoh is asking me how I'm feeling today. When I say, "Fine except for my blood pressure," Dr. Pharaoh's eyes light up as he says, "We had to drive that new kidney, don't worry, you are doing just great."

Without any additional explanation Dr. Pharaoh walks out of my room (so much for chit chat). Then more happy eyes appear by my side, ones that I have been longing to see: it's Debi and my parents (just glad that I'm not dead). Their eyes tell me plenty before any words can be spoken, because I can tell that these eyes love me and they are concerned (me too).

With Debi and my parents all wearing matching pastel head covers and masks it would seem quite funny if they didn't all three look scared. "How is Jimmy?" I finally ask. "Tell him that his left kidney hurts just in case he has been wondering."

My Mom tells me that Jimmy and I are both doing fine, just as my Dad squeezes my finger before he tells me that they have to go in just a minute. Then Debi steps forward and I'm sure that she would give me a kiss if it weren't for her mask, but I'm happy to settle for hearing Debi tell me that she loves me. Then my Father says that Dr. Pharaoh told them that Jimmy's kidney started making urine as soon as they put it in me (you have never seen people get so excited about a little pee).

Debi gives my hand a squeeze and she says that they will come back to visit with me later this evening before telling me one more time that she loves me as they head out the door. Then a song starts playing in my head and I hear The Godfather of Soul singing, "I feel good, like I know that I should" (ooh, yeah!).

Feeling the need to build a little rapport with the nursing staff (in order to dispel any myth that I might have an attitude). I ask Bright Eyes if she had ever known Mr. Huge (a very big businessman in every sense of the word). Mr. Huge had come to D.U.H. in an unsuccessful attempt to save his life after he ran into complications following surgery that he had at another hospital where they had cut a foot out of his intestines trying to remove a foot from his waist.

I start trying to explain to Bright Eyes just exactly who Mr. Huge was but she lets me know in no uncertain terms that she has already made the connection when she says, "I knew him well, he died in that bed" (beam me up Scottie!). This is the only time in my life that I have actually tried levitation but of course nothing happens. Then a male voice chimes in from out in the hall, "He was a nice guy, but his wife is a Bitch with a capital B" (what do you expect when her husband was dying?).

Then proving that timing is everything, the male voice tells me that he is here to take me on a little walk. Had this proposal been made just a few minutes earlier I would have thought that it was an absolute physical impossibility. Coming, as it does, right after hearing that Mr. Huge had died in this bed it seems like a great idea to get out of it. When the Nurse gets me up so that I am sitting on the edge of my bed Bright Eyes adds, "Mr. Huge died because he wouldn't do what he was told" (what was he told: to get well?).

With tubes coming into me and tubes going out, somehow I stagger to my feet, feeling somewhat like the mythical beast Phoenix as I stumble out of this would be grave (hospital bed). I make it out of the door and into the hall with only minimal assistance, but both nurses are right behind me (I hope that they can catch me if I fall). There is no way that I can describe the wonderful feeling that I have in my brain when my eyes are able to look down the vast expanse of the hall.

This humble little entourage heads down the hall one baby step at a time, but the world sure looks fine when you can see it from a standing position. I mutter, "Life is good," as I press on. It is an exhilarating feeling to take your first walk after you were worried that maybe you had laid down for the last time.

I'm shuffling along in the hall with a grin on my face until I get up to the door of the room next to mine. Looking inside the room I'm full of intensity expecting to see some patient lying there in a hospital bed just like every other hospital patient that I have ever seen, but my mind is totally exploded by the sight of the monster that's standing just inside of the door (and he is close enough that he could grab me right now). Oh my God, I am scared and I'd run away except that I am already moving at my top speed. What I see is a man of gargantuan proportions with his head swollen up so large that it is bigger than a basketball (with his features stretched out across it beyond recognition).

I am completely unprepared for the grief that confronts me. I'm frightened by the wild look in the eyes of this patient who is strapped into a hospital bed that has been rotated upright so that he is in a vertical position (just inside the door). The piercing look in the eyes that stare out of that mangled body make me tremble in fear because I'm really not even sure that they are human. Then I hear Bright Eyes telling me his story and apparently just a couple of days ago this was a regular guy. Bright Eyes tells me that the nurses have tilted up his bed so that he can see out into the hall because he is unable to move (that is reassuring).

This poor, pitiful soul is a truck driver, or he was up until, in the middle of a regular day in the course of a normal life, he had backed his eighteen-wheeler down a slight grade into a loading dock so that he could make a delivery.

In his last act as a truck driver this poor guy had climbed down out of his rig and walked around to open up the door on the back of the trailer, when his fate rolled back on him (a case of bad timing). The air brakes on the truck let go with a whoosh, as they failed, allowing the truck to roll back on him, crushing the driver between the trailer and the wall of the loading dock (squeezing all of his dreams from his broken body).

That is how this pitiful soul, with his alert piercing eyes, got here in this specially built bed laying upright (if you can call it that). The bed is tilted upright facing the door so that the truck driver can watch the last of his world pass by before he passes on. I may be this truck driver's last chance encounter. I hope that it isn't my last one too.

Even though no words are spoken, the image of those frantic eyes trapped in that dying body are forever burned into my soul. This guy has to be the King of Pain, (title of a good song) swollen and discolored to the point that I can't even tell his race (not that it matters). The haunting look in those deep-set eyes tells me that this truck driver knows that he is a goner.

Before my audience with the King of Pain I was full of energy and enthusiasm, now the energy has drained from my body to the point that I'm worried that I may not even be able to make it back to my bed. As I shuffle around to leave, I give the King of Pain a hearty thumbs up sign and I know that he understood it because he blinked.

As I work my way slowly back to my bed, I think about the eye contact that I just made with the King of Pain, him with his entire body swollen to inhuman proportions, and me with a dinky little cut about one foot long. I am humbled in the face of such misery (God save the King!).

I feel unworthy to hurt now that I have met the King of Pain (yet I do). I think about what it was like to look deep into those frantic eyes which were so full of expression, and what I saw was a man who is trapped with only one way out (and that is to die). I am haunted because there was something familiar about the desperate look in the King's eyes (I have seen it before in my own mirror). Hit by an emotional tidal wave, I thank God that I have my troubles instead of his.

As I walk through the door to my room, I'm wishing that I didn't have to lay down in this death bed (now that I know the truth about it). I wish that Bright Eyes had never told me about Mr. Huge dying in my bed and I wish that I had never seen the suffering on the other side of that wall. It's embarrassing to show hurt from such a small injury after what I have just seen, yet still, a small gasp slips out of my lips at the sharp pain from my groin as Bright Eyes lifts my feet rather quickly into the bed.

Debi and my parents come into my room for a brief visit a little later on and they tell me that tomorrow morning the doctors are planning to move me back into a regular room where Debi will be able to stay with me more (the better to nurse me). I am all for moving back to a regular room, any room at all, I don't care just get me out of this death bed. After our visit I try to get some rest but every time that I close my eyes all that I can see is the King of Pain with his haunting frantic eyes (good-bye, King).

The morning finally comes and with it I get my ride out of this place back to where the normal people are, back to my original hospital ward where at least they look human. The journey isn't a long one but it's enough for me to start feeling a little like Douglas MacArthur with the, "I shall return," and all of that stuff.

It is great that they give me back my same old room, in fact everything is great; the hospital is great, my doctors are great and it's just great to be alive (you get the idea: this is another stage that I'm going through). I feel like a man that has been shot at and missed, even better than that, I feel blessed. At the top of the manic curve of emotions while at the bottom of physical reserves, I go back to sleep with Debi by my bed (at last I can rest if they will only let me).

As I drift off into what could be the sleep of a lifetime, I hear the squeaking shoes that let me know who the nurse is who is on duty today. I don't even have to open my eyes to know that Nurse Squeaky is here (it is good to be back among friends). Before long John Carter from the lab comes around to draw blood from my arm (it's good to see old friends, even those with sharp needles). The problem is that since the last several days have been ones with very little fluid intake and almost no food, John has to dig deep for the blood that they need.

My arm is hurting as I drift back towards sleep only to be interrupted in my pursuit of rest by the arrival of lunch, which would normally be a humdrum occasion on a hospital ward but now the high doses of prednisone that I am on give me an appetite the size of Texas (I find myself licking each grain of rice from the plate and begging for more). The meager rations disappear, yet still my hunger persists and the staff will not let me have seconds (I guess that no one usually asks for more hospital food).

Everything is going great, even the chocolate milk that Nurse Squeaky has me mix the Cyclosporine in tastes great, (I tell myself) but no manic mood can wish away the nausea that hits me like a freight train as soon as the medicine gets to my stomach. Nurse Squeaky tells me that I will get used to the medicine (I'll bet that's what some shoe salesman told her about that squeak). Then Nurse Squeaky drops the other white shoe as she picks up her medication tray and gets ready to exit the room as she casually adds, "That is unless you develop an allergic reaction to the Cyclosporine."

Nurse Squeaky makes her exit leaving the real nursing to Debi and the suffering to me (I pity the patient who is hospitalized without the help of someone who loves them). Debi puts wet paper towels on my forehead and she uses a real towel to help dry up the sweat that is coming from every pore on my body. Florence Nightingale could never have nursed with any greater degree of tender loving care...

It takes about an hour for the sweats, chills and nausea to subside to a manageable level, which makes me wonder if splitting the Cyclosporine so that I take half of my dosage two times a day would be better than taking it all at one time. There is no way that I can stand this cycle of misery every day for the rest of my life. I call the nurses' station and ask them to have the doctor who is in charge of my medication to call me (little did I know that I might have more success asking Santa for a pony).

Right after lunch there is a buzz of activity down at the other end of the hallway and while I am wondering what's going on, one of the interns stops by my room to tell me that the results from this morning's blood work have just come back from the lab. He tells me that I am one of the lucky ones. After the intern gives me this indication that my kidney is doing fine, he drops the other white shoe as he arches his eyebrows and says with a sigh, "I wish that I could say the same thing for everyone else today." Then, after a pause, he adds, "Now I have to go deliver bad news: this is the worst part of my job."

I am thrilled at the news that my kidney is doing fine. This whole experience is so emotional for me that it seems odd to hear the intern refer objectively to delivering bad news as a part of his "job." This is my initiation into the sadistic daily ritual of the transplant ward where the lab results are the messengers of death or deliverance.

When the results from the blood work come back from the lab each morning is when everyone finds out whether their prayers have been answered or if their dreams have turned into nightmares. If anyone ever needed divine intervention, it's those people who are waiting to hear the lab results on a transplant ward (as a matter of fact, if you ever have unanswered prayers, it's probably because we have been keeping God pretty busy around here).

The suffering that I'm going through today is offset by the fact the Debi and I are not going to have to set up a dialysis machine ever again. This thought alone is enough to sustain my spirits until 9:00 p.m. (the end of visiting hours for the day).

As soon as Debi kisses me goodnight and closes the door behind her, loneliness comes to my side as this is the very first time that I have been left all alone since the transplant. Somehow in the dark I am much more aware of the pain. I know that my pain can't actually be worse just because the light has been turned off and I'm all alone, but that is how it seems (it has to be that I'm just focusing on it now). Relaxation is pain's enemy and tension is its friend, I tell myself on each exhale, but it feels like they cut me open and put a half of a brick in my gut.

Soon after sleep finally takes me the night nurse starts robbing me of the rest that my body craves by waking me up to see how I feel (taking my blood pressure and body temperature every four hours). This goes on all night long, preventing any healing that might have taken place, then for good measure they wake me one more time about five in the morning just to see how much I weigh. There is no way for me to go back to sleep now because I know that it is just about time for that morning reminder of who gets the sharp end of the needle around here. After John comes by to draw my blood it will be time to start worrying about what the results will be when they come back from the lab.

I'm glad to see that it is John who is on duty today. I like his cheerful demeanor; it makes this part of the day just a little easier to handle. My mind drifts away to other concerns as John goes about his work. I think about what a bad job these lab people have, I mean everyone hates to see them coming, I wonder what made a nice guy like John decide to make a career out of waking people up by sticking them with sharp needles. John mentions that I am the only patient that he has ever seen without a shunt in their arm (I am thankful to have one more vein in the rotation as it gives them just a little longer to heal before it is their turn to be stuck again).

After John has left my room with samples of my blood, I smile at the simple pleasure that I alone among all of these transplant patients have two normal arms. On the transplant ward there is a special appreciation for a lot of things that normal people take for granted (like your blood flow going to where God intended).

Death isn't on my mind for a change and that is the way that death works, coming for you when you least expect it (sort of undermines the value of all the worrying we humans do). I'm just minding my own business, thinking about my arm hurting as a way to keep me from focusing on the pain from the transplant (which makes a little hurt more fun to ponder).

Death comes in many forms: right now it's working the transplant ward in the form of the sweet, little old black lady who is cleaning my room without a mask or gloves. Just as I am wondering about this breach of protocol she burst into a coughing fit, hacking uncontrollably spewing millions of assassins into my room.

Horrified, I pull the sheet up over my mouth and nose as I yell to her in a nice but firm voice, "Get out of my room" (that is a hard thing to say in a nice way). In a manner of responding that I would have rather not heard, the cleaning lady points to her throat wheezing, "I gots da strep." Now I'm in a state of total panic, (patient save thy self) pulling the sheet completely over my head while I shout though my shroud, "Get out of my room! Get out now." I am holding my breath as long as I possibly can while the cleaning lady scurries out of my room. I am trying to wait until all of the assassins float to the floor of my room while seething that death gets a free shot at me (with nothing gained from me taking this risk).

When holding my breath is no longer an option I gasp for air under the sheet while I reach out to grab my telephone in an effort to stop this cleaning lady from spreading strep throat all over the transplant ward. Asking the hospital operator to connect me with the director of housekeeping services, I try to be business-like as I sound the alarm. Somewhat surprised that the director would answer her phone this early in the morning, I use my most courteous voice since her cooperation is vital if I'm going to be able to intercept this messenger of death.

Explaining the situation to the director makes it sound like I am accusing housekeeping services of being slack (which I am). In an attempt at comic relief I try to make my point in a humorous manner by saying, "You and I both know that an outbreak of strep throat among the transplant patients with their suppressed immune systems could wipe out the entire herd," but humor is often lost on those who need it most (as it is today).

In the middle of me asking the director to phone the nurses' station on my ward, (in an attempt to let the cleaning lady get well at home) the voice on the other end of the line changes in a cold, abrupt manner stopping me in mid-sentence, saying that the director of housekeeping services is not at her desk at this time, but a note will be made of my call.

It seems a little late in the conversation to be letting me know that the person on the other end of the phone isn't the director of housekeeping services, but I continue trying to complete my mission by trying to get the lady that I am speaking with to understand that this situation requires immediate action.

My insistence that it is urgent that someone call the nurses' station on my ward right now makes the lady on the other end of the phone just as insistent that no one is in the office this early, so I point out that someone is in the office or we wouldn't be having this telephone conversation. This obviously correct observation makes whoever I am talking with all the more defensive, so she cuts me off saying something about how busy they are this time of the morning. More to the heart of the matter she says, "I don't take orders from patients, if you have a problem take it up with your doctor."

So much for diplomacy; my parting shot is intended to disturb her into taking action as I say, "Maybe attitudes like yours are one reason why so many of your patients go home in boxes!" *Click!* She hangs up the phone in my face without any further explanation (go figure).

Never have I seen a hospital staff take swifter action in response to an emergency situation, but do they go stop the employee with strep throat from spreading her infection all over the ward? No, they are too busy wanting to kill the messenger (let no good deed go unpunished).

People start rushing into my room all helter-skelter, led by Dr. Frau, the female intern, who had hurt me during the prostate exam. She is accompanied by two young nurses that I have never seen before (not a glove or a mask between them). As Dr. Frau shouts, "What is wrong with you, don't you know that we have to clean your room?" while the other two nurses glare their concurrence. Retorting loudly, I let them have it, "I'll take my chances any day with a few dust bunnies instead of strep throat." I must have said the magic word because all three of my tormentors storm back out my room without saying anything at all.

Almost immediately the head nurse walks calmly into my room and with a niceness that has been missing from this environment she says, "I understand that you are having a problem with the housekeeping staff." For the first time since my arrival at D.U.H. someone is actually listening to what I am saying. When I tell her that it is inexcusable for D.U.H. not to have a protocol covering the housekeeping employees, to make sure that the sick ones aren't working on the transplant ward, she is in complete agreement with me. She tells me that she is unsure if D.U.H. already has a policy concerning sick employees, but they should.

The positive impact of one caring person in this building full of "professionals" cannot be overstated. The head nurse then proceeds to take the last needle out of my body, which is a truly important milestone in the recovery of any patient who has had any sort of surgical procedure (especially if the issue had ever been in doubt).

Then she asks me if there is any other problem that she should be aware of, so I tell her that I haven't had a bowel movement since transplant, not even so much as a good fart. Making a note of this on my chart she tells me that they will start adding stool softeners to each of my meal trays. She adds that the best thing for that condition is to drink plenty of water and to get some exercise by walking around the ward.

Elated that I can finally get out of my room I set out, urine bag in hand, to walk around the ward. I haven't seen anything except four walls for so long that I can feel the rush of happiness sweeping the recesses of my mind as my eyes focus down the distant hallway.

Slowly placing one foot in front of the other I make my way to the door of the next room putting someone else's life on display. I slowly plod, peering into the drama unfolding behind every open door. Little snippets of a life, that's all that I see as I look in at the people in each room that I walk by. But it is enough for me to tell if these patients are winning or losing their own personal struggle with death, and that is all that matters on the transplant ward.

The first room that I pass by contains a man about my age sleeping flat on his back in bed with a woman sitting dutiful right by his side. Since there are no bags of fluid hanging from aluminum poles next to his bed he must be recovering (good omen I hope). Searching as I am for a comrade-in-arms, I am hoping to find a future life-long friend that can look back with me on this experience at some point in the future and reminisce about how bad things used to be (our bond would be forged in the commonness of our experience). Somehow I feel like a combat veteran surrounded by civilians as I plod on down the hallway towards the next door. Excitement quickens my pace to a crawl as the next open door comes into view, it reveals a woman skinny as a rail, so emaciated that there isn't much of her left to die.

Past the nurses' station I plod in search of something (I'll know what it is when I see it). Patiently plodding, I make it to the first comer of this triangular ward, my eyes eagerly peeking into every open door watching the dramas playing out in other people's lives.

Around the corner, the image of my greatest fear burns into the deepest recesses of my brain when I make the mistake of gazing into room 243. In this room I see an old man locked in mortal combat with death who appears to have the upper hand. Tethered to his bed by all sorts of tubes, this old man doesn't stand much of a chance (my bones shiver because I know that one day I could end up just like that old man). The old man is just lying in his bed looking directly back at me with a pitiful look on his face. I guess that he has nothing left to do in his life but to die. The old man seems to me to be the human equivalent of the poor, pitiful fly who has become trapped by the unseen web and is now waiting only for the spider to come to get its supper.

Frozen in place by the agony that confronts me it is all that I can do to give the old man a quick thumbs up (no words need to be spoken, we both know the deal). Then I cast my glance to the floor and shuffle on around the ward, glad that I have my troubles instead of his.

Moving in a faster shuffle I try to put some distance between me and whatever is about to happen in room 243. Deep in my heart I have to wonder if every person doesn't have a day like that waiting for them somewhere in the future, as we all approach our destinies one day at a time (it gets pretty deep on the transplant ward).

After being disturbed by what I just saw in that last room that I looked into I shuffle over to the far side of the hall away from the next open door as it comes into view (maybe that is why this lady's problems look small in contrast to the old fellow in room 243). With just one bag of fluid standing by her bed she looks quite normal, except for her long-distance stare (lala land, she must have popped in to say hello to the old man next door).

This trip around the transplant ward has revealed a lot of problems that I'm glad are not mine, but I have failed to find any good prospects for a life-long friend. Approaching the last comer before I will be able to see my room, it dawns on me that my entire body is covered with sweat (is it all from the exertion of just one lap around the ward or is part of it the stress of seeing the old man tangled in his tubes waiting for death in room 243).

Heading for the barn my pace quickens to a crawl as I take a glance into the next open door, not with optimism but still with hope, in my search for a friend among the patients who are going through the same sort of personal hell that I am. But I am confronted by death's little helper in the form of a cigarette sticking straight up in the air out of the mouth of the patient who is smoking in bed. The cigarette looks like a distant smoke stack sucking the life out of its owner (no need to get to know this guy, I don't like his odds). There is a strange manner in the way this man pulls the cigarette smoke into his lungs, somewhat like a convict smoking his last cigarette as the firing squad gets ready to aim.

Down at the far end of the hall there is a lot of activity around one certain room with all of the nurses wearing masks and gloves (I'm glad that it isn't my room). With great interest I walk on towards this certain room, straining to make out the small red letters on the little yellow sign that the Nurses have posted on the door of the room that is the center of attention.

Even important signs can sometimes be small, at least this one is, as I have to get right up on it before the meaning becomes clear from that one dreadful word which is printed in small red letters: REJECTION (no wonder it's in red because around here it translates loosely into DEATH AT WORK). Suddenly I am weak in my knees but I plod on to my room and am thankful that there is no yellow sign on the door as I crash back into my bed.

For the first time in my life, I realize why no one ever wants to make friends with the new replacement troops in a combat infantry platoon: it's all because their odds of making it are so slim that it will just drag you down emotionally when they bite the dust, so it is better not to get to know them at all (I have all that I can deal with just trying to stay alive).

Restored as I am, by a short rest, I am compelled to return to the halls driven to make lap after lap as some sort of penance that I must pay along the path to regaining my health. Soon it is early evening, which is accompanied by a quiet period as everyone starts to settle in for the night. As I walk around the ward one sound stands out from the low hum of the distant mechanical room. It is the sound of two people who are locked in earnest debate, their words are not yet clear as I shuffle ever closer to the sound (all the better to hear [I quote the big bad wolf because I feel his presence]).

The first words that I am able to understand tell the whole long story, "It would be a lot cheaper per month," said by the loving young wife to her sick husband who is about to fight for his life. There is only one line of reasoning in any debate that is likely to come up around the transplant ward that has a sentence like "cheaper per month" imbedded in the middle of it. Everything has come back down to money (as it always does).

This is the debate between whether to use the old medicine (Imuran) which is "cheaper per month" or the new medicine (Cyclosporine) which, it would seem to me, is more likely to keep you alive. This is the very same logic that Bill Tulluck and I had to work our way through back when I was at the crossroads of which medicine to use. No longer eager to hear the outcome of this discussion, I hustle away from this guilt trip in progress (death is always cheaper).

Walking back around the ward on my very next lap it's the young wife who is talking, again as the tones become words I hear her say, "Yes, but that only lasts for two years."

I understand the part of the conversation that have I missed. He must have told his wife that Medicare pays for the medicine for the first two years after transplant. At least he is trying to beat the odds. I'm sure that two years seems like a very long time to him at this point in his life (it is). I hustle to get on down the hall so that I am out of hearing range before he can respond because I don't want the sound of his voice ringing in my ears tonight. I know that life has left this unseen man the choice between dying and financial doom (I cringe at the thought of either option, but I know which one is more important to avoid).

Bill Tulluck and I had this very same conversation when my time came to finally decide which medication to pin my hopes on. I still remember Bill's sage advice when he said, "If you don't make the short term, then you don't have to worry about the long term."

Bill's words to me stand in stark contrast to the words that surround this young man in his moment of doubt.

It seems to me as though this unseen young wife may be confusing what would be in her best interest when it's her husband's life that is at stake here. I hope that it all works out for the best I say to myself as I head on down the hallway, but I have a feeling that I'm just whistling my way past the graveyard (better mark this guy off of the list of potential life-long friends). With support like that he is probably headed straight to his grave. Only another transplant patient can really understand what goes on inside of person's mind in a situation like this because, when it comes time to die, we all do it alone.

In all of my laps around this three-cornered ward only one possible friend looks like he might make many reunions, and that is the guy who is in the room right next to mine (the one who was sleeping with his wife by his side). Some of the other patients may possibly make it, but if we are talking probable outcomes the dominant word has got to be dead.

This is just your standard night of suffering on the transplant ward with restless people pretending that the pain isn't so bad and the odds are in their favor. It seems like troubling thoughts always come back to haunt you late at night (at least for me they do). Tonight my worries come in the form of memories as I involuntarily visualize each one of the patients that has crossed my path since the transplant surgery.

Every time that I close my eyes and start drifting off to sleep images of the King of Pain keep tormenting me. The look in the King's eyes still disturbs my soul and the sheer size of his head made him look like some kind of a monster. My dream starts out with me standing way too close to the King, like I'm up in his face for some unknown reason, and I'm filled with fear that he might just reach out and grab me (even though I can tell that he means me no harm).

When I wake up from my bad dream, still afraid, I know exactly what is at the bottom of my powerful fear. I was afraid of his pain coming, as it was, in unimaginable magnitude that no human could fathom, much less stand, and afraid because of the desperate look in the King's piercing eyes (he knew that he was a dead man and so did I). I would guess that the King of Pain is dead by now and it's probably just about time for his funeral visitation (I'll bet that he wasn't expecting me).

Disturbing my sleep, as they come one by one, the next haunting dream is of the Old Man of the Ward trapped in his bed by the web of tubes (his eyes say that he is still alive but the rest of him looks like he is already pretty well dead). In my dream the Old Man of the Ward's eyes look straight into my soul telling me that he knows that he is trapped with nothing to do now except to wait for the spider to come for dinner, and as bad as that is at least he is old. If I am to end up like him, then at least I can't die young (small comfort).

Then there is the lady who was sitting in her bed with that odd little smile on her face and her long-distance stare. I don't think that she has completed her transplant because that kind of joy would be easier to read. She looks more like a donor who is about to donate, but if that was the case then her room would be on the other ward. Besides, she doesn't look strong enough to be giving any organs away (I'm afraid that she may have gotten bad news like go home to die). I'll bet that's the deal; I knew that I had seen that look that she has in her eyes somewhere before, she is resigned to her fate (are you?).

At last the early morning light wakes me up (if you can call that sleeping). I'm thankful for all of my troubles when I compare them to the problems that any of these other people have. Old friends are sure going to be hard to meet around this place. Of course, there is always the young guy whose wife was trying to get him to take the low bid on which medicine might keep him alive (somebody has to draw for inside straights). Maybe he will be the one that beats the odds. I just hope that he knows that rule number one is to play to win. I'm not going to give up on some young guy who I have yet to meet, it's just that I don't like the math.

Then there is always that man who was flat on his back smoking in bed, but like I thought at the time, even though smoking a last cigarette right before the firing squad finishes its work may not shorten your life, it does mean that he has given up (and if he has, then so have I). I'm not even going to think about the chances for that skinny little woman who is so wasted away that most of her is already gone. It looks like my best chance for a future old friend lies with the guy who was sleeping with his wife sitting next to his bed. At least this man has regular odds and with a loving wife by his side, that ought to mean that he has as good of a shot of making it as anybody would (tomorrow I'll make it my business to meet him).

Other than the sleeper, my only plausible hope for a friend would appear to be an outside shot of the young guy who is drawing into the inside straight medicine wise, but then again aren't we all around here (his only problem is that he can't afford to live). Money is something that I don't have to be concerned about unless I'm lucky enough to get out of here. I refuse to worry about the bad luck that comes along with the good luck.

My first indication that "it," as they say, was happening in my life is when "it" didn't happen at all. It is difficult as you may well imagine trying to regain full control of my body's basic functions with nothing but the equivalent of darkness coming from below my new kidney and nothing but pain from anywhere around it. Sitting here trying to feel where there is no feeling I have a better understanding of what Carl Sagan sensed as he sat there pondering the vast blackness of space (come in right leg, do you read me right leg [no reply]).

Right after breakfast (which I consume like a starving man at thanksgiving). Nurse Squeaky comes into my room with her cute little serving tray holding my morning medications. Remembering that yesterday the nausea had nearly beat me, I take out the note pad from the drawer by my bed and write down the time that I chug my Cyclosporine cocktail, in order to time the misery that is sure to follow. Even if I can't quantify the intensity at least we will know the duration of the negative side effects.

The night before transplant, when I was introduced to this ritual of trying not to puke up the wonder drug lest I be labeled as "allergic" (wherever that would lead). I had noted the time when I took my Cyclosporine and when the nausea had finally passed. I checked the time again and according to the clock I had just spent 45 minutes in Hell.

Last night there had seemed to be no need for me to time anything but because the side effects were a lot more severe than they were before. I want to see if I really am "getting used to the medication" like I was told (that would mean the nausea shouldn't last as long as it did in the beginning).

I make note of the time as I take my Cyclosporine dose and don't have to wait long to start timing the nausea because this Cyclosporine stuff is the only liquid that I have ever seen that would bounce (off of the bottom of your stomach). My brain and my body reach different conclusions as to whether saving my life depends on holding the Cyclosporine inside of me or heaving it back up, so a mighty struggle begins to see which one is in charge when my life is on the line.

When the brain prevails and the body surrenders, my pores explode like a million volcanoes (with the heat of hell so easy to feel I must be near the entrance). Nuclear hot flashes with tidal wave sweats sweep over me. I don't know how people stand this (they do stand this, right). Debi quickly brings the latest medical technology to bear (cool wet paper towels on my forehead). I pity the person who must endure this sort of thing alone. The only thing that I can do right now is to push the switch on my hospital bed sending it down to its lowest level in my pitiful attempt to escape the heat that is cooking me (hot air rises so I'm going down).

Keeping one eye on the clock that hangs on the wall in front of my bed I wait for some relief for almost an hour before the sweats finally give way to arctic chills that shake me like a rag doll. I'm almost relieved when I feel the hot flashes coming back for another turn (at least I will thaw out). The cycle starts over but like the waves on a beach that come after high tide the intensity of the sweats and chills are diminishing.

Yet still the nausea is an unbroken constant even after the 45 minutes that I have been trying to stand it (hey, no fair!). What happens to the marathon runner if there is no finish line? Surely these side effects have limits (so do I). I hang on for a full hour, but then I am disappointed to discover that my nausea isn't going by a clock. After an hour and 7 minutes of terrible nausea you would think that the symptoms would gradually diminish, but instead they end all at once as if someone had thrown a switch (good thing, since I couldn't stand much more).

What is going on here? The negative side effects are lasting for a longer period of time; if I were "getting used to the medication" they should be going away. While lying in an exhausted heap in my bed, resting up from my morning medication, it becomes apparent that I can't ponder the observation of the lengthening duration of the nuclear nausea because apparently there are much more important things for me to worry about.

I hear happy chatter down the hall (happy sounds are not natural in hospitals so they merit special attention). This time of morning that happy chatter can mean only one thing, that the guy from the lab (messenger of immanent death) is bringing good news to somebody about the results of their morning blood work. Perhaps the same karma will spread up the hall; we could sure use some good news on this end of the ward.

Looking hopefully towards my door for good news from the lab turns out to be a fruitless endeavor because today I'm greeted with no smiling thumbs up. In fact, John Carter is just watching the floor as he silently goes by my room without so much as a glance (a powerful message without words being said). A different kind of cold shiver runs up my spine (maybe I'm about to be dead). I know this can't be a good sign. Just as I'm saying, "That's odd," to Debi, the sounds of big wooden doors being firmly closed spreads rapidly up the hall, telling me that I'm not the one around here who has the biggest problems today.

I'm concerned as I hear the doors being closed on the rooms near mine but when the door to my room is slammed shut, my mind suddenly thinks of something to worry about (what if the nurse just put a rejection card on my door). No explanation at all as to why all of the doors are being shut seems even worse than the thought that someone else is dead (don't wake me up unless you think it is me that is dead).

Bounding out of my bed in slow motion I know that notification of probable life or death may be posted on the outside of my hospital room door. Trudging the few feet to the closed door in mortal fear of what I maybe about to learn, it is with a trembling hand that I pull open the door and am instantly relieved to see that there is no rejection card on my door.

Hot Dog! There is no card posted on my door! Instantly the terror in my body surges from worry to elation, to the point that I am almost giddy. But before I can turn towards Debi to share my newfound joy, it is shattered by a mean gruff voice that can only come from Nurse Crabb, as she is yelling from halfway down the hall for everyone to hear, "Get back in your room! Can't you see that we need privacy?"

Stunned by the question (no, I couldn't see that you needed privacy) there is a momentary pause which allows me to glance down the hall at a lonely procession of two nurses who are rolling a patient through the swinging doors at the far end of the ward, with the sheet pulled up completely over the patient's face (there goes another unhappy customer). I may miss many old Indian signs but this one is loud and clear (BAD MEDICINE). Guess that a lot of the time there is really nothing that anyone can do (everybody has to die eventually). The form under the sheet is so tiny that it would appear that the skinny little lady down the hall may have just started her last parade (I won't be meeting her after all).

Stumbling back to my bed I hear Debi asking me if it was a fire drill, but I am too blown away to answer her question. The fact that there was no rejection card on my door seems like small potatoes compared to what I just saw down the hall (some things are better left unsaid).

When at long last the nurses go down the hall opening all of the patient doors, (completing the protocol) somehow it all reminds me of an inmate in prison listening to all the cell doors being unlocked by the guards. We are, after all, in a Medical Gulag of sorts, a place that you pause before going to Heaven or Hell (there is probably less suffering in an abattoir).

I have ants in my pants just to get out of this room, so I tell Debi that this is a good time for us to go for our morning walk. Plastic urine bag in hand I head out into the hallway hoping to meet a new friend (a comrade who also knows that the pain of uncertainty can hurt more than a knife). One taste of life makes you want more. "Life is good," I tell Debi as we start our first lap around the ward (I'm just happy to be alive). If you die while you are living on dialysis there may be mixed emotions, (end of the suffering) but now that I have Jimmy's kidney in my side I really want to live (no drug brings a craving as powerful as this).

Since it is still fairly early in the morning no one is out walking in the hall except for Debi and me (in fact, most rooms only have their doors open a few inches). Walking to the end of the hall is a breeze. It is surprising that this puny distance gave me such trouble only one day ago. Maybe this is how healthy people feel (with energy to spare).

Debi and I continue on around the corner quickening our pace to a slow walk as I am still wanting to verify exactly who that was with the sheet over their face this morning. I think that it was probably the skinny little woman, but I wouldn't recognize the old man without all of his tubes. Approaching the room with the skinny little woman I peak inside, expecting a vacancy, so I'm shocked to see the tiny little woman sitting up in bed looking directly at me (very curious).

Hustling on down the hall and around the next corner I am thinking the entire way that the Old Man of The Ward's struggle with his tubes must finally be over (poor man). I'm shocked and amazed that not only is the Old Man not dead, but unbelievably he is standing up next to his bed (dead men don't stand up).

The answer that I seek isn't long in coming as I spot one door at the far end of the hall that is standing wide open. The very door that only yesterday was so important to keep closed now guards nothing (not even a bed). The room which had been at the center of attention just one day ago is now completely deserted, marked only by the little yellow sign that says "REJECTION" (They must have forgotten to take down the sign).

Suddenly my knees buckle under me and I am very tired, gone is the vitality with which my body moved just seconds ago (now all that I want to do is to make it back to my room so that I can collapse in bed). Entering my room totally focused on the bed and the few paces separating me from rest, it startles me to hear a voice from behind me saying in a tone of admonishment, "Where have you been?" It is a tone of voice that only Nurse Crabb would use (I know that I'm in trouble, I just don't know why).

Rushing into my room in order to bring me the results from this morning's blood work I'm sure that Nurse Crabb was genuinely disappointed when she discovered that I wasn't present to hear the bad news. Elaborating about how my blood work isn't as bad as it seems, Nurse Crabb sees the (oh no) look in my eyes, so in a weak attempt to alleviate my fears she says for me not to worry because, "This happens all of the time" (so does death).

Continuing on she tells me that this is just one of those things that transplant patients "get used to living with," only then does she give me the mathematical equivalent of all of this song and dance (I'm getting sicker). The creatinine level in my blood has gone up today, not by much, but it is still a move in the wrong direction (wherever that could lead). While my conscious mind explores every possible thing that could be the source of the problem my subconscious mind already has the situation sized up (this is not a good sign). There are countless things that could be the problem, like perhaps it is only a laboratory variance, something as simple as just a different person working in the lab this morning (sure).

She leaves me with the happy thought that she, "has learned not to get too excited about one day's lab results" (I wouldn't get too excited either if the lab results were hers). What is really worrying me is that the mathematical equivalent of my kidney function indicates almost a 10% decline in function in just one day (could it be that in just nine more days they might be pulling a sheet up over my face).

It is amazing how much the mind influences the body since just a few minutes ago I was feeling like a stud and now I feel as weak as day old dishwater. Down the hall I hear conversations and the sound of many footsteps, which can only mean that the doctors are making their rounds (good because I have a few concerns that need to be addressed).

When the gaggle of wannabe doctors lead by Dr. Pharaoh himself gets to my room, I want to begin our conversation with a little talk about the side effects of Cyclosporine which are lasting longer or the creatinine level going up when down would be better. All the wannabe doctors can talk about is how my bowels still haven't moved (it's like they have yesterday's worries written down on my chart).

Dr. Pharaoh goes on about how the stool softeners have yielded no results, so they are going to put me on laxatives to "get the job done" (medical terminology). Having completed this part of his class, Dr. Pharaoh starts to leave with his young wannabe doctors in tow having never responded to any of my concerns (wouldn't want to ruin tomorrow's class). I persist with verbalizing my concerns to which Dr. Pharaoh gives me evasive answers, skirting the issues, which prompts me to remind him that just a few days ago I was the one who was worried about my bowels not working.

Who am I to question the great Dr. Pharaoh, as my simple comment has frozen all of the wannabe doctors in place, with looks of amazement on all of their faces (like they expect me to be dealt with by Dr. Pharaoh's swift sword). With ice water in his veins Dr. Pharaoh turns to me and says, "Don't worry Mr. Gordon, we will get you back home again" (yeah, let's hope that it's not like the one that you sent home this morning in a box).

Washing up for breakfast it becomes apparent that I have the shakes, like a patient in the advanced stages of Parkinson's disease, with my hands trebling so that shaving is a challenge (can I possibly be this tired so early in the morning or is this the Cyclosporine talking to me).

Still, this might be a good time for another objective opinion from someone who can relate directly to my situation. The one guy that I know of that fits this description is the Sleeper next door because he is probably on the same Cyclosporine dosage that I am on (adjusted for body weight). The Sleeper and I have the same set of doctors following their protocols, as doctors do, so maybe we have the same types of symptoms. I want to go meet the Sleeper as soon as I can, so I shave and put on a fresh pair of pajamas to go pay him a visit.

This mission to go meet the Sleeper originally came up back when I was in search of a friend, and while that is still my primary goal, right now there is something else that I need which the Sleeper is in a unique position to offer (information). I want to talk to the Sleeper to see if he has the shakes like I do, but the main thing on my mind is the nausea. I want to know if he is experiencing the same kind of hell that I am. I'm just checking to see what's normal because I sure wouldn't want to be confused with that certain small percentage of patients who become allergic to the wonder drug Cyclosporine (whatever their odds are they can't be good). I'm going to talk to the one person on this ward who might really understand what the deal is with the tropical sweats and Arctic chills (walk a mile in my slippers).

After cleaning up and dressing in my very best gown (hospital gown, that is). I waddle on over to the Sleeper's room. Two new friends greet my entrance with smiles but no one shakes hands around the transplant ward (lest they spread germs). When I ask the Sleeper, "How bad is your nausea?" he is quick with his answer as he says, "On a zero to ten scale it's a twelve!" (I like this guy). When the Sleeper asks me if I have started to shake, I just hold up my hand and we all break out laughing. Then I tell the Sleeper that the one good side effect of taking high doses of Prednisone is that the hospital food around here tastes great (normal folks have no concept of hospital food tasting great, but the Sleeper knows). When the Sleeper tells me that he isn't getting enough food I tell him to go directly to the source and make friends with the nice black lady who delivers the trays.

As a matter of fact, I thought that perhaps I had found me a future old friend until my next question lets me know that I might have to settle for a life-long friend instead (that may not be a very long time). When I ask the Sleeper, "What is your creatinine level?" he hasn't a clue what I mean, in fact I'm teaching him a new word. So I ask him how somebody gets all the way to the transplant ward without running into the term (but his reasons sound like excuses for dying). Saying good-bye to the Sleeper and his wife I waddle back down the hall towards my room thinking that the Sleeper's odds aren't as good as I thought that they would be.

Back in my hospital room, in an anxious state of mind, I think about what a poor sample of humanity that these doctors have to practice their craft upon. I realize that if the doctors can save any of these people it is to the doctors' credit. Just as I was thinking that a lot of these patients around the transplant ward don't seem to be doing everything that they can do in order to survive, Debi walks into my room immediately brightening my mood just by her smiling eyes. Debi's presence alone dispels the doom and gloom atmosphere that pervades this entire ward. It makes me think that the medical industry might need to work more on creating a happier environment for their patients because it might just improve their odds of survival. Can you imagine how different the interaction around here would be if the nurses had the same attitude as the staff at a five-star hotel (they shouldn't forget who their customers are)?

I tell Debi that my big news for the day is that the nurses have taken out the last needle from my body. (Hallelujah!). I hold up both of my arms displaying my new no needles upgrade because this really is a big step in the right direction, and no one can appreciate it more than Debi (except for me). Happy for any sign of progress Debi and I decide to go for a short walk. I grab up my plastic urine bag and we head out into the hall for a stroll around the ward, perhaps we will meet someone that we can be friends with, or at the very least Debi needs to meet the Sleeper (she can no doubt relate to his wife).

Out in the hall I spot the unattended food cart right away and this mission takes on a new direction (must have food now, my body chants to my brain). I am powerless in the face of these primitive cravings: modern man does not know true hunger, but the transplant patient does (if he's lucky). I hustle on down the hall with Debi by my side, towards my intended destination, the food cart which I know will not be left unattended for long. Debi can barely keep up with me powered as I am by high doses of Prednisone. Debi thinks that the fact that I am moving this fast is a good indication that I am beginning to heal, but I tell her that me moving this fast is a good sign that they are just about to starve me to death.

I didn't recognize it at the time but I was already in the "zone" (High doses of Prednisone are like amphetamines that make you hungry too). As the Prednisone peaks in my blood stream I have a one-track mind: I must satisfy this industrial strength hunger. I'm so hungry that my mind compares my own plight to that of a starving soldier who is out on a foraging patrol. I look longingly at a box of Rice Krispies that some patient is sending back unopened among the dirty dishes on the breakfast trays that are on their way back to the kitchen. I glance into the Sleeper's room as we shuffle past and he is standing up next to his bed talking to his wife (standing up is a good sign). I am totally focused on my mission, which is to acquire food (don't get between me and the Rice Krispies).

The little black lady from food services is collecting all of the breakfast trays as she makes her way around the ward one room at a time. As always, good timing is essential for the success of this mission. I scurry to make my move on the Rice Krispies while the lady from food services is in one of the rooms picking up a tray and the food cart is all alone in the hall (if you don't count me).

Just as I am eyeing my prize the little black lady from food services comes back to the cart with another breakfast tray so I take this opportunity to introduce Debi and myself. I tell the lady from food services that she delivers wonderful meals but the serving sizes are way too small.

Then I point out the little box of Rice Krispies to the lady from food services and ask her if I can have them. I'm certain that the hospital must have some rule that prevents patients from getting extra food, so I take a quick glance up the hall to make sure that no nurse is watching this transaction take place. When the lady from food services hands me that little humble box of cereal, I am moved almost to tears, not so much about the cereal but rather by this simple act of human compassion (something that has been in short supply around here).

To me this seems like a modern version of the story about "The Bells of San Pedro," and this little box of cereal is like the poor woman's church offering that caused the bells to ring after the gifts of kings had left them silent. Victory literally in hand, Debi and I walk back down the hall to my room, keeping the loot hidden (wouldn't want Nurse Crabb to know that I'm breaking protocol).

Passing room 243 I feel compelled to look in at the Old Man of the Ward with all of his tubes, to see if the spider has come yet. When I look into the Old Man's room, I see him lying there in his bed, just staring up at the ceiling (possibly thinking about his younger days). The most frightening part of this visual image is that I know that this could very well be the way that I will end up someday. Of course, I could only end up like that if I am lucky enough to become an old man and I'm not going to worry about the bad luck that comes along with the good luck in life. This is one of those times where you have to dwell on life's possibilities instead its of probabilities. Since we don't know what our future will actually be like we may as well draw ourselves a happy picture when we think about it.

Debi and I make our way on up the hall until we are near the room where I overheard the young couple having the discussion the other day about which medicine would be cheaper to use. The room is totally quiet now as we shuffle on past the open door. I can see that the bed is made up and the patient is gone, but there is his wife sitting next to the empty bed reading her Bible (when she looks up at me I feel guilty for starring into her world). I know the deal this probably means that this guy is under the knife at this very moment (good luck, Dude). Good luck Mrs. Dude, too, because I know that being the wife of a kidney transplant recipient is no picnic either. But her role in this effort to keep her husband alive is just as important as that of any doctor because one thing about staying alive is that you have to want to.

As soon as Mrs. Dude is out of my sight, I go back to thinking about just how good these Rice Krispies are going to taste when I get them back to my room. It would be my guess that this particular box of Rice Krispies might be one of the most appreciated boxes of cereal to come out of that factory in a long time. At last I am back in my room with my coveted Krispies. The fact that I don't have any milk isn't even a concern; it works out even better this way since I want to savor each individual grain of cereal to see if it snaps, crackles or pops.

In a flash the last grains of cereal are being hunted down, one by one, with a certain amount of glee every time that I find one. The only other meal that I remember ever tasting this good was the only watermelon that I ever grew all by myself (don't expect you to understand, it's a Prednisone thing).

Hearing my father's voice out in the hall causes my body to relax away tension that I didn't even know was in me. I guess that's because ever since I was a little child my father (Big Jim) has always been able to handle any situation (let's hope that this is no exception). My body knows that I don't have anything to worry about with Big Jim on the job. Even though not a single word of what is being said out in the hall can be understood I can still tell by the deep resonating tones that it is my Dad who is talking out in the hall. A special love fills the room as soon as my mother opens the door and comes in smiling and talking in happy tones about something (there must be good news).

Mom is telling me that Dad just spoke with my doctors out in the hall and the doctors said that they were, "Pleased with my progress" (any absence of bad news is great news). I am worn out from my walk around the ward so I drift off to sleep feeling safe and secure, but my rest is fleeting because almost immediately Nurse Squeaky wakes me up just to check my blood pressure, et cetera (don't let common sense get in the way of medical protocol).

Since I was resting my parents have decided to go check on Jimmy and I feel like as long as I am already awake, I may as well go for another lap around the ward while I still feel like I have enough energy for the mission. So Debi and I head out down the hallway (to see what there is to see).

When we get to the far end of the ward, I hear distant thunder and feel the rumbling of my intestines coming back to life. Joy to the world! My intestines are alive (I was beginning to wonder). It figures that this would happen when I am at the far end of the hall, so I shuffle as fast as I can and carefully go back to my room where I discover that all of this excitement was over one magnificent fart.

The good news is that this is the highlight of my day, and any day around the transplant ward that isn't filled with worry is considered to be well spent. Another day has been successfully suffered through which puts me that much closer to home. But as I get ready to go to sleep for the night there is one thing bothering me: I still have the taste of Cyclosporine on my lips. I know that when I wake up in the morning Nurse Crabb will have another dose ready for me (yuck!).

Mourning starts before dawn on the transplant ward as I wake up to the sound of quiet crying out in the hall (this is a tough neighborhood). The nurses are surprised to find me already awake when they come around for the early morning weigh-in. I wish that I could just step up on the scale and see how much that I weigh but, just to be "professional," the scale here measures your body weight in kilograms, which is of little value to me this early in the morning.

I can tell that I am dehydrated by how thirsty I feel; what I don't know is that no laxative will work on bowels that are bone dry (duh). These two simple unappreciated facts (weight loss and dehydration) are manifesting themselves in important ways without ever being detected by me, or for that matter my doctors. I am coming directly from the world of a dialysis patient where just one extra glass of water a day carries serious consequences, and it is now clear to me that I have no concept of how much water I should be drinking.

My diet (controlled as it is by medical protocols) should ideally be more moisture oriented instead of being based primarily on calories and fiber. I should be eating things like: watermelon, cantaloupe, peaches, brown rice and blue berries, supplemented with applesauce by the jarful, instead of white grits that are too dry served with eggs that came in a box.

Medical science being what it is seems to think that there is a pill for every problem, but whatever they are giving me to jump start my bowels isn't working worth a hoot. Stool softeners were a good idea except that they were started way too late (the plug is mightier than the pill). John Carter from the lab has come to draw my blood, but with my body so dry he might have better luck searching with Dan Quayle for water in the canals on Mars (mission finally completed, double ouch).

I am beginning to take on a little bit of a 'woe is me' attitude over the pain in my arm, when I realize that I have much bigger things to worry about. I know that if I have just had my morning visit from the lab, then my morning dose of Cyclosporine can't be far behind. I'm just hoping that the nausea doesn't last as long today as it did yesterday. Before I can dwell for very long about things like how long the Nuclear Nausea will last today, Dr. Wienrith intrudes into my little world of woe. One thing that I have learned about being depressed is that it doesn't do much good with an upbeat guy like Dr. Wienrith around to ruin it for you.

Dr. Wienrith is the type of doctor that inspires confidence and he will actually listen to what you are saying, which means that he has the best bedside manner of anyone that I have met while here at D.U.H.. Dr. Wienrith is here today, along with his band of wannabe Urologists, on what would be considered a mission of mercy here on the transplant ward. He is here to remove my Foley Catheter, which means that I would no longer have to carry that little plastic bag of urine wherever I go.

With one slow smooth stroke of his left hand, Dr. Wienrith removes the catheter along with my depression as he throws that tormenting tube in the trash telling me that, "the plumbing is back to normal."

Laying here in my bed looking up at the ceiling makes me think about the Old Man of the Ward down in room 243 since this is what he was doing when we went past his room yesterday morning (I hope that his thoughts were as happy as mine). That's when I realize that for the very first time since my transplant I'm not hooked up to anything at all, so unlike the Old Man of the Ward I can get up out of my bed and just walk away. It's really been since all the way back before I ever started on dialysis that I could look forward to a day free of tubes (free at last).

Getting up on my feet I am almost giddy as I look around the room just to make certain that I haven't forgotten some tube that would be ready to give me a painful reminder if I step out of line. This is one of those times on the road to recovery where they should ring some kind of a bell. I've been in bars before where they would ring a bell when they got a good tip; well, I'll give you a tip: having no tubes is nice. No tube threatens disaster and no needle offers pain (oh, how I have waited for this day!).

I can walk away from my bed without fear the way that God intended (untethered and free). I walk out into the hall a free man, and a happy one too. This is better than winning the lottery, because if you don't win the lottery, at least you aren't dead. I'm getting back to normal and that is worth more than riches to me. Out in the hallway, grinning from ear to ear, I walk around the ward feeling like a pilot coming home from his first solo flight around cloud nine.

Reflecting on my new status in life of being untethered, it amazes me how much my life has changed in just the last five minutes. Then it occurs to me that if the doctors could put down on a graph whether a patient's emotions are positive or negative, that it would be about as accurate as any other medical test that they have to determine if a patient is getting better (or not).

In this moment of frivolity, I have a major insight that they don't teach you in medical school, and that is the Doctors should have the daily patient weight figures displayed in a graph so that trends could be understood at a glance. I am no longer moving like a sick man as I walk down the hall with a spring in my step and a song in my heart, because for the first time since I went on dialysis, staying alive doesn't involve any tubes.

Turning the first corner as I take a lap around the ward, I see the lady from food services at the far end of the hall, delivering the breakfast trays as she creeps her petty pace from room to room (my apologies to the Bard). I'm thinking that whatever God may owe the food lady in height he has certainly made up for in width (this probably goes with a career in food service). Then, while she is still looking directly at me, the lady from food services breaks into a song (Mr. Bluebird is on her shoulder). I like the song as well as her happy demeanor, but it makes the hair stand up on the back of my neck because I know that the fat lady is singing for me. This is a good time for me to make the point that it really isn't over in life as long as the fat lady is still singing and you can get a lot of important things done before the end of the song (thank you, Yogi).

Passing by room 243, on my walk around the ward, I look in to see how the Old Man of the Ward is doing, trapped as he is, by that web of tubes. It is not a very comforting sight. In fact, it makes me think that the Fat Lady is probably singing for the Old Man, because there are more tubes than usual surrounding his bed (good luck Old Man). I can't stop thinking that this could be how I will end up someday (all alone with my tubes and no one to grieve). Right now I just want to live long enough to become an old man. Hi ho, hi ho, it's around the ward I go (passing my own empty room for yet another lap).

I am making good time as I hustle on around the ward again, but when I come back around to my room this time, I see my breakfast tray sitting on the bedside table next to my bed. It is hunger, not fatigue, that brings my first walk without tubes to an end.

Breakfast tastes great thanks more to the pharmacy than the kitchen. These high doses of Prednisone make every mouthful an absolute delight and just as I am scarfing down the last tasty morsel Debi walks into my room. For a change I have something exciting to tell Debi that doesn't mean that my life is in double jeopardy. I jump out of bed displaying my newfound energy and spin around in front of Debi in what would have been an impossible move just yesterday. Then I take Debi in my arms to hug her better than she has been hugged in a long time and I break out into a modified version of an old song by the Mommas & Papas, "All my tubes are gone and the sky is not gray."

That song is not totally accurate because I still do have the Tenckhoff catheter stuck in my side, but since it's not going to be used anymore it doesn't count. I had originally thought that Dr. Pharaoh would take the catheter out when he installed my new kidney, but since it was anchored so firmly in place, he left it alone so that it could be removed by the doctor that put it in.

After finishing another dainty pirouette in front of Debi I hold out my arm and say, "Let's go for a little walk, my dear." Back out into the hall we go, arm in arm, blissfully unaware that at this very moment the forces of darkness have a messenger who is looking for me (sometimes bliss requires ignorance). No two happier people have ever walked in the shadow of death like Debi and I do, but the naivete of our joy is soon apparent when I hear the all too familiar voice of Nurse Spock saying, "I have been looking for you," as if I am in trouble (which I am).

With no apparent concern on her face Nurse Spock tells me to do the impossible when she says, "Don't worry, but..." anytime those three words are used together it really means: don't worry, but you might want to pray. The "but" part today is that my creatinine level keeps going up and the doctors aren't sure why (oh boy!). Nurse Spock continues by telling me that someone from transportation will be here in just a few minutes to take me down to get some X-rays in order to shed some light on the situation. Then Nurse Spock drops the other white shoe when she says, "This may not be rejection." Paralyzed by the fear instilled by the word "rejection," Debi and I just stand there staring blankly at the wall long after Nurse Spock has gone.

Just two minutes ago Debi and I were walking around the ward seemingly without a care in the world, as we celebrated the fact that the doctor had just removed my last tube, now all of a sudden I'm told that my new kidney may or may not be rejecting (we have a problem, Houston). With the word rejection ringing in my ears, I sit wearily on the edge of my bed wondering if there will be one of those little yellow cards saying "rejection" on my hospital room door when they bring me back from getting my X-rays.

Looking at Debi I can see that the cheerfulness has been drained from her body, taking with it the youthful vigor that she had just a couple of minutes ago. As for me, I had thought that I was doing better but we just cleared up that misconception. Trying to reassure Debi with words that seem to ring hollow in the face of this latest news, I reflect on all of the reassurance that Debi has been giving to me. I wish that I could sound more convincing when I tell her that everything will be ok.

There is nothing that Debi or I can do to improve this situation, the only thing that we can do now is pray. This too shall pass, I suppose, I just hope that it passes before I do. I just made up a new adage that I tell Debi, as I manage a weak smile (love multiplies the good in life and divides the bad). We both hug each other without saying anything else (even divided by two there is still plenty of bad to go around today).

Those turn out to be my parting words because the man from transportation is here at my door with a rolling cart to take me down for my x-ray. I tell him that I would rather walk but he tells me that it is against the rules, and besides, he would get in trouble (trump card). As we roll down the hall towards the x-ray room with me lying flat on my back, it seems rather strange that I would have a line from a song playing endlessly in my head, but I do. The song is one of those that they used to sing on the T.V. show Hee Haw, and it goes like this, "deep dark depression, excessive misery, if it weren't for bad luck, I'd have no luck at all" (sing along).

Pausing at the elevators we wait while the doors open up exposing an entourage that is bringing someone back from intensive care. As they roll the patient out of the elevator, I can see that it is the young Dude whose wife was wanting to choose medications based on price. I'm glad to see that he has survived his transplant surgery (way to go, Dude!). I can tell by the big smile on the Young Dude's face that he is pretty pumped up about surviving too. As the Young Dude and I roll along going our separate ways, I know that we are heading to opposite ends of the emotional bell-curve.

Down at x-ray they are checking to see if there is a crimp in the artery that supplies the blood to my new kidney (something that is called a stenosis). As I sit out in the waiting room while they determine exactly what the x-ray means, I'm wishing that Debi was sitting here next to me. If there is an artery that is crimped then my next stop will be for emergency surgery. In a regular life there is no joy in being normal because you take it for granted, but let me tell you that when the doctor comes out to tell me that my x-ray looks normal, I could have jumped up and hugged him. We still don't know what the problem is, but I do know that right now I'm on a cart that is rolling me back to my room instead of to surgery, and that is a good thing.

The emotional roller coaster has been all over the place this morning. but right now it is back up at the top. I know that I still have a problem, but whatever the issue may turn out to be at least no one is about to cut me. As soon as we roll through the swinging doors to my ward, I can see Debi standing by the nurses' station, and when she sees me Debi comes running up the hall to give me a hug. The last time that I saw Debi I was being carted away to an unknown fate, so I'm sure that to Debi it seems odd that I'm smiling, but when she asks me why I answer quite honestly, "It didn't hurt." Rolling on down the hall towards my room I strain for a glimpse of the door to see if it has a little yellow sign on it that would say "rejection," but it doesn't (hallelujah).

Standing up next to my bed I give Debi the strongest hug that my worn-out body can muster, because I can tell that Debi has been crying while I was gone. It is almost amazing how much better I feel emotionally right now considering that I still have the problem, whatever it is, than when I went down to x-ray.

I decide to go into the little tile room to see if this emotional catharsis could lead to my bowels coming back to life, but although I have both the opportunity and the inclination, as my friend Tony would say, "No happening." How do you relax something that you don't have tightened? As if I didn't already have enough problems, I discover something new to worry about. Even though I still can't feel anything on my right side below my waist, except for pain, this time it's a problem that I can see: my right testicle is as big as a golf ball (that can't be good).

While I'm trying to figure out why they aren't still a matched pair there comes a gentle tapping at my bathroom door (poor, pitiful Poe). As I ponder weak and weary, just what could possibly be so important that they would interrupt this, of all things, I hear Nurse Squeaky on the other side of the bathroom door. She is telling me that my morning medications should have been taken almost an hour ago (poor pitiful me). Feeling like an outlaw trapped by the sheriff's posse in a one door adobe hut with no windows I say, "I'll be out in a minute" (at least the outlaw could give up, but that doesn't work on the transplant ward).

216

Out in my room on the bedside table Nurse Squeaky has my medicine tray ready and waiting. All that I have to do, I am told, is to draw up the correct dosage and mix it with the milk (since the patients will be administering their own medication once they are home, the nurses teach you how to do it for yourself as soon as you are able). I draw up the full dose of Cyclosporine from the little brown bottle and mix the wonder drug into the chocolate milk, saying to Nurse Squeaky, "I've done my part" (except for chugging it).

We all know better than to breathe through our nose while swallowing foul tasting medicine, but let me tell you that with something like Cyclosporine you had better not try to breathe the air in your room for the rest of the day. The foul-smelling stuff permeates so thoroughly that you can smell it for hours, and once you have been initiated so that you know what that smell means, the slightest whiff can give you the heaves.

Contemplating the mixture that I'm about to drink, I think that diesel fuel would be a step up as I hold my glass high in the air say, "To Socrates" and chug the beastly brew.

All humor is instantly driven from my body, replaced by my churning stomach wanting to barf this stuff back up to wherever it came from, but I can't do that if I want to live (which I do). My mind quickly contemplates what might happen to transplant patients who lose this struggle with their body's natural instincts (every tissue in my body screams for me to puke while my mind alone says no). Trying to override an involuntary reaction is an unnatural struggle that would normally never take place. This is a struggle of epic proportions, mind verses body; no, it's even bigger than that. This is a fight that is literally between life and death, and it is all going on in my gut.

I walk around the room in order to get some wind in my face while I hold my breath as long as I can, then Nurse Squeaky makes her exit saying, "Call me if you have any problems," as she waves goodbye. I want to say to Nurse Squeaky that if you call a fire in my stomach a problem, then I have one right now. Standing here holding my breath with my stomach protruding, such as it is, I must look like an aging belly dancer working her last gig, because my stomach is contorting while I fight these dry heaves. Holding my nose, I exhale these fowl fumes and then I rush to the far side of the room to gasp for air directly from the heat vent.

You can try this part at home if you would like to by putting some Caster Oil in your mouth (now you can't spit it out or you die). Walking around the room in circles I exhale deeply trying to purge the noxious fumes from my body somewhat like a jet airplane dumping fuel before a crash.

When the mind finally wins this battle of Titans and the body submits to its will, tropical sweats sweep over me as my body goes to plan #2, which opens every pore trying to get this poison out of me any way that it can. Hot to my very core, I lay down in the bed and wonder how anyone can stand this agony every day of their life (unless it is short). I reach over and push the switch to move the bed to its lowest position (since hot air rises, I'm going down).

I seek cooler air down closer to the floor but there is none to be found (oh, how I long for an electric fan). At my wits end I ask Debi to open the door to the hall to let some of this heat out of my room (I feel like I'm in an oven). When Debi tells me that the air inside my room is actually cooler than the air out in the hall, I can't take it anymore, so I get up out of this burning bed and stumble to the window (at least it is December).

Alas, I am trapped since none of the windows will open (not even a vent). I curse the architect who designed this hospital as I press my cheek to the cool glass pane in a futile attempt to quell this fire that is burning inside of me. Just knowing that the fresh, cold December air that God gave us to breathe is just on the other side of this thin pane of glass makes me want to smash something through it (but I know that this would not look good on my administrative review). Doing something like throwing a chair through the window would just give the doctors an excuse to not to feel bad if I were to lie down and die (he was crazy, too bad we put in a kidney when he needed a brain).

Then I stumble over to the sink and begin splashing cold water in my face until I glance up in the mirror where I am confronted by desperate eyes that make me think about the King of Pain (God save the King!). When I think about what the King of Pain had to endure, I can no longer feel quite as sorry for myself (which I guess that I was). If the King of Pain could stand being smushed, then I guess that I can stand being cooked.

When I look closely at the face in my mirror the eyes don't look as desperate now that I have been thinking about the King, but there is no mistaking the weariness as I stagger back to my bed telling Debi that, "It's passing." While I am getting into my bed I start thinking about the Old Man of the Ward. I wonder if this is how he started out and then I think that he might not be as old as he looks (but I'll bet that he is just about as old as he is ever going to get).

Then all of my thoughts are refocused back on to me as I am delivered from the inferno directly to the frozen tundra. Now I am shivering with Arctic chills and I put my hands over the heat vent, but it feels just as cold as everything else. Debi runs out to the nurses' station to get me some blankets, while I go back to the sink to splash hot water on my face (Lord knows I am cold). I try desperately to warm up my body as my energy shivers away at warp speed (beam me up, Scottie!).

The clock on the wall says that I have been suffering in Hell for forty-five minutes, at least that's how much time has passed since I swallowed my medicine. I keep thinking that the negative side effects should come to an end pretty soon if I am "getting used to the medicine." This is how long that I suffered the very first night that I took this medication and the symptoms shouldn't last as long (if I am getting better).

Since I have been able to stand everything that has been thrown at me so far, (nausea, sweats and chills). I know that I can take it for a while longer, but there has to be a limit to how much a person can endure (before they reach the breaking point). I push the button on the side of my bed to call Nurse Squeaky because I have sweated so much that my bed is soaking wet, and some fresh sheets would help my recovery (but other than the little button lighting up nothing happens). Before long the Arctic Chills give way to waves of industrial strength heat and Tropical sweats, but I notice that they aren't quite as bad this time (hooray, it's the sweats that are breaking instead of me).

I am suppressing a laugh just as Debi is coming back into my room with clean sheets and a blanket. I can tell that Debi thinks that laughter is an inappropriate response to a medical nightmare by the puzzled look on her face, but when I tell Debi what I was thinking about, she has a good laugh too (and we both could use it). I told Debi that I was just thinking that, "It feels so hot in here that my brother's kidney probably thinks that it's feeling the blue fires of Hell."

Debi and I are sitting there laughing when all of a sudden, I realize that the nausea is gone and my hot flashes are ending. Immediately I look up at the clock on the wall to see how long it has been since I took the Cyclosporine, and it concerns me to see that I have been suffering for almost an hour. I would have expected the nausea to break before now if I'm getting "used to the medicine" like Nurse Squeaky said that I should.

The main thing about all of this is that I lasted longer than the nausea did. It makes me think about the old saying, "that life is all about getting up one more time than you have been knocked down" (I'm up, are you).

At that very minute one of the young rookie nurses comes into my room and puts my supper tray down in front of me. I can tell that the young nurse is a little offended when I grab my nose with one hand while I fan the fumes coming from the Salisbury steak with my other hand, telling Debi to take it away. I'll bet that young nurse would have even more offended if I had thrown up on her nice white uniform. While Debi is taking the tray out of my room, I am up out of bed in search of a breath of fresh air that doesn't smell like Salisbury steak. I hold my breath as long as I can before I bury my face in the heating vent, waiting for the odor to dissipate.

A wave of mild, dry heaves comes over me which could lead to a lot of bad things, so I leave my position of temporary safety at the heat vent and rush over to the sink in the bathroom to splash cold water on my face (anti-nausea drill number one). When I start to feel just a little bit better, I look up from the sink and into the eyes of the face in my mirror, which looks a good bit older than it did just a few days ago. All kinds of emotions fight for my concern but the one that has my undivided attention right now is loneliness. It seems strange that I feel this lonely because Debi has only been gone for a couple of minutes on her mission to deal with my supper tray, but I wish that she was back here with me right now wiping my forehead with wet paper towels.

I can't think about loneliness without thinking about the Old Man of the Ward, all alone in his bed hooked up to all of those tubes. But the saddest part of it all is that the woman in the Old Man's life won't be walking through his door anymore (I'll gladly take my problems instead of his). I pity anyone who has to die all alone, surrounded by strangers who want to their shift to end.

While I am thinking about the Old Man of the Ward, the nausea comes to an end and I shuffle wearily back to bed, wondering if getting my mind off of myself is the key to breaking the nausea cycle.

Debi watches T.V. while I drift off to sleep for the night, and when the sun starts to come up in the morning, I am pretty happy just to be here to see it. I feel kind of tired this morning. I miss those calories that I couldn't get in me last night and I guess that fighting nausea and chills for an hour really takes a lot out of you.

While I'm shaving, I size up the eyes on the face in my mirror and I chuckle at the thought that those eyes look too tired to have the energy required to look desperate (yet). I'm sort of like the Starship Enterprise operating on "impulse power." (only enough energy to begin moving). Then I stand still and say, "Beam me up, Scottie," but alas, nothing happens except that my stomach growls.

I head out into the hall on a mission to the nurses' station to make sure that Dr. Pharaoh gets the message that I need to see him sometime today (if not this morning, then definitely before he goes home this afternoon). When I see that Nurse Crabb is sitting down doing paperwork behind the counter at the nurses' station, I cringe at the thought of explaining the situation to her in a manner that will bring about a successful conclusion (I get to see Dr. Pharaoh today).

In my most cooperative voice I tell Nurse Crabb that I have some concerns that seem rather urgent to me and I need to see

Dr. Pharaoh just as soon as possible. Nurse Crabb gives me one of those stone faced looks that every policeman practices, as she tells me that Dr. Pharaoh will be working in surgery for most of the day. Then Nurse Crabb lets me know that this conversation is over by looking back down at the form that she had been reading when I walked up to the counter, without even inquiring about the nature of my rather urgent concerns.

My fuse is lit but I don't want to let it show that I'm angry, lest I be labeled as "uncooperative." But if Nurse Crabb were truly professional she would at least find out what it is that is bothering me. I find myself talking to the top of Nurse Crabb's head as I ask her what the proper protocol is for those occasions where a patient has urgent concerns and requests to see a doctor.

Without even looking up to make eye contact with me, Nurse Crabb dials a number on her telephone and holds the receiver up to my face. I take the phone from Nurse Crabb's hand just as a female voice on the other end is saying, "Dr. Pharaoh's office."

When I ask to speak with Dr. Pharaoh, I'm told that he is in surgery today loud enough for Nurse Crabb to hear it, so she looks up at me with a smug little smile that says I told you so. I explain to Dr. Pharaoh's secretary that I need to talk to the doctor sometime today about the lengthening duration of the negative side effects after I take my Cyclosporine. Then, playing for a little show of human compassion, I tell the secretary that I am getting progressively weaker each day. The negative side effects are pulling me down to the point where I don't know how much more I can take. The only response that I get back from her is a flat monotone statement without any hint of compassion that I had been seeking, "I'll see that Dr. Pharaoh gets your message," followed by a dial tone.

Now I know that it isn't Nurse Crabb's fault if I don't get to see my doctor. Earlier I had thought that Nurse Crabb didn't want to disturb Dr. Pharaoh because it made her look bad, but now I realize that she just understood reality better. I thank Nurse Crabb for letting me use her phone and she tells me sweetly, "Anytime" (for all the good that it will do).

I shuffle back to my room thinking about the fact that Nurse Crabb had just been civil if not nice (I hope that she wasn't faking it). I can hear happy noises coming from the Sleeper's room as I shuffle slowly past the open door to his world. The Sleeper is up on his feet and is smiling while my tired, haggard form goes by his door. I am struck by the stark contrast between the Sleeper and myself, and I realize that once again I find myself looking like the wrong end of the Bell-Curve of just who is going to get out of this ward alive.

Debi is in my room when I get back to it and I am glad to see her because it feels good to be loved no matter what else is going on in your life. After I give Debi a great, big hug I tell her that we ought to go for a quick walk around the ward because I have a call in for Dr. Pharaoh to come see me, and I don't want to miss him when he stops by my room.

Debi and I go for an early morning walk but we haven't been very far when I start feeling kind of weak. Right after we walk around the first corner I "hit the wall" just as surely as a Marathon runner on Heartbreak Hill. This naturally happens to me when I am at the furthest point away from my room and I know right away that I'll never make it all the way back to my bed.

I look up and down the hall for a chair to rest my weary bones in but the hall is totally bare. I start thinking about my options, like sitting down on the floor. I labor just to put one foot in front of the other when I see a chair not ten feet away, just inside the open door to the room coming up on my left. I'm so tired that making it even these last ten feet to the chair requires total exertion as I fight to make forward progress while feeling like I am moving in slow motion. The effort is so strenuous that I am breathing hard and I am covered with sweat as I concentrate on my objective, looking at nothing else but the chair as I get closer to it. Any inhibition that I might normally have about walking into someone else's room is completely overshadowed by the need to rest (as my heavy bones sag into the chair).

Momentary panic sweeps over me when I look around the room and realize that I am in the Old Man of the Ward's room. Here I am face to face with one of my deepest fears (ending up just like this

Old Man). The Old Man of the Ward looks pretty surprised to see me sitting in his chair, but he is no more surprised than I am (Debi too). I am too tired to speak but Debi, being the nice person that she is, says, "Hello," to the old man of the ward (after all it is his room). Debi tries to start a conversation by asking the Old Man where he was born, and while I am sitting there waiting for his reply, I can tell that the Old Man isn't all that old (just used up).

It's the Old Man's gray hair and the fact that he is so small and shriveled up that make him look so old. The fact that he is hooked up to so many tubes make the brain measure his age not in how many years he has lived but rather in how many days he has left (not many).

While the Old Man of the Ward is trying to tell us where he is from in a voice so weak and feeble that I can't understand a word that he is saying, all of a sudden it hits me that I am thirsty (very thirsty). It is strange that while my primary need was rest, thirst never entered my mind. Now that I am sitting down I know that I need water (plenty of it and fast). It seems to me that it would be too great of an intrusion to ask the Old Man of the Ward for a drink of water, with him hooked up to all of these tubes he might feel uncomfortable with strange people moving around his room (lest they bump into something that would cause him pain).

I struggle to my feet, thanking the Old Man for the use of his chair, as Debi and I make our exit from his room without ever understanding a word that he said. Out in the hall I turn back around to wave goodbye to the Old Man of the Ward and am almost moved to tears when I realize that he is trying to offer me encouragement with both of his skinny little fists giving me the double thumbs up.

Out in the hallway, as we slowly make our way back towards my room, Debi asks me why I didn't rest longer when I had the chance. I tell Debi that I was afraid that if I rested any longer I might not have the energy to get back up out of that chair, and I have to get back to my room so that I don't miss Dr. Pharaoh when he comes by to see me. Staggering on to my room I am so tired that I don't even turn my head to look into the open doors as we go slowly past them. Right now, there is drama enough in the hall just seeing if I can make it back to my bed without falling down.

Thoughts of my bed beckon my bones until at last the door to my room comes into view, but even this short distance seems to be beyond my physical capabilities, so I concentrate on trying to make it passed one door at a time (which I do). Finally, I can see the bed inside of my room. As I take my little baby steps towards it, the rest that it offers is so appealing that I think that I may never want to get back out of this bed, then a little chill sweeps over my body as I realize that maybe I won't.

Debi brings me some water and as she wipes the sweat off of my forehead with a paper towel, she tries to inspire me by reminding me that back before the transplant I couldn't even drink all of the water that I wanted (guess that I should feel lucky but right now I am just too tired).

Sleep that has for so long been elusive now pulls at my brain, but I must resist the urge to fall asleep or I might miss Dr. Pharaoh when he comes by my room. Hour after hour I watch the clock on the wall but Dr. Pharaoh does not appear. I keep thinking that each lap the clock makes increases the chance that Dr Pharaoh will come soon (but he doesn't).

There is nothing so frustrating as waiting for something that isn't going to happen, especially when it is your life that is at stake. There is an old saying that we would all be wise to note, but I don't have to write it down because it is ringing in my ears, "Make it happen, don't let it happen."

With that in mind I decide to phone downstairs to Dr. Pharaoh's office before they close for the day, just to be sure that he got my message that I need to see him. When I ask the lady who answers the phone in Dr. Pharaoh's office if he is on the way to my room, she answers my question as if they were running a bank when she says, "Dr. Pharaoh leaves at four" (sorry we are closed).

Not getting even so much as a phone call from the doctor who is in charge of saving my life blows my mind. It's not me that is "uncooperative" around here, what I am is infuriated that I have been here all day long and no one has responded to my concerns, which I told them seemed "rather urgent to me." If this is what they call being "professional," I wouldn't be bragging about it. Just what do the doctors mean around here when they say "Call if you need me" (apparently not much).

I turn to Debi and say, "What the hell do these people around here think that we are dealing with, athlete's foot." I quickly phone Dr. Bigg's office hoping to catch him before he can leave for the day, but when I tell his secretary that I'm having some problems so I need to speak with Dr. Bigg, she tells me that he is in an important t meeting as we speak. Then I say, "Lady, this is important, too, because I am about to die." Her only response is to ask me if I would like to leave a message (is the Pope a Catholic?).

I tell Dr. Bigg's secretary that before I ever came to D.U.H. Dr. Bigg had phoned me at my home and told me to call him if there was ever anything that he could do for me while I was here. Then I tell Dr. Bigg's secretary to give him the message that, "I need to see him today," emphasizing that, "This is not a drill!" Then I hang up the phone as I begin to stew in my own juices, ranting to Debi that I am sick of this sorry place and, in general, I am singing the blues to the choir.

When the evening meal is delivered it smells good and I'm hungry, but as I try to sit up in bed to eat, my head comes off of the pillow only a few inches before it collapses back on it. It's hard for me to tell how much of this malaise is due to a lack of energy and how much can be attributed to my low state of morale.

I am depressed at my distress and anyone who finds themselves in a similar situation without also having the blues probably is in need of a check-up from the neck up. I can honestly say that I am feeling lower than a snake's belly because, not only are things going badly, but I am surrounded by indifferent staff members and now I feel abandoned by my doctor (boo! hoo!).

All of this serves to illustrate the point that the emotional needs of the patient need some attention because in a struggle with death your mind and body need to fight as one. I don't know what Dr. Pharaoh's problem is, but I am dealing with a very real crisis; thankfully I have Debi by my side to help me get through it (pity the lonely and pray for the sick).

It's not medical science that worries me, it's medical practice. While I feel abandoned by those whose "profession" this is, Debi's love has been strong. With a lot of tender, loving care Debi gets me to lay on my side while she feeds me my supper one spoonful at a time (until it is all gone).

Not long after I finish eating my supper, I hear someone knocking lightly on my door. I am very pleased indeed to see Dr. Bigg standing there, because if I have ever needed a doctor, it has to be now (hallelujah I'm saved). Dr. Bigg is the kind of man that you would probably enjoy playing golf with because he is pleasant to be around and he smiles a lot.

Dr. Bigg is the kind of man who really seems to care when he asks someone how they are feeling. He also appears to know what he is doing, so I would rather talk to Dr. Bigg about these issues than I would to Dr. Pharaoh anyway; subtle issues, like the duration of time that I feel like puking my guts out after taking my medication (that's one important statistic that doesn't show up on your medical chart).

With my energy and faith both restored, I sit up in my bed to make my case to Dr. Bigg that things are not going well. Dr. Bigg listens with interest as I tell him about the side effects associated with taking the Cyclosporine: Tropical Sweats followed by Arctic Chills, and then there are the shakes; but nothing is as bad as the nausea. The main point that I want to emphasize to Dr. Bigg is that these side effects are getting stronger, not me. I know that a lot of this is subjective but the one thing that can be quantified is: how long my nausea is lasting, and one thing that is certain is that the duration is increasing.

Something needs to change by tomorrow morning, I tell Dr. Bigg, like maybe splitting the medication into two equal doses (half in the morning and half at night). I say to Dr. Bigg that, "These massive doses that are given one time per day are killing me."

Dr. Bigg tells me that he is in somewhat of an awkward position (so am I). Then Dr. Bigg elaborates about how he is the head of the department, but Dr. Pharaoh is the doctor that is directly in charge of my care (he has to consider his office politics). Dr. Bigg

227

seems evasive when all that I am asking is for him to talk with Dr. Pharaoh about my case. Dr. Bigg starts giving me reasons that I should believe in his staff by saying that, "Dr. Pharaoh has five years of clinical experience." Stunned that Dr. Bigg does not appear to share my concerns, I can tell that he must not know that I realize that "clinical" means experience on rats.

I give Dr. Bigg a sharp retort when I say that, "I don't know how many of Dr. Pharaoh's rats ever told him that they felt like they were burning up even though their temperature was normal." The surprised look on Dr. Bigg's face could mean that I have made a good point or that Dr. Bigg is not used to having patients questioning his judgement (a lot of those who might are cold and forever silent).

Dr. Bigg tries to assure me that everything is going fine, even though I know that they aren't. Dr. Bigg does finally say that he will consult with Dr. Pharaoh in the morning to express my concerns.

After Dr. Bigg has left my room I can see that he has given Debi a false sense of security, which I try not to disturb since visiting hours have come to a close for the night according to the announcement being made to that effect over the public address system. Debi looks tired and worn out as she kisses me goodnight (small wonder). I can clearly see the burden that Debi carries so stoically, and though I try to reassure her my words ring hollow because I am just as worried as Debi is.

Sleep that I have been needing for so long now pulls me down into it, but my brain is afraid to let go. This sleep is so seductive that I'm afraid to let go because this could be death's black embrace. Never having died before, I can't be sure that this isn't what it's like.

One thing is for sure, and that is: to live one must sleep. I just have to bet that since I have been waking up every morning for 36 years, I will wake up one more time, so I let go and head into a sleep so deep that the only deeper sleep is permanent.

Chapter 18

THE VISION

DEEP IN DREAMLAND I can see my red E-type V-12 Jaguar (my dreams are in color) coming down Forrest Drive from Columbia with the top down on a beautiful Southern day, when suddenly, I'm in the driver's seat of the Jag looking out at the road up ahead as everything rushes by much more quickly than it should. For some unknown reason I must be going well over 100 m.p.h. on this suburban boulevard while the speed limit, being very realistic, is only 35 m.p.h.

There I am rolling down the road at a high rate of speed when up ahead I can see that the road makes a gentle curve to the right just before it gets to Columbia Athletic Club, that on a normal day wouldn't present any problem, but going this fast I can tell that it's going to be dicey.

I quickly take my foot off of the gas pedal but the Jag's speed keeps increasing, like maybe the accelerator is stuck, so I stomp on the brakes. But the car just keeps on going as if I hadn't done a thing. The Jag keeps on going faster so I push in the clutch to disengage the engine, yet still the Jag rumbles on.

Confused by this total lack of control, I'm wishing that the Jag had come with an ejection seat, but since it didn't all that I can do is to attempt to stay in my lane. I hug the right side of the road to put more pavement between me and the oncoming traffic that has just appeared from around the curve, but I run out of room and my right front wheel hits the curb, sending the Jag somersaulting end over end with me flying right alongside it.

Looking like Superman, I sail through the air right next to my Jag. At first this doesn't seem all that bad because it looks like we will land on the grass instead of the road. Then a shadow blocks the Sun as my Jag comes flipping over on top of me. I realize that this is no place that I want to be: SQUISH! (the Jag has landed right on top of me).

I thought that a person was supposed to wake up from a dream when they were about to be killed. You would wake up if this were an ordinary dream, but from the instant that my Jag came landing on top of me, this dream has turned into a vision from God (I just don't know it yet).

Instantly, I am standing all alone next to the wreak of my Jag in the middle of a field of brown winter grass. I stand very still as I try to understand what is happening to me. I'm not feeling any pain, but I do have a powerful sense of foreboding as I slowly look down on this would be grave.

I am dazzled and frightened to see my shadow dancing when I know that I am standing perfectly still (my shadow has been created by an awesome pale blue light which pulsates way off somewhere behind me). Understanding nothing, I quake in fear in the middle of this field of silence. I'm just glad that I haven't already been smitten by this flickering electric blue light that I fear. I stand frozen in place, much too frightened to even turn around and look for the source of this blue hued fire lest its power deprive me of sight (it may be a nuclear bomb).

Minding my own business, I'm standing there just happy to still be alive, when I notice some stationary people across the field who are standing in a semicircle with me at the center. Why aren't these people coming to help me? It seems weird that they just stand there watching me across this field of woe (I hope they mean me no harm).

It's hard to make out the features of these people in this flickering electric blue light, so I strain to see their faces when the flashes are the brightest, yet still, I can't see who they are. These people seem to have no fear of the power that is flickering behind me, but I tremble in fear and keep looking away from the light.

I am startled to see that the man, who is standing directly in front of me, is smiling. So I glance at the other people across this field of brown grass and I recognize that the one on my left is my mother, so I know that these people mean me no harm. Then I realize that I do know the smiling man who is directly in front of me, it's Steve Dearwent, my old college roommate and high school buddy. Even though Steve isn't saying a word I can tell that he is wanting me to turn around and look at the source of this powerful light that is coming from somewhere way out behind me (quite strange). Then somehow, I know that my mother also wants me to turn around and face towards the light, so it must be ok.

Looking back over my left shoulder while turning around I see no blue light, only a very bright sun in a cloudless blue sky. Then, out on the horizon, something is happening way out in the distance. I strain to perceive what this could be, when I am shocked by a massive bolt of blue lightening bursting out of the ground and pulsating up to the Heavens above with a power that I never dreamed existed.

This electric blue bolt shoots up from the earth into the sky but not quite far enough to touch the sun (which seems to be its objective). Time and again this unbelievable power tries to connect with the sun before flickering back down to the ground, only to explode from the earth again.

Time and again I tremble in fear as this powerful bolt arcs up towards the sun in vain. My gaze is transfixed as I study this hypnotic dance. Then it hits me that this powerful discharge is branching out its electric blue light into five fingers that grasp for the sun, only to miss by the slimiest of margins.

Like Paul on the road to Damascus, I quake in fear before the power of the living God, as the lightning bolt fails to make the connection it desires with the sun. Somehow, I realize that it is me that is the problem keeping this electric hand from grasping the sun by my own lack of faith.

Then I remember that back when Jimmy and I were studying the Bible in his office, when we got to the part about Jesus making the blind man see again, I did believe that even in a totally logical world it really could have occurred (stranger things have happened).

The instant that I realize that I had in fact actually believed without reservation, the lightning bolt finally makes its divine connection and the sun explodes (blinding me with its nuclear white light).

Suddenly I'm back in my hospital bed, still trembling while I stare at the ceiling, wondering if I am living or dead, when a pain in my side lets me know the answer (hallelujah). As soon as I can tell that this isn't the middle of some kind of deal where I float out of my body and up to the ceiling, while watching a bunch of white coated people as they pound on my chest, I sit up in bed with my knees still shaking like a sinner at the Bible Rock Baptist Church on communion day.

The "vision" didn't have anything in it about checking the literature that came in the box with the bottle of Cyclosporine, but it is at that very minute that I remember that the brochure on the medicine is right next to me in the top drawer of the bedside table. Back on the night before transplant, as I was getting the Cyclosporine ready for my very first taste, I never thought much about the literature when it fell out of the box (I figured that my doctor had already read it). It's a good thing that I didn't just throw the literature in the trash because at the time my mind was on other things (Divine intervention).

The first thing that I do, right after thanking God for letting me still be alive, is to open up the drawer on my bedside table in a search for the Holy Grail (of Cyclosporine). Elated when I find the booklet of information that the manufacturer of Cyclosporine provides with each bottle, I flip through the pages of small print in the dim light as if I am directed by the hand of God (which I am).

I don't even stop to read the first couple of pages as I run my finger over the words until I stop without knowing why. The very first paragraph that I read (in apparent total random selection) is under the "adverse side effects" section where it is talking about "nephrotoxicity." Translated into laymen's terms, this means that too much of this wonder drug will kill you, and the interesting thing is that it does this by killing your kidneys first (oh, boy).

Sitting here in my bed I'm trying to understand the meaning of what I just read, when I am interrupted by the early morning routine of waking up all of the patients in order to weigh them. As I step up on the scale, pondering the obvious: the Hospital staff should wait until right before breakfast to weigh all of the patients because they have to wake up then anyway (considering how much we all need a decent night's sleep).

The deeper issue is obscured by my own lack of common sense at not knowing exactly how much I weigh, or the connection between my steady loss of weight and the incredible nausea that now seems to threaten my life.

Normally I could tell you my body weight within two or three pounds because I weigh every day. When my body weight rapidly drops it usually means dehydration. Here at D.U.H., just to show the patient how "professional" they are, the scale is in kilograms, which means nothing to me since I'm used to measuring my weight in pounds.

I probably would still be totally oblivious (dead is about as oblivious as you get) to not only my actual weight but also the message in all of this if (by sheer luck or the hand of God) my weight had been anything other than exactly 76 kilograms. Instead of just writing my weight on her chart without comment, like most of the early morning nurses would do, this nurse's aide sparkles with personality as she says, "Right on the button, 76 kilograms exactly."

It's as if the "Bells of San Pedro" were ringing again, this time it happens when the most insignificant seeming professional (nurse's aide) makes her seemingly unimportant contribution to the mission of keeping me alive (pittance at the altar\telling me my body weight). The connection is made and the "bells" go off in my head (thank you God).

As soon as the young nurse's aide tells me that my weight is exactly 76 kilos, it brings back the memory of the time that I was weighed on the day before my transplant. A small portion of my conscious mind was actively seeking humorous connections in an attempt to keep my body from becoming afraid and depressed. On that particular morning I weighed exactly 81 kilos, which I still remember because it made me laugh when I thought about Etiwan Lumber Company in the low country of South Carolina. Down in the low country the slow southern drawl makes the Indian name Etiwan sound like the number 81. One year the Etiwan Lumber Company even gave out baseball hats to their customers that had a round patch on the front with the number 81 instead of the company name.

Without this humorous connection of Etiwan kilos in my brain, the fact that I now weigh exactly 76 kilos wouldn't mean a thing. Certainly not at 5:30 in the morning, when the only thing that I'm thinking about is getting back to sleep. My ears perk up and goose bumps cover my arms as I realize that I have lost more than ten pounds in just the last few days since my transplant.

Just as soon as the heavy wooden door closes behind the nurse's aide, while she rolls her scales on to the next room, I reach into the drawer of the bedside table and pull out the booklet that had come with the bottle of Cyclosporine. I flip through the pages of small print once more without really knowing precisely what I expect to find, before my finger stops like a dowsing rod on top of the information about "maximum dose per kilogram."

It doesn't take much imagination to multiply the maximum dose per kilogram by 76, but the answer is astounding. I've been taking a lot more Cyclosporine than the manufacturer says is the maximum dosage allowable for my body weight (what the hell is going on?).

Frantically I search through the drawer for the paper that I had used back when I copied down D.U.H.'s Cyclosporine Protocol from the blue notebook that Dr. Pharaoh had said did not exist (eureka! I have found it!). I know that I now have, in my own hands, two key pieces of the puzzle that will give me the answer as to exactly why the nausea from the wonder drug is lasting longer. It may also solve the riddle of why my new kidney isn't working as well as it should.

At that very second, I hear a voice coming from behind me that I know all too well, and my knees start to buckle when Nurse Crabb says, "Good morning, Mr. Gordon." It's never good when Nurse Crabb's voice is dripping with sugar. I feel like a spy caught by the enemy with their secret code book (I'm afraid that Nurse Crabb will confiscate it just like they did with my medicine the first day that I was here). When I turn around to see what Nurse Crabb wants me for, I am actually relieved to see her standing in front of me holding the tray with my morning medications on it.

Thank God that Nurse Crabb isn't wise to my game (I really mean it). She just wants me to take my dose of Cyclosporine like a good little boy. I have to stall for time so that I can read the literature that came with the Cyclosporine and compare it to the protocol that I am holding in my hand. I put a pitiful look on my face as I tell Nurse Crabb that my stomach is feeling a little squeamish just now and I ask her to please come back after a while. Nurse Crabb suspects nothing because in her world patients aren't supposed to think (neither is she).

I wish that I could look over these documents along with Nurse Crabb in some sort of quest for the truth, but I've been around long enough to know that a nurse only follows a doctor's orders (and that's the truth. Besides, an enemy who doesn't know about your plans, is less likely to thwart them.

As soon as Nurse Crabb leaves me alone I pull out the booklet that came with the bottle of Cyclosporine. I flip through the pages without slowing down to read them until my finger scrolls down to the section on recommended dosages. Miraculously stopping once more on the very paragraph that gives the maximum dose per kilogram, I quickly compare it to my copy of D.U.H.'s Cyclosporine protocol.

When I see the exact same number in D.U.H.'s Cyclosporine Protocol, for the initial dosage, and in the literature listed as the maximum allowable dose per kilogram, (of patient body weight). I have a revelation. It hits me like a ton of bricks: my Cyclosporine dose is too high because D.U.H. started me out at the maximum allowable dose per kilogram and they haven't lowered the medication level to allow for the fact that I have lost more than ten pounds.

I feel as though I am being led by a knowing God while I multiply the maximum dose per kilogram, by the 76 kilograms that I currently weigh, to come up with the amount of Cyclosporine that I should be taking (according to D.U.H.'s own protocol). It's a good thing that I feel like God is on my side, because I still have to face Nurse Crabb who has come back into my room with my morning medications on her little tray. Nurse Crabb has brought me my daily dose of poison, but now I am a sanctified man carrying out God's mission (as I see it).

I take my Prednisone like a good little boy but when it comes time for me to take my Cyclosporine, I put up my hand as I tell Nurse Crabb that I will not be taking any Cyclosporine until I talk to Dr. Pharaoh about reducing the dose to reflect the fact that I have lost a lot of weight since transplant. While Nurse Crabb is still processing that information, I add that I had asked to speak with Dr. Pharaoh yesterday morning but he still hasn't even bothered to give me a call. Nurse Crabb turns red like her fondest dream is to hit me upside my head, glaring at me while she utters some practiced words like an evil incantation that I know can have a hidden meaning, "Are you refusing to take your medication?"

I can tell that if I give Nurse Crabb an affirmative answer it will give her a medical reason to medicate me despite my wishes, so instead I tell Nurse Crabb that "I have some concerns that I wish to discuss with my doctor." By the look on Nurse Crabb's face you would think that she had just detected a very bad smell, and Nurse Crabb huffs out of my room without saying a word.

Maybe Nurse Crabb isn't so bad after all. She is going to get Dr. Pharaoh like I asked her to. The hospital probably has some kind of standard protocol for when a patient has a serious concern about their care. I mean everyone is always saying, "If you ever have a question," and all of that (right?). I'm sure that a big hospital like D.U.H. probably has to deal with stuff like this every day.

Wham! The heavy wooden door to my room swings open announcing the arrival of the Medical Storm Troopers (Dr. Frau, followed closely by Nurse Crabb and Nurse Squeaky). As the Medical Storm Troopers stride across the room, I am thinking that

I will have to explain it all once again. Dr. Frau's first sentence lets me know that she has already been briefed, "What are you, some kind of a crazy man?" Dr. Frau screams in my face.

I shout back, "I'm just trying to get D.U.H. to follow its own protocol" (duh). Dr. Frau's face is contorted in anger. Instead of responding to my retort, Dr. Frau, using a more controlled "professional" voice which is clearly loud enough for her two witnesses to hear, says, "Are you refusing a nurse's order to take your medication?" I know a trick question when I hear one, and Dr. Frau appears to be setting me up so that they can have me declared mentally unstable (in need of sedation, restraints, or both). Instead of any form of an affirmative answer which Dr. Frau is apparently seeking, I say, "No, I just asked to speak with Dr. Pharaoh to discuss some concerns that I have, is there a problem with that?"

Dr. Frau looks exasperated that I didn't fall for her trap as she informs me that, "Dr. Pharaoh is in surgery, so he is unavailable today." Then, Dr, Frau repeats her thinly veiled threat, "Are you refusing a nurse's orders to take your medication?" (if at first you don't succeed, try again).

Once again, I feel that Dr. Frau is fishing for any sort of a yes answer, so I respond obliquely, "I will take the entire dose of Cyclosporine which does not exceed the protocol." Dr. Frau is obviously peeved as she tells me that she has no instructions to give me just a portion of my Cyclosporine. Dr. Frau emphatically tells me that I have a choice of taking all of my Cyclosporine or I can take none of it at all and just die (you have to love how Dr. Frau crystalizes the issues).

I call Dr. Frau's bluff by saying, "My original statement still stands, so I guess that means that I'll hurt D.U.H.'s mortality experience like a lot of your other patients." The look of ghastly surprise on Dr. Frau's face is something that was worth living just to see. This medical swat team of sorts now glares at me as if they are about to explode, and then they storm their way out of my room without saying another word.

I make a mental note about teaching hospitals being something like getting your hair done at a beauty school (they guarantee effort, not results). Before I can reflect further on the professional nature of the medical moment that just occurred in my room, the wooden door to the hall swings open again and the entire gang files back into my room for another try.

They enter my room arranged in their pecking order. First is Dr. Pharaoh, (unavailable?) followed closely by Dr. Frau. Then comes the scowling Nurse Crabb and her assistant Nurse Squeaky bringing up the rear. Dr. Frau seems oblivious to the fact that she has just proven herself to be a liar, but that is not the issue that we are assembled here to discuss.

Dr. Frau carries herself with a swagger and based on the smirk that is perched on her face, Dr. Frau must be pretty well satisfied that she is here to see me get my comeuppance. Dr. Pharaoh traverses the room in a few long strides. Without ever even glancing my way, much less acknowledging me verbally, he picks up my file, looking at it for all of ten seconds before saying to Dr. Frau, "Lower his Cyclosporine" blah, blah, blah...

Dr. Pharaoh then exits my room without so much as a 'how are you today?' leaving me and Dr. Frau eye to eye, but the smirk has now traded faces. By not engaging me in conversation Dr. Pharaoh had gotten out of my room without allowing himself to be put in the position of being embarrassed in front of his staff.

I resist the urge to state the obvious, as Dr. Frau and I stand there eyeball to eyeball, without saying a word. Nurse Crabb and Nurse Squeaky look on as if they had just seen a ghost (they have). I don't need to say anything at this point in time, but poor Dr. Frau has to issue instructions to the nurses about lowering my Cyclosporine dose. She can't escape the fact that Dr. Pharaoh had just agreed with me instead of her about the proper dosage, not to mention that this interaction had just proved that Dr. Frau is a certified liar to boot. Dr. Frau does what one might expect from a medical "professional" in a situation like this when she stomps her feet on the floor while she is leaving my room. I'll bet that they never covered this possibility in any class in medical school.

I'm pretty sure that the official "protocol" for a doctor who is responding to a patient's request to discuss some concerns would involve somebody talking to the patient. Pulling Dr. Frau's chain by not saying a word feels pretty good in light of the fact that she stormed in here with every intension of pulling mine.

Silver linings being what they are, I am unaware until much later that the silver lining in this whole experience is that I will never lay eyes on Dr. Frau again. Maybe it really is the official protocol that a medical "professional" gets automatically reassigned if they make a fool out of themselves in front of one of their patients (however, I'm sure that a rule like that would make it pretty hard to staff this place). In the fullness of time, I imagine, Dr. Frau will join that vast legion of medical "professionals" who, when they finally stare death in the eye for themselves, they will be saying "howdy partner."

Originally this morning it had been Nurse Crabb who had brought me my Cyclosporine to take, but now that Dr. Pharaoh has validated my concerns, the duty of bringing me my adjusted dose of Cyclosporine falls to Nurse Squeaky (poop rolls downhill). Being right is of little comfort when the time comes for me to actually chug this foul concoction that is supposed to save my life. I take the glass of chocolate milk laced with Cyclosporine and hold it up like I'm making a toast (which I am) and say, "To my health," before I chug it (what a kick this stuff has). Nurse Squeaky takes her tray and leaves me to suffer on my own with the grin on my face turned upside down.

The nausea that follows when I chug that brew is mild if you compare it to previous days, but it's still a lot worse than what I want to go through every day for the rest of my life (however long that might be). Thank God that the nausea passes quickly today; I still have a bad taste in my mouth but it's coming from my sense of betrayal when I think about how Dr. Frau lied to me about Dr. Pharaoh being in surgery (note: there is nothing in the Hippocratic Oath about telling patients the truth).

If an insurance agent had lied to a client in response to a direct question in front of witnesses, they could lose their insurance license or maybe even go to jail; but when a doctor lies to a patient it goes unnoticed by other medical "professionals" because it is so common ("professional" courtesy). I know that human error can be expected in any endeavor so the overdose itself is easy to forgive, but it is inexcusable for Dr Frau to lie to me when all of the chips are on the line (my life).

I learned something important today, but it's not very reassuring. What I learned is that the medical "professionals" that I have employed to save my life can't be trusted. When I ask them a question now, I know that they will not necessarily be telling me the truth (telling the truth is the first thing that ought to be included in any Patient Bill of Rights).

Debi comes into my room with her eyes full of concern and she has a perplexed look where her smile would normally be. The first thing that Debi asks me is why I am refusing to take my medicine (obliviously, Debi is behind the information curve). While I am in the midst of smugly explaining to Debi that I had a vison from God last night and that, in fact, I had taken all of the medicine that I should have taken, we are interrupted by Nurse Spock.

Nurse Spock's unwelcome news is that the results from this morning's blood work is back from the lab and my creatinine has gone up once again. Then Nurse Spock drops the other white shoe when she adds, "Your body might be rejecting the kidney." Without any further elaboration, and without offering any words of comfort, Transplant Nurse Spock continues on her rounds leaving Debi and I stunned and confused as we ponder what all this could mean (everything). The word "rejecting" cuts through my heart like a knife and apparently bursts Debi's bubble (such as it was). The vast ocean of tears that Debi has been bravely holding back for all of these months now come pouring out all at one time.

If Debi hadn't been crying so loudly I might have started crying myself, but as it is, Debi is crying enough for both of us. It is only my newly discovered belief in Divine intervention that keeps me from joining in on this pity party that is being thrown in my honor, but even though I may not be crying, I'm plenty scared (I'm shaking in my boots even though I am barefooted).

Deciding that a little fresh air would help the situation, I take Debi out for a walk around the ward. While Debi and I are walking past the nurses' station I pick up strange vibes, but it could just be because Debi has that long distance stare on her face like someone that has combat fatigue (which she does). Debi is so blown away right now that she is walking with a stager in her step like she was the one who had the transplant.

Then as Debi and I are shuffling haltingly on down the hall I begin to second guess myself about the reason that I was picking up those strange vibes back down at the nurses' station. It could have been that the nurses were acting weird because the word has gotten out about how I refused to take my Cyclosporine this morning. That little dispute over my morning medication could have caused Dr. Frau to lose face in front of her peers.

My brain is not quite comfortable with that explanation as to why I was picking up strange vibes from the nurses, so I continue to sort through all of the possible reasons why the entire nursing staff would stop talking just as Debi and I happen to be walking past the nurses' station. Then I start thinking about that off the cuff remark that Nurse Spock had made about the possibility that my increasing creatinine levels are an early indication that my body could be rejecting my new kidney. My knees start to wobble when I realize that if Nurse Spock is indeed correct, that I am currently in a state of rejection. Then lowering my Cyclosporine dose like I insisted on doing this morning would be the wrong move and it could have potentially fatal consequences.

As Debi and I walk on around the ward I'm thinking about how bad the nausea has been from the Cyclosporine, and I know that there is no way that I could stand a dose any higher that what I was on. If the kidney is rejecting at that medication level then I might be a cooked goose. Then it hits me that one reason the nurses back at the nurses' station could have been acting strangely is because the word could have gotten out that my body is rejecting my new kidney. If the nurses really do think that my kidney is being rejected then they might be putting one of those little yellow signs that say "REJECTION" on the door to my hospital room right this very minute.

Now Debi and I both have those "long distance stares" on our faces as I urge my weary bones on around the ward as fast as I can shuffle. I am anxious to see if there is one of those dreaded little yellow signs on the door to my room.

When at last the wooden door to my hospital room comes into view and I can see that there is no little yellow sign taped to it, my spirits surge back up. Joy replaces the weariness that had been moving my bones and I dance the last few steps to my room. Debi looks at me like she doesn't understand what made me act like I was so happy when we have so much to worry about. I have learned that joy on the transplant ward can be fleeting and I am living in the moment.

When I enter my room, I discover that my parents are being briefed by Nurse Crabb. There is no telling what Nurse Crabb has been telling my dad after the morning that we have had around here. The first thing that Big Jim (my father) says to me when I walk in the door is, "Son you must listen to your doctors" (he has just been fed the company line). Before I can explain the situation to my father, Nurse Crabb drops the other white shoe when she tells me to call her when I'm finished visiting with my parents because "We have to do the enema thing."

This speaks to the futility of worrying because in all of the months leading up to my transplant, I can assure you that never even one time did I ever worry about the danger that confronts me now. In fact, even now I do not grasp the seriousness of the situation that Nurse Crabb is referring to. You never think that it will come down to something like this but here I am one week after transplant in a life-or-death struggle with a giant turd, and the turd is winning. I am about to discover that all of the King's horses and all of the King's men can't get my bowels moving again.

One part of me wonders if this "enema thing" is some form of retribution for me not taking all of my medication this morning. The staff could be mad that I made them look bad, but I'm ready for the "enema thing" because I'm tired of looking like I'm beginning my third trimester.

When the time comes it is to Nurse Crabb's credit that she doesn't give enemas the way Dr. Frau checks Prostate glands, and I'm glad that Nurse Crabb takes no special pleasure in my discomfort. But for all of her efforts results are not forthcoming. As Nurse Crabb leaves my room she tells me that if nothing happens after lunch, we will try again, adding that some exercise could help.

Here is a health tip for any wannabe doctor who may read this book. If your patient is eating everything on their food tray but their body weight keeps dropping, it may be due to dehydration (an observation that is apparently lost on the staff at D.U.H.).

Coming, as I am, from the world of a dialysis patent where just one week ago I could only drink four glasses of water per day without suffering painful consequences, I have no concept of how much liquid I should be drinking. But I can assure you that I am not drinking anywhere near enough.

All day long I walk around the transplant ward playing Elton John's "Rocket Man" at full blast on my headphones (the same song that I like to play on my stereo back home when I am getting psyched up before I take a long bicycle ride). I especially like the line about "burning off a pair of shoes everyday" since I forgot to bring my bedroom slippers to the hospital. I have to wear a pair of those little pastel paper shoe covers, like they wear over their shoes in surgery, for bedroom slippers and I wear out one pair each day because of all of the walking that I am doing (yet still there is no movement).

The irony of dying from complications related to this problem is not lost on me. I can just see my death certificate where it lists the cause of death, it will say: "full of poop," and Nurse Crabb will say that it figures. Since there is nothing that I can do about most of my problems I concentrate on the one that perhaps I can do something about, but even after spending the entire day walking around the ward nothing happens. Nurse Crabb tells me not to worry because if we have no luck tomorrow morning, they will give me the "atomic bomb of laxatives" (whatever that means).

Although the entire day and throughout the night I have been totally focused on having the big poop when the morning blood work comes back from the lab, I discover that I have even bigger problems than I realized. The blood test results show that my creatinine is still going up, which means that my kidney function is declining.

My spirits sink so low that now once again I have that thousand-yard stare which means combat fatigue (beam me up, Scottie). Second thoughts now fill my mind, maybe Dr. Pharaoh was right the first night that I met him, when he said that I was the type of patient who would end up dying because I messed around with my medicine. Maybe Dr. Pharaoh just went along with reducing my Cyclosporine dosage because I was insisting on it. Everything has greater significance due to my decision not to have a vein reversed for dialysis in case of an emergency, so there is no plan B (if plan A doesn't work, I'm history).

Lying in my bed on the verge of tears my justifiable pity party is just beginning, when it is interrupted by Nurse Crabb who has come into my room with a stack of cards and letters from people that I don't even know (lyric from an old song). I have so much mail that even Nurse Crabb is impressed (and she has seen it all).

As I begin to open this pile of mail, I realize that most of these cards are from people who work for the same company that I work for. One letter is especially touching because it is from a couple that I have never met, yet still they have both given blood in my name at their local Red Cross (tears roll down my face). Several of the letters tell me that their entire church congregation is praying for me. The tears keep flowing down my face like a waterfall, but they are not from depression like they would have been just a few minutes ago. I'm just totally overwhelmed by the love of total strangers.

Now with my spirits restored my mind turns to deal with the issues at hand. Thank God that I had the vision, (literally) because nephrotoxicity sounds a lot better than rejection, and these seem to be the two most likely reasons that my kidney isn't working like it should. This slim thread of hope keeps me going (without hope people give up and die).

Picking up the telephone changes me from helpless pawn (victim) into someone in control (partially) of their destiny. I get long distance information for Washington, D.C. and get the phone number for Walter Reed Army Hospital where I had my childhood surgery. I am thinking (hoping) that perhaps they will give me some information that will be helpful since they will know that I will not become their patient, as I am not in the Army.

Reaching the transplant coordinator at Walter Reed Army Hospital is no problem, so I ask her to let me speak with the doctor that is in charge of their Cyclosporine research. To my surprise they put my call through to a doctor who happens to be female. It's probably a stroke of good luck that I reach a female doctor because what I need now is compassion, a commodity more likely to be found in the fairer sex.

I try to build some rapport with the good doctor before I ask any questions by telling her that I am calling Walter Reed Army Hospital because they saved my life when I was five years old. I am trying to touch some emotional chord in the doctor, lest some cold logic cut our conversation short because I'm running out of options if I don't find help here.

I tell the doctor that I know that I can't be treated at Walter Reed Army Hospital since I am not a government employee and I tell her that I am not seeking advice on my particular case. Rather, I am seeking general information about Cyclosporine, particularly their protocol regarding how much Cyclosporine per kilogram they would be administering to a hypothetical transplant patient in the first couple of weeks after transplant.

My prayers are answered when, to my surprise, I find that this doctor still has a heart even after going through medical school, because she is very helpful and open. She not only gives me Walter Reed's Cyclosporine Reduction Protocol, but she also gives me some direction as to what my next step might be in my quest for information (that could save my life).

In the course of conversation this doctor, whose name I have never heard and whose face I will never see, reaches out to help me from the goodness of her heart. She gives me some vital background information about the research that was done on Cyclosporine, telling me that the research for Cyclosporine using kidneys from cadavers was done by The University of Pittsburgh while the research using kidneys from living related donors, such as I have, was done by the University of Minnesota in Minneapolis, She concludes our conversation with the advice that I ought to be able to get some useful information by calling the transplant coordinator in Minneapolis.

Touched by this act of human compassion I am moved to tears as I hang up the phone. I reflect on how easy it would have been for that doctor at Walter Reed Army Hospital to just turn me away in my moment of need because of some hidden protocol or the potential personal liability (she had nothing to gain and I had everything to lose). I feel personally blessed as though I had just witnessed God at work (I had).

To put this kind act in some sort of perspective, why don't you just call up your local Coca-Cola bottling company and see if you can find out what their secret recipe is. Hospitals don't like to share information among one another because they see each other as business rivals (which they are).

Before I can look over Walter Reed's Cyclosporine Reduction Protocol to see how it compares to the protocol here at D.U.H., the door to the hallway swings open and in walks Nurse Crabb. She has a glass of liquid that looks like ginger ale concentrate (known as the "Atomic Bomb of Laxatives"). It makes me wonder just how someone came up with this stuff to begin with? I mean did some doctor sit down one day to create a wonder laxative, or did they discover that this stuff will have the desired effect by accident one day when some practical joker was fooling around down at the bottling plant.

As I chug the thick, clear goo Nurse Crabb almost breaks into a smile as she gives me a little piece of friendly advice, saying, "Don't go far". Then Nurse Crabb leaves my room closing the heavy wooden door with her foot rather soundly just before the shock wave from the atomic fart would have shut the door by itself. Even with this promising start it all comes to naught when all of the gurgling stops about halfway down and nothing else happens after that one magnificent fart. After waiting patiently for over two hours, I give up hope of any immediate relief, so Debi and I decide to take a lap around the ward (exercise could help).

Walking in the hallway is sort of like driving out on the Interstate Highway in that it is a good place to think and while we are walking it occurs to me that you know that you are in deep trouble when the best that medical science can do for you isn't enough. This most humble of adversaries has become a real problem because no one appears to be monitoring how much liquid that I am drinking (not enough).

The nothingness that occupies my mind is suddenly challenged by Debi asking me what was so bad about this morning's blood tests results. Without ever giving this much thought on the conscious level my subconscious mind has already come up with a course of action that is apparently not in the protocol book here at D.U.H. Debi acts as a perfect sounding board as I tell her that the big deal about this morning's blood work was: for the first time, in addition to my creatinine level being too high, my white blood count is higher than what it has been (this could indicate rejection or I could have some sort of infection).

Always pursue the medical option that has the best chance of you not ending up dead (don't worry about what it all costs because if you don't make it, you can't pay for it). I point out to Debi that for some reason D.U.H. does not have cleaning the surgical wound with hydrogen peroxide in their protocol like Richland Memorial Hospital taught me to do back when I was on peritoneal dialysis. My plan is to add that step to my personal protocol in the hope that by killing some of the microbes around the incision with hydrogen peroxide I might help to lower the white blood cell count that is causing me some concern.

I am more confident in the triumph of science over microbes than I am about medical science's ability to restart my bowels. Even the second dose of the "Atomic Bomb of laxatives" that I took late this afternoon has yielded no results; apparently D.U.H. has no "big medicine" (Indian term) to wake up my bowels. Full of dejection over fears of rejection I get ready to lay my head down to sleep for the night (literally and figuratively).

Chapter 19

FIRE IN THE HOLE!

ROUSTED FROM MY FITFUL SLUMBER by the early morning weighing crew I ponder the news that I now account for only 73.8 kilos of the planetary mass, while I go into the little tile room for a seated stretching routine that yields nothing. Looking into the mirror while I shave gives my mind a chance to dwell on things like whether this is the sort of thing that one prays about, or not, after all, medical science took its best shot twice and all that came of it was one magnificent fart.

I know that God must have a lot of more serious issues to deal with but people can die from this condition too (right). Then I wonder if God could really take care of "business" and I reason that if God could make the blind man see (which he did), then my humbling condition would be no problem at all. But the blind man's faith (belief) in God had also been an important part of the equation.

In two seconds, I am able to assess my own faith by remembering that in my vision, as the huge bolt of lightning was arcing up from the earth in its attempt to touch the sun, one of the critical requirements turned out to be my own personal belief. Once it was established in my own mind that I did in fact have faith the connection was completed, engulfing my world in its blinding white light.

I had believed in the possibility of divine intervention all the way back from the time when Jimmy and I were studying the Bible together in his office and we came to the part where Jesus made the blind man see again. I had to stop reading the Bible for a minute at that point and make up my mind as to whether I could believe this (or not). After careful consideration I had acknowledged to myself that even in a totally logical world devoid of all faith, an act like restoring sight to the blind could be possible.

As I go through the process of replaying the vision in my mind, when I get to the exact instant where the lightning bolt touches the sun and the blinding white light engulfs my world, I snap back to the conscious level. As soon as the devil realizes that he has lost the struggle for this soul, he bolts for the back door as one huge, dark monolith that makes me see the wisdom of commercial grade plumbing (I am a consecrated man).

Going down the hall to find the weighing crew with the scales finds me so happy that it's all that I can do to not shout out, "I'm going to live!" over and over, delivered as it were from the very bowels of Hell. When I get on the scales this time, I weigh almost exactly 72 kilos, which means that I am almost 1.8 kilos lighter than I was just a few minutes ago. Two kilos would be 4.4 pounds, so you have to wonder just how much Cyclosporine I have been gagging down every morning just to keep me from rejecting that.

As I slowly make my way back up the hall to my room, I ponder other questions that have no answers like: does space ever end and did time ever begin? I feel sort of like Carl Sagan must have felt as he pondered the vast cosmos of space, until I walk through the door to my room and I discover that my morning breakfast tray is waiting on me with the scrambled eggs that came in a carton looking like a feast fit for a king.

Normal people living regular lives get hungry but they don't have hunger that takes control of their bodies like the hunger that is powered by high doses of Prednisone. The orange juice has an exquisite taste and the small pat of something that claims to be a substitute for butter transforms the humble white grits into something worth fighting for (I would eat a lot more but they won't give it to me).

This meal restores my energy and I am ready for the challenge when Nurse Squeaky comes into my room with new instructions telling me all about how high doses of Prednisone, like I am taking, can lead to any unused muscle atrophying away in just a few days. We need to go take a few laps up and down the stairs in order to exercise my quadriceps.

With that for motivation and all of my newfound energy coming from the Prednisone, as well as the fine meal that I just ate, I follow Nurse Squeaky down the quite hall to the stairwell. If it's use it or lose it time for my quadriceps I know which option that I want to choose. It reminds me that in life, if you intend to succeed at any endeavor, you don't let it happen you make it happen. If you sit back and let life just happen then all that you will get from life are all the things that are left over after everything worth fighting for is gone (what's left over isn't worth having).

We get to the stairs one squeak at a time, but they aren't coming from me shod as I am in my paper blue footies (I don't squeak, I rustle). This odd duet of *squeak, rustle, squeak* comes to a halt at the bottom of the stairs where Nurse Squeaky instructs me to exercise my legs for as long as I feel comfortable. But I am to go no further than one floor up the stairs before coming back down again, because all of this activity may hit me all at once. Some people become so worn out that they can't make it back to their rooms. With that said, Nurse Squeaky lets me know that the "we" part of this exercise program is now over. She informs me that she is leaving me alone, "because she doesn't do stairs."

I'm so happy that I'm no longer full of poop that I feel like I can float up to the next floor (maybe more). Upstairs and downstairs, time after time, happily I plod thinking that the worst part is behind me. I am beginning the long road back to physical fitness (in a few short hours I will discover that the worst part is behind me, but not in the manner that I had hoped).

Plodding alone in the stairwell without any distractions at hand, my mind begins to make connections between my loss of body weight and the fact that there has been a gradual increase in how nauseated I have felt after taking my Cyclosporine the last couple of days. It all goes hand in hand with the worsening kidney function, indicated by the rising creatinine level in my morning blood test results recently. I now weigh about six pounds less than I did when we had the big brouhaha over my Cyclosporine dose needing to be adjusted downward to compensate for my weight loss.

It does hit me all at once, so to speak, but not in the manner that Nurse Squeaky had expected. What hits me is the realization that I'm being overdosed with Cyclosporine again (no wonder the kidney isn't working like it should), They are probably killing it with too much Cyclosporine (we had a previous class on this but somebody failed to learn the lesson [D.U.H.]).

Up the stairs then down again, I go time after time, lost deep in thought about heavy issues. Like, I wonder how much Cyclosporine a place like Pittsburgh would give to a typical patient ten days after transplant if they weighed, hypothetically speaking, say 72 kilos (just as an example).

While I'm still thinking about how I can be the most tactful when I phone Pittsburgh to find out what their Cyclosporine protocol is something else hits me all at once: somehow my subconscious mind has been counting the number of times that I have walked up and down this one flight of stairs (the count stands at 30). Shocked by the number, I picture walking up and down the stairs of a 30-story office building and I know that it can't be good for you just ten days after having a kidney transplant.

Concern turns into terror on the way back to my room when I discover that my right pajama leg is soaking wet. At first I think it's just some leakage coming from my bladder, but I'm not wet in the right place for that. I'm wet in the area where they cut me to install my new kidney. My pajama leg is soaking wet all the way down to the floor, in fact I'm leaving damp tracks as I walk down the hall, but they are all right footed (very strange).

Oh God! What if I have to go back to surgery to repair something that I pulled out of place going up and down all of those stairs?

To have made it as far as I have only to lose my new kidney over something like being dumb enough to walk up and down 30 flights of stairs torments me as I race down the hall towards my room. Hustling like Pete Rose trying to beat-out a throw to first base, I am hurrying down the hall when I see Nurse Crabb up ahead standing right in front of the nurses' station. She is scowling at me in a hostile manner, like some Southern Sheriff about to give me the old "you in a heap of trouble boy" routine (no one has to tell me that I'm in trouble, this much I know).

When at last I get close enough to hear Nurse Crabb, over the *rustle, squish, rustle* sound that my feet make, I discover that the biggest problem in Nurse Crabb's day is that she has been trying to find me for the last twenty minutes to give me my morning medications. I want to tell Nurse Crabb to take her silly little problem down the hall because I have bigger demons chasing me (and they are gaining).

The last thing that I need right now is for Nurse Crabb to get defensive when I tell her the story about why one of my legs is soaking wet while the other leg is still dry. What I need from Nurse Crabb in the worst sort of way is urgent medical care and advice that only a doctor can give (and only a nurse can get a doctor).

The concept of springing a leak from your side is difficult to comprehend, much less explain. I want Nurse Crabb to hear that I don't think it is her fault, whatever the problem turns out to be, so I start off by telling her that by my own stupidity I may need to be rushed into emergency surgery (a concept that surprises Nurse Crabb a lot less than it does me).

Then I tell Nurse Crabb to please call the doctor right away because I probably have pulled something loose and they may need to re-implant the tube going from the new kidney to my bladder (showing Nurse Crabb my wet pajamas to illustrate the point). Nurse Crabb just says one word before she goes to get my morning medications, and for a change it's reassuring as she says, "Maybe."

The very first thing that I do when I reach my room is to phone Debi because I have some problems that I need to share (come quick, I'm leaking). Yet the phone just rings in the empty room. I missed her (damn). Phoning my parent's room nets the same results (none). They must all be at breakfast (double damn).

Sitting alone in my room watching the secondhand make its laps I worry that an infection could complicate my complications (I wish the doctor would get here post-haste). The second hand's lap count reaches 30, yet still no one comes to my aid. I begin to wonder if back when Nurse Crabb said "maybe" that perhaps she was referring to the possibility that she might actually call a doctor (I think I'll go see).

When I hustle up to the nurses' station I ask Nurse Crabb if she had any luck reaching one of my doctors, and if so, what exactly did he have to say. Nurse Crabb looks totally nonplused as she gazes up from the counter that she is sitting behind, and with a facial expression that indicates that she would rather be doing paperwork than talking with me, Nurse Crabb tells me that the doctor was busy with a patient but he will be coming by my room to see what the problem is as soon as he can.

I just roll my eyes and shuffle back to my room without saying a word. It appears to me that the fact that I have sprung a leak doesn't seem to scare Nurse Crabb nearly as much as it scares me (it's just another day at the office for Nurse Crabb).

Back in my room I start going through the 'woe is me' cycle, and just when I get to the part of the cycle where I start thinking that things can't get much worse than this, the large wooden door to my room swings open and Nurse Crabb walks in carrying my morning medications on her little tray. Then in a move which strikes me as odd, Nurse Crabb takes her foot and closes the door behind her, making a loud noise which seems out of place in a hospital setting (as if to emphasize some point that has yet to be verbalized).

It's plain to see that this bad hombre (Nurse Crabb) means business, but if she is expecting trouble out of a patient, then she is in the wrong room because I'm in no mood to be uncooperative. I am waiting for the doctor, who might be about to rush me in for emergency surgery to fix whatever is causing clear liquid to leak out of my incision in a major sort of way.

So it's time for me to take my daily dose of Cyclosporine? No problem, Boss Lady. After holding the glass up for a toast to my health I chug the vile concoction with a smile. It seems to me that Nurse Crabb is a little piqued as she gathers up her tray and leaves me to suffer alone (me being cooperative probably conflicts with what Nurse Crabb thought that she would get to write on my chart today).

I'm just glad that Nurse Crabb is no longer in my room because I'll bet that if any puke ended up on her white shoes, it would look bad on my administrative review. This liquid concoction that is supposed to save my life starts my stomach jumping as soon as I swallow it. The industrial strength nausea that it triggers is worse than any that I have had to deal with so far, but the worst part is that Debi isn't here to tell me that everything will be alright as she puts wet paper towels on my forehead.

Gritting my teeth to hold the Cyclosporine down as I belch foul fumes from who knows where, the waves of tropical sweats rack my body. Surely the brave French Foreign Legionnaire must have felt something like this while dying for France in the desert with no water in sight. The heat in my room feels oppressive and it is all coming from deep inside of my guts in what feels like a chemical fire, yet still it is the nausea that bothers me the most because I know that if I lose the struggle to keep this medicine down I could lose my life. Can the conscious mind continue to override the involuntary responses of the body indefinitely? (I think not.)

Feeling forsaken, I long for Debi's sweet voice while I keep pushing the button to lower my bed in the hope that I will find some cooler air down below, only to be confused when nothing happens. The bed is already all the way down yet still there is no relief from the heat (oh, what I would give for an electric fan).

Getting up out of bed, I go into the bathroom to splash some cold water on my face, but I choose to not look at my reflection in the mirror. I don't want to know how bad I look. Then all at once there is relief from the heat of the tropical sweats, too bad that it comes in the form of Arctic chills. With chattering teeth and knocking knees I head back to bed for the comfort such as my blanket may provide, when I see a sight that may as well be an angel because that's what Debi is to me.

Armed only with love, Debi has come to do battle with the demons that possess me. Her presence is all of the encouragement that I need, because I know that once the chills begin to replace the sweats the worst part is over. The sweats return before long, but they are not as strong as they were the first time around and

Debi helps me to get through them with just wet paper towels plus a lot of tender loving care. Then, at last, as the sweats finally pass so does the nausea and none too soon. I know that I am near my breaking point (anyway that it can be measured).

Speaking of measuring, I glance up at the clock on the wall so that I can tell how long it has been since I took my Cyclosporine, and I am not surprised to see that these side effects have lasted for almost two full hours. I'd like to get Nurse Crabb to tell me the part again about how I am supposed to be getting used to this wonder drug, because if the side effects last any longer tomorrow, I might not make it.

Each cycle of misery from the side effects of my medication has worn me down and left me weaker while at the same time the side effects themselves are getting stronger and lasting longer. Like the ocean waves working against the largest stone, the outcome is predetermined (if nothing changes). It may be impossible to accurately gauge the intensity of things like nausea and chills, but I can scientifically measure their duration, so I can tell you with some authority that things are getting worse.

Pushing the button beside my bed I call for Nurse Crabb to ask her where the doctor is that was supposed to be coming to examine me over two hours ago to find out why I have sprung a leak. It would have made a greater impression on the doctor if he had come before everything had dried up (now it doesn't look like there is anything wrong). When Nurse Crabb tells me that the doctor is on the way to my room as we speak, I just look over at Debi and say, "My check is in the mail."

In a little while there is a faint knock on my door and I discover that Nurse Crabb has sent an intern to do a doctor's job (the joys of being a patient in a teaching hospital). Now it is my turn to be the wannabe because I wannabe seen by a real doctor. Surely the protocol for a patient who has sprung an unexpected leak from their side would have something in it about notifying a doctor.

If you ever have any condition so bad that an intern can't handle it all alone, then you are really in big trouble. Even if the intern doesn't have a clue about what your problem is or what the solution may be, the intern will just make up an answer if that's what it takes to not bother the real doctor (that's his job).

Now that everything is dry my incision looks normal, but whatever the problem is, it is not on the outside where we are looking. So after the most cursory of examinations the intern tells me that it was probably just some dialysis fluid that my body hadn't yet absorbed, and not a case of the new kidney pulling loose from the bladder like I had feared. The other side of that probably still bothers me, but I'm just glad that whatever the problem is it doesn't require surgery (if the intern is right). It appears as though I have done some of my best worrying over nothing.

Lying in my bed I wonder how a day that started off with such promise (poop de jour) could turn from sugar to shoe leather and back all before lunch, when in walks the Transplant Nurse Spock. Without so much as a how are you today, she announces that my morning blood test results are back showing that my kidney function is still declining. Then Nurse Spock drops the other white shoe: unless things improve they will do a biopsy on Monday.

With that said, Nurse Spock turns to leave my room so I quickly tell her that I may still need to see a real doctor. Even though the intern has checked on me, I walked up thirty flights of stairs this morning and I may have pulled something loose. There was leakage from the incision all over my leg and an x-ray may be required to tell if everything is ok (just to be safe).

Nurse Spock responds by saying "An intern is a real doctor." before she goes on her way without bothering to wait on my response (not that it would matter). It is amazing that Nurse Spock can carry on a conversation like this with a total lack of compassion or interest (that's why I call her Nurse Spock—no offense to Vulcans).

When Nurse Spock leaves my room she closes the large wooden door behind her with a clunk. Then the tears start flowing down Debi's face like a waterfall, but Debi tries her best to suffer in silence, which she does other than a sniffle or two. Brave as Debi has been this is all just a little too much, and I would cry with Debi if I weren't so damned tired. The upside of the downside is that I have a better understanding of just why this day turned from sugar to shoe leather so fast.

Nurse Squeaky comes into my room to check my vital signs and while she is waiting for the thermometer to do its thing, she tells me that she really hopes that the doctors don't have to do a biopsy on my kidney. At least there is one "professional" here (I think) that hasn't been around long enough to lose her compassion for others. As I bask in Nurse Squeaky's apparent compassion, my bubble is burst when Nurse Squeaky continues her monologue by telling me that after the doctors do a biopsy the nurse has to keep direct pressure on the spot where the needle went into the kidney for up to six hours to keep it from bleeding. A few weeks ago the doctors did a biopsy on a patient where the nurse sat in one position for so long that she passed out and fell right on the floor.

Oh great, Nurse Squeaky's compassion isn't for me, it's just that she doesn't want to have to go through all of the trouble involved with keeping pressure on the biopsy site for up to six hours. She knows that duty will be assigned to her (the poor dear). Vital signs verified, patient terrified, Nurse Squeaky leaves my room with her work here complete (for now).

Now motivated more than ever, I call long distance information for Pittsburgh, Pennsylvania, to get the phone number for the transplant clinic at the University of Pittsburgh. I decide to call Pittsburgh before I call Minneapolis just to gain as much knowledge as possible before I play my last card. Working my way through the hospital switchboard to the transplant coordinator is no problem at all (it's about as hard as finding someone at a car dealership who is in sales).

Fortunately, people who become transplant coordinators are usually very caring individuals and this one turns out to be very empathetic so after listening to my story, she transfers my call to a doctor who is supposed to be able to answer my questions about Pittsburgh's Cyclosporine Protocol.

When this doctor turns out to be female, I first think that this is a good thing because it is more likely that a female doctor will be compassionate and therefore easier to talk with. That myth is soon dispelled by her cold, "professional" tone of voice. The personal warmth that I had hoped to find in the doctor that I am counting on to help me save my life is distant at best. I'm lucky to coax the initial Cyclosporine dosage per kilogram from this cold fish (but I do).

I learn one rather profound fact in this short phone conversation: Pittsburgh gives its kidney transplant recipients a lower dose of Cyclosporine after transplant than they do here at D.U.H. In fact, I'm taking more Cyclosporine right now than Pittsburgh would have used on me immediately after the transplant (and at Pittsburgh most of the kidneys are coming from the dead).

I go through the same routine with The University of Minnesota in Minneapolis, but this time I use my communication skills better as I build rapport with the transplant coordinator before I try to get any information out of her. This is the hospital that conducted the original research on living, related transplants, such as mine, and I don't have anywhere else to turn. Luckily, the head honcho that I need to talk with is working today and he is willing to take my phone call. I don't think that there is any way possible that I can relate the incredible tension that I feel as I wait for the doctor to pick up his phone (because I know that this one is for all of the marbles).

The Doctor that takes my call is the chief of staff and puts me at ease right away by telling me that they have never lost a kidney in my category at the University of Minnesota (they probably never had one in my category before). Since Cyclosporine has only been available for a short time, except to patients who were part of a study at one of the research institutions, they have probably never had a desperate phone call from a patient who is currently being treated as an inpatient by another hospital.

I know that no doctor is going to attempt to recommend medical treatment for another doctor's patient, especially over the phone, so I have to probe for details under the guise of seeking general information as opposed to asking for any sort of opinion on my particular case. I feel like this whole experience has to be similar to what it would be like to be one of those people who makes a long journey to seek answers about life's great quandaries from some mystic who lives without plumbing (as if he would know). Here I am at the end of my journey, in that delicate point in time when the wise man is waiting to hear my question, so I ask him, "How much Cyclosporine per kilogram of patient body weight would Minnesota use for the initial preoperative dose".

Then I am quiet because I know that anything else that I say would just complicate the situation. After a brief pause, the doctor gives me a straightforward answer and I'm sitting there thinking *thank you, Lord*, as he goes through their entire Cyclosporine Reduction Protocol. As I write down the information that this doctor is giving me without reservation, it seems miraculous and I say to you: what are the chances of something like this happening without divine intervention? (About the same as the chances of being able to make a blindman see.) After the phone call is over, I reflect on the fact that it was easier to get the Cyclosporine Protocol from Minnesota than it was from the hospital that is treating me. I'm thankful that the doctor was more interested in helping me than he was with some standard procedure.

When I start comparing all of the information that I have it turns out that The University of Minnesota uses an initial dosage of Cyclosporine that is even lower than what they are using in Pittsburgh (this makes sense because at Minnesota the kidneys come from living related donors). There is one tantalizing tidbit of information that seems to be of critical importance: Minnesota's initial preoperative Cyclosporine dose is exactly what D.U.H.'s protocol calls for me to be lowered to on Monday.

It doesn't take a rocket scientist to see that if I have been getting too much medicine (which I have due to my weight loss) and the new kidney isn't working right, (a known side effect of high doses of Cyclosporine) then probably the correct move is to go ahead with the lower dosage tomorrow instead of waiting until Monday.

It's that "probably" word that is causing all of the trouble because medical science doesn't work well with the word "probably" factored in. Unfortunately, what medical science calls for them to do in a situation like this is to punch a small hole in my new kidney in order to cut out a little piece of meat so that they can tell if the problem is rejection.

The trouble with this line of thinking is that the biopsy results will take 48 hours to come back from the lab and that can be a lifetime on the transplant ward. Even after waiting for 48 hours for the biopsy results to come back from the lab, medical science still hasn't been able to completely get rid of that "probably" word because the biopsy results can be labeled as "inconclusive."

Sleep is all that I can think of right now as I am totally exhausted by the stress of the day. I am just beginning to nod off when I am rousted from my rest by the delivery of my supper tray. Debi knows that I missed lunch and she is going to see that this food gets into my body one way or the other. I am so tired (or depressed) that I can't even sit up to eat so Debi feeds me my supper one spoonful at a time, while I lay in bed on my side feeling sorry for myself. I can feel the woe is me cycle coming on (justifiable woe).

My energy is somewhat restored by the food and my spirits also improve, leading me to make the fateful decision to cleanup my wound before going to sleep. Debi and I put on our latex gloves before I pour Hydrogen Peroxide all over the incision (bad move).

At first, I am encouraged as the Hydrogen Peroxide starts bubbling up around each one of my stitches signaling that the microbes are losing this little war. So I pour some more Hydrogen Peroxide on my incision and I don't have to wait long for a reaction, but it's not the one that I was expecting.

Instantly I'm up on my feet jumping around the room like a bullfrog with his butt on fire shouting, "Fire in the hole! Fire in the hole!" Debi looks frightened and bewildered but I can't be much comfort to her right now because I am frightened and bewildered myself. At this point in time, I'm not really sure exactly what happened. I can tell you this much though, it's hard to think clearly when your butt is on fire. All that I can do right now is to keep on dancing around the room to the odd refrain, "Fire in the hole!"

While I am dancing around the room trying to figure out why I am in such acute, unrelenting pain I think about my vision, especially the part when my shadow was dancing in the electric blue light. I wonder if this is what it meant (because my shadow is sure doing some serious dancing now).

I have to keep on dancing as I try to get away from the pain, then finally I realize that the Hydrogen Peroxide must have burned hemorrhoids that I never knew existed. In utter desperation I plop my rear end into the sink with the cold water going full blast. For a split second during my little bull frog dance the pain was so bad that I took momentary comfort from the fact that I had my pistol in my suitcase (pain killer). For the last ten days I have felt absolutely nothing from anything below my waist, but now all of a sudden, every nerve seems to function just fine (communicating that my butt is on fire).

Let me assure you that cold water offers scant relief for a chemical burn, and that is exactly what I am dealing with since the Hydrogen Peroxide has created a case of the atomic hemorrhoids from hell. Never having had any experience with hemorrhoids, I had been unaware of what caused them. But it would appear that my activities of the last few days read like a step-by-step guide of what not to do.

Hopping back into my bed, I push the button for the nurse (as if that would bring help). God help those patients who have a problem while they are in a hospital being treated for something else. When you have a medical problem that isn't covered by some existing doctor's order, good luck on getting prompt treatment. If you are unlucky enough to have something like this happen in a hospital at night, you can just about forget seeing a real doctor until in the morning. Remember that the night shift's motto is: Don't do anything that can be put off until tomorrow (patient heal thyself).

The night nurse comes into my room in response to my call to the nurses' station, so I tell her about the chemical burn creating the "atomic hemorrhoids from hell," explaining that I am in severe pain and I really need help right away. The night nurse leaves my room and after a while I begin to realize that this is probably the extent of the therapy that I am likely to receive.

I turn to Debi in my moment of need, telling her to go get the night nurse and bring her back here dead or alive. In the minutes that I am alone I think about how lucky I am to have Debi by my side, and I pity people like the Old Man of The Ward who have to face things like this alone.

When Debi finally returns with the night nurse in tow the night nurse has all of the body language of the guilty party in a police line-up. So even before she says one word, I can tell that something isn't right. The first thing out of the nurse's mouth is, "The pharmacy is closed until morning."

I am absolutely livid that the night nurse did absolutely nothing after I told her that I was in severe pain and needed help right away. I'd like to ask her what the proper protocol is for a situation like this, but I wouldn't want to be labeled as "uncooperative" (I'd just like her "professional" opinion).

I tell the night nurse that I find it hard to believe that the emergency room at D.U.H. can't even handle a case of hemorrhoids. I can see her body tense up as she gives me her tart reply, "You aren't in the emergency room." This surly remark by the night nurse makes me forget about trying to be tactful, so I just tell her exactly how I feel by saying, "It is very unprofessional that you didn't at least come back to let me know that nothing was being done." She puts on an aloof air as she looks at me and says, "I wrote it in your chart." (Whoopie!)

Then the Night Nurse glares at me as she starts to walk out of my room. Just when I was thinking that she didn't add much to the equation, she turns around to make a rather profound statement before she walks out the door, "If the pharmacy had been open, they would probably just give you some Preparation H." The clock on the wall says that it is now twenty minutes until eleven, so the mission falls to Debi to race out of this internationally known medical facility in search of medical care that can be found at any local Seven-Eleven store (Preparation H).

My only hope is that Debi can win this race against time and make it to the store before it closes for the night to get me a tube of Preparation H (my kingdom for a tube). Looking out of my window I can see Debi as she runs across the parking lot (go Debi go!). My very existence could depend on Debi getting to the store before it closes, because if I don't get some sleep tonight, I will never be able to do what I have to do tomorrow.

I stand there looking out of my window at what would appear to be a peaceful night except for the black Mercedes speeding out of the parking garage (go Debi go!). I feel helpless as I watch the Mercedes speed out of sight and I know that it is time to pray. A lot of things could go wrong with Debi's mission, the store could be closed when she gets there or they might be out of Preparation H.

I decide that I had better say a prayer, but instead of closing my eyes I look up at the night sky full of twinkling stars and I find it easy to have faith. I am marveling at the perfect order in the universe and thinking about how the light left those stars long before I was ever born yet, here I am enjoying their beauty tonight when I see the Mercedes comes roaring back into the parking garage.

Debi is running fast as she makes her way from the parking garage to the front door of the hospital, so I know that the mission must have been a success, because if she had failed there would be no reason to run (hooray for Debi!).

Debi comes rushing into my room all out of breath and hands me the box of Preparation H like it is the baton in a relay race. As I take it from her hand I can tell that something is not quite right, because Debi keeps looking down at the floor and she isn't saying a word, even though the mission was obviously a success.

I pause to ask Debi what's bothering her and she tells me how embarrassing it was for her to go racing into the store just before closing time, just to buy one tube of Preparation H. Then Debi looks into my eyes and she says that the worst part was that the cashier was a good-looking guy about her age.

Chapter 20

COMMAND DECISION

"WHAT WOULD YOU DO IF THIS HAPPENED to you, I'm certain that it happens all the time" (old Beatles song). The early morning weighing crew awakens me to the news that I still am losing weight (not much, yet still, there is less of me today than there was yesterday).

Even though every vein in my arms hurts I am glad to see the guy with the needle from the lab because today this is no ordinary blood test. The only way that I am going to avoid a biopsy of my tender new kidney on Monday is to have the lab results come back showing improving kidney function instead of the steady decline that we have been seeing over the last several days. Of course, the biopsy worries me less than the box (the one that I will go home in if things don't turn around soon).

In the midst of these life and death worries I have to deal with the proverbial pain in the butt, so I phone Debi to ask her to stop by the store on her way into the hospital this morning to pick up another tube of Preparation H because I wouldn't want to run out of it in the middle of the night (plan ahead).

Now back to the song, "what would you do if this did happen to you?" Here I sit fully convinced that the wonder drug that Nurse Crabb will want me to take in less than two hours will put me in the grave just as surely as a lethal injection for a condemned murderer, who would go to blissful sleep while I would end up puking myself to death. In a perfect world I would just share my concerns with my doctor, (that they are killing me slowly) letting him know that due to my continuing weight loss I'm getting more Cyclosporine per kilogram of body weight than the maximum dosage the manufacturer says is allowable (consult the literature that comes in the box with the medicine).

Of course, we have already had that lecture a few days ago. Only begrudgingly did the staff concede the point but they did so without having learned the lesson, because if they had understood the issue, then the amount of Cyclosporine that I would be taking this morning would have been reduced to correspond with my weight loss (just to keep the dose per kilogram of body weight level).

My worst fear is that Nurse Crabb will just mix the Cyclosporine with the chocolate milk at the nurses' station and then bring it to my room (eliminating any opportunity that I might have to reduce the dosage). It is because of this fear that I make a command decision to reduce the Cyclosporine dosage without my doctor's concurrence (through sleight of hand). There is no way that I will be able to survive the side effects of this next overdose. Each day as I have lost weight the overdose has been increasing (dose per kilo). The process of surviving the negative side effects is wearing me down to the point that yesterday I thought that I might pass out (today I'm afraid that I might die).

I don't know what the protocol is around D.U.H. for transplant patients who go down for the count, but most hospitals these days can put in enough tubes to keep the patient alive for a few days (technically). This gives the hospital one last chance to probe the patient's health insurance policy for any remaining benefits.

If I were to go visit the land of Oz (lose consciousness), I'm sure that by the time that I would wake back up the doctors would have already stuck a huge needle into my tender new kidney and cut out a hunk (biopsy). When you get to the point where they need to biopsy your kidney to see if it's rejecting, the bad news would mean that death is calling your name and the good news would mean that they didn't really have to run this test after all (enjoy the blood clot in your new kidney). Sometimes I wonder if the driving force behind the push to do a biopsy on my new kidney this Monday is connected to the fact that it would be a good subject matter for the class.

Try as I might to comfort my troubled mind there is just no escaping from the fact that my new kidney isn't working right. One way to prove this clinically is to see if my creatinine level keeps going up and another way to tell if my new kidney is not working right would be for me to die (the trouble is that both of these outcomes can be a result of more than one problem).

I could be rejecting the kidney that my brother gave me or the kidney might not be functioning correctly due to some other cause (such as too much Cyclosporine). I have to believe that we are not dealing with rejection or my white blood cell count would be a lot higher, and I would think that I would have a fever (but I don't). This is where science gives way to art. It gets down to understanding the probabilities of various outcomes and then having the testosterone to make life or death decisions (the pucker factor isn't as great when the patient is somebody other than yourself).

At times like these you have to hope that your doctor is a good poker player. The pure science part of making this decision wants to be certain before any action is taken but this is an uncertain world. Any doctor would prefer to have their suspicions confirmed by a biopsy and so would I if that would mean that I could be certain whether my kidney is rejecting or not (oh, if life were only that simple).

There are a lot of considerations: for starters it takes two days just to get the results of a biopsy back from the lab and two days on the transplant ward could be two days too late. Even when the report on the biopsy comes back from the lab it might be labeled as "inconclusive," and then I would still be faced with the same quandary that I have now except that I would be two days further down the path to destruction (not to mention the fact that I would have a hole in my tender new kidney).

The thought of going through with a biopsy and then still having no clear course of action indicated makes me want to go with an option that does not involve sticking cold steel into my side. What would the therapy be if the biopsy came back from the lab showing that rejection was not the problem? Let's go ahead and start that therapy now and if it turns out that it was the wrong move, it will be clear to us long before the biopsy results would be back from the lab.

Many times in life one course of action precludes others, for example, trying to play it safe by having the biopsy precludes the optimal outcome which would be for me to get the new kidney that my brother has given to me back home to Blythewood without a bunch of bloody holes in it. Let's just think this biopsy thing through a little more: to begin with, you have to look for the hidden agenda, and doctors do have a hidden agenda of trying to protect themselves from lawsuits. They do this by being able to prove that they ran every conceivable test to show why they made a particular decision just in case things turn out badly and they get sued (C.Y.A.- cover your ass, etc.).

While there is the possibility that rejection is causing the elevated creatinine levels it could also be caused by too much Cyclosporine, so we have to think about which one is more likely given the fact that it is known that I have been receiving more Cyclosporine per kilogram of body weight than the maximum dosage that the drug manufacturer says is permissible (D.U.H.).

Not only is it more likely that too much Cyclosporine is at the root of this problem, but if I am experiencing acute rejection while taking a very high dose of the wonder drug, then what would my probable outcome be? The doctor's logic is caught in the loop that nephrotoxicity from too much Cyclosporine is reversible while sometimes rejection is not (a lot of bad decisions are based on good information).

The real bottom line is that rejection will not impact my life for a couple of days while the impact of an overdose of Cyclosporine will be immediate. I would talk to my doctors about all of this but I am too afraid that they might try to thwart my plans by mixing the Cyclosporine with the chocolate milk before they bring it into my room. I just do not believe that I can stand to be overdosed one more time and I don't think that Nurse Crabb could stand for me to be right one more time either.

Rejection is a maybe thing while the nausea is for certain, and while perhaps I can stand the nausea this time without losing consciousness, I know for sure that I am close to my breaking point. Douglas MacArthur once said that the history of failure in warfare could be summed up in two words, "Too late." Those two words apply to almost any sort of failure in life and I don't intend to sit idly by while my life slips away. The biopsy that is looming ahead for Monday is certain too unless I get back a blood test that says things are improving and like the old cliché' says, "If nothing changes then nothing changes" or as Bill Tulluck's favorite saying goes: "If you always do what you always did you will always get what you always got."

I know that a high dose of steroids can make you aggressive, as well as paranoid, so naturally I'm shaking in my boots (except that I'm barefooted). I am very worried that I may, through my own good intentions, put myself in the ground by doing something stupid. Yet, still, logic on top of logic indicates that I'm right (if I'm sane). The Cyclosporine dosage that I think is most appropriate is exactly what D.U.H. would be lowering me to on Tuesday if things go as planned, and if D.U.H. were to follow their own protocol. However, I must say that when we reduce the dosage to what they would be giving me on Tuesday and we reduce it to allow for my weight loss, we are talking about a lot of Cyclosporine

Another friend of mine introduced me to an old saying that comes to mind, "Just because I am paranoid doesn't mean that people aren't out to get me."

When I compare how much Cyclosporine I would be taking after this contemplated reduction to what the other hospitals would be giving a patient at this stage, it is apparent that I will still be taking more Cyclosporine than what any of the other hospitals would be giving to someone in my category (if I calculated right and if I'm sane).

I wish that I could research this some more but on the transplant ward decisions have to be made in real time, and here comes Nurse Crabb into my room with my morning dose of Cyclosporine on her little tray. Now what would you do if you were convinced that if you took this dose of medication you would puke yourself to death?

Nausea, that's the ticket, (thank you Saturday Night Live) as Nurse Crabb puts the tray with the Cyclosporine down on the bedside table, I put my hand on my stomach and I make a bad face telling Nurse Crabb that I need to wait just a few minutes before I take my medicine because my stomach is upset. Nurse Crabb makes a bad face of her own, as if I'm creating extra work for her (which I am). Then Nurse Crabb goes huffing out of my room still carrying the chocolate milk and the Cyclosporine on her little tray.

Rats! I needed Nurse Crabb to leave the Cyclosporine on my bedside table so that I could take the adjusted dosage instead of the amount that is on my chart. How am I ever going to separate Nurse Crabb from the medicine tray since the protocol calls for her to watch me take my Cyclosporine? I don't have a clue and I don't have much time.

Pacing my room while I wrack my brain for a plan to separate Nurse Crabb from the bottle of Cyclosporine, I keep drawing a blank. (What would you do?) I can't run or hide, neither can I delay this impending doom much longer. As doubts that were lingering deep in my heart bubble to the surface of my conscious mind, they are dismissed but only with great anxiety. I have to put everything else out of my mind so that all of my attention can be focused on this one objective (separating Nurse Crabb from the Cyclosporine). Yet still, for all of my worrying, nothing comes to mind. (What would you do?)

When danger can't be avoided you do desperate things, but one principle must guide your hand: PLAY TO WIN! The only factor working in my favor is the low regard the medical staff has for the patients' ability to think for themselves (they will not be expecting subterfuge).

Back and forth I pace in my room yet still no plan comes to my mind, so I say a quiet prayer in a state of total desperation, which is interrupted by a voice corning over the public address system asking if I feel well enough to take my Cyclosporine now. I answer yes because it's Nurse Squeaky and I know a break when I hear one (thank you, Lord!).

Alright, time is up: everyone reading this book who hasn't thought of a plan to separate the nurse from the bottle of Cyclosporine, don't criticize mine because it is the only thing that I can think of that has any chance of succeeding and it is my life that is on the line.

I go into the bathroom to brush my teeth and shave, leaving the door cracked just enough to peek out (plausible diversion corning up). After a while, Nurse Squeaky comes into my room putting the tray with the chocolate milk and the Cyclosporine down on my bedside table. Not wanting Nurse Squeaky to take the medication tray out of the room with her once she is startled, I bide my time while Nurse Squeaky pours the chocolate milk into the glass and starts taking the top off of the bottle of Cyclosporine.

When I see that Nurse Squeaky has finished taking the top off of the bottle of Cyclosporine, I know that I have the moment that I have been waiting for (it's now or never). Even with the stress of knowing what will happen if I fail going through my mind a knowing smile breaks across my face, because I realize that this gambit wouldn't stand any chance at all if I were dealing with Nurse Crabb (grizzled veteran that she is).

The moment of truth at hand, Plan A swings into action as I flush the toilet to draw Nurse Squeaky's attention this way. I drop my hospital gown to the floor and walk out of the bathroom totally nude, pretending like I don't know that Nurse Squeaky is here. Nurse Squeaky's gasp signals complete surprise (fake look of shock on my face with a real look of shock on Nurse Squeaky's) and in a predictable sort of way Nurse Squeaky bolts out of my room, squealing apologies all the way to the door.

The important point in all of this is that Nurse Squeaky didn't slow down to put the top back on the open bottle of Cyclosporine, in fact, the medicine tray was the last thing on Nurse Squeaky's mind while she was running out of the room.

I hustle across the empty room to the medication tray wearing nothing but a grin and I feel like a spy in the enemy's headquarters. Because if I am discovered before I can complete my mission, the penalty will be the same. I quickly mix the lower dose of Cyclosporine with the chocolate milk and hold the glass up high, toasting to my victory as I chug the lifesaving brew.

The thrill of victory sweeps through me followed closely by hot flashes, but the dreaded nausea never comes (how sweet life is).

This is salvation just as surely as if there were the blood of a lamb smeared upon my door and I am just as grateful. This glorious moment of triumph is interrupted by Nurse Squeaky knocking on my door, so I grab my hospital gown and tell her to come in. Nurse Squeaky's apologies come to an abrupt stop when her eyes hit the empty glass of chocolate milk. Nurse Squeaky has one eyebrow arched as she asks incredulously, "Why did you take your medicine without me?" (I act surprised that she is surprised).

Nurse Squeaky emphatically tells me that she is supposed to watch the patient take the Cyclosporine to make sure that they get the right amount (I know). Nurse Squeaky glares at me during the entire time that she is making her exit with the medication tray. I feel a little bad about having to trick Nurse Squeaky, yet still, if I had been a good boy and taken all of my medicine I would be puking my guts out right this very minute (life is full of imperfect choices).

Feeling vindicated and satisfied to be the master of my own fate once again, the old emotional roller coaster is going up with me enjoying the ride. Into this happy world Debi walks, but it is obvious from the start that something is bothering Debi as she hands me the precious tube of Preparation H. Glad that for a change I can turn my attention to comforting Debi, I hold her in my arms. In my most reassuring tone of voice I tell Debi that everything will turn out ok and that she should try not to worry too much.

Trying to relieve Debi's stress I tell her that it is obvious that she is lost in thought and I would pay two pennies if she would tell me what it is that is bothering her. Debi looks up at me with those big, beautiful eyes and says, "I'm just so humiliated: it was the same clerk," as if that statement would make sense to me. Then Debi goes on to say that, "It was him again," as if that would clarify the issue. At last Debi puts everything in my life back into perspective as she tells me about how embarrassing it had been for her when she went to the cash register to pay for the Preparation H this morning, only to discover that it was the same nice looking guy who had sold her the tube of Preparation H just before closing time last night (to make matters worse, the tube of Preparation H was the only item that Debi was purchasing).

It doesn't matter that I didn't have time to explain to Debi all of the reasons why she shouldn't worry, because that happy world that I had wanted to take Debi to ceased to exist in the blink of an eye when Nurse Spock, the transplant nurse, strides through the open door to my room. She announces that the morning blood test results are back from the lab and tells me: "Your kidney could be rejecting." That one word (rejecting) cuts to the bone in a manner that a healthy person could not fathom. This is probably the part of her job that Nurse Spock likes best (delivering bad news to people that she doesn't like). My guess is that she considers this to be one of the perks of her profession (cold fish that she is).

"There is a good chance that your kidney is rejecting," Nurse Spock continues as she begins to fill me in on all of the details from my blood test this morning. I can see that Debi is beginning to tear up and I feel like crying right along with her as Nurse Spock keeps right on talking in her detached monotone, but I'm still hung up trying to understand the full impact of that one word "rejecting."

Apparently, it is still my increasing creatinine levels that leads Nurse Spock to believe that I could be in the early stages of rejection. Interestingly enough, the one part of my blood work that points away from the rejection theory is that my white blood count has gone down. If I hadn't poured Hydrogen Peroxide all over my wound last night then Dr. Pharaoh might have done a biopsy on me this morning instead of waiting until Monday (ouch).

Trying to act like I'm not panicked when I really am leads me to ask Nurse Spock if there are any reasons, other than rejection, that could result in an elevated creatinine level (like maybe too much Cyclosporine). Hoping that the idea that I'm being over medicated maybe easier to see if it's her own reasoning that brings about the conclusion, I try to lead Nurse Spock in that direction. It seems like just when she has it all sorted out and is about to come to that conclusion, she turns on me with all the defiant emotion of the leading prosecutor at the Salem Witch Trials, saying, "It could be renin produced by your native kidneys. Maybe we will have to cut them out!"

It seems to me that Nurse Spock is doing everything that she can to scare the hell out of me (it's working). "We will not know for sure what the problem is until the biopsy results come back from the lab" Nurse Spock says as she walks back out of my room without even waiting for my response (no doubt in a hurry to continue on her merry rounds).

Looking down the hall I can see Dr. Pharaoh and all of the wannabe doctors going into another room, giving me a few minutes to comfort poor Debi, who is sitting in the chair by my bed with one of those long-distance stares on her face. As I walk across the room towards Debi my knees start to wobble, letting me know that even on the subconscious level I'm shaking in my boots (even though I'm barefooted). Sensing the depths of my own fear just increases my state of high anxiety.

My words of comfort to Debi lack any real conviction and we both know what the deal is, but as we hug in silence our two hearts beat as one (song lyric). Our brief hug is ended by the sound of the doctors coming down the hall with all of those starched white coats rustling together while they murmur amongst themselves.

Dr. Pharaoh enters my room with his normal regal bearing, however his entourage has suddenly stopped talking. By their lack of chatter (these are after all college boys) I can tell that they are concerned that this story may not have a happy ending. How quickly life's pages turn, just five minutes ago my main concern was avoiding an unnecessary biopsy on Monday, now I'm worried that I may really need one today. The results of that one medical procedure represent the fork in the road between misery or victory. (God help me!)

Dr. Pharaoh stands at the foot of my bed and without ever looking into my eyes reads from my chart telling me what I already know. Dr. Pharaoh must send Nurse Spock around the ward ahead of him so that the patients get any bad news before he ever gets to their rooms, to avoid being present while the patient goes through an emotional meltdown (not that it would really bother Dr. Pharaoh).

The "main thing" as Dr. Pharaoh puts it is that my creatinine level continues to go up which could mean that we are seeing the beginning of a rejection cycle, but we can't be sure until we run some more tests. Interrupting Dr. Pharaoh, I ask him if he is referring to a biopsy. Looking into my eyes for the first time since he walked into the room, Dr. Pharaoh tells me that although the creatinine level is a matter of *grave* concern, it is nothing that they don't deal with every day here at D.U.H. Then he tells me that I should just sit back and leave the worrying to him because that's part of his job. All that I can think about is the key word "grave" and how it's my main concern to stay out of one.

Actions speak louder than words, so when Dr. Pharaoh starts to walk out of my room I stop him by hollering, "Hey, you didn't answer my question about the biopsy." Immediately all of the soon to be doctors stop in their tracks and stare at me in silence, as if they know better than to question the mighty Dr. P. Turning back around to face me before he goes into the next room, Dr. Pharaoh says, "Mr. Gordon, I will let you know when I have decided to biopsy your kidney and that will not happen until we do some more x-rays." He disappears into the next room without even waiting long enough for me to say a word (not that it would matter).

I'm sure that to Dr. Pharaoh this is just another day at the office but to me this is the whole ball of wax. I haven't had a chance yet to ask him the question that has been bugging me, so I get the attention of the last young doctor in the line going down the hall, and I tell him to let Dr. Pharaoh know that I want him to come back to my room because I have some concerns.

Mortified that I would put him in this awkward position the young wannabe Doctor points to himself with one of those, who, me, looks on his face and I nod my head to prod him into action. You would think that no one has ever questioned Dr. Pharaoh before because I think that this young doctor looks more frightened than I do.

Now Dr. Pharaoh comes striding back into my room, but this time the young doctors' furtive glances have been replaced by wide eyed stares of amazement while they filter into the room looking like they don't want to miss the fireworks.

Usually when I talk with Dr. Pharaoh I'm lying in bed, but this time we are standing there eyeball to eyeball. I start off with the bottom line by asking him a direct question in front of his students, "Dr. Pharaoh, isn't it possible that my creatinine level is higher because I'm getting too much Cyclosporine?"

You could cut the tension in the air with a knife. The wannabe doctors can't believe that I have confronted Dr. Pharaoh (neither can I). Without any hesitation Dr. Pharaoh gives me my answer, "Sure it could be caused by too much Cyclosporine, but there are a lot of other things that could be the problem, and don't forget that more than one thing can go wrong at the same time."

Stunned by the thought that we could be dealing with more than a simple choice between rejection or too much Cyclosporine, I know that the mighty Dr. Pharaoh speaks the truth. A deep sense of foreboding fills my soul because I know that I did not take as much Cyclosporine this morning as he thinks I did. I wish that I could just fall at Dr. Pharaoh's feet and confess my subterfuge, but I believe that would just be a different way to die.

Then Dr. Pharaoh continues by saying, "Yes, if I were a gambling man I would guess that it could well be too much Cyclosporine, but if we guess wrong and lower the dosage when in actuality we are dealing with rejection: we would blow that kidney right out of there." BOOM! I feel like a grenade just exploded from deep inside of my body (stunning me into silence).

Without waiting for any response Dr. Pharaoh goes out the door and it's just as well because Debi and I both have those long distant stares on our faces as we sit in silence trying to understand what is going on. Oh, what misery there is in my heart. I feel like turning state's evidence and throwing myself on the mercy of the court. I wish that I could tell Dr. Pharaoh about how I made an adjustment to the Cyclosporine dose this morning (just following his own protocol except that I'm following it three days in advance).

I'm too blown away right now to explain the logic behind the act that might kill me (it doesn't seem too smart right now, but at least I'm not puking).

I don't know how long Debi and I had been sitting there in silence but I do know that I was in the middle of a 'woe is me' cycle (justifiable woe). I had just started thinking that things couldn't be much worse than they are right now when the man from transportation knocks on my door ready to cart me (literally) down to x-ray to see if my old kidneys are producing renin ("native kidneys" in the vernacular of the trade).

Oh yeah, that's how things could be worse, my old kidneys could be putting out renin meaning that they need to be cut out of my body while at the same time my new kidney could be rejecting (that's what a bad day on the transplant ward is like). Rolling down the hall towards my destiny I reflect on what is riding on this one x-ray (everything). I have a song playing in my head and it's from the television show, "Hee Haw." "Deep dark depression, excessive misery" (sing along with me) "if it weren't for bad luck I'd have no luck at all."

Chapter 21

ANGEL IN THE EVENING

HAVING SOMETHING DONE at a teaching hospital (such as seeing if your native kidneys are producing renin) means that the person with the experienced hands isn't touching you, but rather they are explaining the procedure to some rookie who is the origin of your pain. To check your native kidneys to see if they are producing renin, the rookie doctor sticks a long plastic needle into the vein in your arm and then tries to thread it to God knows where.

I learned a little about human physiology as the rookie doctor explains to me that the reason the inside of my upper arm feels like something is pulling apart is because blood veins have little valves, (back flow prevention) and what I'm feeling is the needle having trouble getting past these valves without hanging up.

Sometimes knowledge alone isn't enough and experienced hands are what it takes to get the job done. The rookie technician was having a problem threading the needle past a certain point and I'm sure that it was easy for the technician to tell that I was uncomfortable, so to make me feel more at ease he tells me that I might feel some negative sensations (feels like pain to me).

D.U.H. must have a three strikes rule with their medical students because after the rookie technician failed three times to get the little white plastic tube past the valve in my upper arm, the real doctor finally steps in and with one twist of his wrist the sends the little white tube where he intended to send it, completing the test in just a few seconds.

Naturally, I'm curious to find out what the test revealed, but this doctor and the young technician are practicing their poker faces as they refuse to give me any indication of whether or not my native kidneys are producing renin. The unresponsive nature of the doctor and his young technician makes for a rather anxious ride back to my room. If my old kidneys were not putting out renin then what is to be gained by leaving me in the dark, and if my old kidneys are putting out renin then the Doctors could have to go back in to cut them out (oh God). When the man from transportation delivers me back to my room, I find Debi worried sick about what the outcome of the test may mean (welcome to the club).

The squeaking out in the hall announces the arrival of Nurse Squeaky with my lunch tray that I had missed while the doctors were playing the medical equivalent of Go Fish. The fact that she has saved me a food tray makes me feel like she cares about me. For one brief, shining moment I felt a touch of human compassion and wonder if Nurse Crabb had it when she was young too (I doubt it).

Before I can eat two bites of my meal the guy from transportation is back at my door telling me that they need me back down at x-ray to verify that my new kidney is getting the proper blood supply (apparently the artery can get crimped [a stenosis in the vernacular of the trade]). The good news about this test is that it's just an x-ray, the bad news is that they inject some dye in your arm that makes it feel like your brain is cooking. Before long I am once more rolling back to my room (still none the wiser).

Just as the evening meal is being delivered, Nurse Squeaky comes into my room with the news that today's x-ray results were negative. As my heart sinks Nurse Squeaky sees the despondent look on my face, so she quickly informs me that negative results are good news because that means they didn't find any abnormalities (I should have known that in medical terms negative results is a positive). Of course, with the x-rays coming back negative we are back to not being certain exactly what is behind the decline in function of my new kidney, but at least there are two possible reasons that have been ruled out.

After Nurse Squeaky leaves Debi and I just sit staring at each other in silence being so worn down by the events of the day. At this point we aren't even thinking, just vegetating, until Nurse Spock comes into the room. Without any apparent emotions, she delivers the news that since the x-rays today were inconclusive, Dr. Pharaoh will probably want to do a biopsy on the graft tomorrow morning (on the transplant ward even the good news hurts).

Debi and I decide to take a lap around the ward before bedtime just to unwind a little. Down the hall we can hear the happy nattering from the nurses' station, but for some reason it disappears when Debi and I walk by. little hairs on my neck prickle up when I look over at the nurses behind the counter because they are all averting their eyes (they must know that I am going to have a biopsy). What a difference a couple of days of bad blood test results can make.

I hope the subdued reaction from the nurses isn't because they are thinking that I could be rejecting the kidney that my brother gave me (bummer). Once again I don't like the vibes that I'm getting. The nurses might be putting a "REJECTION" card on the door to my room right now. I know that probably no "REJECTION" card will be waiting on me back at my room, yet still, if the biopsy comes back positive the yellow card with the red letters on my door will be the least of my worries. I hate to even think about everything that goes on with the rejection protocol, all kinds of bad stories end with "but the kidney rejected."

Back in my room Debi and I know that my current situation calls for divine intervention, so we pray silently together. I don't know what Debi was praying for, but as for me, I was asking for some kind of a sign to let me know if I am doing the right thing by reducing my medication without my doctor's knowledge. The announcement that visiting hours are over brings the news that tomorrow will be here in three short hours (with a biopsy not far behind). Debi and I hug each other a little tighter and hold each other a little longer than usual tonight because we know what tomorrow may bring.

Quiet desperation grips my soul as I sit alone in my room, too tired to think and too scared to sleep. I sit there in a stupor until there comes a knocking at my door (Poe me). Standing at my door is a man that I have never seen before, who is about the same age that I am, but he is wearing a white doctor's coat while I am wearing pajamas. Without hesitation he walks over to my bed and quietly introduces himself as Michael from the lab.

Just when you think that your heart is sitting on the bottom life proves that it can sink still further. I suppose that Michael has come to talk with me about tomorrow's biopsy, but right off the bat Michael lets me know that this is an unofficial visit that he is making (it feels like someone just took their foot off of my chest). Michael explains to me that because he works in the lab, he is aware that I have been having a hard time of it. Then Michael goes on to tell me that he had a kidney transplant himself three years ago at Pittsburgh, and knows what it is like to be in my position because he had some problems right after surgery also.

Think for a moment that it is about 9:30 p.m. and Michael has just gotten off of work, yet instead of going straight home, he has taken the time to come to visit someone that he has never met and will probably never see again just to ease their (my) anxiety. One human reaching out to another is always touching, but timing is everything. In Michael's visit I see an angel sent here by the Lord in response to my prayer for some kind of a sign (the Lord works in mysterious ways). Michael sits down and begins to tell me all about his own transplant experience.

Apparently, Michael was totally healthy until his car was struck from behind by a truck. Bam! Just like that and his life was forever changed. Michael got his kidney from a cadaver so he was put on high doses of Cyclosporine and he had a tough time of it for the first couple of weeks until the Doctors got to the point that they could reduce the amount of Cyclosporine that Michael had to take.

Michael wants me to know that problems are a natural part of this process and although it might take a couple of years to work everything out, Michael tells me that I will survive. What a wonderful thought: I will survive. Michael telling me that I will survive makes me feel so good that the doctors ought to go out of their way to tell every patient that they will survive just to improve patient moral. No other staff member could have possibly comforted me as well as Michael was able to because, having had a transplant himself, Michael knows what it's like to be in my shoes (even though I am bare footed).

The Doctors understand the physiology but Michael understands the psychology. On top of everything else is the fact that any other staff member would be getting paid to comfort me (It's just their job five days a week ["Rocketman"]). Michael's concerns come from his heart not his head. Michael leaves me never knowing that he was an answer to a prayer, but he was and soon I am fast asleep.

Awakened by fear in the hours before dawn, over and over I hear, "What if I am wrong?"... "Then I am a dead man." Then comes the haunting refrain and I know that this is the truest thought that I have in my brain (Poetry no charge).

Doubting everything except my own self-doubts, I think in endless circles until the guy from the lab comes in wanting blood from this turnup (me). Suddenly I realize that the bad blood test results that I have been worrying about were from before I started lowering the amount of Cyclosporine that I was taking. Spontaneous dosage reduction, that's what the professionals call it when a patient decides to reduce the amount of medication that they are taking. The odds are really fifty-fifty as to the probabilities of whether I screwed up or not, and those happen to be the best odds that I've faced in a long time.

Usually the morning weigh in crew gets to my room before the guy with the sharp needle from the lab, but I guess that since today is Friday everyone wants to get their work done early if they can. The next thing that I know breakfast is being served and that's when it hits me that the morning medications will be coming pretty soon. I have to figure out exactly what it is that I am going to do this morning to separate the nurse from the bottle of Cyclosporine (they would never fall for the same trick two days in a row). Alright dear reader what would you do (think fast).

When the food service lady comes back to pick up my breakfast tray, she takes all of the dirty glasses that have accumulated in my room with her. The proverbial light bulb goes on in my head when I realize that before you can tell if your glass is half empty or half full you have to have a glass (the answer to my dilemma). There are only three clean glasses in my room and I remember that the nurses always use a glass from my room for the chocolate milk they mix the Cyclosporine dose in.

As soon as the food lady is out of my room I leap out of bed, grabbing two of the clean glasses off of the bedside, table tossing the waxy paper bag that covers them in the trash before I peer down the hall to see if the coast is clear. With the tune from the pink panther playing in my head I make my move to get rid of the glasses. Seeing that the food service lady has just gone into the next room I slip out into the hall and casually put the two glasses on her cart before stepping back into my room just as cool as you please.

Grabbing the last glass of any description in my room I get back into my bed with the glass hidden safely under the sheet (you won't find this move in the textbooks kiddies). With a big grin on my face, like the Cheshire cat that I am, I smugly wait for the nurse to bring me my morning medications (I feel pretty confident that Plan B will work because nurses don't expect patients to be able to think for themselves).

I don't have to wait long to find out if Plan B will work because in just a few minutes Nurse Crabb comes into my room with my morning medications on a little tray, announcing her arrival with a firm closing of the large wooden door. Nurse Crabb casts a jaundiced look my way as she asks me, in a sarcastic tone of voice, if my stomach is bothering me today (I answer with a puzzled look).

While it seems like Nurse Crabb has a suspicious mind today, it's a good thing that we came up with Plan B (no glass) because if I were to try Plan A (oops I'm nude). Nurse Crabb probably wouldn't even bat an eye. Seasoned veteran that Nurse Crabb is, I'm sure that she has seen it all before (that's the beauty of Plan B, Nurse Crabb will not see a thing until it's all over).

Even though I have thought everything out I am a little uneasy because Nurse Crabb is a worthy opponent, but I have the element of surprise on my side (I'll take my chances).

Biding my time until just the right moment I act like I'm interested in the drivel on T.V (as if it could compare to the drama in real life). I still remember that yesterday morning, when I told Nurse Crabb that I was feeling a little nauseous, she just picked up the entire medication tray, Cyclosporine bottle and all, taking everything with her as she left my room.

I know that I have to keep Nurse Crabb's mind occupied the whole time until she has taken the top off of the bottle of Cyclosporine because the next step is to pour the chocolate milk into the glass. If Nurse Crabb starts looking around for a clean glass too soon, she might take the medication tray with her when she goes to get a clean glass.

I'm betting that Nurse Crabb will not take a chance of spilling the Cyclosporine by carrying it with her while the top is off of the bottle. And I'm betting that Nurse Crabb will not want to go through all of the trouble to put the top back on the bottle and then put the bottle back in its box, when all she needs to do is to walk out to the nurses' station for a clean glass.

As Nurse Crabb walks over to my bedside table to put down her medication tray I ask her what her "professional opinion" is as to why my kidney is not working as well as it should. For a moment she lights up with one of her very rare smiles as she tells me that she has an agreement with the doctors that she will not do their jobs unless they do her job. Then she looks right at me and speaks in the third person as she says, "Until Dr. Pharaoh starts emptying bedpans, Nurse Crabb will be keeping any opinions to herself'" (all the while taking the top off of the bottle of Cyclosporine).

I have reached a moment of truth (such as it is). Trying not to smile is the hardest part, because I know that Nurse Crabb is going to be hot under the collar in about five seconds as I watch her eyes scanning the room for a clean glass to pour the chocolate milk into (I decide that this is a good time to be interested in T.V. again). After glancing around the room, Nurse Crabb's eyes dart back to mine and with a tone of voice like a Nuremberg prosecutor she says "Where are your clean glasses" (touchy aren't we).

In an effort to distance myself from the despicable act, I keep staring intently at the television while I mumble something about the food service lady cleaning up the dirty glasses when she picked up the breakfast tray. Exasperated, Nurse Crabb huffs out of my room leaving the medication tray on my bedside table (thank you God). I spring into action as I throw off the sheet and leap out of the bed with my secret glass.

I feel like a spy and if Nurse Crabb were to walk back into my room right now I would share a spy's fate, but I'm having fun (and saving my life). Implementing the coup-de-main of Plan B, I pour the chocolate milk into my secret glass faster than you can say Jack Flash, pausing just long enough to accurately measure out the amount of Cyclosporine that I think is most likely to keep me alive. I hold the glass up high in a victory toast before I chug the concoction (Voila, Plan B is a done deal).

Back in bed I reflect upon my smashing success with the only tell-tale signs being the empty glass of chocolate milk and the grin on my face. I didn't have to wait long for this drama to unfold, but this scene is of little importance because the ending is foretold (poetry no charge). What is Nurse Crabb going to do, un-medicate me?

I stare intently at the television while Nurse Crabb comes walking back to the bedside table, where she does a double take when she sees the purloined medication tray. Nurse Crabb stands perfectly still in front of the medication tray while I stifle a giggle (normally there isn't much to laugh at around here). There is a time delay in Nurse Crabb's fuse, about like the delay after you pull the pin out of a grenade, Boom! "What the hell is going on around here?" Nurse Crabb demands. I turn from the television and give Nurse Crabb a baffled look while I state rather matter of factly that I remembered there was a clean glass in the bedside table, so I took my Cyclosporine.

Nurse Crabb stands next to my bed in perfect silence glaring at me as if she would like to whip my butt (and thinks that she could). Nurse Crabb is livid but she still has trouble knowing exactly where to focus her anger. I look up at Nurse Crabb with my head tilted to one side and I give her my best 'what is your point' expression on my face, as I say, "I thought that you wanted me to take my Cyclosporine."

I make no exaggeration when I say that Nurse Crabb shouts back "I do!" (I hope that doesn't mean that we are married). Nurse Crabb's face is red and contorted in anger as she mumbles something about me knowing that she is supposed to watch me take my medicine as she storms out of my room, slamming the big wooden door behind her with authority (I do believe that Nurse Crabb's professionalism is waning). This may be a good time to say that one of the things that you learn playing football is that the people in the wrong color jerseys are supposed to be mad at you (if you are doing a good job).

As for me, well, I'm pretty happy at the way things turned out because I know that if I hadn't of engaged in that second subterfuge, I would be puking my guts out right this very minute. Sitting in my bed basking in the glow of a job well done, I am in an upbeat mood when Debi comes in with her own sparkling personality that anyone would like. It has been so long since both of us have had anything to really feel happy about that makes this minute feel all the better, in fact, for the first time I feel like we are finally over the hump (on the road home).

Debi and I decide to take a walk around the ward and just as we are getting underway, I see my buddy Michael from the lab (part-time Angel) and he gives me a big smile with a hearty thumbs up as we walk past each other in the hall. I know that my morning blood work looks good without any words being said (that would violate the proper protocol).

Good results on my morning blood work will mean that there will be no biopsy on my kidney today. Hooray, the wicked old witch is dead if only for today. Feelings of victory and vindication surge through my brain (Thank You God!). Who wants Friday workmanship on something like a biopsy anyway? It's hard to describe the elation of knowing that someone who was going to stick a big needle into your gut has changed their plans (perhaps it's somewhat like being shot at and missed).

Walk, walk, walk, that is all that I do all day long. Where the energy comes from is a mystery to me, surely it couldn't come from the fake eggs and the smashed corn that passed for grits. Somehow hope must be able to squeeze energy from a body that previously had none.

When Dr. Pharaoh comes sweeping into my room, leading the entourage of soon to be doctors, he has a smile on his face instead of his normal scowl. He uses me as an exhibit for the class today: symbolizing the pinnacle of medical achievement (cheating death). He talks to his young protegees as if I were an inanimate object, saying to the class that, "Mr. Gordon's body has acclimated itself to its new kidney and the medications have come into balance." Then, as if he were just stating the time of day, Dr. Pharaoh says, "if the trend continues until Monday Mr. Gordon may be going home" (alive).

Then, without further ado, Dr. Pharaoh walks out of my room leading the young doctors on to the next patient. The chatter among the young doctors is loud and happy as they file out of my room, as if this is what they went to medical school for (one more life saved). The last intern out the door turns to me with a big smile breaking across his face as he pauses long enough to give me a thumbs up before hustling on down the hall to catch up with the group.

Stunned, I sit on the edge of my bed trying to grasp the reality that all of my hopes and dreams are coming true. My trance is finally broken by the sound of Debi crying happy tears, unable to contain the emotions that bubble up inside of her. Debi and I hug and kiss, sharing a sweet victory that only comes to those who have dared and won.

With all of the tension out of her body Debi is going to take a nap in the big easy chair next to my bed, but as for me, I am too fired up to sleep. So I pick up my Walkman and with Elton John's "Rocketman" playing in my ears, I head out into the hall to take a few laps around the neighborhood. The day passes quickly without the trauma and drama that we have become accustomed to, and I am still walking when the evening meal is delivered (time flies when you are having a good time).

At last, I sleep the sleep of Kings, worry free with sweet dreams. When morning comes, I know that I need a new way to fake out the nurses so that I can adjust my Cyclosporine dosage down to allow for my weight loss.

Now dear reader, if your life depended on separating the nurse from the bottle of Cyclosporine, how would you do it? I can't seem to come up with anything new despite my concerted efforts. With every bite of my breakfast I worry and fret, because I know that the door to my room will swing open any minute now as the endless routine of The Hospital gets around to me.

The key thing to remember in this scenario is that the primary duty of the nurse is to make sure that I take the Cyclosporine in the prescribed amount (which is wrong). I can feel my fate rushing at me like a freight train and fear its arrival. In total desperation I turn to earnest prayer because I can't think of any new strategy to distract the nurse while I do what I have to do with the dosage (without getting caught). My prayer begins with me thanking God for delivering me from both death and my doctors. Then I get right to the bottom line because I know that God has to be pretty busy around this place, so I ask God to show me a way to separate the nurse from my medicine.

Even after my solemn prayer the only plausible strategies that come to my mind are Plan A and Plan B, which have already been done. I don't mind telling you that I was feeling somewhat forsaken when my sea of troubles failed to part. My frantic contemplation is put to a stop by the sound of the metal latch slapping the big wooden door (time is up).

Oh sweet deliverance, I know the answer to a prayer when I see one (the Lord works in mysterious ways). I had forgotten that today is Saturday, so both Nurse Crabb and Nurse Squeaky aren't at work today, leaving my care to a nice Young Nurse who may still be in school. Instantly I know exactly what I have to do this morning to fake out the Young Nurse, and what is even better is that I know how I can handle this situation tomorrow too (Plan A & Plan B).

If I can just make it through this weekend, on Monday D.U.H. is scheduled to reduce my medication level without my help. And if my blood work looks good then I'm out of here. If anyone reading this book still thinks that I shouldn't trick my nurse then they just aren't convinced that one more overdose could be fatal (I have no doubt).

Trying not to smile like the Cheshire Cat that I am I look at the Young Nurse with her innocent eyes, while putting my hand on my stomach and a sick look on my face. I tell the her that I just ate breakfast, so I'm too full to take my medicine right now without getting sick. Her eyes are full of compassion while she tells me that she can come back in a few minutes (refer to your play book because we are running Plan A).

Do I feel guilty about having to trick this nice young nurse? That's like me asking you if you would take a second drink from a glass of sour milk. This is what I'm thinking about while I look back into my room through the small crack in the bathroom door, waiting for just the right moment to run Plan A. I have plenty of time to think while I wait for the young nurse to bring back her medication tray, so I start thinking about my chances of pulling this off. I realize that it's not the odds that worry me, it's the stakes. If I'm right about being over medicated and I successfully run Plan A, then I avoid having a biopsy, but if I'm wrong in my original assumptions I will end up dead.

It's not a hard decision to make because with any other course of action there is no way to avoid puking my guts out (I'm at the end of my rope). If my logic is correct the only thing standing between me and a miserable death is my ability to trick this Young Nurse today & tomorrow (I am committed to the mission). The hard part is making sure that the she leaves the Cyclosporine behind when she runs out of my room.

Let me ask you the reader a question. Would you rather die by a firing squad, or would you rather drink a concoction that would kill you by making you puke yourself to death? Well, on the transplant ward they don't offer the choice of a nice quick firing squad, or there would be a lot more noise around here (if you can't think of a better plan don't criticize mine).

Peering back into my room through the cracked door I wait for events to unfold as the Young Nurse finally returns with her medication tray. Watching closely to make certain that I don't make my move too soon, I wait until she has taken the top off of the bottle of Cyclosporine and poured the chocolate milk into the glass. It's hard to run without spilling everything and grizzled combat veteran that I now am I know this young nurse is going to be running in about five seconds.

Dropping my hospital gown to the tile floor I take a few steps out of the bathroom with a look of faked amazement on my face. In a heartbeat the young nurse predictably goes squealing out of my room, looking genuinely surprised as she apologizes all of the way out the door (I guess the young nurse feels like she should have knocked on my door to be sure that I knew that she was there). I hustle across the room trying not to giggle because I know that my life depends on me finishing my mission before the Young Nurse comes walking back in with reinforcements. I hoist my glass up high in a quick toast, thanking God for letting me live one more day, and then I chug the adjusted dose of the wonder drug.

One thing that I notice is that when you take Cyclosporine in a dose that does not exceed the maximum dose set by the manufacturer, the side effects really are not all that bad (just one or two hot flashes as it bounced off of my stomach). No sooner had I scampered back to the bathroom to retrieve my hospital gown than the young nurse comes knocking loudly on the door to my room. She starts apologizing until her eyes fell on to the empty glass of chocolate milk and everything comes to a stop.

The Young Nurse turns towards me, exclaiming,"Mr. Gordon, I am supposed to watch you take your medication." One of life's lessons that I have come to understand is that when someone needs an answer, it does not always need to be one particular answer, sometimes any old answer will do. I look at the young nurse's concerned eyes with a placid look on my face and tell her that I have been taking the Cyclosporine on my own for the last couple of days (true).

When the results from this morning's blood work come back from the lab, I know that it is judgement day on the transplant ward and it turns out that my kidney is working better than ever (hallelujah time on the sinner's pew). All day long I am on cloud nine and Debi is right by my side as we spend most of the day singing, "We are going to get out of this place if it's the last thing we ever do, girl there is a better place for you and me"(good song). The good blood work means that no one will be hurting me over the weekend, so I don't have any problems until Monday. If things work out right I will be able to avoid the biopsy that has been hanging over my head and I might even be able to go home (oh yeah).

When Sunday morning comes, I wake up early excited at the prospects for running Plan B successfully. I know that Plan B is going to work and so is my kidney (I am a consecrated man). When the young nurse comes into my room with the morning dose of Cyclosporine, I engage her in conversation so that she will not notice that there aren't any clean glasses in my room until the top is off of the bottle of Cyclosporine. She probably won't look for a glass until she is ready to pour the chocolate milk.

The young nurse goes for the old no clean glasses in the room trick (Plan B) hook, line and sinker, in fact, it is so easy that the sense of accomplishment that I get from completing my mission is nowhere near as strong as it was when Nurse Crabb played this same game with me (just saved my life, ho hum). The news that my blood work Sunday indicates that my new kidney is continuing to do better doesn't come as much of a surprise to me since I have been feeling good ever since my blood work started looking better (physiological or psychological, I don't really care).

Debi and I have a nice day and we spend most of it just being in love, while we take long walks around the ward, dreaming about going home (alive). I notice one big difference in our walks around the ward today, something fundamental has changed. Instead of looking into every room, trying to understand what is going on in the life of the current occupant, today I am making an effort to look the other way whenever we pass an open door so that the flame of hope that burns in my heart will not be extinguished by someone else's sorrow (I'm beginning to understand why Nurse Spock always acts so detached). In the beginning I felt compelled to look into every room that we walked past because I didn't understand what was going on, and now I have to look the other way when we walk by an open door because I do understand (good luck my friends).

Late Sunday evening, after visiting hours were over and Debi had gone back to her hotel for the night, I hear a gentle knocking on my door. Dr. Bigg sticks his head around the door with a smile on his face that tells me that this visit is not about anything bad because people do not smile at you when they are delivering bad news (unless it's Nurse Spock). Dr. Bigg sits down in the chair next to my bed and tells me that as long as my blood work looks good in the morning, they are going to let me go home tomorrow (oh, how I have longed to hear those words). I'm sure that no happier news is ever delivered to a man who is leading a normal life, because in a normal life, things don't get this desperate until it's too late for things to get any better.

On the transplant ward you learn to not let yourself get too excited about something as important as going home if there is anything at all that could ruin your plans, but here I am listening to the words that I have been longing to hear and I'm not going to hold my heart back from enjoying the news that I am going home tomorrow. All of my dreams have come true and all of my prayers have been answered.

In this moment of euphoria, as I realize that I am going to escape from this portal to hell, I go out on a limb and explain to Dr. Bigg everything that I have been through. I include how I have taken a reduced dose of Cyclosporine for the last four days. The importance of the correlation between my reduced medication level and my improved kidney function is not lost on Dr. Bigg.

Dr. Bigg knows that I have nothing to gain from this disclosure (I'm doing it all for science). Dr. Bigg thanks me for my candor (perhaps some future patient can avoid the hell that I went through). The thing that amazes Dr. Bigg is that I could do something like take less Cyclosporine than I was supposed to because the nurses are supposed to watch me take my medications to see that something like this does not occur.

It seems to me that Dr. Bigg is looking for a scape goat to blame this success on, so I explain Plan A and Plan B to Dr. Bigg. Fortunately, he has a good sense of humor, so we share a good laugh together before Dr. Bigg heads home from another day at the office and I am on my way home from Hell.

Immediately I phone Debi with the wonderful news that we are going home tomorrow, but she hasn't gotten back to her hotel room yet. I am too excited to sleep, so I get up and start walking around the ward with my mind racing in a hundred different directions as I sing, "I'm going to get out of this place!" in my head. There are only so many ways to say, "Thank you, Lord!" and "Thank you Jimmy!" but I am sure that I cover them all while I walk around the transplant ward contemplating living a normal life again.

Things are pretty quiet on the transplant ward on Sunday nights so it is peaceful in the dimly lit halls while I take my solitary walk. I don't want to look into any of the rooms as I stroll past because tonight, I am living the dream and I don't want it to be ruined by someone else's nightmare. As soon as I turn the first comer I can see that the Old Man of the Ward is needing his nurse because the light above his door is burning like a beacon.

Quickening my pace, I close the distance between me and the Old Man of The Ward's room. When I look into his room, I see the Old Man lying in his bed, trapped by his web of tubes. He is staring forlornly through his open door, looking for help that apparently is slow in coming.

The night nurse isn't hard for me to find, sitting on her ample butt talking to a female patient who doesn't require anything that might be considered work. Taping lightly on the partially open door, as if I need permission to ask the night nurse to fulfill the duties that she is being paid to provide, I tell her that the Old Man needs her. She just rolls her eyes and says, "He always needs something." Then she turns her attention back to the conversation that I had interrupted as if nothing had ever disturbed the chatty flow (which indeed nothing has).

Racing back around the ward to the Old Man's room I peer inside, expecting to see the Old Man looking just like he has always been (flat on his back in bed looking like he is about to draw his last breath). But the current reality in room 243 is far worse than any fear that ever lurked within my worried mind. The Old Man of The Ward is up on his feet in one last defiant struggle with death. Wanting to walk out of this man-made hell has driven the Old Man to strain against his tethers, but the worst part of it all is seeing the confusion on the Old Man's face as he tries to understand the demons that confront him.

If the Old Man is like a fly trapped in his web of tubes then the night nurse who refuses to come to his aid is the black widow maker.

I tell the Old Man to stand still while I go get the head nurse. I start on my mission of mercy, racing back around the ward to the nurses' station where I find the head nurse doing paperwork in her office with the door partially open. I know that the head nurse is the only person who can help the Old Man of the Ward in this his moment of need, because any other regular nurse would just use the public address system to notify the black widow maker that the Old Man in room 243 is needing her again.

It's part of the medical creed that you don't help patients who aren't your responsibility because you might have to make out a report that would create an enemy, who would be anxious to return the favor. Only the head nurse is above the benign neglect that passes for medical care in absence of a doctor's order. More because of the type of people they are instead of the position they hold, head nurses get the job done where others would fail.

Like a bolt of lightning the head nurse runs out of her office and down the hall to the Old Man's of the Ward's room, calling out to her most trusted teammate to come to assist her in room 243. I pity anyone who ever needs help from the weekend night shift at any hospital, especially on a Sunday night because the job description of the night shift is to put everything off until tomorrow. I keep walking around the ward trying to see what is going on with the Old Man of the Ward, but the head nurse keeps the door to room 243 closed while she saves another life (for now).

Chapter 22

MY GOVERNMENT HAS BEEN HERE TRYING TO HELP ME

I AM AWAKE WELL BEFORE DAWN and I am standing over by the window watching the hospital come to life as the staff members make the cold walk from their cars. I'm sure that those workers fail to see the joy in the hum drum activity of everyday life but from my side of the windowpane it sure looks good.

I hear a cheerful voice back behind me saying good morning and even before I turn around I know that it has to be John Carter from the lab here to draw my blood. He is one of the few people around here who is always in an upbeat mood and is surprised to find me awake so early. But on this particular morning I am very glad that Mr. Carter is here because this should be the last time that I ever see him (no offense).

I know that if the results of this blood test turn out to be bad then I won't be going home today, but I'm not going to let that possibility bring me down. I have learned to enjoy the good that comes with the bad in this life, and I'm going to enjoy this day as if it really is the day that I go home (just in case that it is).

I savor the hospital food on my breakfast tray because I know that I'm tasting it for the last time (hallelujah). It doesn't take long to pack the one small suitcase that I brought with me but the thing that I enjoy most is dressing in street clothes. It doesn't even bother me that I can't button my pants because my sweater covers it up (not that I care). I almost look normal and that is what this is all about. The next time that you get up early and get dressed for work think about how lucky you are to be living my dream (to be normal again).

Then Nurse Crabb comes into my room and says, "You are being evicted!" and I know that my morning blood work turned out good. Then Nurse Crabb tells me that Dr. Pharaoh has said that I can go home whenever I'm ready. Oh, what wonderful news, I could almost hug Nurse Crabb I'm so happy!

This glorious news is so momentous that it seems like there should be some kind of fanfare or at least a goodbye visit from my doctor (maybe they could ring a bell at the nurses' station). Then Nurse Crabb turns back towards me as she is getting ready to walk out of my life, and for the first time ever I see Nurse Crabb break into a full smile as she says," Mr. Gordon, take care of yourself, we don't want to see you come back here again." I realize that Nurse Crabb's attempt to be humorous along with her smile is fanfare enough (joy to the world, I'm going home).

It takes a while for Debi to check out of her hotel but she makes it over to my room just in time for us to have one good hug and a kiss before the man from transportation comes knocking on my door to take me downstairs (down elevators). The only thing that I don't like is that the man from transportation has a wheelchair that he is expecting me to ride, but I have been dreaming about walking out of this place on my own power.

The man from transportation is a nice guy and he tells me that if I were to slip and fall it would cost him his job, so reluctantly I accept his offer for a ride. I feel kind of like what Douglas MacArthur might have felt like as he waded ashore in the Philippines (I shall return).

Downstairs (elevators) at the main entrance to the hospital, as soon as I see Debi drive up in the Mercedes, I fulfill my dream by standing up out of the wheelchair and walking through the automatic doors to the outside world under my own power (escaping this portal to hell).

There is a light rain falling from grey skies and looking up at the clouds seems to purify my soul. As Debi is driving us through the hospital parking lot I look off to the left at a little side entrance and I see a disturbing image of four Cadillac station wagons waiting to load their cargo (unhappy customers).

Out on the interstate highway the clouds get darker and the rain picks up, but I just watch the world roll by until we start going down the steep hill just before the bridge over the Haw River gorge. I can see a problem at the bottom of the hill where the asphalt highway has settled more than the concrete bridge creating a huge puddle of water that is causing me some concern.

Little did I know that my closest brush with death lay up ahead and Debi's life hangs in the balance too. An eighteen-wheeler that I didn't even know existed passes us just before we get to the bridge in the left-hand lane traveling down the hill like a bat out of hell. The truck's trailer is sailing along right next to our car when the front wheels of the cab hit the huge puddle sending a wall of water up in the air which lands right on our windshield totally obstructing the view.

In a panic at not being able to see the road Debi locks the brakes just as our wheels hit the puddle, sending the Mercedes sliding sideways on the bridge in the rain between the truck and the guardrail. I know that if we even touch the truck it will send us tumbling right over the guardrail into the gorge.

The brakes are locked up and Debi is too, so I grab the steering wheel with my left hand and scream at the top of my voice, "Take your foot off the brake." It feels really weird to be steering your car from the passenger's side while looking out the side window at the road up ahead but that is the way that life hands me back control of my life (such as it is).

Divine intervention saves the day once again and we roll to a stop in the emergency lane on the far side of the bridge. Sitting in the car with the rain coming down, I wait for Debi to recover her composure. Even though I had to be just as frightened as Debi was,

I know that the danger is over now. Debi still has both hands locked on to the steering wheel as she stares straight ahead into the rain while I try in vain to get Debi out of her trance.

I wait for fifteen minutes in the rain, but Debi will still not utter a word or even turn her head to look my way, and she still has that white knuckle grip on the wheel. I now realize that Debi is in a state of shock and I worry that somebody might hit us from the rear in this rain. So I get out of the Mercedes and walk around the car in the rain to the driver's door, but I can't get Debi to get out of the car.

I take my cold, rain-soaked hand and put it tenderly on Debi's forehead the same sort of way that she would put a wet paper towel on my forehead back in the hospital, and it breaks Debi's trance. Yet still she isn't about to get out of the car, so I coax Debi into crawling over the console into the passenger's seat so that I can get out of the rain.

I never dreamed that I would end up driving home from the hospital but I had been praying to get out of there under my own power, so I'm not complaining. The trip home in the rain is peaceful and Debi slips off to sleep giving me some time to reflect on my current state of affairs.

One of my Father's favorite sayings is that, "Things are never as good as they might appear nor are they as bad as they may seem," and I'm counting on that last part. I now remember all of the money that I owe Uncle Sam for last year's taxes. I had put off worrying about things like money until after the transplant because they would never have been an issue if I had died (I'll take these troubles instead of the ones that I'm leaving behind).

At last, I really am back in the driver's seat of my life and it feels pretty good. (Thank you, Lord! Thank you, Jimmy! Thank you, Debi! Thank you, Mom and Dad!) Thanks to all of my doctors and to all of their dead patients who taught them a lot of what they know.

At long last my eyes fall upon familiar trees and I know that I have made it home. No King has ever felt triumph as sweet as this. These are the thoughts that fill a happy soul as I fulfill all of my dreams by the simple act of pulling into my own driveway one more time.

When you least expect it life has a way of giving you something that doesn't fit within the limits of your expectations, we call them "surprises," and I have a big one waiting on me. When I pull into my driveway and look at my front porch, I am shocked because the whole porch is covered with cardboard boxes piled all over the place. Boxes on top of boxes, what the heck is going on here? It looks like the U.P.S. man unloaded his entire truck at my house (this is December, maybe Santa has a little labor problem).

After pulling into the garage Debi and I walk over to the front porch to investigate the piles of mysterious boxes, only to discover one of the worst scenarios. While we were gone my government has been here trying to help me. Four weeks of dialysis supplies have been delivered and piled all over the porch. I know this was intended to help me, but in reality, at this point in my life these boxes are a burden not a benefit. Two very tired campers have to carry all of these boxes inside the house so the bags of dialysis fluid don't freeze tonight.

While lugging the boxes into the third bedroom I realize that somewhere else across America today there is another burden being delivered to some other family because of this mix-up, since these dialysis supplies don't come cheap (the other burden is in the form of a notice from the I.R.S in some poor taxpayer's mailbox because of the age-old truth: somebody has to pay).

Once we get all of the boxes inside the house, I notice how cold the house is and I discover that the thermostat for the furnace has been left in the "off" position for the last three weeks, allowing the cold air to seep into every wall and every piece of furniture. The concrete slab is freezing cold and it is pulling the heat from my tired body with every step. Fortunately, before going to the hospital I had carefully stacked some wood in the wood burning stove with plenty of kindling ready for a match.

The fire starts to roar leaving Debi and I backed up to the warm stove in a very romantic setting, as if we were camping outdoors cuddled up by the campfire. As romantic as all of this is, I know that we will need a load of firewood because it will take what little firewood that we have to warm up these cold walls.

I phone my friend William Able, the firewood man, and tell him that I need a load of dry firewood (something that is a rare commodity in the middle of winter). When I tell William that I just got home from having a kidney transplant and my house is freezing cold because we left the heat pump off, William tells me that he will get me some wood first thing in the morning (good karma).

This is the first night that Debi and I have had to snuggle and in the cold room under the electric blanket we sleep in each other's arms. The next morning the house is still cold when I get up to go get the newspaper and when I open the front door, I have another surprise, but this is a nice one. There is a load of dry firewood neatly stacked right on my front porch.

William Able unloaded that firewood so quietly that he never even woke me up. I know that took special care and the fact that he didn't even knock on my door for his money brings a tear to the corner of my eye, because I know that everybody needs money right before Christmas (thank you, William).

There was a period of time that my biggest problem seemed to be finding a way to stop the weekly delivery of the dialysis supplies that I did not need. Each time the driver brought a fresh load of supplies I would tell him to let his supervisor know that I have already had my kidney transplant, and what I need is for someone to come pick these supplies up from my house not deliver more of them. After a while my third bedroom was full of dialysis supplies and my great room was overflowing, too, yet still each week more supplies were delivered.

One would think that all of the forces of the universe would be aligned with me in my attempts to get someone to come pick up my dialysis machine and stop the weekly delivery of supplies that are making my house look like a warehouse. Somewhere across America there is someone waiting for a peritoneal dialysis machine to become available to save their life and in a different American home there is a taxpayer who has to pay for all these supplies.

I phoned Dr. Calm's office and I talked to the people at the transplant clinic at D.U.H., yet still every week, just like clockwork the truck comes to deliver my burden (carrying the boxes inside).

Inspired to save some poor taxpayer and some sick kidney patient, I phone the company in Sumter, S.C. that distributes the dialysis supplies. I get past the receptionist to a supervisor who tells me in a nice way that the company could only take instructions from the federal government since they were in charge of administering the dialysis program.

The Feds presumably take their instructions from doctors, so I call Dr. Calm's office one more time to explain what I heard, but the office manager tells me that once the federal government takes over it is out of local hands and that the supplies should stop coming automatically (I agree). When I call back to the transplant clinic at D.U.H. they tell me that I am the only one who has ever had this problem (sure).

Finally, I phone the right place to make these supplies stop coming to my house each week, since it only took one phone call to Congressman Floyd Spence's office to stop this insanity. But I still have a house full of boxes and a dialysis machine that I need to get rid of.

Just as I thought that I was getting my life back to normal, one morning I decided to take my blood pressure before I even got out of bed. Thinking that I would be looking at a very low set of numbers since I had been sleeping, wow, was I in for a shock. My blood pressure was so high that I'm surprised that it didn't blow my head right off of my shoulders.

Just like snapping your fingers my whole world changes and I am thrown back into a life-or-death struggle with high blood pressure. Agonizing over this frightening turn of events I wait for Dr. Calm's office to open so that I can call them for advice. I pass the time by taking my blood pressure every ten minutes and fortunately I can see that my blood pressure is steadily going down for some reason (I wish that I knew why). Dr. Calm tells me that high blood pressure is not something that they would normally expect to see after a successful transplant, so he isn't sure exactly what is going on. Then he tells me that I should phone the transplant clinic at D.U.H. to get their input while I keep monitoring the situation.

Talking to D.U.H. brings no enlightenment, but my blood pressure continues to drop throughout the day leaving me puzzled but not too worried as I go to bed for the night. We don't have the foggiest idea what made my blood pressure spike up this morning or why it came back down this afternoon, but I do know that this calls for a prayer before I drift off to sleep.

After a few hours of sleep I wake up, so I decide that I will take a quick blood pressure reading. My eyes nearly pop out of my head when I see the numbers. Now I'm afraid to go back to sleep but I have to have some rest, so I lay there in bed waiting for tomorrow to come. Hoping for some good news in my life I decide to get a blood pressure reading before I get out of bed, but when I see the numbers I want to leap out of my skin. I've never heard of anyone having blood pressure this high except for me on the night after my transplant.

Afraid that I might be on the verge of a heart attack or a cerebral hemorrhage, I phone Dr. Calm's answering service and ask for the doctor on call to phone me. The doctor who is on call for emergencies returns my call almost right away and I explain the situation that I find myself in with the very high blood pressure readings. He tells me, quite frankly, that he doesn't have any idea as to what is causing my high blood pressure but he recommends taking some kind of action, and I totally agree.

The doctor says that a good place to start would be for me to take a dose of the blood pressure medicine that I was on prior to my transplant and then I should try to get some rest before coming into Dr. Calm's office for him to examine me first thing in the morning. It's hard to sleep when you know that you may never wake up, so I lie restlessly in bed for about an hour before I decide to check my blood pressure again. The numbers are so much higher that they almost scare me to death so, I phone the doctor again to tell him that my blood pressure is still going up (way up).

The doctor on call recommends that I take a second dose of my old blood pressure medicine. Since it is two o'clock in the morning it seems like the only option that we have (if it weren't for bad options, I would have no options at all). This strategy didn't work the first time and it doesn't work the second time, either, because my blood pressure is now up to 215 over 145. I phone the doctor on call for the third time and I don't mind telling you that I'm scared (Debi is terrified).

Doctors don't have magic wands and the doctor on call tells me that he doesn't know what is going on inside my body, so he does not know what to do about it (sound logic). Then he tells me that this would be like me asking my mechanic to fix my car over the phone, and he tells me to be at Dr. Calm's office when they open up at 9:00 a.m. (if I'm still alive).

My brain must be about to explode and I am deflated by the inability of medical science to bring my blood pressure under control, so I get up out of bed even though it is 3:34 a.m. and I am so tired that I could just collapse. My blood pressure, for some strange reason, goes up every time that I lay down and it goes back down when I stand up (but I do not know why). I put some oat meal in the microwave, thinking that perhaps I can pull some of my blood into my digestive system and by that means reduce my overall blood pressure.

I go into the room with my pool table just to hit some balls around the table while I eat my oatmeal and since medical science doesn't seem to be able to do anything to bring my blood pressure down, I turn to prayer. I pray an earnest prayer asking God to help me and because I am alone in the pool room, I pray out loud (like Jimmy would). I eat my oatmeal and shoot some more pool, but pretty soon I'm so tired that I need to sit down. I take my blood pressure again and to my relief my blood pressure has started corning back down (hallelujah).

I am the first person at Dr. Calm's office in the morning and after they open up he examines me right away. By this time my blood pressure is only slightly elevated so Dr. Calm goes ahead and phones the transplant clinic at D.U.H. to discuss my blood pressure problems. But all of the King's horses and all of the King's men have no idea why my blood pressure went up so high last night. Whoever Dr. Calm is talking to at D.U.H. tells him that I am the first patient that has ever had this kind of complication (and lived to report it).

I already know that I'm in a life-or-death struggle again, I just don't know what is making my blood pressure act this way. Thus begins my new schedule of going to bed at night only to have my blood pressure go up so high that I have to get back up out of bed in the middle of the night for "oatmeal hour," as I call my midnight pool shooting practice.

I really hate getting up in the middle of the night when I am so tired, but being tired is better than being dead, so I stick to this routine because it works. I'm just glad that I have discovered that my blood pressure will go back down if I can keep standing up. Why my blood pressure goes up at night and back down during the day is a mystery to my doctors, but that is what happens so I just keep on doing what I have to do to stay alive, and I am getting pretty good at pool.

There is an old saying that pretty well sums up this stage of my life: "There once was a man sitting full of worry when a voice comes to him saying, cheer up things could be worse. So he cheered up and sure enough, things got worse."

I am so tired that I feel like a zombie as I stumble through the day making a couple of sales calls, trying to make my daily bread. I'm making a sales call on Johnny Tillman, who is a nice guy that owns a food distribution business, and since I have to wait a few minutes to see him I decide to phone my house to see if there are any messages on my answering machine.

Then after listening to my cheerful greeting to the world on my answering machine I hit the button to listen to my messages and I hear the last voice on the face of the earth that I would want to hear. The sound of Nurse Spock's voice cuts through me like a knife and she is doing what she does best: delivering bad news (make that really bad news).

Without so much as a hello, Nurse Spock drones along in a tone of voice more suitable for announcing flight departures, but her words couldn't have had more impact if she had shouted them, "Mr. Gordon come to D.U.H. immediately, we all think that your kidney is rejecting."(end of message beep beep).

Just like that my whole world comes tumbling down on top of me and as I hang up the phone I can hear the secretary saying, "Mr. Tillman can see you now." I feel like falling on the floor in a heap and if I thought that would do any good at all, I would try it. I know that when I get to the hospital my room will have one of those little yellow cards on the door that says: "REJECTION" in big red letters.

I go through the motions of a sales call but all that I want to do is to get home to Debi, because I know that even though telling Debi will not change a thing, I also know that it will make me feel better to share my heartache with her.

The sales call on Johnny Tillman ought to be written up in marketing textbooks, not that it was so great, just that it took place at all. I am not able to get Johnny comfortable enough to go ahead and close the deal, probably because I am shaking so much that I look like a crook. I decide to quit while I am ahead when Johnny agrees to take my proposal home over the weekend so that he can review the numbers, because I need to get out of his office before I break down and cry.

Out in my car, racing home to Blythewood, I'm terrified at the unknown. The only thing that is known is that everyone at D.U.H. thinks that my kidney is rejecting. I'm so full of woe that when I think about the fact that I don't have a shunt in my arm for emergency dialysis, it doesn't even bother me because the misery meter is already maxed out.

My tires squeal as I turn into my garage and I go running inside like I'm Paul Revere, but I'm shouting, "I'm Rejecting! I'm Rejecting!" until I can see that Debi already knows. She is crying and I can see that she has already started packing our bags for the trip back to hell. We hug without words as tears stream freely down both of our faces, as we stay locked in an embrace that we know could be our last one here at home in Blythewood.

Out on the interstate highway in a night trip to D.U.H., my motor hums along in a dull, low-pitched monotone that swirls around in my brain mixing with my desperate thoughts. I have never made this trip to D.U.H. in the dark before but it suits my mood. We drive through the darkness in silence except for the hum of the motor drowning out the sound of Debi trying unsuccessfully not to whimper.

It is a big help to have Debi here by my side, yet still I feel pretty lonely as I drive along in the dark. Then it starts to rain and my car seems like it weighs a ton as it makes its way through the storm, then I realize that it isn't my car that feels heavy it is my heart.

As the cold, stone walls of D.U.H. come into view, a chill sweeps over my body as I remember the day that we left here headed home with my new kidney. I was afraid that somehow the hospital building would chase after me, but now I realize that I am chasing the hospital as it spins around on this little dirt ball that we all live on (there is perfect order in the universe even when none is apparent).

Chapter 23

BACK IN HELL AGAIN

YOU DON'T SAY THE TITLE TO THIS CHAPTER you sing it, just like Willie Nelson sings, "On the Road Again," but with a few words changed to suit the occasion.

When an internationally known medical center leaves a message on your answering machine telling you to come to the hospital immediately because they think your kidney is rejecting, then when you get to the hospital you would think that they would be expecting you. Knowing that rejection is a very serious threat I'm sure that the hospital is prepared to spring into action upon my arrival, but the only attention that I'm receiving so far is the third degree from the lady at the admissions desk.

It would seem to me that someone from the transplant clinic would let the admissions office know to be on the lookout for me, but I'm not showing up anywhere in the computer tonight. Transportation should have someone ready to whisk me off to the part of the hospital that handles kidney rejection, but the only rejection treatment around here is coming from the admissions lady who is peering over her glasses as she asks me again who it was that told me to come to D.U.H. right away.

The snooty attitude of the admissions lady reminds me of a front desk clerk at an expensive hotel when they see that your credit card didn't go through; it's really quite similar because the admissions lady isn't looking for my information in her computer, she is trying to find out where the money will come from to pay for my care.

This show-me-the-money mentality irritated me when I experienced it back when I first came here for my transplant, but now being a little better seasoned I just ask the admissions lady to phone Doctor Pharaoh at home to verify everything. The consternation on her face makes a slight smile break across mine.

At night there isn't much going on so transportation has someone come right over to take me to my room. Although I want to walk, the man from transportation tells me that it's protocol for patients who come in rejecting their kidney to ride to the ward so they don't fall down and sue D.U.H.

Seems like a doctor would be deciding if I have to ride in a wheelchair, not a lawyer. I think to myself as I sit down for a ride while poor Debi has to walk. More than anything else right now I'm reeling from hearing how casually I was thrown into the pile of those who are "rejecting their kidney." I guess when we get to the ward my room will have one of those dreaded little yellow cards on the door that say "rejection" in big red letters.

When we get to the ward the head nurse looks at me like I am a load of extra work being dumped on her doorstep (which I guess I am). The good news is that there is no little yellow card on my door, the bad news is that this is an orthopedic ward. I turn to the man from transportation as he is getting ready to leave my room and I say with a weak smile, "Are you sure that the protocol for patients who come to D.U.H. rejecting their kidney says take them to the orthopedic ward?" As he leaves my life the man from transportation utters these words of wisdom, "Protocol calls for me to do what I'm told to do."

No one has even thought about where Debi will spend the night but the big easy chair in the corner of my room solves that problem for tonight (I wonder how many rules that breaks). I don't know what you would expect from an internationally known medical center if you were admitted because you might be rejecting your new kidney, but I expect things to start happening (at least people should be rushing around shouting code yellow while they try to save my life).

Debi and I sit anxiously in my hospital room staring into each other's eyes while we wait for something to happen, but nothing does. I don't want to say anything negative to whoever my nurse is lest I be labeled "uncooperative," but I don't want to be labeled "dead" either. So after a while I decide to walk up to the nurses' station to see what is going on, because Nurse Spock definitely said the word "immediately" in her message on my answering machine.

Being very laid back on the exterior is just a facade because inside my mind every alarm that I have is going off. My body is in complete turmoil as I casually ask the head nurse if someone is coming to pick me up to take me to X-ray or something, to which she responds with these prophetic words, "We do not have any doctor's orders for you." Dumbfounded, I look at her with a puzzled expression on my face and ask if the lab is sending someone to draw my blood for testing? Without even glancing up from her paperwork she mutters, "No doctor's orders," in a way that lets me know that this will be the answer to any question that I am likely to ask, so I just say, "Well, if I am rejecting my kidney a lot of bad things can happen in ten hours."

I turn away from the nurses' station and walk back to my room feeling confused as to why it was so important for me to drive up here tonight. When I walk through the door to my room the first thing that Debi asks me is, "Are they coming?" to which I reply, "No doctor's orders." Debi and I just sit without saying a word as we stare blankly into each other's eyes. I don't know what Debi is thinking but I'm sitting here thinking, "This is how people die."

The extent of the medical care that I receive that night was to be awakened every four hours to check my temperature and blood pressure (I'm certain letting me sleep would have been better for me but a hospital can't make any money at night if they just let you sleep). In the morning it's one of those no breakfast days until after my tests are complete, which would be ok with me except for the fact that I never ate supper last night because of all of the excitement.

Transportation doesn't send anyone to take me to the transplant clinic until 9:25 a.m. because they don't have any doctor's orders (or common sense). I'm steaming mad because Debi and I could take the elevator at the end of the ward down to the first floor and we would be right down the hall from the transplant clinic. In fact, I could have already been at the clinic by now even if I had waited until this morning to drive up from Blythewood. Even though I wake up less than 200 yards from where I need to be, D.U.H. can't seem to get me to the clinic on time.

By the time that we roll into the transplant clinic, the waiting room is teeming with people. This is the same waiting room that I came to the first day that I ever came to D.U.H. for evaluation. There is a hushed chatter coming from the crowd as the brand-new patients stand out like newlyweds, as they smile timidly at everyone while they are filling out the endless forms. I can now look at the waiting room through the eyes of a more veteran patient and even though I am at a more critical stage than many of these patients, I don't have that sense of fear that someone has when they come to the transplant clinic for the very first time (been there).

Seeing that I can distinguish which patients are brand new rookies I turn my attention to the other patients in the waiting room and they seem to fall into a couple of groups; those who are reading (like they are just here for a routine consultation) and then there are those who look much too tense to read (like me). Most of the patients who are not reading are holding hands with the person that is sitting next to them with anxious expressions on their faces, that makes me think that they are waiting for bad news.

Then I hear my name being called and I'm glad that I'm not having to wait in the regular line. As I'm being weighed the nurse with my chart asks me what the problem is and I just say, "That's what I'm here to find out," as I try for a little comic relief. But the nurse must have left her sense of humor at home because, while I'm amused, she is not. A quick test tube of blood from my arm and it's back out into the waiting room I go, where Debi and I anxiously hold hands as if we are waiting on bad news (which we are because if my blood work was looking good then we wouldn't even be here today).

Bad news travels fast and in a few minutes the nurse comes walking up to me followed by a man from transportation pushing an empty wheelchair that I know is for me.

When the nurse makes her way across the waiting room to where we are sitting, she tells me that I am being sent over to "ultrasound." The word "ultra" worries me because anything extreme sounds like it could hurt, so I ask the nurse about the only commodity that I am interested in right now (pain). When I ask the nurse if the ultrasound test will hurt, she answers, "The ultrasound won't hurt," but her tone of voice is not reassuring.

Rolling along in the hall on the way to ultrasound I ponder the inflection the nurse had used when she told me that the ultrasound would not hurt, and I know that I am just waiting for the other white shoe to fall. Three technicians work on me in ultrasound. Fortunately they don't have to stick any sharp needles in my arm but it's still very uncomfortable because, after greasing up the area over my brand new kidney, they start running the unit that transmits the sound waves back and forth over this tender region.

Fear of major pain while I am feeling minor pain keeps me on edge because I don't know what to expect. The three technicians engage me in conversation as they go over the kidney area time after time, distracting me from my pain by letting me see the video screen that displays the image created by the sound waves bouncing through my body. They see my kidney on the display but I just see a black and white mass of fuzzy dots that makes me want to turn the channel.

I ask the technician who is doing most of the talking just what they expect to find, to which he replies by listing a bunch of things that could go wrong like an artery that has crimped up cutting off the blood supply to the kidney. The technician goes on to tell me that they could even find kidney stones or a variety of other conditions that could occur after surgery.

Then the technicians start talking among themselves about something on the screen that apparently only trained eyes can see because it all looks the same to me. Then the technician interprets the fuzzy screen pointing out an area in the center of the monitor that is a little whiter than the rest. He identifies it as a small reservoir of fluid that has leaked into the cavity around my new kidney, compressing everything to the point that the kidney can't do its job.

So the mystery of why my blood pressure went up when I went to sleep at night is solved: that is when the fluid would flow into the surgical cavity around my new kidney and when I would stand back up some of the fluid would drain away to other areas of my body allowing the kidney to work a little better.

This knowledge brings a new concern along with it, so I ask the technician what do they do in a situation like this, but suddenly all three technicians clam up and all of the chatter abruptly comes to an end. Repeating the unanswered question brings an odd response from the technician that I have been talking with because the rapport that we had established between us is gone, replaced by a curt tone of voice as he says quietly, "You will have to ask your doctor."

I rephrase the question to the technician, asking him if a reservoir of fluid compressing the kidney is a serious complication, but I get the same stiff response that I did before (I will have to ask my doctor).

How odd. Until just a minute ago everybody was friendly, now the technicians are acting like medical "professionals" (robots). Perturbed as I am, I put a little edge on my words as I blurt out, "I would ask my doctor if he were present." Then I hear a voice behind me that I am quite familiar with saying, "I'm right here." I know that it is Dr. Pharaoh before I even turn around but I have never seen him like this before, because he looks like a medical Samurai in all of his armor and with all of his weapons (oh God).

To my horror Dr. Pharaoh is in full surgical regalia, covered from head to foot in pale green surgical scrubs. He not only has on a mask and gloves, but he also is wearing a long apron and a clear, plastic "splatter screen" is protecting his face. You know that you are in deep trouble when your doctor is wearing an apron and a splatter screen, because it's your blood that he wants to keep off of his clothes. If you aren't bleeding when you first see your doctor wearing a splatter screen, be patient, because chances are that you will be bleeding soon. Traumatized by this vision of impending pain I now understand how Dracula's victims feel the moment they realize that he has them in his grasp.

Untethered by needles or tubes I sit up right on the table coming face to face with Dr. Pharaoh, and that's when I see what he is holding in his right hand: a large stainless steel syringe that looks like something designed to be used on a horse with the biggest, baddest needle that I have ever seen. Very ominously, the plastic safety cover is off the big needle so everything is ready to pierce mammal flesh (me).

I stammer, "Dr. Pharaoh, what are you going to do with that needle, drain off some of the fluid that is compressing the kidney" (nodding my head towards the implement in his hand)? He answers me in a loud, authoritarian tone of voice saying, "Mr. Gordon, your kidney is malfunctioning and we must find out why." He continues on, "These people are going to put in a small drain tube and I am going to do a biopsy on your kidney to see if it's rejection that we are dealing with."

My mind explodes with every horror story that I have ever heard about biopsies like the poor nurse who passed out after a couple of hours of sitting in the same position as she put pressure over the puncture site to keep it from bleeding (the poor dear). "Hold on a minute here, Dr. Pharaoh, no one ever said anything about a biopsy to me," I say to him, equaling the volume that he had been speaking in.

I can see the amazement in the technician's faces and tell by Dr. Pharaoh's eyes that he isn't used to having his instructions questioned. He answers in an even louder voice, "Mr. Gordon, we are trying to save your life!" Trying to use a little comic relief I say, "Well then, I'm glad to see that we all have the same objective," but nobody's eyes are smiling except for mine.

Fighting for time I tell Dr. Pharaoh that I haven't had any rejection symptoms like fever. The tension in the room proves to be too much for the technicians to bear and as Dr. Pharaoh and I have our little chat they all three quietly leave the room.

Now I have the full might of Dr. Pharaoh directed at me as he says, "Mr. Gordon, more than one thing can be going on at the same time in a person's body, any one of which might kill you if we don't catch it in time." I am still trying to relieve the tension with humor as I say to him, "Well tell them to get in line." Apparently, there is only one sense of humor in the room as he squints behind his mask and splatter screen, saying in the loudest volume yet, "Mr. Gordon are you refusing the biopsy?'

Seeing that building rapport is impossible, I try logic on Dr. Pharaoh. I tell him that I'm not disagreeing with him, but if the problem is that fluid is compressing the kidney and we are putting in a drain tube today, then we ought to know by tomorrow morning's blood test if it's working or not. We will not know the results of the biopsy for 48 hours, so if things do not improve by in the morning, then I would agree with you that the biopsy would be the next logical step.

Once again, I am confronted by Dr. Pharaoh, who repeats himself even louder than he was the first time as he booms, "Mr. Gordon are you refusing the biopsy?" I just look at him standing there with that huge needle in his right hand and I'm glad that I have any choice at all other than being stuck in the gut by that thing. I answer back as if he is hard of hearing telling him slowly and loudly that, "Yes, I am refusing to have the biopsy until tomorrow morning." Dr. Pharaoh does not say one word to me. He just walks out of the room, but his voice is loud enough for me to hear him saying to the technicians, "Patient refuses biopsy."

Looking down at the floor I wonder if I have just killed myself in some kind of pyrrhic victory. Before I can relax the three technicians come back into the room, but now all three of them are dressed in the same medical Samurai gear that Dr. Pharaoh had on right down to the splatter screens (I get rid of one tormenter and he is replaced by three).

"Wait a minute," I say to the three technicians, "let me guess: I'm already dead and this is hell". One of the technicians answers back that, "We will all know in just a minute because if this does not hurt, then you are dead."

I tell them that I'm glad that they found their sense of humor out in the hall and then I say, "I thought we were buddies, but when the fight started, you guys cut out." The technician that seems to be in charge looks at me through his splatter screen saying, "We have just never seen anything like that," and I respond, "Neither have I, neither have I."

Then the technician shows me something he calls the "dilater" you and I would call it a stainless steel ice pick. It's about twenty times bigger than the biopsy needle that I just avoided it and they intend to use the "dilater" to make a hole in my body to insert a drain tube (oh God, please let them not hit my kidney when they puncture me).

The technicians go back over my kidney area with the ultrasound device several times trying to be certain that they do in fact miss the kidney, but still hit the area that the fluid is collecting in. If you have ever seen on T.V. how geologists use explosives to locate pockets of oil down in the ground, well they use the same basic principle that ultrasound uses. I just hope that these technicians are as good at it as the geologists on T.V. were. All three technicians look like they are Jewish and I'm glad, because I figure that there is a high probability that they were in class on the day that they went over this procedure back in medical school.

I want to see what is going on so I lift my head up off of the table, but the technician with that "dilater" in his hand tells me to lay back down so that my abdominal muscles will relax. They are about to insert the drain tube and, as I'm sure that you know, when a masked man has a stainless steel icepick an inch from your gut you have to do what he tells you to do.

Then as I'm trying to relax, the technician braces his hand that is holding the "dilater" against his waist, just like a construction worker would with a jackhammer. Then he leans up on it and I hear a loud "Pop!" that sounds just like when a kid stomps on a maypop. Now I see why they need splatter screens (yuk, I'm all over everything). It feels weird as the warm blood dribbles past the skin that is deadened and on to normal skin (it's warm and there is a lot of it).

A little slurping sound lets me know that the "dilater" has been pulled out of me (hallelujah). Then as one technician compresses the puncture wound the other one slips a white plastic sleeve over the business end of the dilater. Oh, damn, now I understand why the stainless steel icepick is called a " dilater. " That white plastic sleeve is designed to increase the shaft diameter and they are about to increase the size of the hole they just punched into me.

Oh misery upon misery, here we go again. UUUnnngh, oh boy that hurts and even worse it scares the hell out of me. That "dilater" is plunging into me very close to my kidney. I just hope they don't nick it or something. Slurp and the dilater is back out of me, which raises my hopes momentarily, until I see the technicians put an even larger sleeve on the dilater. It's hard to relax when you know that you are about to get stuck in the gut... here we go again, UUUnnngh!

Finally, the technicians put in the drain tube and I'm rolling back to the kidney ward flat on my back, on a gurney hurting just as much as I ever did. Now I have to spend the night at the hospital just to be sure that everything went ok, and if my blood test in the morning doesn't show some improvement, Dr. Pharaoh will stick me with that huge biopsy needle (time to pray).

I'm glad to know that I'm not going back to the orthopedic ward (small comfort) and as we roll onto the kidney ward, I hear the familiar voice of Nurse Crabb barking instructions; it feels good to know that I am back where I belong. When we roll up to the nurses' station, I smile at Nurse Crabb and she looks at me saying, "I thought that I told you not to come back," to which I respond, "I'm just a tourist." (I hope).

When the man from transportation drops me off at my room, I find that Debi is already there waiting on me. It makes my heart feel better when I see her but my gut still hurts. Debi and I hug but I have to lean over to do it so that we don't make contact where they stuck the drain tube in. Then I get settled in my bed and it's plain to see that Debi has been doing a lot of crying, which makes me wonder if the doctors have told Debi something that they haven't told me.

While I am still telling Debi about Dr. Pharaoh and the biopsy fiasco, the young intern (soon to be doctor) who is in charge of the ward today comes into my room to, "Answer any questions that I may have." He is in the right place because one thing that I have plenty of is questions.

The young intern is as yet unjaded by the world within which doctors operate, where their choice of words right down to the care that they give patients is influenced as much by legal minds as medical ones. The first thing that I want to know from the intern is how often does a complication like having fluid compress the kidney occur, and when I hear that it's "rare but not unheard of," I know that they probably don't get much practice on whatever the solution is.

Then I cut right to the chase as I ask the intern what they have on schedule for me tomorrow morning, and when the intern says, "nothing at all is on schedule for you tomorrow so far, and if your blood work looks good in the morning you can go home." It's hard for me to explain the joy that swells up inside of me just knowing that there is a chance that I might be able to go back home tomorrow, but it makes me so happy that I almost cry. When you come into a hospital rejecting your kidney, you know that you may never go home again.

This great news comes as such a surprise that I forget my other questions until a pain from the base of my gut reminds me that I want to get this drain tube out of my life as soon as possible, so I ask the intern to give me some idea about how long the drain tube has to stay in me before it can be removed.

I waited so long just to get free of the Tenckhoff catheter with all of its threat of infection, not to mention how normality is denied to anyone with a tube coming out of them to a point that having the tube removed becomes an objective all of its own. Now, after just a matter of weeks since my last tube was removed, I find myself with another tube jutting from my side (bummer).

The intern has a plausible explanation about how, after a few weeks everything will dry up on its own, and then the drain tube can be removed (sure). Even though the intern's words are like music to my ears, somehow I know that scenario is too good to be true, which leads me to quip, "Save the fairy tale for the rookie patients, just tell me what the strategy is if the fluid will not stop" (let's get real).

The intern is full of enthusiasm as he tells me not to worry because, if the situation persists, they will just inject some chemicals into the area via the drain tube that will burn the tissues enough to make them stick together. It seems appropriate that the intern's two hands come together palm to palm as he illustrates the "stick together" part of all this, because it leaves his hands in the classic prayer position, and I take that as a sign that I had better say my prayers.

The thought of some burning chemicals being injected under my skin around my tender new kidney makes me grimace as I visualize everything (ouch). Since this isn't the movies, I know that this is too simple to work for me, so what I want to know is what happens when the chemical burn doesn't work. The intern looks over to me and says, "Don't worry Mr. Gordon, we can stop a leak."

Then, as I am about to relax with that assurance, the intern adds that, "We just make the solution more concentrated and try again." When I inquire as to the "protocol" in cases where the more concentrated solution fails to have the desired effect, the intern's enthusiasm seems to wane. He shakes his head slowly and says, then we would have to use acid in one last attempt and pray that it works. There is a limit on the number of times that you can do a chemical burn before everything becomes scar tissue in there, then nothing can make it stick together.

When I ask the intern what happens if the acid fails, he mumbles something about how they could always try some sort of "surgical option." I know that the acid burn had better work because I can tell that the intern is grasping at straws when he starts telling me that they could try to find the source of the leaks, maybe cut a square hole in the peritoneal membrane so that at least the fluid wouldn't be able to build up pressure on the kidney.

When the intern finally leaves Debi and I alone with each other, we look into each other's eyes as we contemplate everything that we have been through today. My entire world has changed from what it was just yesterday. About that time, it hits me that the chemical burn stuff is the good news. The bad news that went unsaid was that, if my blood work doesn't "look good" tomorrow morning, then

I will be dealing with rejection and a biopsy (have a nice day). One of the many lessons that life has taught me is to never fight all of your enemies at the same time if you don't have to, because you might lose.

After thinking things over I turn to Debi and I remind her that today in the ultrasound room, when I had asked the technicians if I was already dead and this place was really hell, they had never specifically said that this is not hell. Then a pain shoots up from the base of my gut because I had tensed up when I was thinking about my predicament. Normally a pain wouldn't make me smile, but this one does because I know that it means that I am alive. Debi hugs me as she whimpers just a little while she fights back the tears, and I know that this place is not hell or Debi would not be here with me.

Chapter 24

BURN! BURN! BURN!

THE THOUGHT OF DYING from my own stupidity torments me all night long (patient refuses biopsy). Saying no to a medical test that your doctor wants to run can have a lot of negative repercussions. It scares me to pass up an opportunity to find out if I am dealing with rejection or something as simple as nephrotoxicity from taking too much Cyclosporine, but that doesn't frighten me nearly as much as the image of Dr. Pharaoh standing there with his splatter screen on.

When I think about him stabbing my new kidney with that massive biopsy needle it makes my knees wobble (it has to leave a terrible wound). It takes two days to get back the results from a biopsy and with my luck even then it would be "inconclusive." I know that I made the right choice by avoiding being stabbed in my kidney, not only that, but we will actually know the answer sooner since I reduced my medicine and there is a fifty percent chance that I did the right thing. I like those odds, it's the stakes that I hate (everything).

No monk ever spent a night in more earnest prayer. Self-doubts surface every time that I start to drift off to sleep. If you were a condemned prisoner, would you spend your last night asleep? (I don't think so). I can't sleep either, because plan "B" when you have a kidney transplant is dialysis, and I wouldn't let them put a shunt in my arm. I feel like a pilot in a plane that is on fire (no this is much worse because I could jump out of a plane).

I am awake before the first rays of light filter in from the other side of the world and I know that before long John Carter will be here from the lab to draw my blood. John is surprised to find me awake so early in the morning, in fact I may be more awake than he is, but to him this is just another day at the office but my life is on the line. Debi begins to stir in the big easy chair over in the far comer of the room when John and I start talking, so after he leaves I go to snuggle with Debi for a while (time well spent).

The transplant ward continues its daily routine as the early morning crew comes around to check my weight. Soon the food service lady comes down the hall delivering the morning breakfast tray, but she goes right past my room without giving me any food at all, so I walk out in the hall and ask her if she forgot me this morning. She tells me that there are doctor's orders to hold my breakfast tray. Somehow knowing that even my breakfast is controlled by the outcome of this morning's blood test brings everything into perfect focus as Debi and I snuggle for a little longer while we wait to find out what fate has in store for me.

After a while I go stand by the open door to my room so that I can keep a close watch on the door at the far end of the hall that I know the guy from the lab will come through when he gets here with the results of this morning's blood work. I know how much those results mean to me (everything) and the amazing thing is that to some of the patients here it could mean more.

When the guy from the lab delivers the results to the nurse's station, all of the nurses huddle around (to see if anybody is about to become a body). Then I can see Nurse Squeaky break out of the pack and start walking straight towards me and I know that she already knows my fate. Even before Nurse Squeaky gets close enough for me to hear her shoes I can tell that she is bearing good news by the smile that is on her face.

Nurse Squeaky's words are music to my ears when she says, "You are going home today, just as soon as we can get someone up here from transportation. "Hallelujah!" I shout as I grab Debi for a hug. The thrill of victory fills every cell of my body. After Nurse

Squeaky leaves us alone, Debi and I do a little victory dance around the room, which is interrupted by the food service lady who is bringing me my breakfast tray (life is good).

I look down the hall again hoping to see Dr. Pharaoh making his rounds. Maybe I can be a good lesson for the young doctors this morning that sometimes it's better to do no biopsy at all, then I realize that today is Saturday so they don't make their normal rounds (too bad).

Nurse Crabb comes by my room to tell me goodbye. We have become friends in a strange kind of way; perhaps I have hung around long enough to see the side of Nurse Crabb that she tries not to show (the human side). We have developed a sort of a professional respect for each other because we both take our roles around here very seriously (nurse and patient).

The intern who is in charge of the transplant ward today comes by my room to make sure that I know to call the transplant clinic on Monday to make an appointment for a check-up a month from now. The only other instructions that the intern gives me is to call Dr. Bravo right away if I get a fever or if everything dries-up. This is the same intern who looked tired last night when he came into my room to answer my questions and he has been up all night long, so I tell him that he better take care of himself or someone might try to put a kidney in him.

The man from transportation comes with my ride to the front door and soon Debi and I are out on the interstate highway headed home to Blythewood. All that I can think of is getting home to my dog "Spats" and back to a world where everyday men have everyday problems that don't mean life or death. The true measure of medical success is when the patient's biggest problem is no longer medical (oh, if I could only reach that point).

Then I realize that if the definition of medical success is when you have problems that are bigger than any health issues that you might have, then I guess that I am already somewhat of a success because I really need to make some money soon (so I pray).

When Debi and I finally get home to Blythewood there is one message on our answering machine and I'm afraid to listen to it, because it could be D.U.H. calling to say, "Oops, our mistake, you need to come back." My fear turns to joy when I play back the message because it's Johnny Tillman telling me that he has reviewed the proposal and he wants me to come write him up.

Wow! What a feeling! my prayers are answered now! I don't have a problem in the world until Monday. After crashing in the bed for some really good zzzzs, the next morning Debi and I make a little picnic to eat down on the edge of the little lake that we live on. I love that lake. I know every inch of it, I even have a name for the huge old alligator snapping turtle that I see each summer feeding just out from the Lilly pads. I call him "Bismarck". I used to like sneaking up to where I figured old Bismarck would come up for air, as I would glide along the smooth water in my canoe, not wanting to hurt old Bismarck, but rather just wanting to see the huge old turtle up close. One time I followed his trail of bubbles all the way across the lake to his secret hiding place in the small cove on the other side.

I see old Bismarck out there feeding right now and it makes me feel good to know that life goes on. The old dirt ball is going to spin and boys will always turn into men. I try to live once more only in the present where I have no worries (until Monday and even then, there is the sale to Johnny Tillman to look forward to). The present is a happy place, it's only when I think about all of my future problems that I worry, but I remember Bill Tulluck saying something about future problems having future solutions (I may have bent his phrase but I like the concept).

Today turns into tomorrow, etc., but knowing the way that my life goes it doesn't come as that great of a shock when problems start to develop long before the appointment that was set up for me to go back to D.U.H. to have this tube removed. The first indication that things were not going exactly right is when I see that my blood pressure is up a little, but that could be because I am just worn out. I can make a good case about how my body has a right to feel worn out, so I rest up for a couple of days with plenty of T.L.C. from Debi along with lots of my mother's homemade vegetable soup (with ingredients that came from my father's garden instead of a can).

After a couple of days of the royal treatment I check my blood pressure just to see how good I'm doing and wham, my mind is blown by the super high readings. Hey, this can't be right, what gives? I'm supposed to be getting well. I decide that in the morning Debi and I will drive in to the lab so that I can get a blood test, even though I just had my once-a-week blood test two days ago, something isn't right.

Taking charge gives me a feeling of being in control, but deep down I know that no one is in charge: in fact, no one even knows what the problem is much less what the solution might be. There is only one thing that I can think to do and that is earnest prayer. My brother is my role model for prayer, so I do it his way, which is praying out loud, very loud.

The next morning when I wake up, I look down at my ankles the very first thing, as if I'm looking for reassurance (which I am). What a ghastly sight, swollen ankles like I haven't seen since the transplant. Oh, despair and anguish, Debi gets me my breakfast along with my medicine, but after two bites we leave for the lab.

Down at the lab I'm trying not to look like I am about to panic, but I am. Everyone who works at the lab knows that I was just here a few days ago, since I come here every week. They are aware of my transplant, but today it's not just me that is worried, I can see that they are worried too (oh my).

Alan Oakley is the best phlebotomist that I have ever had draw my blood, so I always get Alan to work on me if I can. It makes me relax when I see him because Alan is not only good at what he does, he is also a good guy who somehow keeps his regular guy attitude in the mist of the fractured lives around him. When Alan tells me not to worry, that it's probably no big deal, I figure that he is in as good a position as anyone to say what the norm is for kidney transplant patients in the first few months at home.

Even though Alan has made me feel better I'm still plenty concerned, so when I get up to the front where I turn in my paperwork I tell the lady behind the counter to run this blood test "stat," which is medical lingo for "right away." I can see by the look on the lady's face when she asks me by whose authority, to which I say "mine" as I try to remind her who the customer is in this equation (she isn't impressed).

I give the lady behind the counter the whole nine yards about how I just had my transplant and now I have this drain tube in my side, but I can't tell if I'm getting through to her about how this blood test does need to be run on a rush basis.

Debi and I go back to Blythewood to wait on the phone call that will surely come any minute but nothing happens. When the phone finally rings Debi answers it right away before handing me the phone as she says, "It's your Mom." The rushed conversation that we have as we try to keep the phone line open in case the call from D.U.H. comes through makes me think about how my Mother has always been there for me in my time of need. After telling my Mother that I will call her as soon as I talk to D.U.H., I hang up the phone to wait again for the phone call that will tell me what to do.

When 5:30 P.M. comes and goes I feel let down that D.U.H. never called (I mean you would think that emergencies like this would get some action by God). Debi and I go up to the grocery store to pick up a few things, lost in a fog we stumble around, neither one of us has much to say. I look at Debi and I'm frightened by what I see, we both look rough, but Debi looks like the one who had a transplant. Nursing me along has worn Debi out, because everything has fallen on her that I would normally do around the house, not to mention taking care of me, which is a job that she takes very seriously.

When we get back home, I go in the house first since Debi has to carry in the groceries and I see at once that there is a message on the telephone answering machine. When I play the message, my skin crawls as I hear Nurse Spock's voice talking in that emotionless monotone of hers, as she tells me that my world is falling apart. "Mr. Gordon, come to D.U.H. immediately. We think that your kidney might be rejecting."

You know, I have had my back to the wall so much that I have discovered that I kind of like the shade up next to the wall. These are almost the same words that Nurse Spock scared the pants off of me with a few days ago. The first time I went rushing up to D.U.H.

in the middle of the night, but nothing happened until the regular clinic hours the next day (fool me once shame on you, fool me twice shame on me). When Debi comes in from the garage with the groceries, she asks me if we had any phone calls? I casually mention that Nurse Spock called to tell me to come the clinic in the morning (ho hum). Driving to D.U.H. in the early morning hours, I am struck by the difference in my attitude on this trip as compared to the last time that Debi and I went rushing back up to D.U.H. in response to a message from Nurse Spock that was worded almost the same way.

The last time that we made this trip I was filled with a fear that bordered on desperation. This time, of course, I'm worried and concerned, but I'm operating without the high anxiety level that pervaded me before. The last time this trip was made at night, that could have made everything more foreboding. Maybe it had something to do with how tired I was or perhaps the surprise made everything seem more threatening. I also remember something that Napoleon said about how even the bravest of the brave would have their heart seized by fear if they were asked to charge the cannon's mouth one too many times. Perhaps the opposite is also true, as I have been so frightened for so long by so many things, that now maybe I have become hard to scare.

The transplant clinic is a timeless place visited by different people with similar problems. I can look at the patients and tell what stage they are going through, and it reminds me of how all the people in Dr. Calm's waiting room looked at me with knowing smiles back in the beginning. When the nurse calls my name and takes me back to see the doctor, I am expecting to be seen by Dr. Pharaoh, but I discover that my case has been handed off like a hot potato and now Dr. Bravo is in charge of my care. The surgery has been deemed a success, which it was, so now it's up to Dr. Bravo to adjust my medications and to take care of any problems that come up (like today).

Dr. Bravo gives me a thorough examination and notices that the area around my new kidney is bloated, then, being a man of few words, says one of them, "fibroid." That word is something that

I understand, because I dealt with those little strands of cream-colored tissue that the body produces to help stop a leak (like the one around my new kidney).

So, it turns out that the issue that was terrifying me was just a plumbing problem (the fibroid strands were stopping up the drain tube). Dr. Bravo does the same thing that a plumber would do but on a much smaller scale when he injects some blood thinner into the drain tube to get everything moving again, and in just a few minutes, Dr. Bravo is telling me that I can go home today. Just as I'm thinking about how good it is to hear those words without having some guy sticking holes in me with an ice pick, Dr. Bravo drops the other white shoe when he says, "Now let's do something to stop those leaks."

Dr. Bravo is explaining that he is about to give me a small chemical burn. Of course, I'm scared because the only experience that I have ever had with that kind of thing was back when I spilled hydrogen peroxide where I shouldn't have. That time I ended up dancing all around the room shouting, "Fire in the hole."

Sensing my fear Dr. Bravo tells me not to worry because this one is the proverbial "piece of cake." Somehow that seems easy for Dr. Bravo to say because I am the one about to be burned. Knowing that you are about to feel pain makes you aware of every sensation, and as the warm fluid flows through the drain tube into the area around my new kidney, I know why they call this a burn. The uncertainty of not knowing how much this chemical burn would hurt makes me suffer more from anxiety than I do from pain. Dr. Bravo leaves the chemicals in me for just three minutes and then he drains them out and tells me that I can go home now.

I'm so happy that I could dance my way out of this hospital (that is if I could just stand up straight). The chemical burn is sort of like getting punched in the gut, but it won't let go so I walk out into the waiting room bent over like I'm eighty years old, but I'm happy to be going home. Debi is pretty surprised to see me walking bent over while I am smiling from ear to ear because those two things don't usually go together, but it's hard not to smile when you are going home.

Out on the interstate highway, as we motor along on the way home, I tell Debi that my kidney area feels like your mouth would feel if you had just tasted alum and you couldn't spit it out. But if that's what it takes to get well, then I'm all for it. All that I have to do now is to wait for a few days so that everything can dry up and then I'm home free (wrong).

The next month is just a repeat of last month with the main difference being the amount of fluid draining into the little rubber bag that the fluid goes into. I mean where in the world does all of this fluid come from (good grief). After the joy of thinking that I'm getting better gives way to the depression of this isn't working, it time to go back to D.U.H. for the second burning.

The only funny thing that happens occurs one day when I am working over in Bishopville with my friend Al Holland. There I was dressed up in my blue suit, making an insurance presentation to a big client, as I fill the role of "expert from afar." That is until the bag of fluid, that is being held up by a safety pin attached to my underwear, falls to the floor right in front of the client. Talk about your awkward pauses, think how shocked he was and how embarrassed I was. I had to shuffle over behind the door and drop my pants while I fastened the pin back before stepping back from behind the door to complete the sale. The hardest part was trying to write and laugh at the same time.

On the trip back up to D.U.H I refuse to become depressed, deciding instead just to choose to believe that this time it will work (it had better). Alas, after going through the same procedure after three weeks, it became apparent that the net result is the same (utter failure). As a matter of fact there is more fluid now than there was in the beginning. What I want to know is where is all of this fluid coming from and where would it go if it were not leaking into the cavity around my new kidney?

Now is the proper time to be worried, because medical science has tried twice to solve this problem without any positive results. Now there is just one option the "big burn," and the worst part is what happens if fate calls strike three (bummer). Gone is my devil may care attitude on the trip back up to D.U.H. for the big burn.

I'm shaking in my boots. Once again everything seems to be riding on this one roll of the dice. The best-case scenario is that I hurt like hell but the leak stops (I will take it).

Up at the clinic while Debi and I wait for my name to be called, we hold hands in earnest as we pray silently together. Scanning the other patients in the waiting room, I can see that we aren't alone in our state of anxiety as there are three other couples that appear to be equally worried (at the transplant clinic there is plenty of misery to go around). When they finally call my name, I almost need the man from transportation to come with his wheelchair because my knees are shaking so bad. It's surprising how hard it is to get your body to walk towards pain.

Back in the examining room as I lay flat on my back looking up at the I.V. bags that hang on the pole next to me, I feel like a convicted murderer waiting on the lethal injection, but instead of going to sleep (forever). I'm about to feel a terrible burn in an attempt to not go to sleep forever.

The Doctor comes in and tells me that they are about to let the contents of this I.V. bag flow through my drain tube into the surgical cavity and after waiting three minutes they will let it all drain out, then I'm all done. I say to the doctor, "Yeah, I will be done like a turkey in the oven." Then as the doctor removes the clamp on the I.V. bag and I know that pain is on the way I tense up (go figure). This leads the doctor to tell me that I can relax, because there are no nerves in the area where the chemical will be so there will be no pain, just a little discomfort.

I tell the doctor that when they said that in medical school they meant that the doctor would have a little discomfort as they watched the patient in pain. First there is a sensation of heat all over my right side and my face breaks out in a full sweat, then my stomach gets nauseous as my body wishes it could puke this stuff out of my system. The I.V. bag is only on-half empty and already I'm not sure if I will be able to stand this procedure (the three minute wait doesn't even start until all of the contents of that I.V. bag are inside of me).

I look up at the doctor and ask him why my side burns like hell if there are no nerves in there (this must be what Jimmy meant when he said that he didn't want any part of him to burn in Hell). The doctor's answer sounds to me like something that he was told in medical school, but he doesn't sound completely sure of himself as he tries to convince me that I don't really feel the pain that I think that I feel. Instead I'm feeling a bunch of strange sensations that my brain interprets as pain (if it walks like a duck, it's a duck). By this time all of the fluid from the I.V. bag has flowed into my side, so the doctor starts timing the three minute wait with what looks to me like a standard kitchen timer (I'm the egg).

If this ever happens to you, I can tell you what your reaction will be; first you will be very still as you hope that if you do not move then it will not hurt (wrong), then you will try to hold your breath for three minutes (you can't) and finally you will end up the same way that I did: panting like a fat hound dog on a hot summer day as you try to cool down the fire that is burning inside of you.

When this three minutes of hell being inside of me is over, the medical technique for getting the fluid back out of my body is to take the empty I.V. bag off of the pole and put it on a chair while I lay on my side waiting for gravity to do its thing. As the doctor is cleaning everything up, he instructs me to not put any heparin in the drain tube and to, "Just let nature take its course."

All the way home that phrase: "Let nature take its course" bothers me. This whole transplant was about not letting nature take its course, it makes me think that the phrase, "Let nature take its course," might be what doctors say to themselves when they run out of ideas. All night long I worry about whether the drain bag will be full or empty when I wake up in the morning. No big fancy medical test will be required to let me know how I'm doing, the bag will tell the tale (it's time to pray). Long before morning I cut on the light to look at the bag, and when I see that it is empty finally at long last I fall asleep (thank you, Lord).

The following week Debi and I go back up to D.U.H. for an ultrasound examine to verify that the fluid is no longer compressing the kidney, but this journey is filled with mild exuberance that would normally be expected on the return leg on a trip such as this. I have complete confidence in the outcome of this test because not only has the drain bag stayed empty, but my blood pressure has been fine. If the kidney is having any problem at all, the blood pressure would be all over the place.

As we exit off the interstate I turn to Debi and say something that she has heard many times but never when there wasn't tension in the air, as I say, "Do you know what this test means?" Looking at my smiling face Debi gives me the answer that I wanted when she says, "Everything," to which I reply, "Right, hot dog!" Debi and I go into the transplant clinic that has always terrified me. We are here to present our winning lottery ticket to the officials, but this is much better, I'm here today to get back my youth.

The smiles on the faces of my buddies at ultrasound confirm my glee, but when I ask them what they concluded they give me the old line about how I need to ask my doctor; then I realize that he is in the room with us in his mask and gloves but without his splatter screen (thank God). In a matter of less than one minute the drain tube is out and I hear the words that I have always hoped for, as the doctor says, "Get a blood test every month and make an appointment to come back to the clinic in six months".

The hugging that Debi and I do in the waiting room has to be good for the morale of the patients. I remember seeing it once before when I first started coming here for the preliminary tests before transplant. Back at that time I didn't understand but now it's all perfectly clear: the hug that I saw then is just like the one that a soldier gives his girlfriend when he steps off the boat that brought him home from winning the war.

I look into Debi's eyes as if we are all alone and I say to her, "We are out of here!" (Hallelujah!)

Chapter 25

WHAT IS KILLING ME?

WANTING DESPERATELY TO GET WELL does not make it happen. After a few months of what passes for good health if you are a transplant patient, things begin to take an ominous turn when my blood pressure starts going up for no apparent reason.

I start taking walks with Debi and Spats, I even quit eating salt, yet still my blood pressure slowly gets worse. My blood work yields not a clue as to the source of my high blood pressure because everything looks normal for me. I'm praying that I haven't sprung a leak again because we have run out of fixes for that.

Before the doctors can figure out what's causing problem number one, I'm hit by problem number two: swollen ankles. When I woke up this morning and lifted up the sheet to look at my ankles I was in for a shock (damn they were big).

The first order of business is to rush down to the lab to get some blood drawn to see if we can find out what's going on. The good news about my blood work today is that there is bad news (my creatinine is high). I hope that maybe somehow things will reach a plateau and not get any worse (it's called denial).

Everything that I have ever gone through served only to get me where I am today (how was that thought, Yogi). Medical problems of unknown origins are the most frightening kind, because if you don't figure them out in time (you know the deal). Right now this transplant business looks like it's one part science and two parts art.

The usual suspects: rejection (too little medicine), nephrotoxicity (too much medicine), infection, and fluid leaking into the surgical cavity all become the focus of lively conjecture because any one of these could easily kill me, the combination of any two would... (oh, perish the thought). I feel sure that medical science can handle any of these issues if only we knew which one to treat. Another trip to ultrasound is scheduled so that we can find out if fluid has started slowly seeping back into the area around my new kidney, compressing it to the point where it's function is impaired (do you know what this test means? [everything]).

The truth, such as it is, will not be long in coming because as soon as the ultra-sound technician makes a few passes over my new kidney he will either see a fluid reservoir or he will not. There is no delay involved like there is when you are waiting for blood test results to come back from the lab. It's almost as if you are looking into your future when the technicians peer into their crystal ball (image on the monitor). There is definitely tension in the air as my buddies in the ultra-sound unit get ready to do their thing, because these guys know that if they find a fluid reservoir near my new kidney my goose is cooked.

As the T.V. monitor flickers to life I don't even waste my time looking at it since to my untrained eye it's just a bunch of white and grey static. I'm doing some monitoring of my own and I get my information in "real time," even ahead of the audio interpretation that comes from the technician who is running the show. It's the technician's eyes that I focus my attention on as they stare intently into the screen, totally unaware of my gaze. I don't want to see any wide-eyed, shocked expression come over the technician's face, what I want to see is eyes that look calm and relaxed.

The ultra-sound exam seems to go a lot faster when they aren't hurting you, so after just a couple of minutes of high anxiety the technician who is doing the scanning breaks the silence by saying, "My, my, my, I sure do pretty work." Then the other technician says to him, consider yourself high-fived and I know that this is good news.

We still don't know what's causing my problems but since we have run out of options for stopping leaks, I'll take some of the unknown (thank you). If this isn't the problem then what the heck is? One thing that I've learned is that no matter how bad things seem, they can always get worse (or better). The doctors are clueless through no fault of their own, so Debi and I go back to Blythewood while the doctors monitor the situation (waiting for death to make the first move).

Bill Tulluck and I decide to sponsor a business retreat for our insurance agents at the Caravel Hotel in Myrtle Beach, South Carolina. Sometimes life is a beach, so make sure that you enjoy it. On Friday as Debi and I drive to Myrtle Beach our spirits are good but I can tell by how much my ankles are swollen that things are getting worse because it's not even lunch time and my ankles are already larger than I would expect them to be late at night.

Saturday morning during the business session it is my job to introduce the speakers which means that while they are talking, I get to wait out in the hall and it's a good thing because the whole morning I feel like I'm about to have a heart attack. I don't mean at some theoretical point in the future, I mean right now (the big Mamoo)! Out in the hall I loosen my tie and drink as much water as possible, but I know that I can't keep going on like this (I have to get to the bottom of this problem before I end up in the bottom of my grave).

Everything about the beach retreat is emotional for me, all the speeches seem to be full of passion and the bonds of friendship that this group has would make any fraternity proud. About the point where I'm thinking about all of this, I realize that I'm going through the "last time syndrome" again (this could be the last time that Debi and I have a weekend together at Myrtle Beach, etc.).

At the very end of our beach retreat on Saturday night there are about 65 of us in the meeting room standing in a big circle singing the Star-Spangled Banner while we all hold hands to close things out. Just when I'm thinking that this song couldn't possibly be any more emotional, Bill Tulluck starts the crowd swaying back and forth together (not a dry eye in the house).

On Monday morning when I phone Dr. C. to tell him about how I have been feeling, he gets his office to make me an appointment with Dr. Stan Juk, who is one of the best cardiologists in Columbia. Dr. Juk saved my father's life not long ago when my father had a pace-maker put in, so I feel very comfortable with him on the case.

The American medical system is expensive, but say what you will, when the chips are on the line it comes through. I say this because I'm able to get an appointment to get a thallium tread mill test with Dr. Juk first thing tomorrow morning (in a lot of countries with socialized medicine there would have been a long wait and in a lot of other countries the capabilities don't even exist). I know that Dr. C. and Dr. Juk are pulling some strings to get me in this soon but I will take any help that I can get in this unequal struggle.

There is a special depression that comes over people who have had a heart attack, and as a matter of fact, a lot of the time the repair to the heart is easier than the psychological baggage that comes with the territory (I've got the blues). I know when it's time to pray and this is another one of those prayers that needs to be said loudly (Jimmy would be proud). "Oh, please Lord, let them find out what is killing me but don't let it be my heart" (goes my earnest prayer). The what-ifs are too bad to contemplate.

The thallium treadmill test is an experience in its own right. First the doctors pump your veins full of a dye with nuclear markers in it, then they see if making you run on a treadmill will kill you (if you don't die on the treadmill, then your heart isn't all that bad).

There is an awkward thirty-minute wait after the thallium treadmill test is complete while the doctors process the images that will show them whether you will live or die. This test gives the doctors the exact size of the openings in the arteries that go to your heart and small openings mean that you have been killing yourself one meal at a time (by-pass time).

This is another one of those medical exams that mean everything. Why can't I just be a regular Joe with normal problems like the rent is due or your daughter needs braces, instead of stuff like you might be rejecting your kidney and you need a coronary by-pass too.

I'm sitting there in the waiting room with Debi wishing that I could have a normal life (is that asking too much) when Dr. Juk calls me back to his office. I'm pretty damned worried so I'm glad that Dr. Juk gets right to the point when he tells me that he doesn't know what is causing my symptoms, but it is not my heart (hallelujah). I know that this is the up part of the emotional roller coaster and things could head back down again because we still don't even know what the real issue is, but all of that worrying can wait for another day because right now I am going to enjoy the ride (not having blocked arteries feels pretty sweet to me).

When it turns out that my heart is normal and healthy it seems prudent to Dr. C. that I go have a glucose tolerance test, an idea which meets with some resistance from me since I had one just a few months ago. But Dr. C. tells me that sometimes a kidney transplant can cause a person to become diabetic, plus there is some family history of diabetes on my mother's side.

Diabetes is a really bad deal, in fact some people end up losing a leg, but no one grabs their pancreas and keels over dead so there isn't any depression to deal with like there was when the issue was my heart. The glucose tolerance test makes for a miserable day, but diabetes can make for a miserable life, so I'm pretty damned happy when my results look normal.

I still wish that the doctors understood what my problem is but it doesn't look like it will kill me today, so I won't worry about it until tomorrow. One positive aspect of today is that I don't have diabetes and another good thing is that I will not have to take another glucose tolerance test (yuk).

Debi and I make another trip up to D.U.H. to check on my declining state of health. I find out at the transplant clinic that when doctors can't find anything wrong, then it's time to check for the big "C" (Cancer). My mother has a friend named Cat Huggins who has been a surgical nurse for a number of years and Cat always says that, "by the time that cancer shows itself it is usually too late." As Debi and I walk through the hospital on our way to the oncology clinic, I can't help but think about what this test means (everything). If Cat is right, I might not have to worry about my kidney anymore because cancer would probably kill me first.

Inside the oncology clinic there are a bunch of skinny people waiting to see the doctor and they are all staring right at us even after I have checked in with the receptionist. I recognize the staring phenomenon because it is exactly like the experience that I had the very first time that I went to the dialysis clinic (misery loves company). Even the nurses look at me funny as they take me back for a chest x-ray (they know that I have come here because I might have cancer).

I tell the nurse running the x-ray machine that she might need a large x-ray negative because a lot of the time when I have a chest x-ray they end up having to do it all over again because, when I inhale, my chest expands so much that part of my lung doesn't show up on the film. The nurse who is running the x-ray machine looks at me like she thinks that I must have just fallen off of a turnip truck as she says, "I do this every day." Then the nurse takes control of the conversation (using volume to convey authority) saying, "Take in a full breath and hold it, don't breathe or move," completing the x-ray as if I had never said a word.

Out in the waiting room Debi and I make small talk while we wait to find out if I have lung cancer. I see the young nurse walking across the waiting room in my direction and it makes me uneasy because I wouldn't think that they have had enough time to analyze anything. I can tell that Debi sees the nurse coming too, by how hard that she is squeezing my hand. When the young nurse comes up and tells me that they want to take another x-ray, my heart sinks (they don't take more x-rays if your lungs look good). With one last look back into Debi's eyes I follow the young nurse back to confirm my doom (or not).

When we get back to the x-ray room, I ask the young nurse if they have seen a spot on my lungs? She tells me that the doctor hasn't looked at anything because part of my lung was off of the film, so they have to take it over using a wider plate. The depression that had gripped me as I walked back to the x-ray room melts away when I picture the expression on the face of the "professional" nurse that was running the x-ray machine when she sees that I'm back again, but I'm told that she has gone to take an early lunch (sure).

As I walk back to tell Debi the good news (that there is no bad news). I can tell that Debi is confused by the smile on my face as I sit back down next to her. When I tell Debi that the problem was that I had more lungs than they had film, she doesn't find it as funny as I do. At long last we get the news that the doctors don't see any dark spots on my lungs (if lung cancer was the option then I'm glad that we are still dealing with the unknown).

As Debi and I leave the oncology area on our way back to the kidney transplant clinic I am overcome by a feeling that we are headed to a far better place than the one that we just left and the reason is clear: hope is still alive over at the transplant clinic. The best piece of advice that I could give to anyone who finds out that they have advanced cancer is to stay in denial as long as you can. I know that what I have to deal with over at the transplant clinic is no bowl of cherries, but it's not lung cancer either. I don't need some sophisticated medical test to tell me that we are fast approaching a point where some tough decisions are going to have to be made because my ankles are swelling again.

Back at the transplant clinic when my turn comes to see the Dr. Bravo, I can tell that something is bothering him before he even says one word. Looking down at the floor as he talks Dr. Bravo tells me that he needs to do a biopsy on my kidney today. An explosion of emotion rips through my head sending me reeling in disbelief (I thought that we had already dealt with the biopsy threat). Then the Dr. Bravo starts explaining his logic by telling me that since all of my other tests have turned out ok, we must be dealing with either rejection or nephrotoxicity and the only way to find out is to do a biopsy.

Everything that I have been through up to this point has only taken me back to the beginning. It occurs to me that maybe they should teach the young doctors how to play poker in medical school but of course doctors can't take chances because of lawyers. This cover yourself mentality among doctors means that a lot fewer tough decisions get made and a lot more medical tests end up being done (sound of cash registers ringing). The problem is that it's my kidney that they are talking about punching holes in.

It is at about this point that I realize that lack of emotion is not something that they actually teach in medical school, rather it is something that you learn on your on to protect yourself. I have been up and down the emotional roller coaster so much that my emotions refuse to become involved this time around.

What we are faced with now is nothing more than a math problem, what potential complication has the highest probability of being the one that is killing me: rejection (too little medicine) or nephrotoxicity (too much Cyclosporine). The answer seems clear to me. If my kidney is rejecting at these high doses of Cyclosporine then there may not be much that anyone can do for me because the side effects are unbearable if I take much more. In addition to that logic there has been no history of rejection in my case, yet, and we have had a problem with the kidney not working right due to the Cyclosporine dosage being too high (is this a trick question).

With no more emotion than that of a professional poker player who is playing for funsies, I ask Dr. Bravo what he would do if the biopsy were to come back indicating that the problem was nephrotoxicity. After I hear that Dr. Bravo's strategy would be to lower the Cyclosporine dosage, I hear the voice of my stepdaughter going off in my brain saying the word "Duh?"

I am not worried about being sued if I don't have a biopsy, I'm worried about the biopsy itself. I know that it is time for a command decision, so, without hesitation I tell Dr. Bravo that I want to just go ahead and lower the Cyclosporine level without doing the biopsy. Dr. Bravo looks at me over his glasses and says, " Mr. Gordon, are you refusing the biopsy?" I explain to Dr. Bravo that I am electing not to have a biopsy done at this time. Dr. Bravo doesn't say a word directly to me, he just pulls out his hand-held tape recorder and records the time and date along with the fact that, "Mr. Gordon has refused a biopsy."

After receiving Dr. Bravo's instructions to reduce the amount of Cyclosporine that I am taking I stumble back out into the clinic waiting room, glad that Debi is here with me for the drive back home. Although the decision to not have a biopsy was made without emotion it wasn't done without fear (what happens if that was the wrong move).

When the day rolls around for me to have my next routine blood test I have a troubled mind, but I know that we will find out the answer to this riddle just as surely from the blood test as we would have from a biopsy. If my blood work turns out to be ok, then we have taken the right course of action without anyone puncturing my kidney. If it turns out that I was dealing with rejection then I have made what could be a fatal mistake (nephrotoxicity is reversible, sometimes, rejection is not). I can't fault Dr. Bravo's logic or my own (the die is cast).

My spirit is uneasy as Debi and I spend the afternoon waiting on the phone to ring. I know that Alan Oakley, my friend at the lab, will phone me just as soon as the results are known. There isn't much conversation between me and Debi this afternoon because we each know what the other one is thinking (this blood test means everything).

When the phone call from the lab finally comes, I have to write the numbers down as Alan gives them to me because I am too scared to think. The critical measurement in all of this is my creatinine level. Just thinking about the implications of what the wrong numbers would mean to my life keeps me in turmoil as Alan goes over the results of the blood test with me.

When Alan reads my creatinine level my heart sinks to the floor (it's higher than it should be). Now I'm on pins and needles waiting to hear what my white blood count is, because if it is rejection that is messing up my kidney, then an increase in white blood cells would be seen as a confirming piece of evidence (that I am just about dead). When I hear that my white blood count has remained stable a wave of relief sweeps through me and I shout "Hallelujah!"

because this means that the jury is still out. We still don't know what is going on in my body but at least we can't confirm that the kidney is rejecting (be thankful for small favors).

As I hang up the phone anxiety fills my soul because, while the logic of refusing a biopsy before I lowered my Cyclosporine dosage this morning hasn't changed, the stakes involved have gone up dramatically (if I made the wrong choice). I know that the change in my Cyclosporine dosage this morning has nothing to do with the results of this blood work because it is too soon for that change to have any measurable effect. The body is like a giant ship coming into port in that it takes a long time for course corrections to alter its path. In fact, the higher creatinine level just shows that there is a crisis that required immediate action, now we have to pray that I did the right thing (the die is cast).

Worry could consume this entire day if I would let it, but I'm not. That would be an incredible waste when good days are in such short supply, so I project all of my worries into the future by saying, "I don't have any troubles until tomorrow." That is when I will get my blood tested again, which makes it a true statement, otherwise it wouldn't do any good. There are no decisions that have to be made on this day, there is nothing that needs to be done. I'm going to try and enjoy Debi's company until I get the results of my blood test tomorrow (there will be plenty to worry about then).

It doesn't take long for tomorrow to come and when it does, the first thing that I do when I wake up is to look down at my ankles to see if they are swollen (they are not). Two bites of breakfast is all that I can manage because I am excited about going to get my blood test. I am expecting to see some improvement in my numbers because my ankles look normal (hallelujah).

This is the day that I set aside to worry and I put it to good use, watching the clock tick the time away waiting for the phone to ring, so that I can get today's blood work results from Alan (this test means everything). Finally, Alan calls from the lab with today's results and I am shaking in my boots until he reads my creatinine level, which has gone back down to where I would expect it to be (my ankles were right, hallelujah). Even my white blood count is right where it should be, I feel like a double lottery winner (I am).

Hanging up the phone I grab Debi and we dance around the house as I shout, "Ain't no boogers out tonight," (old childhood game played down South). Euphoria runs wild and I make no effort to rein it in because I have waited a long time for a day like this where things go well and I'm going to enjoy it. This really is better than winning the lottery because I get to live (being dead is worse than not being rich).

I didn't know it at the time, but this was a cycle that would repeat it's self where my creatinine level would start drifting higher, but we weren't sure why. We gave consideration to all of the usual suspects, (rejection, infection, compression) but upon closer scrutiny none of them seemed to be the issue.

One thing that is known about Cyclosporine is that too much of it can be toxic to the kidneys and that is one thing that could account for my declining kidney function. One answer would be to stick a huge needle into my new kidney and cut out a hunk to look at under a microscope. That's what my doctors want to do. If I went ahead with the biopsy and the results came back showing that I was getting too much Cyclosporine our response would be to reduce the dosage (duh). Given the same quandary by life with no new information, I make the same choice once again (avoid the biopsy).

When we would reduce the Cyclosporine dosage my kidney function always improved and my creatinine level would decline, but after a few weeks things would start to get worse again. Emotionally, the cycle went something like: elation, joy, hope, disappointment, and then desperation (I could feel death reeling me in). Stuck in the doldrums between sickness and health, we marked the first anniversary of our transplant thankful that I was alive, but aware that my status could change. I was just stumbling forward in the course of a regular day trying to make a living, when I got an unexpected phone call from Nurse Spock letting me know that Dr. Bravo wants to see me at the transplant clinic right away.

Early the next morning, rolling along on the interstate highway heading to D.U.H., I ponder my fate. I know that I am in a heap of trouble or Nurse Spock never would have called, but there was no way for me to tell that I was making the trip to D.U.H. for the very last time.

Debi and I check in with the nurse at the transplant clinic and sit down to start waiting for them to call my name. I guess that you could say that I'm feeling a little philosophical as I sit there thinking about how the unknown nature of my problem is like trying to guess the answer when you don't even know the question.

As soon as I heard my name being called right away, I looked over at Debi and said, "Uh oh." Then the nurse with my file starts leading me away but instead of taking me back to the examining rooms, she heads down the carpeted hallway that leads to Dr. Bravo's office. A chill runs up my spine because I know that Dr. Bravo doesn't want to examine, he wants to explain.

I go in and sit down, and as Dr. Bravo starts to talk, I realize that he doesn't look very confident (but then again, neither am I). It turns out that we are back to the beginning again, where Dr. Bravo wants to do a biopsy (I don't). Dr. Bravo has everything set up to put me back in the hospital today, but I'm not sold on this mission as I have a few questions of my own.

I ask Dr. Bravo what he would think if we did a biopsy today that lead us to reduce the medication, but after a couple of weeks my creatinine level started going back up while my white blood count stayed about the same. Dr. Bravo fidgets around staring down at the carpet while he thinks about what he is going to say, turning ever so slowly in his swivel chair to the point where I am looking straight at the back of his head, then he says, "Well, you could have developed an allergic reaction to the Cyclosporine."

Like a sinner who has just heard the voice of God I know that Dr. Bravo is speaking the truth. It's such a devastating turn of events that I have never even contemplated this what if. my muscles turn to Jell-o as I picture Dr. Pharaoh in his splatter screen waiting on me and I tremble in fear, but I still have one more question for Dr. Bravo before they cart me away, "What is your strategy if it turns out that I am in fact allergic to Cyclosporine?"

Dr. Bravo's eyes immediately go back to the floor as he tells me that I would be taken off of Cyclosporine and switched over to Imuran (the old drug). Every hair on my body stands up after all that I have heard about how Cyclosporine is supposed to be a wonder drug, (revolutionizing the transplant field) to be told that I might have to be taken off of it is a devastating blow (worst case scenario).

If the old drugs worked just as well then Cyclosporine wouldn't have been seen as such an advancement. There is a part of me that wants to stand up and say to Dr. Bravo, "Ok, that does it, you're fired" (but I don't do it). I know one thing; if door number one leads that way (biopsy and the old drugs) then I am going through door number two. I almost startle myself when I do stand up and say, "I'll have to consider my options, I'll call you in a few days." Dr. Bravo looks up at me totally dumfounded and says, "What options are you talking about?" and I tell Dr. Bravo that it is time for a second opinion, but I don't mean my own.

In a zombie trance I stumble back out into the waiting room and walk over to where Debi is sitting. I can still hear my childhood Doctor (Dr. Reed) telling me a year and a half ago to get my transplant wherever they would give me Cyclosporine (if I wanted to live). I do want to live more now than ever (doesn't death have anything better to do? I'm only thirty-seven).

Right now, I just hope that I can get out of this waiting room before I break down and cry (it wouldn't be good for patient morale). Debi can't understand why we are leaving since we have only been here for a short time, but I can't explain anything other than she has to drive. I am like a shell-shocked soldier with battle fatigue (now I know how Debi felt after the Haw River bridge). All the way home I stare blankly out of the passenger side window watching the hills roll by (my eyes work but not my brain).

Back in Blythewood I lower the Cyclosporine dosage on my own (I know that I am going out on a limb but this tree is on fire). I have to be near to the dosage level where the Cyclosporine will not keep the kidney from rejecting, but something has to change or I will end up dead (soon). This is like being on the circus trapeze performing without a net because I know that if lowering the Cyclosporine dosage this time doesn't work, I won't be able to try this gambit again without crossing that invisible line that separates the living from the dead.

When I go in for my next blood test (there is no such thing as routine) there is no ominous feeling hanging over my head because I know that even if my blood work comes back looking good, that doesn't mean that I am off of the hook. It usually takes a couple of weeks before my creatinine starts going back up, so for a change this blood test doesn't seem to mean everything (unless it turns out bad).

During the day while I am waiting for the results to come back from the lab, I phone the University of Minnesota to find out when I can see the doctor that I had the brief phone conversation with right after my transplant surgery, just in case my blood work says that bad things are happening. I liked the way that doctor talked and how confident he was that my situation could be managed. Not only was the doctor at Minnesota easy to communicate with, but he also sounded like he knew what he was talking about. Unfortunately, the doctor that I want to talk to in Minnesota is out of the country until next week, and when transplants go bad, that can be a lifetime (or end thereof).

Dejected, but not desperate, I phone the University of Pittsburgh as a fallback position that I don't expect to need. They tell me that all that I have to do to be seen by a doctor is to show up at their transplant clinic any morning between eight and eleven.

When the lab has the results of today's blood chemistries ready, Alan calls me with the bad news. It is so extreme that I am totally blown away (statistically I'm just about dead). It's a good thing that I had thought over my options earlier in the day because I am too devastated to do any thinking right now. Before I even tell Debi what Alan said, I phone Columbia Metropolitan Airport to see if they have any flights to Pittsburgh today. It turns out that they have just one flight and it takes off in less than an hour, about the same amount of time that it takes for me to drive to the airport if everything goes ok.

Debi looks pretty exasperated and most of her normal energy has flowed out of her body as she stands there telling me that there is no way for us to make it to the airport on time, but Debi's expression perks up when I ask her if she has ever seen a plane leave on time. The only thing that I grab before we rush out the door is my medicine and a coat, there isn't even time to feel sorry for myself (if we want to catch that plane). I would sure feel better if Debi could come to Pittsburgh with me, but somebody has to stay home to take care of the dog (not to mention that money is getting scarce).

Out on the interstate highway as we speed to make the flight I am pulled over by a highway patrolman and precious seconds tick away while he walks up to my car, but when I tell the trooper that I have to catch a plane to save my life, he just waves his hand and says, "Drive on" and we do. We come screeching to a stop in front of the airport and run over to the ticket counter where I find out that the plane is getting ready to pull away from the gate, but the ticket agent tells me that they will hold the plane for me if I will hurry. What a break! It makes me so happy I could shout!

Debi and I look into each other's eyes before I board the plane with an intensity that comes from knowing that this could be the last time we ever see each other. While Debi and I are kissing goodbye, the thought crosses my mind that I could be going to Pittsburgh to die, and the thought of not having Debi with me makes it feel ten times worse.

The flight to Pittsburgh is on one of those small commuter planes and everything is normal until we get ready to land, then the pilot announces over the public address system that everyone should buckle their seatbelt because we are going to land during a snowstorm and there will be some turbulence up ahead. That was the understatement of the year because as we descend the plane was tossed around and the passengers were pretty well shaken (in more ways than one). I could see everyone looking around to see who they were going to die with, and I could see the expressions of horror on their faces as they confronted their own mortality (they didn't like it).

The frightened passengers look just like the rookies when they show up for their first day at the transplant clinic and I can tell that it confuses them when they see my smiling face staring back at them. But I know that a fast death in a plane crash could be far better than a slow death in a hospital bed. The plane lands with a thud and a bounce but at least we are all safe (everyone except for me). The passengers break out in spontaneous applause and I notice that I am clapping loudest of all. Maybe that means that deep down inside of me I still want to live (I do).

Once we get into the terminal, I discover that getting to Pittsburgh is only half of the journey because it is snowing so hard that none of the cab drivers want to take a fare all the way to the hospital (especially at night). Pleading my case of medical emergency and offering a $100 tip, I find one cabby who is up to the task.

The cabby tells me that he would take me to hell for a $100 tip, and going with the lighter side of emotion I tell the cabby that if I wanted to go to hell that I would just drive myself because I know the way. When we get out on the highway, I can tell that the fears of the other cab drivers were not unfounded because we drive past a large bus that is stuck in the snow and there are cars strewn all over the place.

My cabby is a "professional" in the best sort of way because he has prepared for such a day, and thanks to his tire chains, we plow through the storm to a hotel just a few blocks from the hospital. You should have seen the expression on the face of my cabby when I actually gave him the tip that I had offered on top of the humongous fare.

As soon as I get to my room, I phone Debi and I listen to her sweet voice with little tears in my eyes until we are both about ready to fall asleep (being away from Debi is so strange that I put the two pillows off of the other bed next to me under the covers). The next morning I am awake well before dawn. Time just drags when you are waiting on the sun. I stall around as long as I can, but I still get to the hospital about an hour too early so I go into a coffee shop that sits right across the street from the hospital's main entrance. I sit there watching the people as they go into work in the freezing cold, wishing that I was one of them (regular people with regular problems).

When I walk across that frozen street and start up the stairs in front of the hospital doors, I feel like an infant about to be left on the stoop because I am so all alone (I am a stranger in a strange land). I don't know anyone's name who works in this hospital, in fact, I don't even know anyone that lives in this state (Pennsylvania). I am just showing up at their door hoping that they can save my life (praying).

Once I get to the transplant clinic things seem to be more in order because I see people playing familiar roles. Even here in this strange setting, the patients fall into different groups. The rookies are the easiest ones to spot because they are the only ones smiling, and that's because they don't understand (yet). I'm standing in line with several rookies because we need the same forms, but that's where the similarities end because we are as different as combat veterans are to the green replacement troops.

Once I sit back down to fill out the forms, I start looking around the waiting room at the other patients looking for someone that might be in the same boat as me. I see plenty of skinny people that are probably all on dialysis and I see several other patients who have big puffy faces that you would expect on people who are on very high doses of Prednisone. That indicates that these patients have had their transplants recently. There are also some couples sitting down holding hands with concerned looks on their faces, and then there is me. I'm the only one in the waiting room who is all alone and I wonder if this is how the Old Man of the Ward got his start (cringe).

There are a number of people in this room who look like they have had all of the emotion wrung out of them, but at least they are not alone. Then I hear my name being called and fear ripples through my brain when I think about what I am about to go through.

When I walk into the examining room the doctor is already there and I want to make a good impression on him because my life is in his hands. I don't say anything at first, as the doctor gives me a thorough examination, but I think that he might be Filipino.

Then after the doctor has checked all of the physical parameters, he looks at me and says, "What the trouble is?" That's when I realize that I am at yet another teaching hospital, and good grief, they have an intern working on me. The language barrier is so bad between us that I end up pointing to my swollen ankles while I say, "Need doctor," and the intern looks at me earnestly and says, "Me doctor" (beam me up, Scotty).

Some things have a universal language like kidney disease and the intern clearly understands what swollen ankles mean, especially in conjunction with the word Cyclosporine, but even though he seems to understand most of what I am saying some of the nuances may be lost. The Filipino intern does a darn good job of drawing some blood, then he leaves me to stew in my own juices. I am alone for a very long time, which gives me plenty of time to think about how when you come to a hospital with a complicated medical situation you expect to see the Doctor that has the most experience, or at least one that speaks the language. I appear to just be someone that this intern can practice on that won't count against the hospital's mortality ratio if things don't work out.

Then in the middle of my pity party I hear the intern's distinctive broken English coming from the room next to the one that I'm in, and because of the hard terrazzo floor I can hear every word that he says (for all the good that will do). The Filipino intern is explaining my predicament to the real doctor who happens to be a woman. The intern is making a good case that I'm getting too much Cyclosporine so he recommends lowering the dosage (just like I would).

Then I hear words that I will never forget as the female Doctor says, "Sure, unless the patient is really rejecting, then if you cut back on the Cyclosporine you are talking about a dead man in just a matter of days." Then I hear the word "biopsy" and it cuts to the bone (that's a very bad thing and I'm a long way from home).

Stunned, I can't even listen to the rest of the conversation as I am too blown away by what I have already heard. When the intern comes back to talk to me, I understand the word biopsy well enough, so I ask the intern what his strategy would be if the biopsy did not show any signs of rejection, but lowering the Cyclosporine level only helped for a few days before the same thing started happening again.

The intern tries to explain things to me in his broken English and I understand the words allergic and Cyclosporine, so I get the idea. When I ask what Pittsburgh would do, the intern doesn't look too sure of himself. Basically, his answer is pretty much like D.U.H.'s to this situation (use the old drugs).

Then I ask the intern if he knows of any other institutions that might have a different approach to this problem. The young intern tells me something that a more experienced doctor might never have mentioned because it is being done at one of this hospital's competitors.

It's like the story about the Bells of San Pedro all over again, as I see the hand of God working in all of this. The intern starts telling me that the University of Minnesota has been experimenting with tri-therapy in cases like this (Prednisone, Imuran and Cyclosporine all in lower doses).

I have come here to be saved and I have ended up being enlightened, which is just as good because now I know what I have to do (get to Minnesota). The irony that this young Filipino doctor with whom I can barely converse would end up being the one that sets me on the right course after D.U.H. had been on the case for over a year, blows my mind and to me there can only be one explanation (thank you, God). On the flight back home to South Carolina I keep thinking about where I would be right now if I hadn't decided to get another opinion, and I tremble.

When I get off of the plane in Columbia, Debi comes running into my arms. I'm sure that the other passengers must think that we have been apart for a very long time but even though we were only apart for one night, Debi and I both know that it could have been forever.

Chapter 26

PLAN ZEBRA

IT WILL ONLY BE A FEW DAYS until the doctor in Minnesota returns to the clinic, but it seems like an eternity and it could be if my kidney shuts down (judging from my swollen ankles that is a distinct possibility). I have phoned the transplant clinic at the University of Minnesota two different times and I'm certain that I want to go there, but it doesn't give me a good feeling to be relying on total strangers to save my life.

When the time comes for me to actually say goodbye to Debi at the airport, I give her one last hug before boarding the plane and once I have her in my arms, I don't want to let go because we both know that I may not be coming back. In the back of my mind, I keep thinking about how I had such high hopes for the mission to Pittsburgh, but in the end their approach to the problem was very similar to what D.U.H. had in mind. If that strategy wasn't going to work at D.U.H., then it wouldn't work at Pittsburgh. If Minnesota doesn't have any new tricks then all of this is just wasted motion.

The reason that I am so worried this time is that I know that this mission to Minnesota represents Plan Zebra in the story of my life, and you don't get down to Plan Zebra until you have exhausted all of your other options. This must be the way that a soldier would feel when it comes time for him to go onboard the ship that will take him away from his girlfriend and off to war. This trip to Minnesota is in the middle of March but winter still has the twin cities in a deep freeze as I begin my journey. It doesn't really matter what the weather is like, anyway, because Plan Zebra is something that you have to do come hell or high water.

Flying over Chicago I look down at the endless suburbs with all of the yards covered in snow and I think about how in each house there is a family locked in their own little struggle with the world. As the cab takes me to the hospital in Minneapolis the one thing that amazes me as we drive through the city are the huge mounds of brown slush that have been piled up in the comers of the gas stations over the course of the winter, standing in mute testimony to the bitter winters that these hardy Minnesotans endure.

Standing outside the hospital as I am about to walk through the automatic doors at the main entrance, I pause for a moment to reflect on the situation that I am in. I feel all alone because I am. If the doctors here in Minneapolis can't help me, then I may never walk back out of these doors again.

When I find the admissions desk, much to my surprise, they recognize my name and they tell me that they have been expecting me (wow! what a difference from what I had experienced when I went to D.U.H. for my transplant). I had only been seated for a few minutes when I heard my name being called by a professionally dressed lady who stood out from the rest of the hospital staff because most of them are dressed in pastel green uniforms with the obligatory white coats.

The professionally dressed lady introduces herself as Vicky, the transplant coordinator here at the University of Minnesota and she is carrying a large manila folder that has my name printed on it. Vicky asks me if I would like to ride up to my room in a wheelchair and I am thrilled that I get to walk up to the ward on my own two feet. I haven't even gotten to the ward yet but I can already tell that I have come to the right place because the people seem nice and they also appear to know what they are doing.

When we get to the ward Vicky takes me up to the nurses' station and introduces me to the head nurse who greets me with a smile. After Vicky gives my file to the head nurse, she tells me goodbye and the nurse shows me to my room like I am some sort of a V.I.P.

The procedure that a hospital goes through while admitting its patients is pretty much the same from one place to the next with one notable difference: up here in Minneapolis they didn't confiscate my medications that I brought with me.

The man from the lab comes to my room to draw some blood from my arm so that the doctors can see what is going on. He does it very efficiently but without the entertainment value of a visit from my old buddy John Carter back at D.U.H. I sort of miss the old gang back at D.U.H. where I knew how everyone fits into the scheme of things.

It's just a waiting game for now while I wait for the results of my blood work to come back from the lab (time to pray). Then before long I hear a knock on my door and I know that it is judgement day.

I'm surprised by the youth of the doctor that comes into my room to discuss my blood test results (they scare the heck out of me, but they don't seem to alarm the doctor). I'm relieved to hear that the next step would be to take some x-rays because that shouldn't hurt. Just as I am savoring the joy associated with the avoidance of pain, I hear the doctor talking rather abstractly about how they are going to stop my Cyclosporine for one day just to see how my body reacts.

Wow! That's a frightening concept: taking me off of Cyclosporine completely for one day What if my body reacts by rejecting my new kidney? (That would solve the mystery of what has been killing me.) When the doctor leaves me alone in my room, I know that I had better say my prayers (and I do). Then I decide to phone Debi while there is a little break in the action and I am telling her about how the staff here in Minnesota seems to be "professional" in the best sense of the word when I hear a faint commotion out in the hall.

My big news to Debi is that I have been able to wear my blue jeans so far without anyone hassling me (that ought to put things in perspective for her). After Debi and I say goodbye, I go over to the door and open it just enough to peek through the crack to see what the noise was all about down at the end of the hall.

It is obvious that something is going on because there are six or seven doctors milling around in the hall and then I see two men in business suits pushing a low cart on to the elevator when the doors open up. Then I see the crushed velvet body bag that is riding on their cart and I realize that they are from a funeral home (so this is no delivery). As the elevator doors start to close, I think about the shattered dreams inside of that bag and I say a quick prayer for the loved ones who are about to get bad news and those who have to tell them.

As soon as this incongruous entourage of dark suits and white coats disperses from the hall, I start thinking about the crossroads of life again and how it really was judgement day (but not for me). Then I think that the medical term "body" is probably slang for a patient without health insurance. I wonder if the medical protocol for this situation calls for all of the doctors involved to reassemble in the cafeteria for coffee to get their stories straight. I mean they all seemed to leave at one time without anyone saying a word.

Now it's just me alone in the hall and somehow I am drawn down the hall by a force that I don't understand, until I am standing in front of the elevators where everyone disappeared. As I turn around I see the open door that is compelling me to come look inside. The sign above the door says "x-ray" and something tells me in a powerful way that this is the place where life's most dreaded of all events has just taken place, and for some reason I need to look inside.

Peering into the empty room my eyes search for the source of whatever it is that is pulling me in. The floor is littered with empty syringes and I can tell that a mighty struggle has taken place, then I see the two terrible images of death at work. Across the darkened x-ray room there is a white light coming from two fluorescent screens that have the last x-rays taken of the recently deceased. The two x-rays seem to be staring at me from across the dimly lit room like the eyes of an icon at some pagan shrine.

The two images are x-rays of the top view of a patient's brain who must have been laying right there in front of me on the black table below the x-ray machine when events unfolded such as they did. The story is plain enough to see with the x-ray on the left being a normal brain except for a very dark area in the center of the x-ray where the two lobes of the brain join together. This small black line about the size of your little finger was the beginning of the end for the man in the crushed velvet bag.

The second x-ray though is the one that makes my skin crawl because it is the only time that I have ever seen an image of death in motion. Everything looks the same as image number one except that the dark line in the center has gotten longer and it has made a right turn. This shows the hand of death taking hold of this patient's brain and there wasn't much that anyone could do at that point (except watch).

The dark area in the center of the brain is a river of blood with a tributary forking into the crevasse on the right side of the brain (end of story). Looking at both x-rays together I can see death in action and it scares the hell out of me to think that tomorrow morning I will have an appointment to lay down on that same black altar where death just did its thing. I've never seen an actual image of death before, but there it is like a small black hand turning out the lights on the list of things that never got done.

All night long the images of those two x-rays torment me as I think about the potential consequences of not taking my Cyclosporine for a day. I tremble at my prospects for tomorrow, but at least I am about to get the answer that I came here for. This ought to settle it once and for all, whether my kidney is rejecting or my doctors have been choking it with too much Cyclosporine (unless it's something that we haven't even considered like cancer of the kidney [Oh, God!]).

The first hint of morning is the sharp end of the needle taking some of my blood for the lab to see if I'm doing better (or not). Once again I have everything riding on this one blood test. Just as I was thinking that there couldn't be much more pressure than this life proves that I was wrong about that when my nurse comes walking into my room to let me know that I might want to get up and shower because the biopsy team will be here soon.

I'm out of my bed in a flash, fully awake now I know that I have to do something fast or they will stick a huge needle into my tinder new kidney and tear out a chunk. I want to avoid that big needle like you would a robber's knife, but my doctor has to agree with me or the hospital might not take my case at all. In my most respectful tone of voice, I tell the nurse that I want to talk to the doctor to see if a biopsy is required in my case. Even though the nurse says not a word, both her eyebrows arch-up like a cat's back at the sight of a dog.

Trapped like a rat. That's how I feel. I wish that I could just run out of my room and blend into the crowd but this isn't the movies. I can run out of my room but not away from my doom (so why bother). MacGyver could avoid that biopsy needle just using objects that he would find in this room, that's what I'm thinking while my eyes scan the room looking for tools to use in the war on pain. My eyes are drawn to my pad of lined notebook paper and I know that will be my ticket out of here (with no extra holes).

I pick up my pen and I start drawing a graph that is supposed to show the relationship of a reduction in Cyclosporine dosage to an improvement in kidney function as measured by my creatinine level. This graph goes back for a period of about six months and since I am making this graph up as I go, I take out all of the confusing stuff that D.U. H. had to deal with. It's not like they have the time to check on my sources and besides, I illustrate the primary issue which is, after a brief improvement the kidney function starts to decline again and in each cycle things get worse than they were before (that's what brings me here).

I'm not trying to prove any points. I'm trying to avoid the one on the end of that huge biopsy needle. I'm shocked that the doctors up here want to do a biopsy. Since they took me off of Cyclosporine for a full day the answer should be readily apparent very soon (sooner than the biopsy results would come back from the lab).

If the doctors are correct in their judgement (which I agree with) that the decline in my kidney function is related to the high dose of Cyclosporine, then pretty soon a blood test should indicate that my kidney is working better, just as soon as those toxins start exiting out of my body. And if that turns out to be faulty logic, then I ought to start blowing the tops off of the thermometers around here (fever).

I know that the doctors around here are just following the hospital's protocol, so I need to provide a credible answer for why this doctor should make an exception from their standard operating procedures. If things don't work out, I may not be around to back up his story and in medical school they tell the young doctors to pay attention, because the law school has a class for this occasion too.

I know that a lot of medical decisions are made because of what someone learned in law school and I didn't come to this hospital to get any legal opinions. Right now, I just want to avoid pain. It's one of my favorite basic instincts.

When the doctor comes into my room I am relieved to see that he isn't wearing a splatter screen and since there is no audience, we can talk about the issues man to man. This is the best opportunity that I have had to make my case to an open mind that the probable cause of my poor kidney function comes in a bottle. It's easy to communicate when there is no blame to place and no ass to cover.

I back up my logic with the graph that I made and I feel like a gladiator pleading with the emperor to spare my life from the coliseum floor, as I try my best to avoid the biopsy needle (like I would a sword). Then I hear the words that I know mean that I am being spared (if only for a while).

I am stunned when the doctor says, "I don't blame you." I feel like a five-year-old who has just been told that he is getting a pony for Christmas as I listen to the doctor telling me that my morning blood test results looked pretty good, so we can postpone any decision on a biopsy until this afternoon, after I get back from having some x-rays done.

The thought of that black x-ray table waiting on me sends shivers up my spine because I know that is where that man died last night (on what was his judgement day). I feel like an Inca who is next in line at the altar as he watches the body of the guy that was in front of him as it rolls down the steps.

Last night it seemed like that black x-ray table was the last place that I would want to be but it turns out that the x-ray table was only next to last. When it gets down to being penetrated by an x-ray or the biggest needle that you ever saw, the choice is as clear as it gets. Yet still, it gives me the willies when I climb up on that cold black x-ray table with my life on the line.

Trying to make conversation with the x-ray technicians I ask them if they were working last night when the guy had the cerebral hemorrhage. Both x-ray technicians have a ghastly look on their faces as they recall the events that they had been trying to repress.

One of the technicians starts talking in an animated way that makes me think that he is probably gay until he put both hands on his hips as he says, "It was just awful" (then I was certain). The technician looks exasperated as he tells me that he didn't know that anything was wrong until he developed the film, he just thought that the patient had drifted off to sleep. When they realized he was gone they did everything that they could (to run up the bill?).

Then the x-ray-tech says, "That guy was complaining at work about headaches, so one of his friends brought him in." After a silent pause the x-ray-tech adds "That guy will probably end up in some textbooks," then he adds that the x-ray-tech who was working with him last night couldn't even come into work today (neither could the patient). After taking the last x-ray that they need, the x-ray-tech tells me to stay in the waiting room while they wait for the film to develop and I wonder if those were the last words that the patient, who drifted off to heaven ever heard.

Out in the waiting room I say an earnest prayer that the x-ray technicians don't see the dark hand of death in my x-rays. I keep thinking about how the x-ray-tech didn't even know that the patient who had the cerebral hemorrhage was about to die as he was hearing the patient's last words. That is, until the x-ray-tech looked at the film to see if it had developed correctly, and I would be willing to bet that the x-ray-tech has already seen my film (my fate is known, but not to me). These x-rays mean life or death to me, just as much as they did to the man who died on the x-ray machine last night (I just hope that I have a different result).

When I see the nurse making her way across the waiting room, I know that she is coming for me and my heart is up in my throat until I hear her say, "You can go back to your room now." I peer deep into the nurse's eyes to see if her pupils are dilated or constricted because surely if something bad was wrong it would put tension in her eyes, but alas all that I see is a blank stare.

As I walk back to my room I am tormented by self-doubts about influencing the doctor's decision about doing a biopsy with the graph that I made up, but then when I contemplate the cold steel needle being shoved into my tender new kidney I know that some risks are worth taking. It could be that a biopsy is just the thing that I need to clear everything up, but let's not forget that all of the pain and damage that would ensue came in the pursuit of a diagnosis (not a cure).

Back in my room I pace the floor with my gaze drifting out through my window to the streets below that look so peaceful with their fresh coat of snow. I can see the people down on the city streets going about their lives with regular worries while I am up here grappling with life-or-death issues. I envy them all and I just wish that I could get lost in the hum-drum of a normal life where hopefully your biggest concern is whether the dry cleaners close at 5:30 or 6:00. I would consider myself "cured," so to speak, when the day finally comes when my number one problem has nothing to do with my health.

Life happens one day at a time and over the course of a lifetime every one of those people that I am watching drive past this hospital will face a day like this of their own. Remember that our objective on this earth should not be just to survive but rather to live (none of us is going to get out alive). I wish that Debi could be with me now because I'm going to need her if the doctor comes in here wearing a splatter screen. I know that I am out of wiggle room. If this doctor says that I have to have a biopsy, then I won't have any other choice.

In poker you are gambling against a single "if," (if my cards are better than his) if you want to factor in your chances with a double "if," just imagine making those same bets without ever looking at your cards. Here I sit facing a triple "if," because I am waiting to hear about the results of this morning's blood work which ought to reveal how my body is responding to skipping my Cyclosporine yesterday. Of course, my x-ray had better not show that death has a grip on my kidney. If I make it past those two hurdles then all that I have to worry about is the biopsy (except for the unknown).

I'm sitting there thinking about how I don't like these odds when I hear a knock at my door and I know that it is judgement day for me. The door swings open and a gray-headed doctor walks into my room with a clip board in his hand and I'm just thankful that it isn't a biopsy needle that he is carrying.

I can barely stand the tension in these first few silent seconds while I wait for the doctor to tell me what he came here to say. I feel like the pilgrim who has struggled to the top of the mountain to hear words of wisdom from the medical guru (that's it exactly). It turns out that this doctor says the very words that I have been dying to hear, "Your blood work as well as your x-rays look pretty much like we would expect to see, so we are going to change your medication, and if your blood work looks ok in the morning, "YOU CAN GO HOME."

I don't know why doctors never give patients high-fives because an occasion of this significance ought to be accompanied by a little fanfare. I keep a straight face because the doctor does but as soon as he is gone I dance around the room saying, "Thank you, Lord!" I need to hug Debi except that she isn't here, so I call her at home to give ger the glorious news: I'M GOING HOME (ALIVE).

The ironic thing is that in a regular life that kind of thing happens to everyone every single day, but it isn't appreciated until it is taken away. The important things in life were listed in a fairly appropriate order by the words that were written on that pewter ashtray that I bought for ten bucks down in Charleston: HEALTH, LOVE &WEALTH AND TIME TO ENJOY THEM. You will discover that happiness is easy to find but it is hard to recognize.

I am so overcome by the rush of relief that I drift off in somewhat of a daze and I feel like Dorothy in 'The Wizard of Oz,' so I click my heels together while I say, "There's no place like home, there's no place like home" (and there isn't but what I have discovered is that sometimes you can go home again).

Then I think of a question that I failed to ask so I call up to the nurses' station where I leave word for the doctor to stop back by my room before he leaves the ward and in about two minutes he comes walking back into my room. I just get right to the bottom line of my fears when I blurt out, "No biopsy?" The gray-haired doctor looks straight into my eyes and says "If your blood work looks good in the morning then you are out of here."

I could have 'left well enough alone' as my Dad would say, I should be satisfied to be going back home without a puncture wound in my side, but I have one more question for this medical guru. So, I just cut to the chase and I ask this gray-haired doctor "What makes all of the hospitals so quick to want to do a biopsy when there may be times that it isn't a medical necessity?"

Truth follows silence, so I sit quietly through the pause in our conversation and the doctor looks down at the floor. He tells me in slow, measured tones that the insurance companies are so afraid that transplant patients will become paranoid and want to almost live in the hospital, that they don't like to pay for inpatient follow up visits unless a biopsy is performed. The vastness of what goes unsaid makes me wonder if the insurance companies may be trying to reduce demand for hospital visits by insisting on administering pain.

After everything that I have been through with all of these various hospitals and clinics over the last two years, you would think that I should at least understand who is in charge of deciding what medical care that a patient ultimately ends up receiving (wrong). In the beginning, when I was quite naïve, I thought that the doctors made all of the medical decisions based solely on what they learned back in medical school. But along the way I discovered that the doctors alter their treatment recommendations because of what their lawyers tell them to do in case they get sued (CYA).

I had always thought that the doctors were the top dogs in the hospital hierarchy but now I know that the MDs are being controlled by the MBAs. Your future medical care is being determined over at the school of business administration in what would be called a profitable business model. Over at the medical school they see what is theoretically possible but over at the business school they determine what your health insurance policy will actually pay for and the law school figures out how to settle disputes (after you are dead).

I guess that I shouldn't be too surprised that control goes back to those in charge of the money, but the great facade of caring put out to the public by the medical industry makes me think about the Wizard of Oz standing behind the curtains pulling the strings (oh no, Auntie Em, the hospital is a business after all).

I know that I have one more blood test in the morning that could break my heart but I'm not going to ruin today by worrying about tomorrow (make sure that you don't either). Besides, in the past, lowering the Cyclosporine dosage has always made my kidney work better (for a while).

In the morning I am awake well before dawn and in my assessment of my situation I figure that the trip to the airport in this snowstorm represents a greater risk than my final blood test (and I am right). When the man from the lab comes around to draw my blood I know that this one blood test is the only thing that is standing between me and the rest of my life, so I look at the guy who is holding the needle and I say, "let's get it on." After the man from the lab has left with my blood samples I decide to pass the time by talking to God because, after all, that is who saved me.

After a while the door to my room swings open and there stands a nurse whose smile is telegraphing the message even before she says, "Pack your bags because we need this room for sick people." I could have hugged the nurse! I feel like dancing around the room and in fact, after she is gone that is precisely what I do, thinking about my shadow as it dances in the sun.

Out at the airport they de-ice the plane two times because it is snowing so hard and as we rumble down the runway, I can see seven snowplows working out on the tarmac as we lumber by. I can feel the resistance as the wheels of the plane push through the snow and as we get near to the end of the runway, I glance around the plane and I'm glad to see that there are a lot of empty seats. I have a life to live and this plane feels heavy so I say in my head, "up Donder up Blitzen" (come on plane lets fly). The scattered applause when the plane becomes airborne lets me know that I wasn't the only one who was feeling concerned.

As we fly up through the thick snow clouds, I look out of my window into the totally diffused sunlight which gets brighter and whiter as we approach the tops of the clouds, making me feel particularly close to God as we burst through the top of the clouds and the sun bathes our plane in its golden rays. My trance is broken by the sound of the pilot making an announcement over the public address system telling the passengers that he just got the word that the airport has been closed because of the snow and we were the last plane that was able to leave (more applause).

The long flight home is good for my soul because it gives me plenty of time to think (and pray). The only special favor that I ask God to do is to let me be normal again (not that I ever was). Please just let me live my life like a regular man whose biggest worry isn't wondering if he will be waking up in the morning (goes my plea). When the plane touches down in Columbia, I am the only one who lets out a cheer. I guess that I'm just happy to be alive and besides, I know that Debi will be waiting for me.

As I walk into the terminal building from the plane, I can see Debi right away and we fly into each other's arms, kissing as if we were the only two people around.

The drive home to Blythewood is like a balm for my brain as my gaze falls upon familiar trees glistening with a light dusting of snow. The last thing that I expected was the unexpected, when we turned into our driveway at home, because I have done it a thousand times before. But today I am greeted by a magnificent sight with everything covered in white except for the little bursts of yellow from bunches of daffodils that are poking their sturdy little blossoms up through the snow.

There are moments in this world where we all try to grasp the essence of our existence but we don't need to seek out any mystics to explain the meaning of life when we have such a perfect example in the simple daffodils, with their golden buttercups showing us what we should all be striving to do: BLOOMING IN THE FACE OF ADVERSITY.

October, 1983

RANK	AGENT NAME	PREMIUM	FACE AMOUNT
1.	CAYETANO ERLINDA G	8,058.12	1,105,000
2.	RICHARD CLAYTON	7,852.70	1,005,300
3.	RANDALL J. YEOMANS	7,776.04	1,663,000
4.	PEN WHITE	7,457.25	1,578,000
5.	JORDAN-III-CHARLES LOVETT	7,447.08	1,702,800
6.	MOE GREGORY SAMUEL	7,279.68	1,357,000
7.	DUFAULT ROBERT J	7,227.90	1,724,000
8.	RICHARD SHAW	7,206.24	1,680,000
9.	TED BRIGHT	7,204.44	1,454,500
10.	JEFFREY H WATEPS	6,780.90	1,134,500
11.	MITCHELL BENNY M	6,702.72	559,000
12.	SANDERS CLAUDE	6,886.00	765,000
13.	OLLIFF MYRA DO	6,602.84	1,470,000
14.	ALLEN WALTER STEPHEN	6,425.90	644,500
15.	STONEKING JAMES MICHAEL	6,343.08	1,035,000
16.	GRAVITT JAMES E	6,333.91	2,384,000
17.	LEVIS WILLIE CLYDE	6,317.40	703,025
18.	NATHA DUNKIN	6,255.30	1,251,100
19.	MENDES ROBERT J	6,146.27	887,000
20.	LONTELLO JAMES C	6,134.48	1,277,000
21.	DAVID COCCIA	6,124.92	740,725
22.	DON GORDON	5,758.80	1,000,000
23.	STURTEVANT DAVID M	5,577.90	705,315
24.	COULTER LONNIE JERRY	5,054.52	1,540,000
25.	GARRETT GRACE W	5,054.92	843,500
26.	MILLER CHARLES J	5,374.28	1,045,100
27.	TOLBERT JR-BRYANT N	5,353.70	1,217,000
28.	URSILLO RONALD D	5,338.84	685,175
29.	THOMAS E BALLARD	5,280.00	779,000
30.	WOODLE GARY L	5,233.44	779,500
31.	J KOD JONES	5,217.00	1,051,000
32.	POWELL WILLIAM H UN	5,100.04	882,000
33.	KEVIN QUIGLEY	5,096.84	728,500
34.	SHOWCAS SR RICHARD	4,991.10	836,000
35.	KESSELL LEONARD F	4,959.60	1,002,000
36.	STARR GUY THEODORE	4,933.20	757,000
37.	LITTLE BELINDA LOU	4,893.12	650,000
38.	GILES RICHARD ALONZO	4,477.04	186,500
39.	SNOW JOHN EUGENE	4,477.28	116,500

DIALYSIS

November, 1983

RANK	AGENT NAME	PREMIUM	FACE AMOUNT
1.	CAYETANO ERLINDA G	15,801.20	1,105,000
2.	PATRICIA D LAND	7,803.52	1,172,000
3.	MCKENZIE ELROY III-PVP	7,380.44	790,250
4.	WILLIE GILGERT	7,061.96	815,854
5.	STEINKER GEORGE R	6,309.24	1,043,000
6.	JOEL TEAGUE	6,309.24	784,000
7.	BONUS M SHADE	6,929.02	917,500
8.	TED BRIGHT	6,411.88	1,088,500
9.	ARTHUR J DESCHENE	6,956.40	838,000
10.	MUELLER LEONARD M	6,902.19	1,436,270
11.	LINDLEY ROBERT EDWARD	6,843.32	861,000
12.	STRONGE III LEO A	6,720.86	787,128
13.	LONDON SYLVIA A	6,721.84	870,000
14.	SESSONS ADA LEVERNE	6,615.80	650,000
15.	STARDANCE	6,531.70	612,900
16.	STONEKING JAMES MICHAEL	6,491.90	630,000
17.	MEANS HOWARD L	6,441.10	395,000
18.	WILLIAM CHARLES MATHEW	6,390.70	788,000
19.	PRYNARD RUGH	6,310.48	1,204,280
20.	PORTER JAMES E	6,360.82	855,000
21.	FLOYD FLYNN	6,181.58	720,000
22.	EBB LOVELL	6,174.28	440,000
23.	BRADSHAW JONAS B	5,958.76	591,000
24.	LETTIRIO JOHN EDWARD	5,928.52	501,000
25.	MARTIN JR GEORGE J	5,930.00	632,000
26.	LAMBERT ELLIOT L	5,900.80	1,025,000
27.	KEVIN QUIGLEY	5,889.25	764,500
28.	ART VILLAS	5,832.90	755,000
29.	DON L DOMINICK	5,780.90	800,000
30.	POPE RONALD DAVID	5,751.08	495,000
31.	THOMAS L LEATHERWOOD	5,718.68	1,090,000
32.	MUELLER JOANNIE E	5,648.92	402,400
33.	CAYETANO ERLINDA G	5,580.72	440,750
34.	HAMILTON RAYMOND E	5,579.44	440,000
35.	MITCHELL KENNETH LEE	5,547.60	387,000
36.	HUFF LISA MARIE	5,447.60	241,500
37.	HAWKINS JAMES MANDEL	5,434.84	717,587

TRANSPLANT

December, 1983

RANK	AGENT NAME	PREMIUM	FACE AMOUNT
1.	INGRAM JOHN PATRICK	9,742.40	1,779,000
2.	LEVIS JAMES C	8,591.64	895,500
3.	LENDI JAMES E	6,819.32	763,047
4.	THOMAS E BALLARD	6,670.32	805,636
5.	BROWN JOHN F	5,953.23	229,377
6.	CEREIO BINI S	5,602.90	536,489
7.	NOYMA DONALD L	5,529.70	815,000
8.	JIM LELAND	5,091.16	1,909,000
9.	HILL JOE DORYA	5,045.86	914,000
10.	SNEEZE BARRI E	5,028.64	423,769
11.	LEACH KATY BELLAMY	5,024.11	560,000
12.	RICHARD CLINTON	5,982.78	1,226,512
13.	SESSONS ADA LEVERNE	5,261.86	1,101,030
14.	URSILLO EDWARD R	5,349.84	617,015
15.	LONDON SILVIA	5,385.47	519,000
16.	TED WELDON	5,258.12	853,500
17.	ASHFORD OLIVIA ELAINE	5,401.54	869,000
18.	RANDALL J YEOMANS	4,378.32	5,196,000
19.	BOB TURLEY	4,937.32	1,160,000
20.	KEN SUMMERS	4,878.44	1,459,000
21.	ARMAMENTH ARKEN	4,128.86	1,048,600
22.	RICHARD B JEANREST	4,851.70	737,200
23.	CATH COURT GERALD	4,759.46	364,834
24.	MICHELITTI JOHN	4,634.81	365,290
25.	CAGENAS RONALD LOYAND	4,478.79	527,000
26.	JOEL TEAGUE	4,413.58	1,103,000
27.	COULTER LONNIE JERRY	4,406.62	1,013,200
28.	TED BRIGHT	4,371.72	1,018,200
29.	WOODLE GARY L	4,348.84	918,120
30.	MENDES ROBERT J	4,325.92	236,000
31.	JOSEPH GROVES	4,163.28	871,020
32.	CAYATI ANTONIO C	4,127.28	893,000
33.	NATHAN DUNKIN	4,157.08	887,100
34.	DON GORDON	4,144.72	860,000
35.	IVAN D EARLE	3,935.04	507,400
36.	OLLIFF MYRA DO	3,744.85	475,500
37.	MUELLER LEONARD M PVP	3,706.90	350,636
38.	ORLANDO DILE FLEX	3,960.48	555,000
39.	RICHARDS JR CLARENCE T	3,654.96	441,000
40.	G SONNELL WILLIAM H RVP	3,652.42	707,350
41.	PEGGY LEON	3,560.90	365,230
42.	CODY LOUGIN JOSEPH	3,987.90	734,000
43.	SUINE RICHARD BINGEL	3,554.90	509,600
44.	CHARLES ANGLE	3,548.18	688,200
45.	WILLIAMS ARTHUR	3,527.10	828,100
46.	KEITH MICHAEL CRAIG	3,493.70	765,100
47.	WILLIAM H ISLAND LYMP	3,451.28	1,145,100
48.	JANICE XOLEN	3,376.61	313,500
49.	FAIRINGTON GARBETH S	3,357.44	460,105

DIVORCE

February, 1984

BLOOMING IN
THE FACE OF
ADVERSITY

REMOVAL OF TENCHOFF

March, 1984

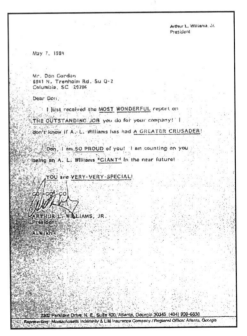

Arthur L. Williams, Jr.
President

May 7, 1984

Mr. Don Gordon
6841 N. Trenholm Rd. Su Q-2
Columbia, SC 29206

Dear Don,

I just received the MOST WONDERFUL report on THE OUTSTANDING JOB you do for your company! I don't know if A. L. Williams has had A GREATER CRUSADER!

Don, I am SO PROUD of you! I am counting on you being an A. L. Williams "GIANT" in the near future!

YOU are VERY-VERY-SPECIAL!

ARTHUR L. WILLIAMS, JR.
President

ALW/kh

2302 Parklake Drive, N. E., Suite 400, Atlanta, Georgia 30345 (404) 908-6930
Representing: Massachusetts Indemnity & Life Insurance Company / Regional Office: Atlanta, Georgia

EPILOGUE

THEY DON'T RING ANY BELLS in the transplant business when they finally get everything just right so I was praying to God for a sign that I had been healed (which I had). So I took it as a good sign when I noticed that the bluebirds were building a nest in the bluebird box that was in the cedar tree just outside of my sunroom in Blythewood (Bluebird of happiness and all). As I waited on the other white shoe to drop several weeks went by (which is a good sign).

One morning I see my pair of Bluebirds pitching a fit as they fly around their nest chirping loudly so I know that something is terribly wrong and I put down my coffee rushing outside to investigate the problem in bird land.

This birdhouse is designed with two nails that you pull out to clean out the box at the end of each season so I grabbed the nails and pulled (completing the connection that God had intended). Out drops a big old Blacksnake that had just eaten its breakfast.

Horrified and heartbroken I yell at the snake but I don't harm it for doing the things that Blacksnakes do. Mumbling things that I can't write here I walk around the house to go get my mail pondering what the old Indian sign means when the Blacksnake eats your Bluebird of happiness chicks (I know that it can't be good).

When I open the mailbox, I find one rather ominous looking envelope appropriately trimmed in black from the Internal Revenue Service holding the official notification that I owe them more money than I have in the world.

The cosmic significance of these events is still unknown to me as I walk back into my house to the sound of my ringing telephone. I pick up the insistent receiver, saying "hell-o" and I am greeted by a voice saying, "I is your Revenue Officer." In that flicker of an instant I knew that this was the sign that I have been praying for because at last the Lord has blessed me with the troubles of an everyday man. Surely, I must be healed (and I was). I answer back with a song in my heart, "I be your taxpayer" (thank you, God).

When I hung up the phone after scheduling my personal interview with the I.R.S. I could tell that the world was working just exactly as it should, because I have a house full of dialysis supplies and we all know that means that some poor taxpayer has to pay.

* * *

* * *

Debi and I were married two years after our transplant.

December 7th 2023, will mark the 40th anniversary of my brave brother's gift of life to me and both of us are still in good health.

The only advice that I would like to leave you with is that in the course of human endeavor there are but two choices that a man or woman can make. You must choose between letting things happen or making things happen. If you go through life letting things happen you will only end up with whatever was left over after everything that was worth fighting for is gone.

To succeed in life, you must MAKE THINGS HAPPEN and to be happy you must live like lilies in the field. It is our quandary in life to figure out how to do both (best wishes).

God Speed,
Don Gordon

THE BEGINNING

I HAVE DECIDED TO END MY BOOK WITH A PRAYER because at some point in your Life that may be the best hope that you have so here is a prayer that had a lot of impact on me and I would like to dedicate it to all of you everyday Heros.

I asked for strength that I might achieve.

I was made weak that I might learn humbly to obey.

I asked for health that I might do greater things.

I was given infirmity that I might do better things.

I asked for riches that I might be happy; I was given poverty that I might be wise.

I asked for power that I might have the praise of men.

I was given weakness that I might feel the need of God.

I asked for all things that I might enjoy life; I was given life that I might enjoy all things.

I got nothing that I asked for; but everything that I hoped for.

Almost despite myself my unspoken prayers were answered; I am, among all men, most richly blessed.

Prayer of an unknown Confederate Soldier.

ABOUT THE AUTHOR

BORN IN THE CAPITOL CITY OF COLUMBIA, Don Gordon is a native South Carolinian. Although his early years were spent in California, Japan, Washington, DC, and Puerto Rico, he returned home to finish High School. He later attended the University of South Carolina where he earned his B.S. in Marketing. While at USC, he was a student senator, fraternity president (Alpha), Junior Class Treasurer, and fraternity football all-star Middle Linebacker.

His Business Career began in Columbia where he owned and operated a small business for 11 years. After selling his business (which is still in operation), Gordon spent many years in the Financial Service industry, eventually serving as Senior Vice President. Other career moves included Champion Communication in Greenville South Carolina, that pioneered Internet Telephones. Most recently Gordon worked as a Medical Sales Representative providing Doctors with a cheek swab that enabled them to know in advance if a patient would metabolize various medications in the expected manner (or not).

Growing up under the threat of "impending doom," resulting from his health issues, gave Gordon a "fear of missing out coupled with a sense of urgency." He became a risk taker because there was no safe way for him. "In the end," says Gordon, "the knowledge that there is no safety in life was a great gift for me as it freed me from the shackles of a comforting myth."

The author can be contacted by email at

istillmissthatdog@gmail.com

AVAILABLE FROM SHOTWELL PUBLISHING

If you enjoyed this book, perhaps some of our other titles will pique your interest. The following titles are now available for your reading pleasure... Enjoy!

MARK C. ATKINS

WOMEN IN COMBAT
Feminism Goes to War

JOYCE BENNETT

MARYLAND, MY MARYLAND
The Cultural Cleansing of a Small Southern State

GARRY BOWERS

SLAVERY AND THE CIVIL WAR
What Your History Teacher Didn't Tell You

DIXIE DAYS
Reminiscences Of A Southern Boyhood

JERRY BREWER

DISMANTLING THE REPUBLIC

ANDREW P. CALHOUN, JR.

MY OWN DARLING WIFE
Letters from a Confederate Volunteer

JOHN CHODES

SEGREGATION
Federal Policy or Racism?

WASHINGTON'S KKK
The Union League during Southern Reconstruction

PAUL C. GRAHAM

CONFEDERAPHOBIA
An American Epidemic

WHEN THE YANKEES COME
Former South Carolina Slaves Remember Sherman's Invasion

JOSEPH JAY

SACRED CONVICTION
The South's Stand for Biblical Authority

SUZANNE PARFITT JOHNSON

MAXCY GREGG'S SPORTING JOURNALS 1842 - 1858

JAMES RONALD KENNEDY

DIXIE RISING: Rules for Rebels

WHEN REBEL WAS COOL
Growing Up in Dixie, 1950-1965

JAMES R. & WALTER D. KENNEDY

PUNISHED WITH POVERTY
The Suffering South – Prosperity to Poverty and the Continuing Struggle, 2nd ed.

THE SOUTH WAS RIGHT!

YANKEE EMPIRE
Aggressive Abroad and Despotic at Home

PHILIP LEIGH

THE DEVIL'S TOWN
Hot Springs During the Gangster Era

U.S. GRANT'S FAILED PRESIDENCY

LEWIS LIBERMAN

SNOWFLAKE BUDDIES
ABC Leftism for Kids!

JACK MARQUARDT

AROUND THE WORLD IN EIGHTY YEARS
Confessions of a Connecticut Confederate

GREEN ALTAR BOOKS
(Literary Imprint)

CATHARINE SAVAGE BROSMAN

AN AESTHETIC EDUCATION
and Other Stories

CHAINED TREE, CHAINED OWLS: Poems

RANDALL IVEY

A NEW ENGLAND ROMANCE
and Other SOUTHERN Stories

JAMES EVERETT KIBLER

TILLER

THOMAS MOORE

A FATAL MERCY
The Man Who Lost The Civil War

KAREN STOKES

BELLES
A Carolina Love Story

CAROLINA TWILIGHT

HONOR IN THE DUST

THE IMMORTALS

THE SOLDIER'S GHOST
A Tale of Charleston

WILLIAM A. THOMAS, JR.
RUNAWAY HALEY
An Imagined Family Saga

GOLD-BUG
(Mystery & Suspense Imprint)

MICHAEL ANDREW GRISSOM

BILLIE JO

BRANDI PERRY

SPLINTERED
A New Orleans Tale

MARTIN L. WILSON

TO JEKYLL AND HIDE

Showed instead of shown

p. 51 Saddest

14-
51.

Made in the USA
Columbia, SC
22 June 2021